Perspectives in Pragmatics, Philosophy & Psychology

Volume 31

Francesca Santulli • Chiara Degano

Agreement in Argumentation

A Discursive Perspective

🐎 Springer

Francesca Santulli (iD)
Department of Linguistics and
Comparative Cultural Studies
Università Ca' Foscari
Venezia, Italy

Chiara Degano (iD)
Department of Languages, Literatures,
and Cultures
Università degli Studi di Roma Tre
Rome, Italy

ISSN 2214-3807   ISSN 2214-3815   (electronic)
Perspectives in Pragmatics, Philosophy & Psychology
ISBN 978-3-031-16292-3   ISBN 978-3-031-16293-0   (eBook)
https://doi.org/10.1007/978-3-031-16293-0

This Springer imprint is published by the registered company Springer Nature Switzerland AG
The registered company address is: Gewerbestrasse 11, 6330 Cham, Switzerland

In memory of Donella Antelmi,
a brilliant researcher and a dear friend

Introduction[1]

In 1959, long before the development of discourse analysis as a discipline, the French linguist Émile Benveniste gave a definition of discourse (*discours*) as interaction with a persuasive component: "Discourse must be understood in its widest sense: every utterance assuming a speaker and a hearer, and in the speaker, the intention of influencing the other in some way" (Benveniste, 1959/1971, p. 209). This definition suggests that argumentation as a text type is pervasive in actual discourse, and, on the other hand, given the dialogic character of discourse, it has to be considered in the context of a communicative interaction. Accepting Benveniste's approach as a starting point, we believe that argumentation and discourse are inherently linked, and therefore adopt a discursive viewpoint to tackle the question of agreement as a crucial component of argumentative practices.

In these introductory remarks, we shall briefly discuss the most relevant traits of the notion of discourse; we shall then focus on argumentation in discourse, and in particular on the role of agreement.

Discourse

The definition by Benveniste quoted above emphasizes the pragmatic character of discourse, which is conceived as an event—and in this respect opposed to *histoire*, (etymologically) intended as the narrative of events. This interpretation of discourse as an event characterizes also Foucault's approach (Foucault, 1970), which can be considered the philosophical counterpart of Benveniste's linguistic analysis. In the second half of the twentieth century, French scholars gradually developed a new line

---

[1] The overall design of the volume was conceived jointly by the two authors, who have penned together the Introduction and the Conclusions. The other chapters were distributed as follows: Santulli wrote Chaps. 1 and 4; Sects. 3.1, 3.2, 3.5; 6.1, 6.3, and 6.4; Degano wrote Chaps. 2 and 5; Sects. 3.3, 3.4, 3.6, 3.7, and 6.2.

of research combining the analysis of texts with social and political interests, and drawing inspiration from philosophy, psychoanalysis, and epistemology. These investigations mainly focused on the social use of language and on political texts, aiming to single out linguistic markers of ideological manipulation. Mere analysis is however only one aspect of discursive studies. As emphasized by Maingueneau (1991), not only does language allow the manifestation of hidden ideas, but its use is part of a *practice*, which accounts for the creation of discursive objects and events. The French *Analyse du Discours* has developed from this line of research, recognizing as fundamental analytical tools the theory of enunciation by Benveniste and Bakhtin's genre theory. In our view, the initial development of French discourse analytical studies crucially emphasizes the linguistic component, which has sometimes been given less prominence in what has been called the Anglo-Saxon strand of this area of research (Antelmi, 2011).

Various disciplines and methodologies have gradually been involved in the analysis of discourse: text linguistics, pragmatics, conversation analysis, argumentation theory, and rhetoric, to name a few, mostly within the linguistic framework of Halliday's functional grammar and socio-semiotic approach. Considering the diversity of principles and tools exploited in the actual analysis of discursive phenomena, it is not surprising that a single, universally accepted definition of discourse is difficult to find. Besides the interactive nature of discourse mentioned by Benveniste, there are however some constant elements that characterize the notion—namely, its being a *process* rather than a structure, and, above all, an active social *practice* (van Dijk, 1997). Fairclough clearly distinguishes between text and discourse:

> I shall use the term *discourse* to refer to the whole process of social interaction of which a text is just a part. This process includes in addition to the text the *process of production*, of which the text is a product, and the *process of interpretation*, for which the text is a resource. Text analysis is correspondingly only a part of discourse analysis, which also includes the analysis of productive and interpretative processes (Fairclough, 1989, p. 24).

Van Dijk, on the other hand, offers a quite comprehensive definition:

> [. . .] discourse is a multidimensional social phenomenon. It is at the same time a linguistic (verbal, grammatical) object (meaningful sequences of words or sentences), an action (such as an assertion or a threat), a form of social interaction (like a conversation), a social practice (such as a lecture), a mental representation (a meaning, a mental model, an opinion, knowledge), an interactional or communicative event or activity (like a parliamentary debate), a cultural product (like a telenovela) or even an economic commodity that is being sold and bought (like a novel) (van Dijk, 2009, p. 67).

Action as a crucial component of discourse was already emphasized by Foucault (1970), who analysed the origins of discourse and its use in right and magic, in an ancient era when words were not judged for their truth value but were able to perform effective rituals. Without using the word, Foucault actually referred to the *performative* value of utterances: historically, this function of language was dominant before the development of rational thought, which in turn shifted the emphasis from the enunciation onto the utterance and its connection with reference. The *creative* power of discourse has remote and well-entrenched roots.

Beyond textual research, discourse studies have therefore a constant pragmatic component, which is however insufficient to capture the distinguishing features of a discursive approach. As a matter of fact, discourse is the expression, and at the same time is the unifying element, of a *discourse community* (Maingueneau, 2009). In this social perspective, each discursive phenomenon is part of *interdiscourse*, in which it seeks *positioning*, thus displaying a persuasive component—albeit covert (Amossy, 2006). Last but not least, discourse has a twofold connection with the context in which it occurs: on the one side, it is the product of time/space constraints; on the other, it is one of the most important agents of modification of those same constraints (Antelmi, 2012). Thus, beyond the analysis of texts and of language use, discourse analysis aims to investigate the functioning of discourses in society. In its *critical* version (CDA), it has mainly focused on how different forms of manipulation and social control are enacted in discourse (Fairclough, 1989) with a strong emphasis on political engagement and commitment against ideological supremacy (van Dijk, 2009, Wodak, 2009).

In the genre analysis strand of discursive studies, instead, the focus has been on how factors of the context, especially the communicative purpose (Bhatia, 1993), impact on texts, setting in relation the contexts, the cognitive structure that underpins a given genre, and its textual realizations. Rhetorical moves and steps (Swales, 1990) are the textual units through which generic communicative purposes are conventionally realized, having recourse to a range of equally conventional linguistic traits (Swales, 1990, Bhatia, 2004). Within each genre, some moves are more constitutive than others, allowing the very identification of the genre, while other moves are more peripheral and are not necessarily realized in texts. Originally, genre analysis placed emphasis on the constitutive elements of a given genre, which confer stability to it, while subsequently attention was turned to destabilizing forces like interdiscursivity (cf., among others, Candlin and Maley, 1997), hybridization between genres, and the user's creative manipulation, whereby a given genre could be bent to different uses from those originally conceived, mostly in response to a more or less covert persuasive intent.

Argumentation in Discourse

Though, as we have seen, the argumentative component of discourse was mentioned in Benveniste's definition, which dates back before the earliest manifestations of discourse studies, argumentation has been mainly studied in its narrow interpretation, focusing on the processes that make a thesis acceptable on the basis of a series of arguments. The arguer offers reasons (in the form of propositions) in favour (or against) a statement (another proposition). In this perspective, argumentation theory is prescriptive and aims to study the formal patterns adopted to support a thesis, judging their soundness and possibly disclosing fallacies.

The realm of argumentation has expanded when it has started to be considered within the rhetorical framework, as an instrument of persuasion. The rebirth of rhetoric in the twentieth century has moved along a "dialectical line" (Piazza, 2004), marked by the publication of the *Traité de l'argumentation. La nouvelle rhétorique*, by Perelman/Olbrechts-Tyteca (1958). In this theoretical framework, argumentation is not an impersonal dialectical exercise but is always addressed to an interlocutor, and its aim is to obtain the adherence of a given audience to the thesis put forth by the arguer. In other words, argumentation and its validity must be judged in context.

Such an assumption underpins Toulmin's distinction between field-invariant and field-dependent arguments (Toulmin, 1958), which challenges the formal logic notion that a standard set of principles can be applied to all cases of argumentation regardless of the context. According to Toulmin, such an approach is hardly applicable to real-life uses of arguments, because even if formal validity is not field-dependent, judgements of acceptability do vary across fields, and greatly depend on the types of backing that are conventionally exploited in the field. At the same time, he also held that the differences in the linguistic forms given to arguments in different fields is an important source of information for argumentation theory, decrying the logicians' practice of cramping all the different occurrences in language use into predetermined forms:

> A biologist would hardly ever utter the words 'All whales are mammals'; though sentences such as 'Whales are mammals' or 'The whale is a mammal' might quite naturally come from his lips or his pen... [B]acking by enumerative observation is one thing, backing by taxonomic classification another; and our choices of idiom, though perhaps subtle, reflect these differences fairly exactly (Toulmin, 1958/2003, p. 109).

In the last few decades of the twentieth century, a new approach developed to argumentation theory combining a formal normative orientation with a pragmatic concern: pragma-dialectics. In subsequent evolution of the model, a rhetorical component was injected alongside the original dialectical one. With the notion of *strategic manoeuvring* (van Eemeren, 2010), pragma-dialectics intended to reconcile the two components, as originally conceived by Aristotle, thus moving away from formal logicians' distrust towards rhetoric. Strategic manoeuvring rests on the idea that rhetorical effectiveness is not necessarily reached at the expense of dialectical rigour. Reinserting rhetoric into argumentation enhanced the role of the context in which argumentation takes place since only in context can the three aspects of strategic manoeuvring be considered: of all the possible topics that arguers might use, the choice of the most effective arguments (1. topical selection) is driven by what they think will be most effective for an intended audience (2. adaptation to the audience), on the ground of their mental representation of it. The linguistic form given to the topics (3. presentational choices) will be chosen accordingly to maximize the possibilities that the audience will accept them. At the same time, the rekindled attention for the audience has shifted attention to what is specific to argumentation in different settings or fields of activity, bringing the scope of argumentation theory closer to that of (socio)linguistics and discourse analysis. While the dialectical component of pragma-dialectics pushed for a search of the common traits of argumentation, whatever the conditions in which it takes place (an effort that produced the critical discussion model: van Eemeren/Grootendorst,

1984), the attention for argumentation in context places emphasis on what is different in each context.

As a result of its new orientation to the context, pragma-dialectics set out to study strategic manoeuvring in relation to specific activity types and their institutional constraints with a view to identifying prototypical patterns (van Eemeren, et al. 2014). Activity types—a concept similar to that of genre as understood in genre analysis—cluster into broader categories, named "genres" (van Eemeren and Garssen, 2009, p. 3, in line, broadly speaking, with Aristotle's tradition), namely adjudication, deliberation, disputation, and communion seeking, each having "institutionally distinctive argumentative properties" (van Eemeren et al., 2014, p. 560). Differences between genres are determined by their institutional purpose, where "institutional" and "institutionalized" are not understood as exclusively related to formal organizations, but to "all socially and culturally established communicative practices that are formally or informally conventionalized". (*Ibidem*). Just to give an example of genre differences, starting points in adjudication tend to be explicitly elicited and refer to codified rules, whereas in deliberation they generally remain implicit and are intersubjective (van Eemeren et al., 2014, p. 557).

For the purpose of this book, it is particularly important to focus on the approach to argumentation studies that developed in contraposition to the analysis of the linguistic construction of arguments (*l'argumentation dans la langue:* Anscombre/ Ducrot, 1983) to consider *l'argumentation dans le discours* (Amossy, 2006). In this view, argumentation is an intrinsic *dimension* of discourse though only in some cases discourse has an argumentative *aim*. The construction and representation of meanings in discourse is the result of a deliberate choice of the speaker, who thus orients the reception of the interlocutor and promotes their view of the world. Any utterance has an argumentative component (Amossy, 2005, 2009) and the function of argumentation is not limited to persuasion proper, as it can be used to reinforce or slightly modify a point of view, or to stimulate reflection on something. The study of argumentation in discourse considers a wide range of texts where no specific thesis is supported, but certain values and viewpoints are promoted, thus expanding the scope of research across genres and domains—from literature to the news, from private correspondence to fiction, etc.

However, mere transmission of one's point of view, with no intention of modifying the position of the interlocutor, should not be mistaken with the process of persuasion proper, which starts from the explicit will of obtaining the adhesion of the interlocutor and relies on the conscious adoption of specific strategies. In other words, "il faut dans cette optique différencier la dimension argumentative de la visée argumentative" (Amossy, 2005). In this respect, the notion of genre plays a fundamental role: "La notion de genre de discours définie par l'analyse de discours dans la mouvance de Bakhtine ne permet pas seulement d'élargir le champ de la rhétorique classique: elle mène à repenser la notion d'argumentation" (Amossy, 2009). As a matter of fact, not only is argumentation part of discourse in general, but it develops in the realm of different practices and communicative exchanges and takes different forms in relation to the genre where it occurs.

In this respect, there are genres that have an overt argumentative aim (as, in ancient rhetoric, the deliberative or the judiciary), but the presence of argumentation in discourse should be analysed in a scalar dimension, along a continuum of explicitness and of actual relevance. On the one hand, defendant's and plaintiff's statements, parliamentary debates, advertisements, and other forms of propaganda are considered typical examples of argumentative genres. On the other hand, textual-linguistic analysis has revealed the presence of argumentative traits (ranging from mere evaluation to explicit reasoning) in a wide choice of different genres—from scientific communication to the news—traditionally believed to be immune to persuasive intentions. Though we do not fully agree with the view according to which *any* utterance has an argumentative component, we do believe in the *inter-personal* character of discourse, implying the respective positioning of the interlocutors and, more often than not, a certain degree of promotion of one's image and, possibly, convictions. In other words, the total absence of any persuasive aim is, in most contexts of communication, more an exception than a rule.

Agreement

When thinking about argumentation, the first thing that comes to mind is disagreement, associated with the defending of different positions and possibly prevailing. Quite counterintuitively, though, it is agreement that makes argumentation possible: without an initial area of agreement, it is quite pointless to embark on a discussion for solving a difference of opinion. Nor can persuasion be obtained if the arguer does not share some preliminary premises with their audience. If argumentation is analysed beyond its formal, logical value and is considered in the context of real-life exchanges, as part of processes aimed to obtain adhesion of the audience to the arguer's thesis, it is evident that this effort would be vain in the absence of a common ground of agreement.

Actually, in any form of dialogical exchange, effective communication between the interlocutors relies on the possibility of sharing a series of "premises": a common language, knowledge of the context, meanings and fundamental values. Moreover, whenever the aim of persuasion expands in discourse, "the more common ground there exists between the arguers, the better the prospects for a statement to be successful" (Kraus, 2012). Kraus takes an inventory of the different denominations and conceptions of "common ground" in argumentation and pragmatics: "shared knowledge" (Johnson and Blair, 2006); "mutual knowledge" or "mutually manifest cognitive environment" (Sperber and Wilson, 1986); "the normative environment the arguers inhabit together" (Goodwin, 2005); "common sense" (Billig, 1991); "communal links, foremost among which are shared values or beliefs" (Billig, 1996); "common knowledge" (Walton, 2001); "general knowledge shared by the speaker, hearer and audience" (Walton, 1996).

A similar notion was at the basis of the persuasive process in ancient rhetoric. Besides argument schemes, Aristotle emphasized the importance of *endoxa*, or widely shared opinions, which are exploited as premises to argumentation proper. These premises play a crucial role, and their adequacy depends on the audience they are meant for. This approach to preliminary agreement confirms the interactional and pragmatic character of argumentation in rhetoric.

In the perspective of more recent approaches to argumentation, the problem of preliminary agreement has been posed in two main areas: agreement on premises in general terms (the New Rhetoric), and more specifically, agreement on starting points (pragma-dialectics).

Agreement in Discourse

The discursive representation of the premises offered for preliminary agreement is crucial in the perspective of persuasion, which implies the actual addressing of an audience, in line with the rhetorical tradition from Aristotle to Perelman. Actually, the rhetorical system includes both *inventio* and *elocutio*. In the Aristotelian presentation, the two aspects (usually indicated as *parts* or, more properly, *stages* of the process) were inseparable and equally relevant. Only later have two different interpretations of rhetoric developed, causing the divorce between "rhetoric of proofs" and "rhetoric of tropes" (Piazza, 2004, p. 46). This separation—both in research and in actual practice—of logic-argumentative structures from the use of figurative language has been a constant in the long period of decline of rhetoric and has also characterized its twentieth-century renaissance. In the last few decades, a renewed effort to re-establish and re-evaluate the unity of rhetoric has led to a more comprehensive view, in line with the original character of the discipline, which proves useful in the perspective of discourse. When argumentation is analysed as a discursive phenomenon, it is difficult to separate it from rhetoric.

In this volume, we intend to explore how the quest for agreement is enacted in discourse, focusing on both the construction of a common ground with the audience and the premises in argument schemes.

In Chap. 1, the discussion starts from the crucial Aristotelian concepts of the probabilistic nature of argumentation oriented to persuasion, and the unity of the means of proof (logos, ethos, and pathos). The probabilistic character of argumentation brings to the centre of the stage ethos as a discursive phenomenon, which for Aristotle is the most important proof, being the prerequisite for acceptance of any argumentative stance. For its importance and discursive character, current approaches to argumentation and rhetoric have given prominence to ethos, analysing it also in relation to the notions of face and politeness. Although centred on the speaker, ethos is fundamental for establishing a relation with the addressees, and indeed contributes to the construction of the audience as intended in the New Rhetoric. Here the audience is a primary concern for the Authors, and its construction through the exploitation of objects of agreement is the preliminary step to argumentation proper. As argumentation moves away from formal reasoning, it is all the more important for the arguer to be aware of the audience and win their trust.

In the last section of the chapter, agreement will be explored with reference to the concept of loci, considered in its different uses leading to terminological overlaps, and of their procedural role in argumentation.

In Chap. 2, we turn attention to agreement from an argumentative perspective, with specific regard to the pragma-dialectical approach and the Argumentum Model of Topics (AMT). Two aspects are singled out for their relevance to the notion of agreement, namely starting points and argument schemes. With regard to starting points, we will clarify their relationship with supporting arguments. In the critical discussion model, the opening stage is devoted to establishing starting points, thus identifying a zone of agreement among the parties, even if in actual argumentation this step may not be explicitly realized. The argumentation stage, instead, is associated with the defence of the standpoint by means of supporting arguments and their critical dialectical testing by the parties. This separation in the heuristic model of the critical discussion seems to imply that in real-life argumentation, starting points can be either explicitly formulated or tacitly assumed, but in either case they are set apart from the supporting argument. However, this understanding cannot be confirmed at closer scrutiny, as suggested both by some incidental remarks in the literature and by the discussion of some examples. As van Eemeren himself points out, material starting points are often only inferable from the fact that they are used argumentatively in the argumentation stage. Starting points are then discussed in relation to the rule for the critical discussion applicable to the opening stage. The chapter highlights how the Burden of Proof rule can be violated, conveying the impression that the defence of a standpoint rests on preliminarily established starting points. Finally, schemes are brought to bear on the notion of agreement, by focusing on how the pragma-dialectical model and the AMT model, respectively, conceptualize and operatively represent schemes, with special regard to unexpressed premises.

The discursive perspective imposes detailed analysis of the linguistic structures functional to the construction of identities, representations, and values. For this reason, in Chap. 3 we shall examine the most frequently used strategies exploited in actual discourse instances. To obtain agreement, it is indispensable to single out the actors and to construct narratives concerning both arguer and audience, which often involve common experience and bring forth the existence of founding, shared values. In this respect, transitivity plays a fundamental role as a system determining "who does what to whom". Pronouns are crucial for the identification of the main characters (arguer, audience, their community, as well as the other), while tenses contribute to the historical representation of facts and modality to the modulation of illocutionary force. Lexical choices, on the other hand, are functional to the representation and evaluation of all subjects and objects involved, and of their qualities. Considering that agreement is constructed as a preliminary step to argumentation proper and therefore not subject to direct and open backing (and rebuttal), implicit meaning is often exploited: among the most frequent structures, presupposition, concession, and dissociation are interesting from the linguistic point of view, as they mainly occur in consistent and recognizable forms. Nor can the dialogic character of argumentation be neglected, insofar as it allows the representation of different actors and, at the same time, more or less explicit confrontation with an *ad hoc*-constructed opposite viewpoint. Finally, patterns of figuration (and metaphoric meaning in the first place) do contribute to the argumentative process, especially when it appeals to both rational and emotional involvement.

A discourse analytical approach is not conceivable without actual textual work. The second part of the book provides examples of how a choice of texts can be investigated to single out the main rhetorical and argumentative strategies exploited to construct agreement in its different manifestations. As mentioned above, context and genre are fundamental to qualify the persuasive effort of the enunciator, and for this reason it seems convenient to focus on a selection of texts produced in a single domain and belonging to well-recognizable genres. We have opted for political discourse, in the context of post-war US presidential campaigns.

Genres of Political Discourse: The Reasons For a Choice

The domain of politics is undoubtedly imbued with argumentative/rhetorical discourse. Historically, rhetoric and politics were born in the same cultural context, i.e. the Greek *polis*, where public debate was an essential part of the actions aiming at effective government and solution of common problems. Genres of political discourse generally display an overt persuasive aim, in particular when they belong to the area of deliberation. It has been argued that their analysis can lead to revisiting some central issues concerning properties common to most communicative genres (Cap and Okluska, 2013). In political discourse, the tensions between generic aims and textual forms, context and its interpretation, stability and variation, diversification and hybridization are usually more evident. In it, the three main aspects highlighted (with different emphasis) in the most common definitions of genre co-exist—namely the goals of communication, the expectations of the addressees and the characteristics of texts, corresponding to the ideational, interpersonal, and textual metafunction of language, respectively (Santulli, 2012). Yet interpersonal relations seem to play a special role, as politics is the domain of aggregation of groups and construction of support towards achieving a certain goal. In this perspective, preliminary agreement between arguer and audience is inevitably sought, as it can be the key to obtain persuasion and have the audience perform certain actions, which, in different contexts, can ensure the arguer victory over the adversaries.

Among the numerous genres represented in the domain of politics, we chose to exclude those which show evident elements of hybridization or of rapid evolution, among them all genres including strong multimodal and intermodal components or a marked trend to migrate across different channels. The selected genres function as "conventionalized communicative practices whose conventionalization serves to meet the institutional exigencies of the communicative domain in response to which they have developed" (van Eemeren, 2010, pp. 139–45). This allows a relative stability of both textual and contextual features throughout our corpus, which in turn enhances the possibilities for intrageneric comparison, to single out similarities and differences among individual texts. On the other hand, we thought that the chronological dimension would give us the opportunity to detect the evolution of a given genre, as well as the preservation of constant traits that belong to its distinguishing features.

All this considered, we have privileged genres which produce recurring instances at regular time intervals and in a limited number, which makes it possible to spot and follow any evolutionary trend.

The geopolitical context we have chosen is post-war US politics, focusing on the Presidential electoral campaign as a macro-act with a single final goal (winning the election to become President), including a series of different discursive practices, some of them highly institutionalized, which in turn can be broken down in their constitutive components and (micro)structures. In this respect, "hierarchies of communicative acting are virtually infinite because intentionality and goal-enactment levels are infinite in the first place, and thus relatively "stabilized" genres can be potentially identified at more than one level of a given hierarchical structure—as long as the analyst sees some rationale to identify them" (Cap and Okluska, 2013, p. 10).

Within the Presidential campaign, we have singled out two crucial moments lying at the limits of its time frame, namely the official announcement of a candidacy and the ceremony where the new President is sworn in. Two important speeches are delivered by the candidate (then President) on these occasions, the Presidential Announcement and the Inaugural Address: the former marks the beginning of the electoral commitment, the latter is the first official act after the Presidential oath.

Both are typical institutionalized genres though with a different degree of stability and rituality. Both rely on a canon of unwritten norms but are differently enacted by challenging candidates (who do not belong to the party of the President in office) and incumbent candidates (including both incumbent Presidents running for a second term and candidates belonging to the same party as the President in office). Since World War II, there have been 14 different Presidents in the USA, most of them winning a second term. Truman took office for his first term before the end of the war, Johnson and Ford were Vice-Presidents who took over after death or impeachment of the President in office. Apart from them, the sequence shows a constant alternation between a Republican and a Democratic president, excluding George Bush, who succeeded Ronald Reagan. On the whole, in the last 70 years, there have been ten challenging candidates who managed to win the elections, most of them after two terms of the incumbent presidency. Five of them were Republicans, five were Democrats. For this research, we have chosen to consider the five decades between 1960 and 2010, form Eisenhower to Barack Obama.

Chapter 4 deals with the Presidential Announcement, which hinges on the performative act of *announcing* a candidacy, entailing a justification of the decision to run. Here the persuasive effort of the arguer aims to show his adequacy to the role, on the basis of a shared evaluation of both contextual factors and personal biography. Despite the evolution of the genre across the decades, the crucial role of ethos is a constant, while facts and values are recurrently exploited as objects of agreement.

Chapter 5 concerns the Inaugural Address, the genre that officially sanctions the beginning of the new presidency. While during the campaign the discourse is markedly argumentative and aimed at marking differences among candidates, in the Inaugural the president speaks for the first time with an institutional voice and seeks to establish agreement also with the part of the electorate that did not vote for him. The chapter preliminarily focuses on the constitutive moves of the genre in order to achieve a general understanding of its institutional aim, and then, on this ground, identifies prototypical argument schemes.

In Chapter 6, we have chosen to give an example of a dialogic genre, which emphasizes the adversarial component, and therefore more frequently offers examples of argumentation proper: the Presidential Debate. The analysis takes into consideration the first debate broadcast in the history of US Presidential elections, confronting John Kennedy as challenging candidate and Richard Nixon, who was the incumbent Vice-President.

In our analysis, strategies for the construction of agreement will be investigated, with a view to identifying recurring patterns of exploitation of linguistic elements and structures. Besides lexis and figurative language, pronominal choices, modality, implicit meaning have a significant impact on the organization of discourse and, as a consequence, on its capacity to mould the real world.

References

Amossy, R. (2005). The argumentative dimension of discourse. In F. van Eemeren & P. Houtlosser (Eds.), *Practices of Argumentation* (pp. 87–98). John Benjamins.

Amossy, R. (2006). *L'argumentation dans le discours*. Armand Collins.

Amossy, R. (2009). Repenser l'argumentation à travers les genres de discours. In V. Atayan & D. Pirazzini (Eds.), *Argumentation: théorie - langue - discours* (pp. 237–248). Peter Lang.

Anscombre, J.-C., & Ducrot, O. (1983). *L'argumentation dans la langue*. Mardaga.

Antelmi, D. (2011). L'analisi del discorso in Italia. *Italienisch, 65*, 87–98.

Antelmi, D. (2012). *Comunicazione e analisi del discorso*. UTET.

Benveniste, É. (1959). La relation de temps dans le verbe français. *Bulletin de la Société de Linguistique* (LIV/1) [English translation in: Id. (1971). *Problems in General Linguistics* (p. 205-216). Miami: University of Miami Press].

Bhatia, V. K. (1993). *Analysing Genre: Language Use in Professional Settings*. Longman.

Bhatia, V. K. (2004). *Worlds of Written Discourse: A Genre-Based View*. Continuum.

Billig, M. (1996). *Arguing and Thinking: A Rhetorical Approach to Social Psychology* (new ed.). Cambridge University Press.

Billing, M. (1991). *Ideology and Opinions: Studies in Rhetorical Psychology*. Sage.

Candlin, C. N., & Maley, Y. (1997). Intertextuality and interdiscursivity in the discourse of alternative dispute resolution. In B. L. Gunnarsson, P. Linell, &

B. Nordberg (Eds.), *The construction of professional discourse* (pp. 201–222). Routledge.

Cap, P., & Okluska, U. (Eds.). (2013). *Analyzing Genres in Political Communication*. John Bejamins.

Fairclough, N. (1989). *Language and Power*. Longman.

Foucault, M. (1970). *L'ordre du discours*. Gallimard.

Goodwin, J. (2005). Designing premises. In F. H. van Eemeren & P. Houtlosser (Eds.), *Argumentation in practice* (pp. 99–114). John Benjamins.

Johnson, R., & Blair, J. A. (2006). *Logical Self-Defence*. International Debate Education Association.

Kraus, M. (2012). Cultural diversity, cognitive breaks and deep disagreement: Polemic argument. In F. van Eemeren & B. Garssen (Eds.), *Topical Themes in Argumentation Theory* (pp. 91–107). Springer.

Maingueneau, D. (1991). *L'analyse du discours. Introduction aux lectures de l'archive*. Hachette.

Maingueneau, D. (2009). *Les terms clés de l'analyse du discurs*. Éditions du Seuils.

Perelman, Ch. & Olbrechts-Tyteca, L. (1958). *Traité de l'argumentation. La nouvelle rhétorique*. Presses Universitaires de France [English translation by J. Wilkinson & P. Weaver (1969): *The New Rhetoric. A Treatise on Argumentation*. University of Notre Dame Press].

Piazza, F. (2004). *Linguaggio, persuasione e verità. La retorica nel Novecento*. Carocci.

Santulli, F. (2012). Genre variation and genre change: Theory and application. In G. Garzone, P. Catenaccio, & C. Degano (Eds.), *Genre Change in the Contemporary World* (pp. 277–294). Peter Lang.

Sperber, D., & Wilson, D. (1986). *Relevance*. Harvard University Press.

Swales, M. (1990). *Genre Analysis*. Cambridge University Press.

Toulmin, S. E. (1958/2003). *The Uses of Arguments*. Cambridge University Press.

van Dijk, T. (1997). *Discourse as Structure and Process*. Sage.

van Dijk, T. (2009). Critical Discourse Studies: A sociocognitive approach. In R. Wodak & M. Meyer (Eds.), *Methods for Critical Discourse Analysis* (pp. 62–78). Sage.

van Eemeren, F. H. (2010). *Strategic Manoeuvering in Argumentative Discourse: Extending the Pragma-Dialectical Theory of Argumentation*. John Benjamins.

van Eemeren, F. H., & Garssen, B. (Eds.). (2009). *Pondering on problems of argumentation: twenty essays on theoretical issues*. Springer.

van Eemeren, F. H., & Grootendorst, R. (1984). *Speech Acts in Argumentative Discussions*. Foris.

van Eemeren, F. H., Garssen, B., Krabbe, E. C. W., Snoeck Henkemans, A. F., Verheij, B., & Wagemans, J. H. M. (2014). *Handbook of Argumentation Theory*. Springer.

Walton, D. (1996). *Argument structure: A Pragmatic Theory*. University of Toronto Press.

Walton, D. (2001). Enthymemes, common knowledge, and plausible inference. *Philosophy and Rhetoric, 34*, 93–112.

Wodak, R. (2009). *The Discourse of Politics in Action*. Palgrave Macmillan.

Contents

List of Figures

Chapter 1
Agreement and Persuasion

Abstract This Chapter explores the notion of agreement from the point of view of rhetoric, adopting a mainly historical approach. It starts from the assumption that it is possible to single out two moments in the process of persuasion when agreement on the premises plays a fundamental role: a preliminary stage, in which a common ground between arguer and audience is established, on the one hand; the exploitation of premises in actual argumentative sequences on the other. The former is examined with reference to the Aristotelian concept of ethos, which is the prerequisite for acceptance of any argumentative stance. For its importance and discursive character, current approaches to argumentation and rhetoric have given prominence to ethos, analysing it also in relation to the notions of face and politeness. Although centred on the speaker, ethos is fundamental for establishing a relation with the addressees, and indeed contributes to the construction of the audience (and *agreement* with it) as intended in the New Rhetoric. The Chapter then focuses on actual argumentative sequences, analysing the role of agreement with reference to the concepts of *topos* and *endoxon*, examining both their original meaning and subsequent interpretations.

Before considering agreement from the point of view of rhetoric, a few preliminary observations on the relationship between rhetoric and pragmatics can be useful, as an introduction to the exploitation of typically pragmatic concepts, which in many cases have their natural predecessors in the ancient rhetorical system.[1] Both rhetoric and pragmatics focus on language use, and include contextual factors in their analyses, with special attention for the subjects involved in the communicative exchange. Both are concerned with language as a form of action. Yet, they seem to look at the same object from different, and complementary, viewpoints. On the one hand, pragmatics is mainly concerned with illocution, and the very notion of speech act is defined in terms of the intentions of the speaker; rhetoric, on the other, focuses on the effects of the linguistic performance, thus emphasising perlocution (Venier, 2008: 95). As the

---

[1] A parallel analysis of the main aspects of rhetoric and pragmatics is carried out by Venier (2008), in an interesting volume including a discussion focused on the development of pragmatic research in Italy.

art of persuasion through discourse, rhetoric is defined on the basis of a discursive aim that does not correspond to a single speech act. Strictly speaking, it is impossible to *perform* the act of persuading. **I persuade you of this* is not a performative, and may be considered an ill-formed utterance, which gains meaning if transposed into a past or a future dimension (as the constative utterance describing a past achievement, e.g. *She persuaded them,* or announcing a future commitment, e.g. *I will persuade them*) or enriched with a modal component (e.g.: *I want to/can persuade* etc.). However, if we consider persuasion not as the final achievement of discursive practices but as the process through which those very practices are enacted, its pragmatic nature becomes self-evident. Shifting from the level of (micro)speech acts to that of discourse as a macro-act,[2] fundamental pragmatic notions can be applied to the rhetorical analysis, and they often turn out to be nothing else but the modern counterpart of ancient concepts and instruments (Kienpointner, 2017). The discussion of the fundamentals of agreement, stemming from the constitutive con-traposition of the interlocutors, will show how deeply some crucial tenets of modern pragmatics are rooted in the ancient rhetorical system (already delineated by Aris-totle), how new notions draw inspiration from old practices, and ultimately, how recognising the intertwining of the two disciplines can shed new light on discursive investigations.

Being a discipline founded on perlocution, rhetoric is oriented to the attainment of its final aim, which is a form of agreement. Namely, a persuasive process aims to obtain the adhesion of the interlocutor to the thesis of the speaker. In this funda-mental objective lies the difference between demonstrative and argumentative sequences, insofar as the former aim to prove the truth of the conclusions on the basis of the truth of the premises, while the latter pursue adhesion to the conclusions transferring to them the adhesion obtained on the premises (Perelman, 1977). Therefore, the whole rhetorical problem is a question of agreement. A rhetorical macro-act is successful when the audience adheres to the thesis of the arguer, and this is the ultimate measure of the effectiveness of discourse.

Yet, if we examine the process of persuasion more closely, it is possible to single out two crucial moments when agreement *on the premises* plays a fundamental role: a preliminary stage, in which a common ground between arguer and audience is established; and the exploitation of premises in actual argumentative sequences. Both aspects will be analysed in the following paragraphs: the problem of agreement will be firstly examined in the rhetorical perspective of ethos, with a focus on the opening parts of a speech (Sect. 1.1); it will then be analysed in the context of the New Rhetoric, where the construction of the audience and the choice of objects of agreement play a crucial role (Sect. 1.2); finally, the discussion will move to the role of *topoi* (and *endoxa*) as the source of arguments (Sect. 1.3).

---

[2]Van Dijk (1992: 215) defines a macro speech act as: "the global speech act performed by the utterance of a whole discourse, and executed by a sequence of possibly different speech acts".

1.1 Agreement as a Rhetorical Problem

1.1.1 Rhetoric as Persuasive Discourse

When trying to define the scope and distinguishing character of rhetoric, Reboul (1994) focuses on its interpretation as the art of persuasion through discourse. In this definition, the aim of persuasion, which is universally recognized as an essential feature of rhetoric, is further specified by two crucial words, *art* and *discourse*, which respectively emphasise its methodological approach and its linguistic nature.

Born, and already fully developed in Aristotle's work, rhetoric as a *techne* looks at persuasion as a complex but fully integrated process, and systematically examines the mechanisms of language in the perspective of persuasion. A crucial element in this unitary approach is the existence of forms of non-necessary truth on the one hand,[3] and the inseparable connections among the different means exploited to reach a persuasive goal on the other.[4] Rhetorical truth emerges in an area where things can be different from what they are—in opposition to the realm of necessity, where things cannot be different from what they are. This is the domain of primarily non-apophantic uses of language, and linguistic actions are performed with the aim of persuasion. In this process, numerous elements co-exist and interact to form a cohesive whole, and can be singled out and separated only for the sake of clarity and pedagogical explanation. The importance of these aspects will emerge in what follows, in connection with both preliminary agreement and premises for argumentation proper.

Quite evidently, reaching agreement through a persuasive process implies the existence of a *disagreement space*, an original difference of opinions, which in turn can occur only because there is no absolute truth. Demonstrative reasoning does not concern persuasion, because its conclusions are the inevitable consequence of undisputable premises. In the realm of rhetoric and of non-apophantic language, instead, things can be different from what they are and occur only "for the most part" (*hos epí to polú*). This concept is crucial in Aristotle's thought, and marks the domain of human action, where human behaviour is capable of modifying reality and can design the course of the events. *Hos epí to polú* knowledge is not deceiving nor approximate, and is not secondary to knowledge based on necessity. It is not possible to establish a hierarchical order between the two different approaches to knowledge, which merely depend on the objects involved and must therefore be

---

[3]This concept is usually connected to the distinction between demonstrative and persuasive reasoning, the former being based on the principles of formal logic, the latter developed in the realm of probability and starting from probable premises.

[4]These two aspects of Aristotle's thought are emphasised in the comment on his *Rhetoric* by Piazza (2008, but also 2004), which is considered one of the most acute and comprehensive produced in the last few decades. In the course of this chapter, frequent reference will be made to the observations of the Italian researcher.

adequate to the different contexts—it would simply be absurd to expect persuasive reasoning from a mathematician or a demonstration from a rhetorician. [5]

The premises exploited in argumentation are only probable, but this circumstance does not compromise its soundness and its value:

> Since *few of the premises from which rhetorical deductions are composed are necessary* (for most of the things that judgments and investigations are concerned with admit of being otherwise [...]), and since things that happen for the most part and are possible must be deduced from other such things, and necessary ones from necessary ones (and this is also clear to us from the *Analytics*), it is evident that while some of the premises on the basis of which enthymemes are stated will be necessary, *the majority will hold for the most part.* [...] *A likelihood is what comes about for the most part*, not however simply so, as some people define it, but rather [1] when it concerns things that admit of being otherwise, [2] standing in relation to that in relation to which it is a likelihood as the universal stands to the particular (Rh. 1357a: 9; emphasis added).[6]

In ancient rhetoric a crucial role is played by the notion of *eikós* ('likelihood'), whose interpretation has however been heavily influenced by an anti-rhetoric attitude. With the disqualification of rhetoric, which reached its climax in the second half of the XIX century, the concept was given negative evaluation, emphasising the distance between *eikós* and truth. Yet the etymological analysis of the word used by Aristotle shows that its original meaning referred to what happens in usual conditions and is therefore adequate to those conditions (Piazza, 2008: 54–59).[7] *Eikós* is not the opposite of truth (*alethés*), but should rather be conceived as an intermediate term between what is extraordinary and what is necessary. It indicates what happens "for the most part". The three notions form a sort of *continuum*, which does not discriminate between true and false, as there can be truth in extraordinary, probable or necessary things—albeit with different degrees of probability. Lack of necessity does not necessarily imply falsehood, and a different conviction is only the consequence of a rationalistic attitude, which has long privileged the idea of the immediate, self-evident nature of truth. This is one of the main reasons for the decline of rhetoric, which is inherently founded on probability, as necessity would simply pre-empt the possibility of persuasion.

The *discursive* nature of rhetoric implies that persuasion is a question of finding adequate linguistic expressions, capable of producing the desired perlocutive effect. The linguistic problem is obviously rooted in a pragmatic dimension. There is a subject (*I*) who addresses one or more subjects (*you*), using speech to reach a goal, thus emphasising the constitutive role of deixis in communication. Language cannot

---

[5]This example is taken from Aristotle's *Nicomachean Ethics* (1094b, 25).

[6]In all the quotations from Aristotle's Rhetoric (Rh.) the page number refers to the English translation by C. D. C. Reeve (2018).

[7]The negative evaluation of the notion of *eikós* is particularly evident in the Italian context, reinforced by a traditional, but questionable translation choice. The word *verosimile*, literally referring to what is "similar to the truth" emphasises the distance between what is *eikós* and what is true, as if a "likelihood" *only* had the appearance of truth and were actually (though implicitly) false.

be separated from the speaker, and this pragmatic dimension makes it possible to go beyond Saussure's opposition between *langue* and *parole*, as clearly shown in the pioneering studies by Benveniste (1966).[8] Personal deixis, in particular, accounts for the identification of the characters involved in the discursive performance: the arguer, using language through the appropriation of the first-person singular pronoun, indirectly generates their deictic counterpart, *you*, as object of the linguistic action. In rhetorical terms, the audience seems to be the most important element, as it guides the choices of the speaker and becomes a measure of the effectiveness of the discursive process itself. Furthermore, the nature and role of the audience is at the basis of Aristotle's classification of genres.

1.1.2 Genres

For Aristotle, there are three kinds (*eidos*) of rhetoric, corresponding to three types of listeners (Rh. 1358b). At the beginning of the first book of his Rhetoric, he singles out the three genres, emphasising that discourse is made up of three elements: the speaker, the thing spoken about, and the addressee. The aim of discourse is linked to this third element, and its different manifestations lead to the classification of genres. The listener *must* be either spectator or judge, and as a judge can consider either past or future events. The judge of future events is the member of an assembly, while the judge of past events is the member of a court; the spectator, on the other hand, judges the ability of the speaker. As a consequence, there are three genres (*genos*): the deliberative, the judiciary, and the epideictic. The first is based on exhortation or dissuasion, as the speaker either encourages or discourages a given course of action, and deliberation consequently concerns future events, through the evaluation of what is advantageous or harmful. A judiciary action involves either accusation or defence, referring to past events, and aiming to single out either just or unjust behaviour. Finally, the epideictic genre consists in either praise or blame, in order to distinguish what is noble from what is shameful. This classification implies that, depending on the genre and therefore on the character of the audience, different elements and values are involved in the persuasive process. For example, if arguers aim to praise or blame, they will not consider if an action is advantageous, while before the assembly fairness can be neglected, as the aim is to encourage advantageous and discourage disadvantageous behaviour. The Aristotelian classification stems from a very general principle, but it is evident that, in the political situation of the Greek *polis,* it referred to actual text production, which required appropriate use of argumentative schemes and stylistic devices. Norms governing the production of effective forms of discourse were genre-specific, i.e. context-based, as the three different genres corresponded to specific social situations, each having its aims and characteristics.

---

[8]This aspect will be discussed more extensively in Chap. 3.

In modern theories of genre, the Aristotelian focus on the audience can be easily recognised. Indicated in text analysis as an important element to single out different registers (Halliday, 1985), integrated into the notion of intertextuality to account for its paradigmatic dimension (de Beaugrande & Dressler, 1981), genre has been differently defined, but the aim(s) of communication have always been taken into consideration, and even considered as the main (if not exclusive) element for classification (Swales, 1990), in a genuinely pragmatic context (Miller, 1984). Actually, the emphasis on the goals of discourse should not lead to neglect a crucial, and complementary, feature: namely, the expectations of the addressees. This aspect is emphasised in Jauss' concept of genre as *Erwartungshorizont* ('horizon of expectations', Jauss, 1977), which is effectively exploited in discourse analysis, well beyond the realm of the reception of literary texts where it originated.

The focus on the audience in genre analysis (Bhatia, 2004)—and, more generally, in discourse analysis—is tightly intertwined with the persuasive nature of discourse, which is widely pervasive and occurs in texts across different genres, including those lacking an overt persuasive aim.[9] It has been noted that there is an argumentative dimension in discourse, to be distinguished from actual argumentative reasoning, which cannot be eliminated and inherently (albeit often implicitly) characterises interpersonal communication (Amossy, 2005; cf. *supra*, Introduction). From this point of view, the identification of genres from the point of view of the listener is the first step in the process of persuasion, as the fundamental rules governing discourse production stem from generic differences, as determined by the role of the addressees (cf. Aristotle) or, more generally speaking, by their expectations. In other words, the prerequisite for obtaining agreement is adequate and accurate consideration of the audience.

1.1.3   Ethos

Within a given discourse genre, arguers have however different means of proof to support their thesis. The traditional classification, based on Aristotle's approach, singles out three kinds (*eidos*) of persuasion: the first depending on the character of the speaker (*ethos*), the second relying on the ability to dispose the listener in some way (*pathos*), and the third consisting in discourse itself (*logos*) (Rh. 1356 a). They evidently correspond to the three constitutive elements of a discursive interaction, i.e. the speaker, the listener, and discourse itself.

It is important to emphasise that the three different means of proof are all obtained *through discourse* (*dia tou logou*), and are therefore purely linguistic in nature. Moreover, they are all equally evaluated, and an effective persuasive process must

---

[9]The relevance of persuasion in genre analysis is emphasised in research focused on the diachronic perspective: it has been suggested that the effort to keep persuasion covert in discourse crucially contributes to the evolution of genres (Halmari & Virtanen, 2005).

include all of them, in a close interaction. It is the decline of rhetoric—in the context of rationalism—that led to a prejudice against ethos and pathos, as elements of "emotional" (if not "irrational") nature, and therefore opposed to logos, as the expression of authentic rational reasoning. This interpretation, however, does not belong to Aristotle's view. Each of the three means of proof can be exploited in an argumentative process aiming to persuasion, and the good arguer must be able to use all of them, and possibly decide if one has to prevail in a given context.[10] Their evaluation, again, ultimately depends on the audience.[11]

Ethos, however, is in some respect the strongest argument, as it is able to generate trust (Rh. 1356a). Persuasion is obtained through ethos when the speaker is trustworthy, a quality that is all the more important in the case of disputable truths, i.e. when different opinions can legitimately be put forth, as a reliable person is *in general* able to raise approval more strongly and more immediately. Therefore, the importance of reliability in the persuasive process is not the consequence of a poor attitude to reasoning of the listener, as is assumed in rationalistic approaches, but depends on the very nature of argumentation. Whenever matters can be discussed and leave room for different interpretations, we are naturally inclined to give credit to people we trust, and this is not an irrational behaviour.[12]

However, the adhesion of the listener must be obtained through discourse, and not through previous opinions concerning the character of the speaker: we trust "decent speakers" more, "this should come about through the speech, however, not through prior belief that the speaker is of a certain quality" (*Rh.*: 1356a, 9–10).[13] Ethos is a proof—and possibly the most important proof—insofar as it is a discursive phenomenon; it results from what is said and how it is said, and not from previous knowledge, prejudices or fame independent of discourse.[14]

Quite interestingly, when Aristotle introduces *topoi*, as the elements from which argumentative reasoning develops, he immediately goes beyond the purely logical dimension, emphasising the importance of self-representation of the speaker and of

---

[10] The interdependence of the three Aristotelian means of proof is discussed by Piazza (2004: 155-59).

[11] For example, ethos is more important in deliberation, while pathos plays a more relevant role in the judiciary (Rh. 1377b, 30).

[12] This aspect is extensively analysed by Piazza (2004: 159-161; 2008: 92-94).

[13] All comments on Aristotle's Rhetoric emphasise this aspect (cf., for all, Kennedy, 1991), which is not a constant in the ancient rhetorical tradition.

[14] Yet it is to be noted that pre-discursive ethos is imbued with discursive values and often constructed through discourse. *Doxa* ('fame') does not actually lie outside discourse in general, but simply outside the speech delivered in a given situation (Piazza, 2008: 98). A good example of discursive strategies intentionally adopted to construct a positive *doxa*, which in its turn is part of pre-discursive ethos in dialogue, is offered by a character in the Italian novel *I promessi sposi* ('The Betrothed') by A. Manzoni. *Conte zio* ('the Uncle Count') is a master in using words to construct his own image of powerful nobleman emphasising his political connections well beyond actual fact, and then exploiting it when confronting his interlocutors (Santulli, 2009).

the attitude of the audience (Rh. 1377b).[15] In particular, the persuasive strength of the speaker stems from three positive characters: *phronesis* (wisdom), *areté* (virtue), *eunoia* (goodwill), three good causes for believing in what someone claims (Rh. 1378a, 8). Each of them concerns a different aspect of the credibility of the arguer: the intellectual, the moral and the interactional sphere, respectively. *Phronesis* is the capacity of forming correct opinions about the matter under discussion to find adequate means to reach the desired objectives, while *areté* is what makes us choose a fair objective and therefore makes us appear just and honest. Finally, *eunoia* is a special feeling towards the audience, not really friendship but a sort of prerequisite to it, which makes the arguer desire the good for their audience.

The nature and role of these qualities is explained from the negative point of view, considering what happens when they are absent, and in connection to lying, or saying what is false. 'False' advice is due to these three causes, or at least one of them: arguers may reason incorrectly for lack of wisdom; though thinking correctly, they may not say the truth for wickedness; finally, there are speakers who, being wise and honest, are not benevolent and therefore do not suggest what they know is better (Rh. 1378a). There is no contradiction between beliefs stemming from truth and those based on the reliability of the arguer; rather, the three ethical qualities enhance persuasive strength in the speaker, and thus make discourse more persuasive, *because* their presence is indicative of truthfulness. The character of the speaker as a means of proof is not of moral nature, but refers to their ability to appear trustworthy, and therefore persuasive. These qualities must be displayed from the very beginning: when discussing the organization of a speech in Book III of his Rhetoric, Aristotle focuses on the Introduction, where appeals to the listener are based on producing in them goodwill and attention (Rh. 1415a). These in turn "will lead to ease of learning (*eumatheian*), if the speaker wishes it, including his appearing to be a decent person. For the listener pay more attention to such people" (Rh. 1415a: 35–39). Attention, goodwill and ease of learning are crucial prerequisites for the arguer to obtain agreement: they persist throughout the speech and reflect positively on argumentation proper.

The connection of rhetorical ethos with crucial concepts in modern pragmatics appears to be fully justified, if we consider how the notion has been accommodated in the context of linguistic research, parallel to the growing interest for rhetoric that extends from linguistics proper to argumentation studies and discourse analysis. Ethos has been studied in the argumentative framework, mainly focusing on informal fallacies (s., among others, van Eemeren & Grootendorst, 2004, Walton et al., 2008), and in the discursive perspective of argumentation, integrating rhetoric with sociology and pragmatics (Amossy, 2001, 2009, 2010). Pragmatics has obviously been a privileged area for a discussion about ethos, paving the way for an 'extended'

---

[15] "For it makes a great difference with a view to persuading—especially in deliberative speeches, but next in judicial ones—both that the speaker appear to be of a certain quality and that his listeners take him to be disposed in a certain way toward them, and if, in addition, they too will be disposed in a certain way" (Rh. 1377b: 55).

interpretation of rhetoric itself (Adam, 1999) that moves from a revaluation of the discipline to widen its scope and include its application to a wide choice of genres.

The role of the three fundamental characters (wisdom, virtue, goodwill) and the question of truth can be re-examined in the light of the principles of communicative interaction and cooperation in conversation (Grice, 1975), on the one side, and in connection with the felicity conditions of speech acts (Austin, 1962) on the other. Venier (2008) suggests that a balanced exploitation of the three Aristotelian characters can be compared to a conversation that complies with the Maxims of Conversation, while the arguer who chooses to create an imbalance (and, for example, to privilege a character to the detriment of the others) behaves similarly to one who deliberately flouts the Maxims. According to Venier, this makes it possible to interpret the rhetorical system in the light of Grice's model of conversation. The Maxims, as a synthesis of the principles guiding an effective exchange, actually reflect the behaviour of the speaker and can be considered the modern counterpart of the norms governing the production of persuasive discourse in ancient rhetoric. On the other hand, when Austin discusses the conditions that hinder the felicitous performance of a speech act, he includes a crucial condition, which depends on the speaker, namely sincerity. In performing an act, the speaker shows sincerity as a conventional character, which is the precondition for the success of a communicative exchange. Sincerity, in its turn, is parallel to ethos, as embodied in the characters of the arguer, which are inherently part of discourse, as we do not even lend our ears, if we do not give credit to the speaker.

The linguistic manifestation of the characters of the arguer is a crucial thread that runs across discourse. The characters indicated by Aristotle have a certain degree of conventionality (Barthes, 1970): wisdom implies careful consideration of pros and cons in a certain situation; virtue is manifested as a sort of braveness and frankness; benevolence is translated into agreeableness, and marks the desire to obtain communion with the audience. We can interpret these traits as conventional norms of discursive behaviour in a given cultural context, namely the civilization in which rhetorical principles originated. Not differently from topoi, they are culture-specific, though it is possible to single out recurring elements across different cultures. The very existence of norms for self-presentation is one of the most interesting legacies of the rhetorical approach. If we extend these considerations from the arguer (as 'public' speaker) to any speaker involved in a conversational exchange, the rhetorical problem can be linked to the concept of face (and face-work), within the paradigm of politeness.

Considering that the (re)presentation of the Self and the Other is a constitutive aspect of any linguistic interaction, the rhetorical perspective on ethos can naturally be integrated into the linguistic approach typical of the enunciation theory (Benveniste 1966). In discourse analysis, this has led to the concept of *discursive ethos* (as opposed to *pre-discursive ethos*) (Maingueneau, 1999, 2016),[16] which accepts the Aristotelian notion of ethos as a means of proof obtained *through*

---

[16]The relationship between constructed and pre-existing image of a speaker in ancient rhetoric is examined by Žmavc (2012), who emphasises the differences between the Greek (Aristotelian) and

discourse, emphasising that further elements deriving from the real character of the arguer are not relevant for linguistic analysis. Moreover, the modern version of ethos does not include reference to the three elements singled out in ancient rhetoric, but is more comprehensively conceived as the self-representation of the speaker in discourse, which implies at the same time the existence (and the active role) of the Other, as co-enunciator. Ethos is always constructed and represented for an addressee, it is, according to Auchlin (2000: 76), a "hologramme expérientiel" which is shown in enunciation and is processed both in the production and in the reception of discourse. This expansion of the ethotic dimension makes it possible to recognise and investigate ethos in any type of text, beyond the realm of the three rhetorical genres.

A parallel between this modern interpretation of ethos and the pragmatic concept of face is established by Antelmi (2011), who integrates the two aspects into the paradigm of politeness. One of the crucial problems with the notion of politeness—namely its alleged universal value—is investigated by Antelmi in the light of the connections between face and ethos. As is well known, face is a principle that governs actual strategies of politeness, though it is differently interpreted in different contexts and cultures. Goffman's original definition of face (1967) as the positive social value that each participant in a dialogic communicative exchange recognizes and defends gives it a cross-cultural value, independent of specific linguistic and cultural norms.

Ethos has a wider scope than politeness, as it refers to the image of the speaker in discourse and through discourse in any kind of context, both in dialogue and in monologic speeches, in oral as well as in written texts across genres. Even in contexts where *face-work* and the negotiation between interlocutors is impossible, ethos is always present, as the enunciator inevitably conveys a self-image and, at the same time, implicitly constructs the image of the co-enunciator. Thus, the construction of the audience can be seen as a question of ethos. [17]

1.2 Agreement in the New Rhetoric

The rebirth of Rhetoric in the XX century, conventionally marked by the publication of the *Treatise on Argumentation—The New Rhetoric* (Perelman & Olbrechts-Tyteca, 1958, from now on NR), is strongly characterized by a focus on the audience. The NR was explicitly conceived as a turning point in the history of Western thought, as shown in its opening lines:

---

the Roman approach, affirming that in the latter rhetorical ethos "almost entirely consists of the speaker's pre-existing reputation and the authority that comes from it" (2012: 186).

[17] According to Antelmi (2011), ethos—having a wider scope than face—can be useful as a measure for politeness.

> The publication of a treatise devoted to argumentation and this subject's connection with the ancient tradition of Greek rhetoric and dialectic constitutes a *break with a concept of reason and reasoning due to Descartes* which has set its mark on Western philosophy for the last three centuries (NR: 1; emphasis in the original).[18]

The fundamental message of Perelman and Olbrechts-Tyteca lies in their refusal to identify reason with self-evident truth and formal reasoning. In line with the authentic Aristotelian tradition, they put forth a general theory of argumentation, whose scope extends beyond the realm of demonstration and includes all types of discourse, independently of its domain and its audience. One of the reasons why the word *rhetoric* is included in the subtitle of this book (and preferred to *dialectics*) is Perelman and Olbrechts-Tyteca's will to emphasize the fact that "*it is in terms of an audience than an argumentation develops*" (NR: 5; emphasis in the original). The audience, in other words, is not an external and possibly fortuitous element, but inherently belongs to argumentation (Piazza, 2004: 58). Differently from ancient rhetoricians, Perelman and Olbrechts-Tyteca do not aim to develop persuasive capacities in their disciples, but want to understand the mechanisms of thought, focusing on the analysis of argumentative structures. They examine neither *memoria* nor *actio*, and do not exclude written texts from their investigation. Yet they preserve the fundamental concept of *audience*, which extends from listeners (who physically belong to the context of communication) to readers, and therefore implies that a writer is not different from a speaker, insofar as their discourse is always conditioned by the persons they intend to address.

A theory of argumentation aims to study "the discursive techniques allowing us *to induce or to increase the mind's adherence to the theses presented for its assent*" (NR: 4, emphasis in the original). For this very reason, argumentation presupposes the presence of an *intellectual contact*, of a community of minds that must exist in a given context:

> There must first of all be agreement, in principle, on the formation of this intellectual community, and, after that, on the fact of debating a specific question together: now this does not come about automatically (NR: 14).

Thus, obtaining preliminary agreement is a specific goal for any arguer.

The pivotal role of the audience clearly emerges in the organization of the NR. Starting from the different implications of demonstration and argumentation, in Part One (*The Framework of Argumentation*) Perelman and Olbrechts-Tyteca introduce the relation between speaker and addressees, and discuss the very notion of audience. The problem of preliminary agreement (inextricably intertwined with the idea of *construction* of the audience) is then investigated in Part Two (*The Starting Point of Argument*), which includes a chapter totally devoted to *Agreement*, and then examines the selection of data and the discursive forms for their presentation. *Ethos* is explicitly mentioned in Part Three (*The Techniques of Argumentation*), among the arguments based on the structure of reality. Rhetorical figures contribute

---

[18]In all the quotations from Perelman and Olbrechts-Tyteca' *New Rhetoric* (NR) the page number refers to English translation by John Wilkinson & Purcell Weaver (1969).

to the process of agreement, as they are selected and exploited with a view to meeting the expectations of the addressees, which makes it possible for them to play an actual argumentative role. In what follows, the discussion will start from ethos (Sect. 1.2.1), it will then focus on the audience and its construction (Sect. 1.2.2) and on the objects of agreement (Sect. 1.2.3). The role of figures as linguistic means exploited to enhance agreement in argumentation will be examined in Chap. 3 (Sect. 3.7).

1.2.1 Agreement and Ethos

Ethos as a crucial element in the relation between speaker and addressees is not explicitly discussed in the NR. It is not even mentioned in the opening parts of the treatise and is only evoked in the section devoted to the techniques of argumentation. Here the focus is on the interaction between speaker and *speech* (§ 72), examined among the arguments "based on the structure of reality", and in particular those rooted in a link of *coexistence* (NR, Part III, Ch. 2, section B). In this framework, the relationship between speaker and speech is of the "act-person type". It is so strong that "irrespective of his wishes [...], a speaker runs the risk that the hearer will regard him as intimately connected with his speech" (NR: 317). The person is therefore part of the *context* of a speech, being actually "the best context for evaluating the meaning and the significance of an assertion" (*Ibid.*). Evidently, it is a question of ethos.

Ethos is explicitly mentioned in the context of the speaker-speech relation with reference to practical recommendations given by ancient rhetoricians in order to gain respect, goodwill and sympathy. The effort of the *speaker* is to inspire confidence, as without it the *speech* would merit no credence. According to Perelman and Olbrechts-Tyteca, "what the ancients used to call *oratorical ethos* can be summed up as the impression which the speaker, by means of words, gives of himself" (NR: 319). They quote La Bruyère to offer an example of how the person of the speaker can play a prominent role in persuasion:

> A worldly or irreligious cleric who goes up into the pulpit is just a phrasemonger. On the other hand, there are saintly men whose character, alone, carries the power of persuasion. They appear, and the whole multitude which is going to hear them is already moved and, as it were, persuaded by their presence (La Bruyère, *Caractères*, quoted in NR: 319).

It is important to emphasise that for Perelman and Olbrechts-Tyteca the role of the speaker, and the interaction between speaker and speech:

> is perhaps the most characteristic part of argumentation as opposed to demonstration. In formal deduction, the role of the speaker is reduced to a minimum; it increases progressively as the language used is more removed from univocity and as context, intentions, and ends gain in importance (NR: 317).

The person as a crucial element of the context is decisive for the interpretation and evaluation of utterances, and can shed new light even on reported words as "in the process of repetition [the arguer] always adopts toward them a position in some way new, even if only in the degree of importance he attaches to them" (*Ibidem*). Yet the role of the person is less important when their statements are part of a consolidated system, as the system itself (and the positioning of the statements in the system) is a guide to their interpretation. This is what typically happens in certain forms of scientific communication.

Scientific communication is mentioned in the first Part of the treatise, when Perelman and Olbrechts-Tyteca aim to investigate the conditions that make a contact of minds possible in a wide range of social situations, from serious debates to trivial everyday conversation. To do so, they initially focus on the analysis of scientific communication and suggest that most scientists believe that sheer presentation of facts is sufficient to raise the interest of their readers. Yet this approach is the consequence of a typically rationalistic "illusion", namely the idea that "facts speak for themselves and make such an indelible imprint on any human mind that the latter is forced to give its adherence regardless of its inclination" (NR: 17, § 3). Although this conviction is deceptive in nature, scientists writing for a journal or speaking before a group of peers can rely on an exceptional commonality of knowledge, method and approach that justifies them to disregard the quest for preliminary agreement.[19] The importance of ethos is thus parallel to the importance of agreement: they both gain momentum when the arguer moves away from the realm of formal reasoning and indisputably shared mechanisms to venture into the uncertain and still unexplored land of possibilities.

As mentioned above, in the NR the problem of the audience is amply discussed in the opening sections. When examining the speaker-speech relation (§ 72), however, Perelman and Olbrechts-Tyteca extend this link of coexistence to the audience, and refer back to the first part of the treatise (§§ 5–6). Ultimately, the conclusion of the analysis of the speaker-speech-audience coexistence shows the interconnection of the three elements:

> The interdependence of act and person in the audience influences the effect of argumentation. Reference to this connection between act and hearer can be superimposed on the arguments expressed, as well as on the connection between speaker and speech, and can interfere with these elements (NR: 321).

1.2.2   The Audience and its Construction

In the New Rhetoric, the link between speaker and audience plays a fundamental role, not only in the preliminary stages but across the whole argumentative process.

---

[19] From the point of view of contemporary science, it can be noticed that there are differences among disciplines and domains: the approach of formal sciences (as logic and mathematics), natural sciences (as chemistry or biology), and social sciences (as sociology or linguistics) varies, corresponding to different degrees of commitment in the construction of agreement and in the exploitation of ethotic means of proof.

As stated in § 3: "For since argumentation aims at securing the adherence of those to whom it is addressed, it is, in its entirety, relative to the audience to be influenced" (NR: 19).

The definition of audience put forth by Perelman and Olbrechts-Tyteca is a direct consequence of this approach, as, for the purposes of persuasion, the audience is effectively identified as *"the ensemble of those whom the speaker wishes to influence by his argumentation"* (*Ibidem*, emphasis in the original). The emphasis on the intention of the speaker clearly connects the rhetorical model to the pragmatic interpretation of persuasion and to contextual factors. In the identification of the audience, however, material criteria are insufficient to describe the context and to determine what constitutes a speaker's audience. The audience is the result of a deliberate act of the arguer, who selects their ideal addressees, an ensemble that has no physical counterpart, but is rather a "thought construction of the arguer" (van Eemeren et al., 1996: 97). The knowledge of the audience—which is "a condition preliminary to all effectual argumentation" (NR: 20)—is therefore a form of self-awareness, insofar as the speaker 'constructs' their own audience, and must be aware of all the aspects of the process, from the rationale of their choice to the means to be exploited to put it into effect.

An adequate construction of the audience starts with the choice of the addressees, through a selection of the (social, economic, cultural etc.) features that identify them. In this process, it is important to be aware of the inevitably composite nature of an audience, as it is impossible to imagine a perfectly homogeneous group, no matter how small it may be.[20] When knowledge of the members of this ensemble is adequate—including the different roles played by sub-groups or individuals—it is possible to focus on the problem of its conditioning. As a matter of fact, "knowledge of an audience cannot be conceived independently of the knowledge of how to influence it. [. . .] knowledge of an audience is also knowledge of how to bring about its conditioning, as well as of the amount of conditioning achieved at any moment of the discourse" (NR: 23). Conditioning through the speech (which is the matter discussed in the NR) cannot occur without adaptation of the speaker to their audience, which is tantamount to adapting the speech to the audience. Obviously, this is nothing new in rhetoric. As discussed above, in Aristotle's Rhetoric the classification of genres and their connection with specific argumentative and stylistic means relies on the nature of their different audiences. The measure of effective argumentation ultimately lies in its being adequate for a given audience.

The extremely complex nature of the audience on the one side, and its crucial role on the other, are the reasons why "there is such a tremendous interest in a technique of argumentation that would apply to any kinds of audiences" (TA: 26), beyond historical and local differences. The ideal of finding means acceptable for all actually

---

[20]In this respect, it is worth mentioning the distinction put forth by van Eemeren (2010: 110) between a multiple audience (with differences of opinion concerning a standpoint) and a mixed audience (with differences concerning the starting points), the latter being particularly difficult to tackle in relation to the construction of agreement.

re-introduces the opposition between opinion and truth. According to Perelman and Olbrechts-Tyteca, it is the debate over the problem of objectivity that gave rise to the distinction between *convincing* and *persuading*. This distinction is re-examined in the context of a theory of argumentation based on the role of the audience.

In this framework, conviction is the result of argumentation that can be accepted by any rational being, while persuasion relies on arguments that claim validity only for a particular audience. In current language use, the two terms have different semantic implications, as persuasion usually evokes a strong emotional involvement, in opposition to conviction that brings forth the rational approach to argumentation, suggesting objectivity and universal validity. This distinction, however, is a delicate matter, as it ultimately depends on the idea of rationality—rationality of the speaker and, as a consequence, of their audience. It is reminiscent of the Kantian opposition (different in principle, but similar in its consequences) between *Überzeugung* and *Überredung* (*conviction* and *persuasion*, respectively) but does not imply the acceptance of the distinction between objective and subjective beliefs. On the contrary, as a purely rhetorical notion the opposition between conviction and persuasion relies on the nature of the audience, and "expresses indirectly the connection that is frequently established, though in a confused way, between persuasion and action, on the one hand, and, on the other, between conviction and intelligence" (NR: 29). The conviction-persuasion distinction is the foundation for the opposition between *the universal* and *a particular* audience.

The universal audience ideally includes all mankind, as stated by Perelman and Olberchts-Tyteca, who try to provide an empirical definition, describing it as "the whole of mankind, or at least, of all normal, adult persons" (NR: 30). It is addressed with *convincing* arguments while a particular audience is an ensemble of subjects addressed with *persuasive* reasoning. It is however difficult to draw a sharp line between convincing and persuading. The universal audience is an abstract concept: on the one hand, the universal audience of a given arguer is the result of their concept of rationality, and can therefore be considered the manifestation of a particular audience; on the other hand, a particular audience can represent an idea of rationality and therefore play the role that is typical of the universal audience. For example, a scientific community, in a given domain, can be for a scientist *their* embodiment of the concept of universal audience, as a peer group sharing their knowledge of the outer world as well as the fundamentals of the discipline and the methods for research. It can also occur, though, that this audience is not assimilated to the universal audience, as the arguer may want to keep it separate from the rest of mankind, and treat it as a model to be imitated by others. In other words, it is difficult to keep the *universal* audience apart from a *particular* audience. This difficulty stems from the character of the distinction, which is the result of a choice of the arguer, who selects the audience, constructs its image, and decides how to address it. A particular audience is nothing more than a "fortuitous" manifestation of the universal audience (van Eemeren et al., 1996: 100).

In order to defend a thesis with sound arguments, arguers must preliminarily select the audience they intend to address and then, through an accurate analysis of its characters, choose the arguments that have more probabilities to be accepted, so that their argumentation will be effective (and, as a consequence, valid). Therefore, argumentation is not evaluated with the instruments of formal logic nor from an aesthetic point of view, thus avoiding ethical issues and shifting the process into a pragmatic dimension, where speech acts are effectively performed by the speaker.

1.2.3   Objects of Agreement

Given the crucial role of the audience, the first task of the arguer is to catch the attention of the addressees and keep it alive. They must adapt to the expectations and the needs of the addressees, establishing a contact with them. This quest for agreement can be interpreted as an effort of self-positioning of the arguer in the context of the beliefs held by their audience (Venier, 2008: 76). At the basis of argumentation there is the creation of a common ground shared by the arguer and the audience, made up of a range of solid premises, whence argumentation proper can develop. There must be *agreement on the premises*.[21] From start to finish, argumentation is concerned with the agreement of the audience, exploiting what is supposed to be accepted by the addressees. In this process, the choice of premises and their formulation have a crucial value, as they are the actual foundation of arguments, and they are not subject to discussion, presupposing the adherence of the audience. They prepare for the argumentative stage, and represent the first crucial step in persuasion. Their selection and the way they are presented are the key to agreement, which relies on adherence to the premises in absence of actual argumentative effort.

In the NR, the discussion starts with the types of agreement that can serve as premises, dividing these "objects of agreement" into two classes: one concerning the *real* (facts, truths, and presumptions), and the other concerning the *preferable* (values, hierarchies, and loci). This classification is connected to the analysis of the audience we have already examined:

> The conceptions people form of the real can vary widely, depending on the philosophic views they profess. However, everything in argumentation that is deemed to relate to the real is characterized by a claim of validity vis-à-vis the universal audience. On the contrary, all that pertains to the preferable, that which determines our choices and does not conform to a pre-existent reality, will be connected with a specific viewpoint which is necessarily identified with some particular audience, though it may be a large one (NR: 66).

The choice of the objects to be exploited is obviously functional to obtaining the adherence of a given audience, and this confirms that the first and foremost task of the arguer is to select their audience, having a clear mental picture of its distinguishing traits to find out what is more adequate for them.

Objects of agreement are not subject to argumentation, but there may be differences in the way they are presented to the selected audience. In the realm of the real,

---

[21] In pragma-dialectics this is the *starting point rule* (cf., for ex., van Eemeren & Grootendorst, 2004: 193).

facts and truths are opposed to presumptions. [22] The former are statements for which it is possible to postulate universal agreement, though the possibility of confuting them is not totally excluded. If agreement on them is not obtained, these objects are not accepted as premises but are brought up for discussion, so that they are no longer treated as facts but as opinions. Presumptions, on the other hand, do imply that something is true or real, as they are linked to what is "normal and likely" (NR: 71), and therefore can claim the agreement of the universal audience, but the addressees expect their adherence to be reinforced through other elements.

In the realm of the preferable, objects of agreement are linked to the preferences of a given particular audience. Values are naturally subject to differences of opinion and can therefore be exploited to contrapose different groups—or audiences. Hierarchies of values are even more important than values themselves; they concern the possibility of grading different values or the degree of acceptance of a given value:

> Most values are indeed shared by a great number of audiences, and a particular audience is characterized less by which values it accepts than by the way it grades them. Values may be admitted by many different audiences, but the degree of their acceptance will vary from one audience to another. A hierarchy which should not be disregarded is established by the intensity with which one value is adhered to as compared to another. [. . .] In most cases, not only are the values adhered with different degrees of intensity, but the audience admits principles by which the values can be graded (NR: 81).[23]

Agreement on values is particularly important, as it stems from a choice of the arguer, who justifies it to obtain the adherence of the addressees. It is agreement on values that makes a common action possible. Though there are values that seem to have universal validity, their apparent universal applicability fades away when they are brought into focus more sharply. We all pursue the Good, but we may have different opinions about what it actually consists of.

Therefore, the divide between facts and values is not clear-cut. Suffice it to think of how differently historical facts can be told; whenever a narrative is assumed as a premise it becomes a fact, though it is imbued with values that influence the way reality is interpreted. In a wider perspective:

> A statement can be understood as relating to what is commonly considered a fact or to what is considered a value, depending on its place in the speech, on what it enunciates, refutes, or corrects. Also, the status of statements evolves: when inserted into a system of beliefs for which universal validity is claimed, values may be treated as facts or truths (NR: 75-76).

Values can be presented as universal notions, thus increasing the dimension of the selected audience, but through a sharper definition they can also be transformed into the banner of a more limited group.

> In the course of the argumentation, and sometimes by a rather slow process, it may perhaps come to be recognized that one is dealing with objects of agreement that cannot make a claim

---

[22] Actually, truths are more complex systems, which imply the connection of different facts, as is the case of scientific theories or philosophic conceptions.

[23] The third type of premises belonging to the realm of the preferable, *loci*, will be treated *infra*, Sect. 1.3.1.

to the adherence of the universal audience. But if this is, as we claim, the characteristic of values, what about such things as the *True*, the *Good*, the *Beautiful*, and the *Absolute*, which are readily considered as universal or absolute values?

The claim to universal agreement, as far as they are concerned, seems to us to be due solely to their generality. They can be regarded as valid for a universal audience only on condition that their content not be specified; as soon as we try to go into details, we meet only the adherence of particular audiences (*Ibidem*).

In other words, it is the arguer who marks the boundary between universal and particular audience and through their choices determines the validity of their argumentative strategies. The selection and exploitation of objects of agreement is therefore not a neutral process, as they are at the basis of argumentation and crucially contribute to its persuasive effect. Yet, as objects of agreement are not subject to discussion, they are often left in the realm of implicit meaning. It often occurs that they are not openly and explicitly presented but are rather conveyed through more subtle and less perceivable strategies.

The very choice of facts to be used as objects of agreement is a form of interpretation of reality, but the adoption of appropriate strategies can transform a personal point of view into a shared perspective, thus giving rise to an unquestionable representation of reality, which is assumed as truth. On the other hand, different linguistic and textual forms of evaluation are an effective means not only to give voice to, but also to construct a shared set of values. In numerous contexts, the identification of the values of a group is completed with the de-valuation of an adversary group (the 'enemy'), which in turn emphasises the shared positive traits. The most common and effective of these widely exploited linguistic strategies will be discussed in Chap. 3.

1.3   Agreement as an Argumentative Problem

1.3.1   Loci *in NR*

As illustrated above, in NR loci are introduced and discussed only as a form of support to values, to be exploited to construct agreement with the audience. This is explicitly stated in the opening lines of § 21:

When a speaker wants to establish values or hierarchies or to intensify the adherence they gain, he may consolidate them by connecting them with other values or hierarchies, but he may also resort to premises of a very general nature which we shall term *loci*. These are the τόποι of Greek writers, from which come the *Topics*, treatises devoted to dialectical reasoning (NR: 83).

Perelman and Olbrechts-Tyteca define loci as "headings under which arguments can be classified", and consider them as a precious instrument for the speaker, who can thus easily find useful elements for their speech. The advantage apparently lies in their accessibility, as they group materials that can then be retrieved whenever necessary. Accordingly, ancient rhetoricians frequently presented them as "store-houses for arguments" (*Ibidem*).

As pointed out by Rigotti and Greco (2019: 178), Perelman and Olbrechts-Tyteca acknowledge that with the decline of rhetoric the study of loci has progressively lost its argumentative focus, giving prominence to the oratorical aspects, so that when we consider a locus (and in particular *loci communes*), "we notice only its banality and fail to appreciate its argumentative value" (TA: 84). Yet, Rigotti and Greco empha-size that—despite these introductory remarks—the TA does not contribute to restor-ing a more traditional approach to loci, offering instead a "reductive" interpretation of their role. Namely, Perelman and Olbrechts-Tyteca do not treat loci as "relations (*habitudines* [...]) that generate principles of support for real arguments", but for the Authors loci "seem to be assimilated with rather generically defined 'general pre-mises'" (Rigotti & Greco, 2019: 179).

In the NR, loci are merely considered as a means to obtain preliminary agreement. Perelman and Olbrechts-Tyteca briefly illustrate the Aristotelian classification of *topoi*, but emphasise that their approach is different, first of all because they do not intend to commit to a metaphysical system. Moreover, they only consider loci in relation to values and hierarchies, in the realm of the preferable:

> As we distinguish the types of objects of agreement which relate to the real from those which relate to the preferable, we shall only apply the term *loci* to *premises of a general nature that can serve as the bases for values and hierarchies. Loci* of this kind are treated by Aristotle under the heading of *loci* relating to accident. Such *loci* form *the most general premises, actually often merely implied*, that play a part in the justification of most choices we make (NR: 84; emphasis added).

Perelman and Olbrechts-Tyteca do not aim at drawing up a list of these loci. They affirm that such an attempt (if ever feasible) lies outside the scope of their treatise, which excludes metaphysical speculation and is limited to the analysis of concrete arguments. Agreement may stem from *general* loci that are accepted by the inter-locutors, but these can be differently exploited and reconstructed, and are never beyond justification. Therefore, Perelman and Olbrechts-Tyteca find it more inter-esting to examine "more specific loci", which are accepted in different cultural contexts and can characterize them. The general nature of loci is itself illusory, as "each locus can be confronted by one which is contrary to it: thus, to the classical locus of superiority of the lasting, one may oppose the romantic locus of the superiority of that which is precarious and fleeting" (NR: 85). As a consequence, it is possible to oppose different cultures and societies on the basis of "the intensity with which they adhere to one or the other of a pair of antithetical loci". (*Ibidem*). Against this background, a series of loci is examined in the NR, starting from loci of quantity and of quality, to end up with the identification of a "classical outlook" opposed to a "romantic outlook" (§ 25). All of this is dealt with in the framework of useful considerations for the actual exploitation of loci in connection with a given audience in a given situation. These observations conclude the discussion of loci, which is confined to Part Two of the treatise.

For Rigotti and Greco (2019) a further clue to the "reductive interpretation" of loci put forth in the NR is the fact that Perelman and Olbrechts-Tyteca, when treating argumentative schemes (Part Three, which is the core of the book), do not connect their discussion with their previous observations about loci:

> [...] the topical tradition is left in the background. In particular, Perelman and Olbrechts-Tyteca propose an original criterion for classification of argumentative schemes, which has nothing in common with the criterion they had given for classifying loci: as if the two concepts are a complete disjunction (Rigotti & Greco, 2019: 179).

Nonetheless, when Perelman and Olbrechts-Tyteca examine argumentative schemes, the notion of loci somehow resurfaces, as the schemes can be "considered as *loci* of argumentation, because only agreement on their validity can justify their application to particular cases" (NR: 190). And, from the point of view of agreement:

> Our analysis of argumentation will deal first with what is taken as the starting point of arguments and afterwards with the way in which arguments are developed through a whole set of associative and dissociative processes. This division of the subject is indispensable to our examination and should not be misunderstood. The unfolding as well as the starting point of the argumentation presuppose indeed the agreement of the audience. *This agreement is sometimes on explicit premises, sometimes on the particular connecting link used in the argument or on the manner of using these links*: from start to finish, analysis of argumentation is concerned with what is supposed to be accepted by the hearers (NR: 65; emphasis added).

These are the opening lines of the chapter devoted to *Agreement* (Part Two, Ch. 1), which make it clear that agreement is not confined to the general premises (those examined in Part Two), but extends to the whole argumentative process. Similarly, loci as "objects" of agreement are seen not only as functional to reinforcing values, but they can be *identified* with the schemes themselves, characterized by processes of association and dissociation, classified and analysed in Part Three of the treatise (Kienpointner, 2006: 212). This identification is implicitly suggested also by Rigotti and Greco (2019), who lament the lack of connections between the two parts of the treatise, but conclude their brief examination of argumentative schemes in the NR affirming: "Perelman and Olbrechts-Tyteca's *classification of loci* is of great interest because of the detail with which each single argumentative scheme is discussed, including a variety of examples" (Rigotti & Greco, 2019: 180, emphasis added). Rigotti and Greco's observations are by no means isolated, as confirmed by the fact that the NR has frequently been indicated as an important contribution to the modern theory of topics (Walton et al., 2008). Given the long-standing difficulties in interpreting the position of loci in the NR, there seems to be a problem of terminology.

1.3.2 **Topos/Locus *and* Endoxa**

A systematic review of the notion of *locus* (the Latin counterpart of the Greek term, *topos*),[24] including different theoretical implications and different denominations, lies outside the scope of the present discussion. Suffice it to emphasise that the polysemy of the word on the one side, and the use of other terms with similar meaning on the other, have contributed to generate difficulties in the interpretation and application of the concept. Leff (2006) summarizes his years-long research in the subject emphasising the ambiguous and multi-faceted nature of the notion. He also mentions the differences between the dialectical and the rhetorical tradition as a source of the ambiguities emerging in the use of the word *topos*, and concludes that, given the hypothetical nature of rhetoric, in its realm *topoi* have a specific character and are meant for specific audiences.

In contemporary argumentation studies, the principles that are exploited for justification of statements are usually classified as argumentation (or argument) schemes and correspond to *topoi* (Garssen, 2001) or *general topoi* (Wagemans, 2011). Actually, a "precursor" of the modern term is Aristotle's *common topos* (Braet, 2005), a metaphor literally indicating the place whence arguments can be drawn: "Ancient and modern approaches share one feature: topoi, or loci, or argument schemes, are always intended as abstract structures that generate or support (depending on the theory involved) a variety of arguments in real-life argumentation" (Rigotti & Greco, 2019: xii).[25] It is important to emphasise, however, that for Aristotle they are not universally valid formal rules, nor undisputable and necessary knowledge. Rather, they belong to the realm of *hos epí to polú*, or 'true for the most part', which implies that they behave as rules admitting exceptions (Piazza, 2008: 73). As a consequence, they show different degrees of reliability, and can also compete with one another, so that, under given circumstances, two different (if not opposite) topoi can be both acceptable.

An extensive discussion of the notion of topos from Aristotle to modern argumentation theories is offered by Rigotti and Greco (2019) as a premise to their AMT (Argumentum Model of Topics). The analysis of the polysemy of the word *topos* in Aristotle, mostly based on the *Topica* but also with reference to the *Rhetoric*, leads to singling out different types of argumentative procedures, which can be grouped under three headings: (i) dialectical, (ii) rhetorical, and (iii) sophistic, the latter referring to 'fallacious' procedures, the other deserving further comment.

---

[24] Though *locus* is the Latin counterpart of the Greek term *topos*, the two notions should not be fully overlapped. Actually, one of the achievements of the Latin tradition starting with Cicero and Boethius was "to systematize and specify the meaning of what a locus is, leaving aside the Aristotelian terminological vagueness" (Rigotti & Greco, 2019: 18).

[25] Despite this predominant interpretation, it is worth mentioning the reconstruction by de Pater (1965: 147 f., cited in Kienpointner, 2021), who singled out two functions for Aristotelian topoi, namely that of seats of arguments (*sedes argumentorum*) on the one hand and, on the other, that of guaranteeing the plausibility of the shift form arguments to conclusions. With reference to the latter, they remind of Toulmin's concept of *inference warrant* (Toulmin, 1958: 104 f.).

(i) The *dialectical* level refers both to inferential constructs (the crucial interpretation of a topos as a place, lat. *Locus*), which in their turn include *topoi from*
(i.e. the source of an argument) and *topoi around* (or those concerning reasoning
about something, as for ex. a definition), and to interactional rules, which are at
the basis of effective strategies to conduct a discussion (Rigotti & Greco, 2019:
17–56). Interactional rules, developed by Aristotle as dialectical strategies to be
adopted in a mainly dialogical context, are crucial for persuasion. Concealing
one's thesis, reformulating weak points that may emerge as a consequence of
any objections, carefully ordering and presenting the premises to increase the
adherence of the addresses are some examples that show the role of interactional
rules in persuasion. From the point of view of agreement, it is particularly
important to focus on the choice and exploitation of premises in the context of
the enthymeme—the rhetorical syllogism characterized by the implicitness of
some of its premises (Rh. 1357a).[26] This specific aspect of the enthymeme
makes it easier to hide the link between premises and thesis, so that the
addressee may concede premises without realising their implications for the
adherence to the thesis, and thus making its acceptance easier insofar as it stems
from the accepted premises.

(ii) The *rhetorical* level, quite obviously, emphasises the practical aspect of the
notion, as topoi are crucial in persuasive discourse, and are often formulated in
the form of advice to the arguers. In Rhetoric II, 23 Aristotle lists 28 different
general topoi, which do not exactly correspond to those discussed in the *Topica*
(Rubinelli, 2009).[27] Topoi are at the basis of the enthymeme, but they can be
exploited also beyond the realm of proper logical reasoning. For example, in
Book II, when discussing the role of passions (II, 3), Aristotle mentions topoi
that "those who wish to make their listeners mild-mannered should speak from"
(Rh.1380b). In general terms, it is interesting to note that Aristotle uses *element*
as a synonym for *topos*. In Book II, when discussing the enthymeme (II, 22), he
states: "let us now speak of the elements of enthymemes. And *by element and*

---

[26]The enthymeme is traditionally defined as a shortened (or rhetorical) syllogism, a form of
deductive reasoning which is complementary to the inductive nature of the example. *Enthymema*
and *paradeigma* are actually introduced by Aristotle as two different types of argument, to be
selected on the basis of the context. Yet, in the *Rhetoric*, the enthymeme is the form of rhetorical
argumentation par excellence, which comprises all the reasons given by the arguer to persuade the
audience of the truth of their thesis. This interpretation corresponds to the original meaning of the
word (Piazza, 2000). The shortened form of the enthymeme does not imply it being imperfect, but is
simply the result of a rhetorical strategy aiming to make presentation simple, attractive and not
redundant, in line with the general rules governing persuasive discourse (Rh. 1357a).

[27]In some modern approaches to argumentation, researchers have sometimes tried to produce lists
of argumentation schemes, which are often the result of the analysis of argumentative texts. This
effort has been criticised as a "misuse" of the concept of topos, particularly frequent in the realm of
Critical Discourse Analysis (Zagar, 2011). Eriksson has tried to revive the ancient tradition,
focusing on the pedagogical value of topoi and their crucial role in helping "the communicator to
find materials and arguments as well as helping the listener and the critic to understand and evaluate
messages" (Eriksson, 2012: 219).

topic, I mean the same thing" (Rh. 1396b: 97; emphasis added). Further on (Rh. II, 26), he affirms: "For I mean *the same thing by element and topic*, since an element or topic is *something into the province of which many enthymemes fall*" (Rh. 1403a: 111; emphasis added), and thus gives us a sort of definition of the synonymic terms. A topos, having a general character and therefore a wide range of application, can be the starting point for a large number of different enthymemes, the *seat* (Lat. *sedes*) of the arguments, a source from which the arguer can draw them. In this perspective, it is worth mentioning the critical synthesis of rhetorical principles developed by Boethius, who introduced an explicit distinction between *locus* and *maxims*, the latter being the numerous different propositions that can be derived from one single locus, which make it possible to reduce the number of loci and rationalize their classification.[28]

The exploitation of general argumentative schemes is not sufficient to obtain adherence from the audience. Namely, general schemes are not limited to specific contents and can be applied across different cultures. In this respect, the study of topoi takes into consideration the general rules governing human reasoning. Yet, to persuade in a given context it is necessary to know the "way of thinking" of the audience, the specific values shared and the opinions accepted by the majority of the addressed group—in Aristotelian terms, the *endoxa*.

A general definition of *endoxa* is offered by Aristotle in the *Topica*, emphasising that they refer to opinions accepted by most people, or by most wise men, or by the most renowned wise men (Top. 100b 21–23). Therefore, they are not simple opinions, but authoritative opinions widely shared by a given community, as evident from the etymology of the word *doxa* ('fame'). They should not be given a negative value (Berti, 2002; Piazza, 2004, 2008), as is the case in the anti-rhetorical tradition. It is the negative attitude towards rhetoric that led to a negative interpretation of *endoxa*, as a sort of "mass opinions" to be exploited with a manipulative goal. Actually, *endoxon* is no pejorative term.[29] In order to catch the attention of the addressees and produce goodwill and ease of learning, the arguer must be fully aware of their way of thinking. The ultimate starting point of any argumentation must be a shared set of premises, however limited or general in their contents. Without this, argumentation cannot be developed, and communication itself is impossible. Moreover, while in a dialectical confrontation each premise must be explicitly accepted by the interlocutor, in monological rhetorical discourse the arguer must carefully choose their premises on the basis of their knowledge of the audience (Piazza, 2008: 65). However, resorting to *endoxa* does not necessarily imply that arguers are obliged to adapt to the ideas of the audience, as they can choose from a wide range of different *endoxa*, which can even be exploited against one another.

---

[28] For an accurate synthesis of Boethius' work and a discussion of its implications s. Rigotti and Greco (2019: 66–91).

[29] Aristotle's reference to the wise or the most renowned wise, actually introduces a normative element. *Endoxa* are not mere opinions of the mass, but represent what is common sense for lay people, for experts, even for the most distinguished experts.

This circumstance is the logical consequence of the non-necessary character of premises in argumentation, discussed above.

> So one should not speak on the basis of all the things that seem to be so but on the basis of definite ones—for example, those accepted by the judges or of those they approve. And in fact it should be clear that *what is said appears so to all or to most*. And one should not only draw the conclusion from what is necessary, but also from *what holds for the most part* (*Rh.* 1395b: 95, emphasis added).

The arguer will choose their premises after accurate consideration of their intended audience, as the value of *endoxa* can only be measured against the character and the values of the audience. In the context of argumentation (as opposed to demonstrative reasoning), premises derive from "knowledge for the most part" (*hos epí to polú*). And persuasion inherently is argumentation in context.

To sum up, when considering the argumentative value of premises two different notions emerge as a legacy from ancient rhetoric: *topos/locus* and *endoxon*, roughly corresponding to argument(ative) scheme and shared opinion, respectively. Both are crucial in the process of persuasion, both in logical (enthymematic) reasoning and as elements of other means of proof (ethos and pathos, which are usually more extensively exploited in the initial and final part of a speech). The difference between the two types of premises (re-interpreted as procedural vs. material starting points) is clearly presented and skilfully exploited in the AMT, which will be discussed in detail in the next Chapter.

From the discursive point of view, it is important to emphasise that the often implicit character of premises makes it particularly interesting to investigate how they are introduced, which textual and linguistic devices are more frequently exploited to convey meanings that play a pivotal role in persuasive discourse. This will be dealt with in Chap. 3.

References

Adam, J.-M. (1999). *Linguistique textuelle. Des genres de discours aux textes*. Nathan.

Amossy, R. (2001). Ethos at crossroads of disciplines: Rhetoric, pragmatics, sociology. *Poetics Today, 22/1*, 1–23.

Amossy, R. (2005). The argumentative dimension of discourse. In F. van Eemeren & P. Houtlosser (Eds.), *Practices of argumentation* (pp. 87–98). John Benjamins.

Amossy, R. (2009). Repenser l'argumentation à travers les genres de discours. In V. Atayan & D. Pirazzini (Eds.), *Argumentation: théorie—langue—discours* (pp. 237–248). Peter Lang.

Amossy, R. (2010). *La presentation de soi. Ethos et identité verbale*. Presses Universitaires de France.

Antelmi, D. (2011). Faccia, cortesia, ethos: interazione ed immagine di sé. In G. Held & U. Helfrich (Eds.), *Cortesia Politesse Cortesía* (pp. 75–92). Peter Lang.

Aristotle, *Ars Rhetorica* (Rh.). English translation by C.D.C. Reeve (2018). *Rhetoric*. Indianapolis & Cambridge: Hacket Publishing Company.

Auchlin, A. (2000). Ethos et expérience du discours: quelques remarques. In M. Wauthion & A.-C. Simon (Eds.), *Politesse et idéologie. Rencontres de pragmatique et de rhétorique conversationnelles*. Peeters.

Austin, J. (1962). *How to do things with words*. Oxford University Press.

Barthes, R. (1970). *L'ancienne rhétorique. Communications (XVI) (reprint in Id. [1985], L'aventure sémiologique)*. Seuil.

Benveniste, É. (1966). *Problèmes de linguistique générale*. Gallimard.

Berti, E. (2002). Il valore epistemologico degli endoxa secondo Aristotele. In *Seminario de Filosofia*, Instituto de Filosofia, Pontificia Universidad Catòlica de Chile, vol 14–15, pp. 111–128.

Bhatia, V. K. (2004). *Worlds of written discourse. A genre-based view*. Continuum International.

Braet, A. C. (2005). The common topic in Aristotle's rhetoric: Precursor of the argumentation scheme. *Argumentation, 19*, 65–83.

de Beaugrande, R.-A., & Dressler, W. (1981). *Einführung in die Textlinguistik*. Niemeyer Verlag.

de Pater, W. A. (1965). *La Topique de Aristote et la dialectique platonicienne*. Éditions St. Paul.

Eriksson, A. (2012). Argumentative *topoi* for refutation and confirmation. In F. H. van Eemeren & B. Garssen (Eds.), *Topical themes in argumentation theory* (pp. 209–220). Springer.

Garssen, B. (2001). Argument schemes. In F. H. van Eemeren (Ed.), *Crucial concepts in argumentation Therory* (pp. 81–99). Amsterdam University Press.

Goffman, E. (1967). *Interactional ritual*. Doubleday.

Grice, H. P. (1975). Logic and conversation. In P. Cole & J. Morgan (Eds.), *Syntax and semantics, III, speech acts* (pp. 22–40). Academic.

Halliday, M. A. K. (1985). *An introduction to functional grammar*. Arnold.

Halmari, H., & Virtanen, T. (2005). *Persuasion across genres*. John Benjamins.

Jauss, H.-R. (1977). *Alterität und Modernität der mittelalterlichen Literatur*. Fink Verlag.

Kennedy, G. A. (1991). *Introduction to Aristotle, on rhetoric. A theory of civic discourse*. Oxford University Press.

Kienpointner, M. (2006). Die Argumentationsmuster der Neuen Rhetorik. In J. Kopperschmidt (Ed.), (Hg.) *Die Neue Rhetorik* (pp. 211–226). Fink.

Kienpointner, M. (2017). Rhetorik as Vorläufer. In T. Nieher, J. Kilian, & M. Wengeler (Eds.), (Hg.) *Sprache und Politik* (pp. 20–33). Hempen.

Kienpointner, M. (2021). Rhetorik. In C. Rapp & K. Corcilius (Eds.), (Hg.) *Aristoteles Handbuch* (pp. 593–598). Metzler.

Leff, M. (2006). Up from theory: Or I fought the *topoi* and the *topoi* won. *Rhetoric Society Quarterly, 36*, 203–211.

Maingueneau, D. (1999). Ethos, scénographie, incorporation. In R. Amossy (Ed.), *Images de soi dans le discours. La construction de l'ethos* (pp. 75–100). Delachaux et Niestlé.

Maingueneau, D. (2016). *L'ethos en analyse du discours*. L'Harmattan.

Miller, C. (1984). Genre as a social action. *Quarterly Journal of Speech, 70*, 151–167.

Perelman, C. (1977). *L'empire rhétorique. Rhétorique et argumentation*. Librairie Philosophique J. Vrin.

Perelman, Ch. & Olbrechts-Tyteca, L. (1958). *Traité de l'argumentation. La nouvelle rhétorique*. Paris: Presses Universitaires de France [English translation by J. Wilkinson & P. Weaver (1969): *The New Rhetoric. A Treatise on Argumentation*. Notre Dame (Ind.): University of Notre Dame Press].

Piazza, F. (2000). *Il corpo della persuasione. L'entimema nella retorica greca*. Novecento.

Piazza, F. (2004). *Linguaggio, persuasione e verità. La retorica nel Novecento*. Carocci.

Piazza, F. (2008). *La retorica di Aristotele*. Carocci.

Reboul, O. (1994). *Introduction à la rhétorique. Théorie et pratique*. Presses Universitaires de France.

Rigotti, E., & Greco, S. (2019). *Inference in argumentation. A topics-based approach to argument schemes*. Springer.

Rubinelli, S. (2009). *Ars Topica. The classical technique of constructing arguments from Aristotle to Cicero*. Springer.

Santulli, F. (2009). Le ragioni di Attilio. *La lingua italiana, V*, 69–80.

Swales, M. (1990). *Genre analysis*. Cambridge University Press.

Toulmin, S. E. (1958). *The uses of arguments*. Cambridge University Press.

van Dijk, T. A. (1992). *Text and context: Explorations in the semantics and pragmatics of discourse*. Longman.

van Eemeren, F. H. (2010). *Strategic manoeuvering in argumentative discourse: Extending the pragma-dialectical theory of argumentation*. John Benjamins.

van Eemeren, F. H., et al. (1996). *Fundamentals of argumentation theory. Handboook of historical backgrounds and contemporary developments*. Erlbaum.

van Eemeren, F. H., & Grootendorst, R. (2004). *A systematic theory of agumentation: The praga-dialectal approach*. Cambridge University Press.

Venier, F. (2008). *Il potere del discorso. Retorica e pragmatica linguistica*. Carocci.

Wagemans, J. (2011). Arguments schemes, *topoi*, and laws of logic. In F. H. van Eemeren et al. (Eds.), *Proceedings from the seventh international conference of the international society for the study of argumentation* (pp. 1934–1939). Sic Sat.

Walton, D., Reed, C., & Macagno, F. (2008). *Argumentation schemes*. Cambridge University Press.

Zagar, I. (2011). The use and misuse of *topoi*: Critical discourse analysis and discourse-historical approach. In F. H. van Eemeren et al. (Eds.), *Proceedings from the seventh international conference of the international society for the study of argumentation* (pp. 2032–2046). Sic Sat.

Žmavc, J. (2012). The *ethos* of classical rhetoric: From *epieikeia* to *auctoritas*. In F. H. van Eemeren & B. Garssen (Eds.), *Topical themes in argumentation theory* (pp. 181–191). Springer.

Chapter 2
Agreement: An Argumentation Perspective

Abstract The Chapter offers an account of how agreement is dealt with in the pragma-dialectical approach and in the Argumentum Model of Topics. The account sets off with a discussion of the opening stage of the critical discussion model, as the one most inherently related to agreement. It is the stage dedicated to establishing starting points, i.e. facts and values that are, or are cast as, objects of agreement which are exploited argumentatively. In real-discourse counterparts of the critical discussion model, the opening stage often remains implicit, because premises are simply entailed, as is typically the case in enthymemes. Such implicitness may be exploited by the protagonist to leave controversial starting points out of focus, surreptitiously treating them as agreed facts or opinions. From the opening stage the discussion passes to argument schemes, with the related notion of topoi, as the inferential patterns whereby the agreement elicited or tacitly assumed on the premises should be transferred to the conclusion. It is in schemes/topoi that starting points, whether preliminarily established or not, are brought to bear in the defense of standpoints/conclusions. It is argued that reconstructing argumentation through formal models favors the identification of those nodes of discourse where efforts to secure agreement concentrate.

While in the previous chapter agreement was considered from the perspective of rhetoric and the New Rhetoric, here it will be addressed with reference to the pragma-dialectical approach to argumentation. One of the tenets of argumentation theory at large and of pragma-dialectics in particular is that only if there is an initial area of agreement between the parties can they profitably engage in argumentation. The possibility of leveraging on agreement is crucial to strategic maneuvering, so much so that it might be seen as a sort of an X factor in argumentation, and as such it can be quite ineffable. The pragma-dialectical approach refers to propositions that the parties preliminarily agree on as *starting points*, conceiving them as roughly equivalent to Perelman and Olbrechts-Tyteca's *objects of agreement*. Establishing starting points is the core issue of the opening stage, but decisive as it may be, this is something that in the real-life counterpart to the model of the critical discussion often remains implicit. Most times people do not state their starting points, which are simply entailed in their arguments, with the result that the whole defense of a standpoint may rest on a basis that is not as steadfast as reasonableness would have it. This point is clearly illustrated by the words of an expert invited to a radio show, where the theme was the cultural level and argumentation capacity of the average 'no vax' champions.[1] The guest, an epidemiologist, asserted that contrary to expectations, no-vax advocates are typically not ignorant, having indeed enough culture as to allow them to produce logical-deductive argumentation against vaccination. The problem, according to him, is not a lack of cognitive/cultural instruments, but the fact that they start from wrong premises. And a person who choses premises in a wrong way, but can argue, is perfectly capable of logical-deductive reasoning, thus producing argumentation that is formally valid, but rests on wrong premises, and thus leads to a wrong conclusion. The problem then lies in how they chose their premises; those who are used to choosing factual premises, will select 'correct' premises also in the case of vaccines. Those who select premises that simply suit their intent, basically premises they like, will in all likelihood chose false premises.

The epidemiologist evidently assumes that there exist wrong and correct premises. This presupposition is possibly natural enough for the hard sciences, and a few other spheres like religion and morality, which can aspire to the truth, the right and the good. In all other realms, where the preferable is the yardstick for deliberation, the premises are chosen from common knowledge, intended as "a common commitment store" of two parties engaging in rational argumentation (Walton & Macagno, 2006: 1). It is most often on the basis of common knowledge that premises are accepted, and not because the participants in the discussion are in a position to verify them, or to assess them against scientific evidence (*Ibidem*: 9). Beyond the specificity of the no-vax debate, this episode seizes the gist of argumentation: even in the face of scientific evidence, without agreement on the premises even the best arguments are blunted. What made it impossible for pro-vax and no-vax to engage in a profitable discussion was first and foremost a misalignment on one of the founding principles of contemporary complex societies, i.e. trust in expert opinion. In the face of ever-expanding scientific and technical expertise, nobody can expect to be knowledgeable in all fields of human activities, and we all need to trust the communities of specialists whenever we need services that are beyond our capacity. Arguments from expert opinion are therefore at the basis of much of scientific communication addressed to a lay audience, resting on the topos *if experts say that a given course of action, within the purview of their competence should be taken, then we should do as they say*. However, those entrenched in staunch no-vax positions would simply not trust the scientific community and their motives, which preempts any possibility of preliminarily finding agreement on a fundamental procedural starting point, let alone of persuading them to accept arguments built on that basis.

Common knowledge is not different from the ancient rhetoric's notion of *endoxa* (Walton & Macagno, 2005: 1, see also Sect. 1.3.2), including not only facts, but also opinions (and by extension also value-judgements) and generalizations, which form

---

[1] From a radio show aired on December 22, 2020, *Radio 24* .

the background of a community. Given the physiological subjectivity of premises in so many fields of life, investigating premises is key when trying to understand how people manage to win arguments, at least as far as argumentation proper can go in that respect. Once premises have been chosen, a great part of the job is done, but because the choice of premises can be made implicitly, it may easily elude critical scrutiny. Generally, any issue which becomes an object of discussion is set in a given frame, and the objects of agreement will often implicitly come with the frame, so that arguers may rest on them in the argumentation stage (i.e. when supporting arguments are brought in defense of the standpoint and are critically tested) without the need of linguistic codification. When argumentation gets to this stage, the choice of premises has already been left behind, and although it is always possible for the parties to go back to a previous stage to reframe the issue, there are good chances that they will indeed focus on the arguments themselves, which are more evident, without challenging the starting points. It is exactly for such an implicit nature that it is all the more important to draw attention to the starting points for argumentation and to how agreement on them is sought.

2.1   Agreement: The Point of the *Opening Stage*

Argumentation is about transferring acceptability from arguments to the standpoint they are meant to support (Hitchcock & Wagemans, 2011: 185). Starting from a situation of distance between the parties with regard to the standpoint, the protagonist chooses arguments that will presumably be acceptable to the other party, in the hope that once the arguments have been accepted, also the standpoint will. The acceptability of arguments is sometimes established explicitly, eliciting consensus on one or more starting points, but most times it is tacitly assumed (van Eemeren, 2010: 61) as part of the pragmatic commitments[2] (van Eemeren & Houtlosser, 2002b) of a given argumentative situation or on the ground of the *endoxa,* i.e. views and opinions accepted by most people.

   The identification of areas of agreement falls in the purview of the *opening stage* according to the critical discussion model (van Eemeren & Grootendorst, 2004). The critical discussion model, intended as a heuristic model for the reconstruction of argumentation, and not as a normative or descriptive sequence of moves in real-life

---

[2]Reconstructing what people say and intend to convey in argumentative discourse entails the identification of the parties' 'dialectical' commitments to certain propositions. The dialectical commitments "can be derived from the 'pragmatic' commitments that are inherent in the way in which they have expressed themselves in the discourse, whether explicitly or implicitly." Pragmatic commitments, i.e. unexpressed propositions the parties can be held accountable for, can be reconstructed decodifying implicatures and further implicit meanings on the basis of (among others) Searle' speech act theory and Grice's Cooperative Principle and maxims (van Eemeren & Houtlosser, 2002b) <https://rozenbergquarterly.com/issa-proceedings-2002-a-pracmatic-view-of-the-burden-of-proof/>

argumentation, includes four stages. The confrontation stage is where a difference of opinion emerges between two parties; the opening stage is devoted to establishing agreement on the starting points; the argumentation stage is concerned with dialectical testing of the strength of the other party's arguments through "a systematic exchange [...] of critical attacks by the antagonist and argumentative defences by the protagonist" (van Eemeren, 2013: 67); the concluding stage is where a "winner" is declared, at least in line of principle.

From an agreement perspective, the opening stage is the most relevant. Here, the parties distribute the roles of protagonist and antagonist, undertaking the obligation, respectively, of defending a standpoint and responding critically to the standpoint and its defense (van Eemeren et al., 2014: 529). At the same time, it is the stage in which some common commitments are identified, which will be in force during the discussion. The participants thus try to find out whether their "zone of agreement is sufficiently broad to conduct a fruitful discussion" (van Eemeren & Grootendorst, 2004: 60), otherwise any attempt at resolving a difference of opinion is doomed to fail. Agreement can be procedural or substantive, drawing on the distinction between procedural starting points, i.e. rules and norms regulating the exchange between the questioner and the answerer, accompanied by some strategic advice (van Eemeren, 2013: 67), and material starting points, which are generally drawn from the *endoxa*.

Procedural starting points generally relate to what makes contributions formally acceptable (e.g. commitment to logical reasoning, appeal to reasonableness, or compliance with specific institutional requirements, as in court cases). From the pragma-dialectical perspective they consist of ten rules for a critical discussion (van Eemeren, 2013: 67), one of which pertains specifically to the opening stage. This will be dealt with in Sect. 2.2. As for substantive starting points, they come in the two categories of descriptive and normative starting points, in a reprise of Perelman and Olbrechts-Tyteca's classification of the objects of agreement (cf. Sect. 1.2.3). Descriptive starting points comprise facts, truths and presumptions, while normative ones point to the sphere of the 'preferable', including values, value hierarchies and loci (van Eemeren, 2010: 110).

The strategic advantage of a correct identification of a starting point lies in the fact that once the other party or the audience have committed to it, they can be held to such commitment in the argumentation and concluding stage (van Eemeren, 2010: 110). Strategic maneuvering in the opening stage, therefore, consists in finding starting points that the other party, as a thought construction of the arguer, is willing to avow, or at least to starting points which cannot be comfortably disavowed. Two examples of strategic maneuvering with starting points are briefly discussed below. Both of them come from fiction, which offers a good reflection of real-life argumentation, while embracing a variety of situations far broader that one can expect to find in one particular real-life argumentative activity type.

The first example is taken from Jason Reitman's movie *Thank you for smoking* (2005), where Nick Naylor is a lobbyist for the US Tobacco Organization. The first time he is seen in action is during a talk show on the health damage caused by nicotine, where he defends the 'bad guys'. Among other guests there are a 15-year-old former smoker diagnosed with cancer and a representative of an NGO targeting the tobacco industry. Highjacking the order planned by the host and taking the floor before any other speaker, Naylor manages to turn a hostile audience into a supportive one. A first outbreak in conquering the goodwill of the audience comes before that, and consists in the establishment of a starting point, which he knows his audience would easily commit to: "We can all agree that there's nothing more important than American children". This proposition is not exploited argumentatively in the rest of the discussion, but certainly makes a strong object of agreement with the audience. The supporting argument he brings forth immediately afterwards is quite of another tone, stating that cigarette companies are the first ones who have no interest in causing the death of young smokers, as in this way they would lose customers. Cynical as this argument is, it rests on implicit starting points that the audience will not challenge, i.e. that companies are after profit, and profit depends on their customers. The argument can be reconstructed as follows:

> 1. The tobacco industry is not responsible for the death of young smokers
> 1.1 the tobacco industry does not want young smokers to die
> 1.1.1 if young smokers die, the cigarette companies lose customers
> (1.1.1' companies depend on their customers for profit)

In actual facts, the argument is not properly sound, as there is a logical gap in the reasoning: the fact that tobacco industry does not want young smokers to die does not pre-empt the risk of their death, and therefore does not exclude the responsibility of the tobacco industry. However, if the logical gap in the arguments put forth by one of the parties is not challenged by the antagonist, the argument can be taken as accepted.

In the next example, the antagonist's commitment to a starting point is elicited explicitly and the starting point is then used as an accepted premise in an enthymematic argument. It is an example of court litigation, taken from Ian McEwan's novel *The Children Act* (2014). In the excerpt a lawyer, Grieve, is defending the right of Henry Adam, a 17-year-old Jehovah witness, to refuse blood transfusion, in compliance with his religion. The antagonist is a doctor who seeks the High Court's authorization to give Adam a transfusion that would save his life:

> Grieve said, "You accept, do you not, Mr. Carter, that the freedom of choice of medical treatment is a fundamental human right in adults?"
> "I do."
> "And treatment without consent would constitute a trespass of the person, or indeed an assault of that person."
> "I agree."
> "And Adam is close to being an adult, as the law defines it in such instances." (McEwan, 2014, 68).

Following the critical discussion model, their exchange can be reconstructed as follows: Grieve's standpoint is that the court should recognize Adam's right to refuse a transfusion, and the argument supporting this standpoint is that it is perfectly legal to refuse medical treatment for adults, jointly with the argument that his client can be considered an adult as the law defines it (as he is becoming of age in a few months, and is mature by his age standard). The lawyer elicits his interlocutor's explicit commitment to the starting point that "the freedom of choice of medical treatment is a fundamental human right in adults" and, consequently, that imposing medical treatment would be a crime, thus pre-empting a refutation of the freedom of choice argument, and leaving as a matter of disagreement only whether Adam can be considered adult.

In the example above, the opening stage is explicitly realized insofar as commitment to the starting points is openly elicited. The starting point is used argumentatively in a syllogistic reasoning, where the freedom of medical treatment choice for adults is the major premise, and the proposition that Adam is close to being an adult is used as a minor premise. However, it is often the case that the argumentation stage is explicitly realized while an agreement on the starting points is simply taken for granted. What is worthy of notice is that it is quite unusual for opening and argumentation stage to be both explicitly formulated, as the effect would be one of redundancy. The fact that the critical discussion model envisages one stage dedicated specifically to starting points may suggest that they are something different— and disjointed—from the arguments put forth in the argumentation stage. In fact, starting points are part of the supporting arguments. That starting points and arguments are not separate entities is taken for granted in the argumentation literature as shown, for example, by the following quotation: "It occurs more often than not that the starting points on which an argument is based are expressed only through the fact that they are used in the argumentation, instead of being somehow introduced beforehand" (van Eemeren et al., 2007: 108). In yet another point, van Eemeren et al. refer to indicators that "point to an argument, and thus to an argumentatively used starting point" (2007: 110). Argumentatively used starting points, therefore, *are* supporting arguments. On the other hand, though, not all arguments can be considered starting points, as they are not commonly shared and require themselves further support, as is the case with subordinative argumentation, where an argument is defended in turn by another argument.

The following example illustrates the proposition that starting points are not qualitatively different from supporting arguments. It is an excerpt from a doctor-patient interaction, used by van Eemeren et al. to illustrate the use of questions as "an implicit request to accept a proposition as a starting point" (2007: 93):

> Patient: It's none of their business how I live. They should only [. . .]
> Psychiatrist: Are you still living with your parents?
> Patient: Yes.
> Psychiatrist: Are they paying for everything you need?
> Patient: Yes.
> Psychiatrist: Then, how can they not interfere with your life?

The two initial questions are asked to elicit agreement on the patient's material dependence on his parents. These material starting points will be implicitly recalled as supporting arguments by the final rhetorical question. The first two questions correspond to the opening stage of the critical discussion going on between the psychiatrist and the patient. However, they also serve as the arguments used in defence of the psychiatrist's standpoint, as made clear by the following reconstruction:

1 Your parents have a right to interfere with your life

1.1 you live with your parents, who pay for everything you need
(1.1' as long as parents maintain their offspring, they have a right to somehow control their life)

The reconstruction shows that the starting points *are* supporting arguments, whose acceptability had been ascertained beforehand. Eliciting the antagonist's commitment to them before expressing the standpoint, makes it impossible for the antagonist to withdraw such commitment once their role as supporting arguments becomes evident. Conversely, when the acceptability of the propositions used as arguments in defence of a standpoint is not determined beforehand, they are more susceptible to challenge.

2.2   Rules and Argumentative Profiles in the Opening Stage

Further characterization of the opening stage comes from the rules for a critical discussion that are specifically related to it, and to the argumentative profiles that in a dialectical dialogue can occur there. Both these constructs are oriented towards dialectical rigor, setting out the conditions that should be met to preempt the risk of derailment into unreasonableness.

The *critical discussion rules* are functional norms or standards that define how the parties ought to behave in order to solve a difference of opinion, while the infringement of such rules would represent what in other approaches to argumentation is considered a fallacy, insofar as it hinders the solution of the controversy (van Eemeren, 2010: 193).[3] The rules thus embody the normative nature of pragma-dialectics and compliance with them would satisfy the dialectical demands for rigor and reasonableness, while not denying that each party also pursues effectiveness, as envisaged by the notion of strategic maneuvering (van Eemeren & Houtlosser, 2002a, 2006). The ideal balance between the two antithetical forces of dialectical rigor and rhetorical effectiveness is kept in the course of a discussion if the parties manage to maintain their commitment to reasonableness, without being overruled by the pursuit of effectiveness at any cost. In this sense, all derailments of strategic maneuvering are seen as fallacies.

Of the ten rules of the critical discussion, the one pertaining specifically to the opening stage is the *Obligation to Defend Rule* (Rule number 2) stating that "discussants who advance a standpoint may not refuse to defend this standpoint

---

[3] The problem with the traditional treatment of fallacies, according to the pragma-dialectical view (van Eemeren, 2010: 196 and ff.) is a failure to account for the fact that the boundaries between sound and fallacious strategic maneuvering are not always clear-cut. Much depends on the context in which the argumentation takes place: what is deemed unacceptable by the standards of a given activity type may be perfectly acceptable in the context of another activity type.

when requested to do so" (van Eemeren, 2010: 214).[4] Such rule is violated if the protagonist shifts the burden of proof to the other party, expecting them to prove the standpoint wrong, or if the burden of proof is evaded, as is the case when a standpoint is surreptitiously presented as self-evident, and therefore not needing to be defended. The burden of proof is attached to some of the speech acts performed in argumentative discourse, namely the assertives used to advance a standpoint or a sub-standpoint, i.e. a supporting argument that needs defending itself (van Eemeren, 2010: 214). The assertives performed to establish a starting point, instead, do not carry an obligation to defend, as their acceptability rests on the "intersubjective agreement" of the parties, irrespectively of whether acceptability is established on an "epistemological, ethical, ideological, juridical, esthetical or other" ground (van Eemeren, 2010: 217). For example, a politician claiming that a change of government is needed has an obligation to defend this claim by pointing out problems in the current state of things that can be blamed onto the government, while they do not have to defend the implicit starting point that in democracy a change of government is possible at general elections.

Once a burden of proof has been generated, it must be met by means of argumentation, resting exclusively on the starting points established beforehand in the opening stage or added subsequently in the course of the discussion "as a result of a successful defense of sub-standpoints in the argumentation stage" (van Eemeren, 2010: 216). It is wort remarking here, indeed, that in real-life argumentation the empirical counterparts of the critical discussion stages may not come in the same order as the stages in the model, nor do they all need to be realized.

More specifically, a burden of proof is created when there are indications that a speech act performed by one party in not acceptable to the other. Judgements of acceptability may rest on general principles of communication like Grice's maxims. The presumption holds that an assertion advanced in the discourse is acceptable (Jackson 1995), unless the interlocutor doubts acceptability either for some independent reason, or because they think the other party is not complying with the cooperative principle. Alternatively, the speaker themselves may reckon that the interlocutor may not accept it. Van Eemeren (2010: 226) makes the presumption of acceptability dependent on the notion of 'pragmatic *status quo*', i.e. "the list of premises implicitly or explicitly accepted by the parties involved in the discussion", which are not necessarily coincident with common knowledge beyond that discussion. The pragmatic *status quo* goes unchallenged, and therefore the speaker is exempted from taking the burden of proof, until they perform a speech act that is obviously at odds with the set of shared premises. If we reconsider the psychiatrist example discussed above, the psychiatrist explicitly elicits the patients' agreement on two material starting points that in all likelihood he already knows to be true (as a

---

[4]Another rule that partly impinges on starting points is the Unexpressed Premise Rule "a party may not falsely present something as a premise that has been left unexpressed, or deny a premise that has been left implicit" (van Eemeren, 2010: 194), but this pertains to the argumentation stage, and therefore is not considered here.

matter of fact, also the previous two questions were rhetorical questions). What is left implicit, thanks to the enthymematic form of the argument (Sect. 1.3.2), is the major premise that until parents maintain their son, they have a right to interfere with his life, which incidentally is the only premise the patient may disagree with, and consequently would require a preliminary agreement. This shows that when agreement is explicitly elicited beforehand, this might even be a distracting strategy aimed to divert attention from another premise whose status as a starting point should be agreed with the other party, because it is more controversial. By using three rhetorical—conducive—questions in a row, the psychiatrist induces the patient to believe that all the possible premises have been agreed on, whereas in fact the most important and dangerous one for the patient has been eluded.

Coming to the *argumentative profiles*, they are intended as "step-by-step specification of the moves that can help to accomplish a specific task in a certain stage or substage of the discussion that the participants have to perform in the opening stage" (van Eemeren et al., 2007: 18). They were devised drawing on Walton and Krabbe's *profiles of dialogue* (Walton, 1989; Krabbe, 1992; Walton & Krabbe, 1995; Krabbe, 1999), i.e. goal-oriented sequences of moves and countermoves forming a normative model of dialogue (Krabbe, 1999: 2).

In the opening stage of the critical discussion, dialectical profiles concern both procedural starting points and the establishment of material starting points. The parties determine which utterances must be defended by whom, thus assigning the burden of proof: the party who takes the burden of proof will act as the protagonist, while the other commits to critically respond, acting as the antagonist. At the same time, the parties will decide which propositions can be considered starting points, which therefore do not require a defense (van Eemeren et al., 2007: 63). The argumentative profile for the deliberation on starting points is schematically represented as follows (Fig. 2.1):

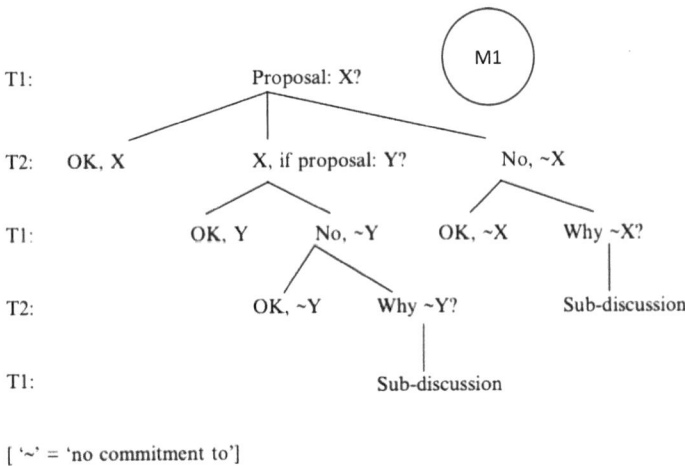

['~' = 'no commitment to']

Fig. 2.1 Dialectical core profile for establishing a starting point

The only possible move (M1) that can be made to start such deliberation is for the protagonist (T1) to suggest that the other party (T2) accept a given proposition as a starting point for the discussion. T2 can accept the proposal *tout court*, fail to accept it or accept it partially, imposing restrictions on their acceptance, such as that T1 should accept also another proposition, Y, as a starting point for the discussion. This scenario opens up two possibilities: T1 accepts the restrictions or rejects them. If reject is the case, T2 can simply accept it or ask for clarification, opening to subdiscussion.

Such an approach is clearly hardly applicable to argumentation in discourse, where most or all of these moves would probably be left implicit, especially in the case of monologic argumentation. This calls for attention to be turned to how agreement is implicitly or explicitly constructed in discourse, which is the theme of Chap. 3.

2.3 Indicators of Starting Points from a Pragma-Dialectical Perspective

Since real-life argumentation hardly ever displays such a redundancy of explicit preliminary deliberation, it will be interesting to see whether and how these notions can be useful for the analysis of agreement in discourse, and especially of monologic argumentation, where both acceptance and rejection can only be the projection of the speaker or writer, absent a real interlocutor who can actively take part in the discussion. One way in which profiles can certainly contribute to the analysis of agreement in discourse is by helping to find indicators of starting points. Since dialectical profiles spell out the moves that are dialectically relevant in a particular stage of a critical discussion, their formulation may point to words associated with a given move, which therefore can be considered indicators of that move. Of course, no certain one-to-one relation can be established between the occurrence of a word and the potentially associated move (Degano, 2016), and besides that, moves can be realized without explicit indicators. As van Eemeren et al. point out (2007: 19),

> We imagine the indicators to be different types of points on a scale which ranges from explicit verbal indicators, such as, 'I put forward the following standpoint ...', to a little less explicit, but still rather solid verbal indicators, such as 'I have two arguments supporting this ...', to more abstract functional indicators, such as the class of speech acts the move is regarded to be part of, to formal indicators, such as the grammatical mood of the sentence in which the move is made, and finally to a total absence of indicators.

Nevertheless, identifying indicators fits in a linguistic approach to argumentation, both because it draws attention to the linguistic realization of arguments and because indicators are needed if a quantitative perspective is adopted for the analysis of argumentation. As far as the linguistic realization of arguments is concerned, the presence of indicators can be significant. Although establishing starting points beforehand does not change the matter of the reasoning, the fact that the arguer feels the need to do so can be relevant from a discursive viewpoint. As a matter of fact, it is worth asking why speakers may want to signal through any type of indicator that they are proposing that something be accepted as a starting point or that a given proposition is being used as such. Expressions to *propose* that a given statement should be accepted as a starting point include informative and rhetorical questions (van Eemeren et al., 2007: 19). Expressions used to *cast* a proposition as an accepted starting point may present the starting point as accepted by the parties (e.g. *as you said yourself, we agree that*), but also as generally accepted (e.g. *everybody knows that, nobody would deny that*), irrefutable (e.g. *it is clear that, it is self-evident that*), obvious (*obviously, naturally*). In some cases, the proposition cast as a starting point can simply be presupposed.

Under the Cooperative Principle, asserting a proposition implicates that the speaker commits to its truth, so the expression of certainty is redundant and constitutes a violation of the maxim of quantity, and as such it may generate the implicature that the listener should accept that proposition as well (van Eemeren et al., 2007: 33). Such an implicature may in fact cast a doubt on the acceptability of the proposition, betraying, so to say, the speaker's fear that the proposition can meet the listener's criticism: "the speaker would not have to implicate that the listener should accept the asserted proposition if he took it for granted that the listener would do so anyway" (*Ibidem*). Conversely, presuppositions entail the acceptability of a proposition, without drawing attention to its status of shared starting point, thus increasing the likelihood that the proposition goes unnoticed, and therefore is not met with criticism.

2.4   Agreement beyond the Opening Stage: Schemes and Topoi

The interlocked nature of starting points and supporting arguments (see Sect. 2.1) calls for an account of starting points that takes into consideration the notion of schemes. Originally introduced by Perelman and Olbrechts-Tyteca (1958), the concept of *argumentation scheme* presents overlaps with the classical notion of *topoi*, which, while still lacking a unified definition, can be considered the "historical forerunners of schemes" (Walton et al., 2008: 276. Cf. Sect. 1.3.2). Schemes are tools of modern argumentation theory defined as "an abstract characterization of the way in which in a particular type of argumentation a premise used in support of a standpoint is related to that standpoint in order to bring about a transfer of acceptance from that premise to the standpoint" (van Eemeren et al., 2014: 19).

Both topoi and schemes account for the *acceptability transfer principle* (ATP), i.e. the inference on the ground of which "accepting the argument renders the standpoint acceptable" (Wagemans, 2010: 1935), as synthetically represented below:

1   STP
1.1   ARG
1.1'   ATP (1.1→1)

Germane concepts are unexpressed premise, or *warrant* in Toulmin's model (2003), but also the pragma-dialectical "pragmatic optimum" (see Garssen, 2001: Ch. 3; van Eemeren & Grootendorst, 1992, Ch. 6), or "pragmatic principle of support" (van Eemeren & Garssen, 2009: xvi). In spite of terminological differences, all these labels refer to a correct way of transferring acceptability from the argument to the standpoint. So central is this notion that in pragma-dialectics schemes are actually seen as a "representation of the principle of support that is used when in the argumentation a reason is advanced for accepting a standpoint" (van Eemeren & Garssen, 2009: xvi).

How does all this relate to our understanding of starting points in the perspective of agreement? The crucial element is acceptability, which can be transferred from the argument(s) to the standpoint only if the argument is accepted first. In syllogisms intended as in the Aristotelian Analytics acceptability is a matter of logic: deduction (*sullogismós*) is speech in which "certain things having been supposed [i.e. premises], something different from those supposed [i.e. the conclusion] results of necessity because of their being so" (*Prior Analytics* I.2, 24b18–20). The necessity condition entails that it would be impossible for a conclusion to be false if the premises are true (Smith, 2000). Most of real-life argumentation, though, cannot count on generalizations that are necessarily valid. Acceptability is to be sought in the realm of the non-compulsive, the credible, the plausible, in other words, of rhetoric, having in mind a particular audience (cf. Chap. 1). The arguments falling in this dimension often rest on general premises that are true only to an extent. Such premises are referred to as defeasible or enthymematic generalizations, which are "true only for the most part", until an exception disproves them (Walton et al., 2008: 230–231).

As Wageman's ATP representation shows, starting points come in focus, only if the inferential component, which is normally implicit, is made explicit in the reconstruction of argumentation. Different approaches exist to the representation of schemes in contemporary argumentation theories. If we take Walton et al.'s compendium (2008), for example, the traditional terminology is used of major premise, minor premise, and conclusion. The argument from cause to effect, for example, is formulated as follows:

> *Major premise*: generally, if A occurs, then B/will (might) occur.
> *Minor premise*: in this case A occurs (might occur)
> *Conclusion*: therefore, in this case, B will (might) occur (Walton et al., 2008: 328).

The major premise is what states the inferential reasoning that connects the minor premise with the conclusion. The other party will accept the conclusion only if they agree both on the general validity of the reasoning pattern set out by the major premise, and on the particular validity of the minor premise.

In pragma-dialectics, argumentative schemes are formulated using conventions derived from logics, and are divided into three general categories, which differ from each other for the type of inferential reasoning that connects the supporting argument and the standpoint: symptomatic schemes, causal schemes, and schemes based on a relation of analogy (van Eemeren et al., 2002). For the sake of comparison with Walton et al.'s schemes (2008), the pragma-dialectical causal scheme is represented as follows:

> Y is true of X [standpoint],
> because Z is true of X [supporting argument]
> and Z leads to Y [inference linking the supporting argument and the conclusion, or ATP].

Here the traditional presentation order is reversed; the first line represents the standpoint, where a property is attributed to a referent; the second is the supporting argument, and the third line is the one concerned with the inferential reasoning, i.e. the "pragmatic principle of support" (van Eemeren & Garssen, 2009: xvi). The presentation order, however, has no consequences in the production of real-life arguments, since the schemes have simply a heuristic function, not being concerned at all with the actual arrangement and wording of contents.

In a later work, Hitchcock and Wagemans (2011) propose that the three main schemes should be reduced to two super types: a *predicate-transfer scheme*, which conflates symptomatic and causal argumentation, and a *referent-transfer scheme*, which accounts for forms of reasoning based on a similarity between two referents. In *predicate-transfer schemes* possession of a given property (Z)—what they call *predicate*—by a referent (X) is sufficient to justify a claim that the same referent possesses a different property (Y):

1. Y is true of X

1.1 Z true of X (Hitchcock & Wagemans, 2011: 197)

This type is exemplified by the all too famous argument:

> 1 Being an animal (P) is true of Socrates (R).
> 1.1 Being a man (Q) is true of Socrates (R).
> 1.1' Accepting that Socrates is a man renders acceptable that Socrates is an animal (Q is true of R→P is true of R). [ATP]

Here different symbols are used, which calls for some disambiguation: Q is equivalent to 'a given property' (Z), R to 'referent' (X), and P to 'another quality possessed by the referent'(Y).[5]

The reasoning is valid, or acceptable, only if there is agreement on the specific fact that the referent actually has property Q, and on the general classification principle whereby human beings are animals (ATP).

---

[5]To make the matches more immediately visible, the following representation contains both sets of symbols:
> 1 Being an animal (P/Y) is true of Socrates (R/X)
> 1.1 Being a man (Q/Z) is true of Socrates (R/X).

In *referent transfer schemes*, instead, "possession of a property by a referent is sufficient to justify a claim that a different referent possesses the same property" (Hitchcock & Wagemans, 2011: 198).

1 Y true of X

1.1 Y true of Z

A typical example of this second type is the precedent principle in Common Law, which binds judges to decide new cases following the judgements rendered by their colleagues in previous cases that present analogies with the new one, on the ground that similar cases should receive similar treatment. In extremely simplified terms, new court decisions grounded on comparable precedents rest on a reasoning that goes as follows:

1 Decision Y is made with regard to case X

1.1 the same / a similar decision was made with regard to case Z

Agreement with the standpoint (1.) can only be built starting from agreement on the 'facts' that decision Y was actually made in previous case Z, something which can be objectively verified against published decisions, and that case Z is really relevant, i.e. similar, to the case at issue (X).

Bringing all this to bear on our topic of discussion, topoi and schemes can be profitably put to use for the analysis of agreement construction as in the first place they impose an order on what would otherwise be a content-driven reading of real-life argumentative discourse. This order allows attaching to the contents a specific function in the argumentative process, which in turn makes it possible to identify where efforts are (or should be) concentrated in order to try and establish agreement on the starting points. Either in their original tripartite classification or in Wageman and Hitchcock's reduced binary proposal, the pragma-dialectical schemes have the advantage of being applicable to an infinite number of real-life uses of arguments. Thanks to their abstract formulation, the list is highly manageable, and as the different schemes use the same streamlined codification, one can single out common traits across them. One such common trait is that agreement pivots on (i) the minor premise, and particularly on the property that is not mentioned in the standpoint, e.g. Z; (ii) the inferential relation linking it to the standpoint, i.e. the Acceptance Transfer Principle, as a means to pass from given knowledge to new knowledge (*res dubia*), or in the realm of rhetoric, to extend acceptability from a proposition that already qualifies as accepted to another proposition whose acceptability is dubious. As Greco points out, the *from. . .to* relation is crucial to an understanding of loci as a source of argumentative inference, in so far as it sums up the passage from known to unknown, i.e. from acquired knowledge to new knowledge on a *res dubia* (Greco, 2017: 32).

As a standpoint is for its nature non-shared, the receiver is more likely to put it through critical testing. The premises, on the other hand, are often discursively presented as factual, or anyway as already accepted by both parties, which requires greater alertness, on the part of the receiver, to decide whether they can legitimately be considered starting points. Furthermore, for the very fact that the inferential transfer of acceptance is generally derived by the receiver might create the impression that the receivers themselves are responsible for the judgement, which reduces critical alertness. According to an adaptive mechanism, we tend to trust our judgement more that the judgement of others (Lombardi Vallauri 2021).

2.4.1   Topoi in Pragma-Dialectics

The pragma-dialectical schemes entail, in a way, the notion of topos, but do not codify it as such. Several topoi or finer-grained argumentation schemes listed in other typologies correspond to a variant or sub-type of one of the three main argumentation schemes included in the pragma-dialectical typology (Garssen, 1997: 246).[6] Below are indicated some of the subtypes mentioned in various works of pragma-dialectical scholars (van Eemeren & Grootendorst, 1992: 97; Garssen, 1997; van Eemeren et al., 2002: 98, 101–102; van Eemeren et al., 2007) (Table 2.1):

Table 2.1 Pragma-dialectical argument schemes and their subtypes

Argumentation based on a symptomatic relation:
Argumentation presenting something as an inherent quality
Argumentation presenting something as a characteristic part of something more general
Argumentation based on meaning or definition
Argumentation from authority
Argumentation from example
Argumentation based on analogy:
Making a comparison
Giving an example
Referring to a model
Argumentation based on the principle of fairness
Argumentation based on the rule of justice
Argumentation based on the principle or reciprocity
Argumentation based on a causal relation:
Argumentation pointing to the consequences of a course of action
Argumentation presenting something as a means to a certain end
Argumentation emphasizing the nobility of the goal in order to justify the means
Pragmatic argumentation

---

[6] Garssen made this claim based on a review of the following typologies: Perelman and Olbrechts-Tyteca (1958), Hastings (1962), McBurney and Mills (1964), Schellens (1985), Kienpointner (1992) and Freeley (1993).

Subtypes of argument schemes in the pragma-dialectical account of argumentation are equivalent, then, to what other approaches call topoi or to the schemes
featured in longer lists like Perelman and Olbrechts-Tyteca's (1958) and Walton
et al.'s (2008). Although neither the representation of the structure of argumentation,
nor that of argument schemes presuppose the explicitation of the topos, some
maxims (the *if-then* components of topoi according to Rigotti and Greco Morasso's
AMT model—cf. next section) are taken into account in the *discursive description* of
the different subtypes of argument schemes. As mentioned earlier, maxims can be
identified only with regard to specific subtypes of argument schemes, because, as
Rigotti and Greco Morasso point out "maxims are specific argumentative principles
at work in concrete applications of argument schemes" (2010: 507). The three main
pragma-dialectical schemes are formulated too abstractly for that, and the same
holds for Hitchcock and Wagemans' classification. However, the topos could be
explicitly represented in the pragma-dialectical schemes, as shown by Wagemans
below:

   1 Being an animal (P) is true of Socrates (R).
   1.1 Being a man (Q) is true of Socrates (R).
   1.1' Accepting that Socrates is a man renders acceptable that Socrates is an animal (Q is true
       of R→P is true of R). [ATP]
   1.1'.1 The *topos* "What belongs to a species, also belongs to the genus" applies. (Wagemans,
       2010: 1938).

The topos therefore provides backing to the ATP, but conventionally it is not
represented. It is already entailed in the ATP/pragmatic principle of support, which
is roughly equivalent to the *if-then* component of more traditional representations
(cf. Walton et al., 2008, above), or maxim in traditional approaches. The maxim is
more specific than the topos—indeed different maxims can be derived from the same
topos—but reliance on a maxim inherently points to the topos itself. For this reason,
making the topos explicit might then be perceived as redundant.

   The Socrates example falls in the realm of logical demonstration and as such, its
standpoint is not really susceptible to challenge, but supposing that someone should
doubt that Socrates is an animal, the supporting argument (i.e. the expressed
premise) *1.1 Being a man (Q) is true of Socrates (R)* together with the unexpressed
topos *What belongs to a species, also belongs to the genus* would defend the claim.
The argumentation would go as follows: Socrates is an animal. Why? Because he is a
man. And why should being a man make him an animal? Because what belongs to a
species (man) also belongs to the immediately higher-ranking category, i.e. the
genus (animals). Going back to agreement, this line of reasoning can only be
accepted if the antagonist shares some background knowledge about the biological
classification of living organisms, which is not explicitly recalled in the discussion,
but is assumed. Included in this background knowledge there must be the proposition that men are animals, which is activated and made relevant by the ATP.
Agreement, therefore, should be elicited or assumed for the material premise *being
a man is true of Socrates*, and for the procedural premise *what belongs to a species,
also belongs to the genus*. The latter, in turn, entails accepted knowledge of the facts
that in the classification of living organisms 'man' comes as the species, and species

with similar characteristics are grouped under the same genus. Such deeply embedded accepted knowledge amounts to the *endoxon*.

2.4.2 Topoi in the Argumentum Model of Topics

Starting points receive special attention in the Argumentum Model of Topics (Rigotti, 2006, 2009; Rigotti & Greco-Morasso, 2010), which while not being in disagreement with pragma-dialectics, aims to further explain how implicit starting points (or premises) can be reconstructed. Quoting from the originators of the AMT, its relationship with pragma-dialectics can be seen in these terms:

> We suggest to re-read the distinction proposed by the pragma-dialectical approach between procedural and material starting points in the opening stage [...]; we take the liberty of applying it as an instrument to specify how, in argument schemes, there is a dimension overcoming the logical principle (Rigotti & Greco-Morasso, 2010: 493).

The dimension "overcoming the logical principle" relates to the connection of the inferential component to its material starting points, which is the

> source of the force of the statement presented as an argument in relation to the statement presented as a standpoint; 'the force that forces' us to acknowledge it is an argument in support of that specific standpoint (Rigotti & Greco-Morasso, 2010: 500).

Following AMT conventions, all the elements of a topos, implicit or explicit, are plotted along two intersecting diagonal lines. Before the intersection, each line accounts for different aspects of the reasoning, one dealing with the procedural starting point, and the other with the material starting point (Fig. 2.2).

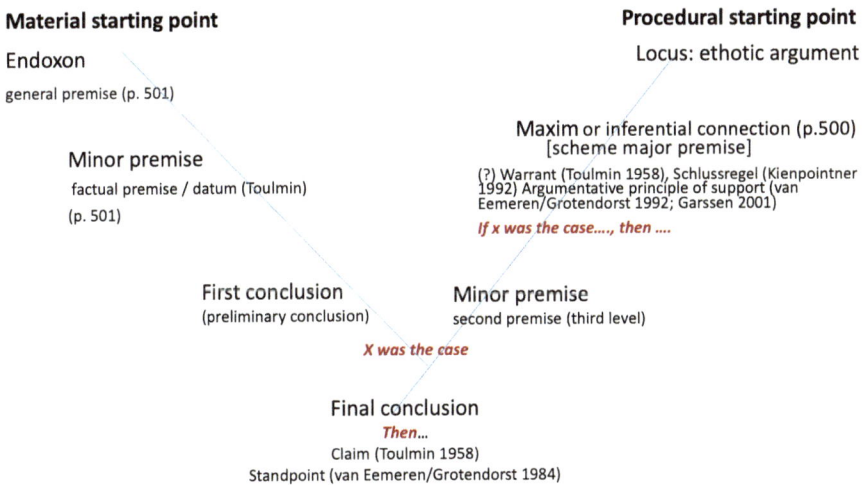

Material starting point   **Procedural starting point**

Endoxon   Locus: ethotic argument

general premise (p. 501)

                                                             Maxim or inferential connection (p.500)
                                                             [scheme major premise]

  Minor premise

    factual premise / datum (Toulmin)   (?) Warrant (Toulmin 1958), Schlussregel (Kienpointner
                                                             1992) Argumentative principle of support (van
    (p. 501)   Eemeren/Grotendorst 1992; Garssen 2001)

                                                             If x was the case...., then ....

        First conclusion   Minor premise
        (preliminary conclusion)   second premise (third level)

                   X was the case

              Final conclusion
                   Then...
              Claim (Toulmin 1958)
         Standpoint (van Eemeren/Grotendorst 1984)

Fig. 2.2 AMT model, adapted from (Rigotti & Greco-Morasso, 2010: 508), to which the page numbers in the Figure are referred

The procedural starting point is the locus (cf. Sect. 1.3.2, n. 23 for the difference between *topos* and *locus*), from which a maxim (the *if-then* pattern) is derived. The maxim functions as a procedural general premise that must be taken together with a minor premise to reach the conclusion. What the AMT calls maxim is comparable to the notion of *warrant* in Toulmin (2003), of *Schlussregel* for Kienpointner (1992), and to the pragma-dialectical concept of 'argumentative principle of support' (Garssen, 2001; van Eemeren & Grootendorst, 1992). All these terms refer to the *if... then* inferential connection that forms the core of the topos. The minor premise is located at the intersection of the two diagonals, as it partakes in both: it performs the function of the minor premise along the procedural line, but it is derived from material starting points. In Rigotti and Greco-Morasso's words, "it derives from the material starting point, but it is equally exploited by the procedural starting point being associated to the maxim as a second premise" (2010: 501–502), and so it anchors the procedural abstract reasoning to the case in point. Along the other diagonal, the material starting points are arranged according, again, to a major-minor premise structure: the *endoxon* performs the part of the major premise, which together with a factual minor premise leads to the (preliminary) conclusion. Such preliminary conclusion functions, as stated above, as the procedural minor premise that, together with the maxim, supports the final conclusion.

An example of AMT taken from real life mediation, a form of Alternative Dispute Resolution, is discussed by Bigi and Greco Morasso (2012: 1138). Here, the media-tor's standpoint is that the commercial and personal relationship between two former friends and business partners is worth maintaining. This is defended using an argument that rests on the locus from termination, with the maxim stating 'If something is a value, it must not be interrupted', and the minor premise being 'the interpersonal relationship between the two parties is a value'. This is a preliminary conclusion deriving from the *endoxon* 'Friendship is a kind of human relationship which consti-tutes a real value' and the *datum* 'We were friends before we were partners", which relates to previously elicited evidence. The topos is represented below:

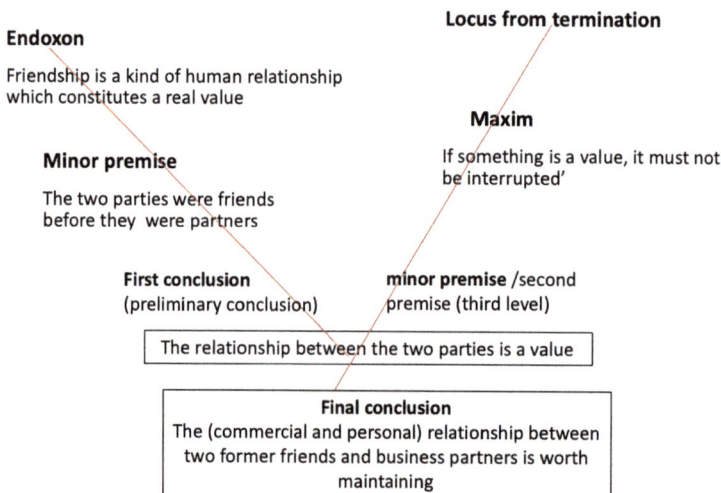

Locus from termination

Endoxon

Friendship is a kind of human relationship
which constitutes a real value

Maxim

If something is a value, it must not
be interrupted'

Minor premise

The two parties were friends
before they were partners

First conclusion   **minor premise** /second
(preliminary conclusion)   premise (third level)

| The relationship between the two parties is a value |

| **Final conclusion**
The (commercial and personal) relationship between
two former friends and business partners is worth
maintaining |

The model may be seen as entailing a certain degree of redundancy, since the material and the procedural reconstruction relate to the same linguistic material, which is, so to say, reconstructed twice. Likewise, distinguishing between a preliminary and a final conclusion may seem somewhat artificial, as it requires an over-segmentation of thought. At the same time, reconstructing the material premises as formally valid argumentation entails a good extent of reformulation, as is also the case with the reconstruction of pragma-dialectical schemes.

Other approaches to topoi are more content-based, as is the case of the Discourse-Historical Approach (Reisigl & Wodak, 2001; Reisigl, 2014), which focuses on patterns of justification that are recurrently used in a given field of social action. The point of analysing topoi in the Discourse Historical Approach is mostly that of finding the ideological implications attached to them. Topoi retain their function as a conclusion rule that warrants the passage from the premises to a conclusion (Reisigl, 2014: 84), but the inferential reasoning is simply derived from the linguistic data, without recourse to highly formalized models. An example of a recurrent topos identified by Reisigl in political discourse is the "Topos of repaying the diligent and good workers/nationals", from which the following conclusion rule is derived: "If you vote for my party, or we get the power, then the diligent and good workers will be repaid" (Reisigl, 2014: 79).

For the sake of comparison, the inferential principle of the friendship argument that was reconstructed above following the AMT conventions could be more simply formulated as "If friendship is a kind of human relation which is a real value, then it must not be interrupted", which entails the endoxon *Friendship is a real value*. In this way, both the material and the procedural/inferential aspects are reconstructed more linearly and concisely, without requiring much rewording.

If simplicity is certainly a value, the complexity inherent in more formalized models may nonetheless be worth the effort, especially in the investigation of agreement. In authentic argumentation, which is often enthymematic, one or more premises will only be entailed, which contributes to casting them as starting points that are already accepted by the audience, whether this be true or not. In this respect, the more a model brings to the fore what was left implicit, the more can it contribute to spotting those contents that are implicitly treated as objects of agreement. Even the 'redundancy' of the AMT can be compensated for by the clarity it brings to the reconstruction. Separating the procedural and the material components may indeed enhance the perception that not only the contents but also the inferential aspects can be challenged, if they are not actually shared. Both the material and the procedural starting points are chosen from the 'common knowledge' of a community, broadly intended as not only facts and opinions, but also procedural reasoning patterns, be they called schemes, loci or maxims.

Such models are not necessarily intuitive, but a trained eye would less likely let surreptitious starting points slip through the net of critical scrutiny. What none of them includes is the dimension of discursive effectiveness—the aspect of strategic maneuvering that deals with presentational choices (van Eemeren, 2010) –, which pertains to how the propositional content of the argument should be presented to enhance the chances that it will be accepted by the interlocutor, or an audience at large. The next chapter will address this aspect, drawing on linguistics, with a focus on those categories that can be more relevant to the pursuit of agreement.

References

Bigi, S., & Greco Morasso, S. (2012). Keywords, frames and the reconstruction of material starting points in argumentation. *Journal of Pragmatics, 44*, 1135–1149.

Degano, C. (2016). Corpus linguistics and argumentation. *Journal of Argumentation in Context, 5/2*, 113–138.

Freeley, A. J. (1993). *Argumentation and debate: Critical thinking for reasoned decision making* (8th ed.). Wadsworth.

Garssen, B. J. (2001). Argument schemes. In F. H. van Eemeren (Ed.), *Crucial concepts in argumentation theory* (pp. 81–99). Amsterdam University Press.

Garssen, B. J. (1997). *Argumentatieschema's in pragma-dialectisch perspectief: Een theoretisch en empirisch onderzoek*. [Argumentation schemes in a pragma-dialectical perspective: A theoretical and empirical study]. IFOTT.

Greco, S. (2017). La dimensione inferenziale nell'argomentazione. In P. Nanni, E. Rigotti, & C. Wolfsgruber (Eds.), *Argomentare: per un rapporto ragionevole con la realtà* (pp. 25–53). Fondazione per la sussidiarietà.

Hastings, A. C. (1962). *A reformulation of the modes of reasoning in argumentation*. Unpublished doctoral dissertation. Northwestern University.

Hitchcock, D. L., & Wagemans, J. H. M. (2011). The pragma-dialectical account of argument schemes. In E. T. Feteris, B. J. Garssen, & A. F. Snoeck Henkemans (Eds.), *Keeping in touch with pragma-dialectics* (pp. 185–205). Benjamins.

Jackson, S. (1995). Fallacies and heuristics. In F. H. van Eemeren, R. Grootendorst, J. A. Blair, & C. A. Willard (Eds.), *Analysis and evaluation* (Proceedings of the third ISSA conference on argumentation) (Vol. II, pp. 257–269). Sic Sat.

Kienpointner, M. (1992). *Alltagslogik: Struktur und Funktion von Argumentationsmustern*. Frommann Holzboog.

Krabbe, E. C. (1999). Profiles of dialogue. In J. Gerbrandy, M. Marx, M. de Rijke, & Y. Venema (Eds.), *Essays dedicated to Johan van Benthem on the occasion of his 50th birthday*. Amsterdam University Press/Vossius Press.

Krabbe, E. C. (1992). So what? Profiles for relevant criticism in persuasion. *Argumentation, 6*, 271–283.

Lombardi Vallauri, E. (2021). Presupposition, attention and cognitive load. *Journal of Pragmatics, 183*, 15–28.

McBurney, J. H., & Mills, G. E. (1964). *Argumentation and debate: Techniques of a free society*. Macmillan.

McEwan, I. (2014). *The children act*. Vintage.

Perelman, C., & Olbrechts-Tyteca, L. (1958). *Traité de l'argumentation. La nouvelle rhétorique*. Presses Universitaires de France. [English translation by J. Wilkinson & P. Weaver (1969): *The New Rhetoric. A Treatise on Argumentation*. Notre Dame (Ind.): University of Notre Dame Press].

Reisigl, M. (2014). Argumentation analysis and the discourse-historical approach. A methodological framework. In C. Hart & P. Cap (Eds.), *Contemporary critical discourse studies* (pp. 67–96). Bloomsbury.

Reisigl, M., & Wodak, R. (2001). *Discourse and discrimination: Rhetorics of racism and antisemitism*. Routledge.

Rigotti, E. (2006). Relevance of context-bound loci to topical potential in the argumentation stage. *Argumentation, 20*, 519–540.

Rigotti, E. (2009). Whether and how classical topics can be revived in the contemporary theory of argumentation. In F. H. van Eemeren & B. Garssen (Eds.), *Pondering on problems of argumentation* (pp. 157–178). Springer.

Rigotti, E., & Greco-Morasso, S. (2010). Comparing the argumentum model of topics to other contemporary approaches to argument schemes: The procedural and material components. *Argumentation, 24*, 489–512.

Schellens, P. J. (1985). *Redelijke argumenten: Een onderzoek naar normen voor kritische lezers.* [Reasonable argumentation: A study of norms for a critical reader]. Foris.

Smith, R. (2000). Aristotle's logic. In E. N. Zalta (Ed.), *Stanford encyclopedia of philosophy.* <https://plato.stanford.edu/archives/fall2020/entries/aristotle-logic/>

Toulmin, S. E. (2003). *The uses of argument.* Updated edition. Cambridge: Cambridge University Press. [1958.]

van Eemeren, F. H. (2010). *Strategic Maneuvering in argumentative discourse: Extending the pragma-dialectical theory of argumentation.* John Benjamins.

van Eemeren, F. H. (2013). In what sense do modern argumentation theories relate to Aristotle? The case of pragma-dialectics. *Argumentation, 27*, 49–70.

van Eemeren, F. H., & Garssen, B. (2009). Problems of argumentation: An introduction. In F. H. van Eemeren & B. Garssen (Eds.), *Pondering on problems of argumentation* (pp. xi–xxi). Springer.

van Eemeren, F. H., Garssen, B., Krabbe, E. C. W., Snoeck Henkemans, A. F., Verheij, B., & Wagemans, J. H. M. (2014). *Handbook of argumentation theory.* Springer.

van Eemeren, F. H., & Grootendorst, R. (1992). *Argumentation, communication, and fallacies: A pragma-dialectical perspective.* Erlbaum.

van Eemeren, F. H., & Grootendorst, R. (2004). *A systematic theory of argumentation. The pragma-dialectical approach.* Cambridge University Press.

van Eemeren, F. H., Grootendorst, R., & Snoeck Henkemans, A. F. (2002). *Argumentation: Analysis, evaluation, presentation.* Erlbaum.

van Eemeren, F. H., & Houtlosser, P. (2002a). Strategic maneuvering in argumentative discourse: Maintaining a delicate balance. In F. H. van Eemeren & P. Houtlosser (Eds.), *Dialectic and rhetoric. The warp and woof of argumentation analysis* (pp. 131–159). Kluwer Academic.

van Eemeren, F.H., & Houtlosser, P. (2002b). A pragmatic view of the burden of proof. *ISSA Proceedings 2002* <https://rozenbergquarterly.com/issa-proceedings-2002-a-pracmatic-view-of-the-burden-of-proof/>.

van Eemeren, F. H., & Houtlosser, P. (2006). Strategic maneuvering: A synthetic recapitulation. *Argumentation, 20*, 381–392.

van Eemeren, F. H., Houtlosser, P., & Snoeck Henkemans, A. F. (2007). *Argumentative indicators in discourse: A pragma-dialectical study.* Springer.

Wagemans, J. H. M. (2010). Argument schemes, Topoi, and Laws of Logic. *ISSA Proceedings* <http://Rozenbergquarterly.Com/Issa-Proceedings-2010-Argument-Schemes-Topoi-And-Laws-Of-Logic/> (7.10.2019).

Walton, D., & Macagno, F. (2005). Common knowledge and argumentation schemes. *Studies in Communication Sciences, 5*(2), 1–22.

Walton, D., Reed, C., & Macagno, F. (2008). *Argumentation schemes.* Cambridge University Press.

Walton, D. (1989). *Informal logic.* Cambridge University Press.

Walton, D., & Macagno, F. (2006). Argumentative reasoning patterns. *Proceedings of the ECAI* (Università di Trento, Riva del Garda, 28 August – 2 September). Available at SSRN: https://ssrn.com/abstract=1751683 or https://doi.org/10.2139/ssrn.1751683

Walton, D., & Krabbe, E. C. W. (1995). *Commitment in dialogue: Basic concepts of interpersonal reasoning.* State University of New York Press.

Chapter 3
Agreement through Language

Abstract Representations of reality in discourse embed facts, values and identities, which are all codified linguistically. The Chapter offers a comprehensive toolkit of linguistic and discursive categories that can be used strategically to seek agreement against the backdrop of the beliefs and identities of both the arguer and the intended audience. The tools are broadly framed in the Socio-Semiotic approach, with prominence given to the interpersonal metafunction, an aspect of discourse that more than others contributes to the construction of ethos—both the orator's and the audience's. The contents are arranged according to an order that shies away from specific models stratified in the last few decades, as after all discursive representations are the result of actual language choices, which boil down to morpho-syntactic and lexical signs and the implicit pragmatic potential attached to them. Hinging on the system of transitivity, the chapter deals with pronouns, tenses and modality; with lexis (including connotation and figurative language) as well as with those items that activate implicit meanings. Finally, the dialogic dimension of discourse is addressed, by considering concessions, reported discourse and negation.

The rhetorical approach to persuasion is inherently discursive. In the work of ancient rhetoricians, the means of proof that are at the core of the rhetoric craft proceeded *through speech* (Aristotle, Rh. 1356a), nor has the approach changed in the New Rhetoric (Perelman & Olbrechts-Tyteca, 1958): "Our treatise will consider only the *discursive means* of obtaining the adherence of minds: in the sequel, only the technique which uses language to persuade and convince will be examined" (NR: 8).[1] This principle of the primacy of language applies also to the construction of agreement as a preliminary step in all argumentative (and persuasive) processes. As already said above (Sect. 1.2.3), textual and linguistic strategies are crucial in the construction of agreement, as they not only represent and communicate shared premises, but actually contribute to creating identities, facts, values and beliefs to be exploited in persuasion. The linguistic approach is particularly relevant in the

---

[1] In all the quotations from Perelman and Olbrechts-Tyteca' *New Rhetoric* (NR) the page number refers to English translation by John Wilkinson and Purcell Weaver (1969).

© The Author(s), under exclusive license to Springer Nature Switzerland AG 2022
F. Santulli, C. Degano, *Agreement in Argumentation*, Perspectives in Pragmatics, Philosophy & Psychology 31, https://doi.org/10.1007/978-3-031-16293-0_3

perspective of discourse analysis, which is rooted into the assumption of the generating power of words. In this Chapter, some of the most common and effective linguistic strategies functional to the construction of agreement will be examined, with the aim of exploring the connections between forms and functions that play a pivotal role in the creation of a common ground, thus generating a preliminary adhesion of the audience, which can then be extended to the theses defended by the arguer.

3.1   Agreement on Identities: Pronouns

Given the pragmatic nature of discourse, the presence and the representation of the enunciator (and the enunciatee) is the first element to take into consideration. As mentioned in the Introduction, the very notion of discourse (*discours*) is introduced by Benveniste (1959/1971: 209) in opposition to history (*histoire*), thus distinguishing two complementary planes of utterance. Each of them prototypically includes only one group of the verb tenses, and displays a different use of personal pronouns. History characterizes the narration of past events: "Events that took place at a certain moment of time are presented *without any intervention of the speaker* in the narration" (*Ibidem*: 206, emphasis added). Therefore, the historical utterance prototypically only includes the anaphoric pronoun, i.e. the third person, which is actually a non-person and has no deictic link with the situation of enunciation.[2] It is to be noted here that Benveniste uses *person* in the sense attributed to it in pragmatics with reference to the context of enunciation, where persons proper are just the enunciator (*I*) and the enunciatee (*you*). Even if a third party is present in the context where the interaction takes place, the fact that he/she is codified as a third person excludes him/her from the direct I-you relation. On the plane of discourse, on the contrary, the speaker takes possession of language, and propagates their presence to all the linguistic elements of grammatical agreement, person and verb in the first place. Benveniste had already examined the role of person in discourse in a previous essay (Benveniste, 1946), founding his argumentation on an extensive review of grammatical descriptions in different traditions (ranging from Arabic to Sanskrit to Greek and Roman grammarians) and on an interesting analysis of actual linguistic data, i.e. the forms that, in a wide choice of languages, mark the differences among the various persons and personal pronouns. Combining this linguistic analysis with theoretical reasoning, Benveniste singles out the opposition between the (so-called) third person on the one hand, and the first and second persons on the other. As a matter of fact, the third person is usually morphologically different from the other two. It is also remarkable that it is indicated as 'the one who is absent' by Arab grammarians, thus revealing a disparity between third person and the other two persons ('the one who speaks' and 'the one who is addressed'). The form that is,

---

[2]Historical narration in the first person represents a hybrid form.

according to Benveniste, improperly called third person does contain an indication of a statement about someone, but is not related to a specific 'person'—"the third person is not a 'person': it is really the verbal form whose function is to express the *non-person*" (Benveniste, 1946/1971: 198). First and second persons, on the other hand, are characterized by "specific oneness", as the speaking subject and the addressee are unique each time, and by their being reversible. The opposition between actual persons (I-you) and the non-person (he/she) is named *correlation of personality*, as *I-you* possess the sign of person, while *he* lacks it. Within the I-you opposition, the two persons are distinguished in that *I* is *internal* to the statement and external to *you*, though remaining within the dialogic situation which characterizes discourse. *I* establishes a relation with *you*, as the only imaginable person outside it. *I* is therefore the *subjective person*, opposed to the *non-subjective person*—what Benveniste called *correlation of subjectivity* (cf. *Ibidem*: 201).

The focus on the relations of person shows that Benveniste's approach is pragmatic, as it concerns the link between the utterance and its context of enunciation; the expression of persons crucially contributes to defining the role of participants in the communicative event and their mutual positioning. In this respect, it is important to distinguish between a purely pragmatic interpretation and a sociolinguistic approach. Wilson, in an essay focused on the use of pronouns in political discourse (1990: 47), emphasised that the selection of a form in a given context is a sociolinguistic choice, (e.g. *tu-vous* in French), while the use of a form having a conventional meaning in a context where it acquires different semantic implications (e.g. *we* in the royal plural, as discussed later on) is a question of pragmatics. Though the sociolinguistic and the pragmatic layers may overlap in actual communication, the distinction is useful to single out manipulative language use typical of persuasive discourse, which is usually subtler in comparison with open and explicit sociolinguistic choices—for example those concerning the selection of different forms of address. The latter have been frequently studied in sociolinguistics, as an instrument to establish and display the relationship between the interlocutors. In the wake of Brown and Gilman's well-known essay (1960), pronominal choices have been examined for their interpersonal role, functional to expressing power vs solidarity, to characterizing the position of speakers in a given context and establishing conversational roles and social hierarchies (Silverstein, 1976, 2003).

On the other hand, the pragmatic approach focuses on the first person: research has investigated the different forms of self-presentation, frequently drawing inspiration from Goffman's work, and in particular exploiting the concepts of framing and footing (Goffman, 1974, 1981). Only starting from the first person as the deictic origin of the utterance is it possible to introduce alternative forms, comprising the second person (as the addressed interlocutor) and the non-person, which in turn makes it possible to introduce different subjects and forms that are syntactically described as 'impersonal'. Pronominal choices are functional to creating perspectives in which the image of the speaker and of their relationship with their own utterances materialises. Thus, different 'figures' are introduced in discourse, as if they were characters on a stage, and a given interpretation of the event can be promoted.

Since, as discussed so-far, pronominal choices are deeply embedded in the context of situation, and depend on the speaker's intention more than on given lexico-semantic relations, pronominal choices are crucial for establishing agreement through the construction of ethos within the speaker-receiver relation. A first important difference in enunciation stems from the opposition between the use of personal deixis and definite description. The speaker can choose to present themselves through the first person pronoun (singular or plural, as will be discussed later), but can also opt for a more neutral presentation, introducing nouns that semantically include them, but make it possible to avoid an explicitly personal interpretation.

A good example of this strategy can be found in press releases, a genre typical of corporate (and also institutional) communication. In these texts the enunciator, i.e. the company, often chooses to avoid personal deixis (*we*) and uses a definite description (*the company*). This strategy has been interpreted as an effort of the writer to abandon their own perspective and adopt that of the journalist who will use the release for their article. Jakobs (2003) considers this choice an important element to reach the actual goal of the text, i.e. obtaining the publication of the news with a minimum of reformulation. Expanding and adapting the notion of keying (Goffman, 1974), this global strategy is named *pre-keying*.

The context of production and the aim of a press release make it possible to give a straightforward justification for the use of definite descriptions. These, however, can also be chosen to promote a positive evaluation of the enunciator, reducing their responsibility and forwarding a given interpretation of facts. In this respect, an interesting example is offered by another genre produced in the domain of corporate communication, namely the letter to the shareholders. In a study by Garzone (2005a), a large corpus of texts was examined, finding that personal deixis is amply used; in particular the first-person plural can refer to the Board of Directors, to the whole company, and even include the shareholders, who may also be addressed with the second person (as, for example, in *your company*). Yet the personal forms that refer to the enunciator are more frequent when the actions performed need to be emphasised, in terms of efforts made and results obtained (e.g. *we were able to increase revenues*), while negative data are presented impersonally, to reduce the responsibility of the characters involved (e.g. *profits dropped*).

The examples mentioned above, stemming from genres that have a relevant persuasive component, show how the preference for definite descriptions can influence the perception of the addressees and contribute to the interpretation of facts promoted by the enunciator. Yet the pronominal strategies for self-presentation are even more important, as they concern the identification of the actors involved in the communicative event, both addresser and addressees, and their mutual relationship.

As we have already discussed, in persuasive discourse, and particularly in the domain of politics, the character of the speaker is crucial. To obtain adhesion—and, before that, agreement—the speaker must be present in discourse. *I* is the explicit reference to the enunciating subject, and its use brings it to the foreground. *I* is the form chosen for autodiegetic narrative, which is frequent and sometimes indispensable in numerous genres of political communication. Moreover, the first-person singular can be used also in homodiegetic narrative, when the enunciator tells facts they witnessed, often to transform them into a commonly accepted historical truth. Quite obviously, it is also functional to the expression of personal beliefs, to be assumed as shared values of a group.

The presence of *I* implies the existence of a dialogic setting, and materializes *you* as enunciatee. This is crucial for the construction of the audience and its relation to the speaker, which in turn bears on the possibility to win their agreement. The narrative of one's own story is part of an ethotic effort of self-presentation, but is also an opportunity to promote exemplary actions and convictions. If a personal narrative (e.g. a candidate's autobiography) is cast as part of a wider historical background (e.g. the American dream), where *I* meets *you*, shared facts and values conjure up a new entity, prototypically encoded by the pronoun *we*.

The nature of pronouns and their role in the enunciation have been investigated mainly for the singular forms, but the passage from singular to plural does not involve a simple pluralization. As emphasised by Benveniste, in most languages, the morphology of plural pronominal forms has no regular correspondence with the singular, nor is there any correspondence with nominal paradigms (Benveniste, 1946/1991: 201 f.). The case of the first person, which is the most interesting, has particularly complex implications from both a semantic and a pragmatic point of view. First of all, *we* is not the plural of *I*, because the subjectivity of the first person singular and its oneness exclude pluralization—"*we* is not a multiplication of identical subjects but a *junction* between *I* and the 'non-I', no matter what the content of this 'non-I' may be" (*Ibidem:* 202). This fundamental assumption (already claimed by Jespersen, 1924) has been widely accepted as a starting point in research;[3] the plural form must be interpreted as an addition of heterogeneous terms, a *junction* (as stated by Benveniste) of the speaking subject with someone else. Urban (1986) represented the semantics of the first person plural as a series of circles, which progressively expand to include more subjects: in the innermost circle there is only I + one other, while the outermost comprises I + all mankind.

The semantic interpretation of *we* emphasises the vagueness of its meaning, as the boundaries of we-reference are fully blurred. In the framework of this inherent vagueness, special mention is deserved by two opposite but not contradictory functions of the first-person plural singled out by Benvenise. On the one hand, the use of *we* expands the *I* and amplifies it "into a person that is more massive, more solemn, and less defined" (Benveniste, 1946/1991: 203). This is the so-called 'royal-we', or *pluralis majestatis*. On the other, "the use of *we* blurs the too sharp assertion of *I* into a broader and more diffuse expression: it is the 'we' of the author or orator" (*Ibidem*). This use is often denominated *pluralis modestiae,* as it reduces the dominance of the speaking subject and indicates a shared responsibility (Siewierska, 2004).

---

[3] An exception is the so-called *choral usage*, "when several persons are co-author of the same speech act" (Daniel, 2005: 10), which however occurs on few occasions (for example, when more authors write a paper together) and has therefore a marginal role. It can be noted that, even in such a context, *we* is not a true pluralization of *I*, as each participant to the speech acts speaks for themselves, and a homogeneous multiplication of the first person identity is still impossible.

Furthermore, an important distinction can be made between two uses of the first-person plural: exclusive (I + them) vs inclusive (I + you), which in many languages have dedicated morphological markers. In these languages, ambiguity can be avoided, but in languages that have only one form, this can be interpreted differently, as plurality concerns only the number of individuals present in a given syntactic function and not whether they are enunciators or not (Prieto, 1977). The first person inherently includes the enunciator, but in the plural the enunciator can be united to one or more enunciators or to one or more non-enunciators. This opposition has been analysed in a more comprehensive perspective (including the possibility of applying it also to the second person), with reference to a wide choice of typologically different languages (Filimova, 2005).

The exploitation of first-person plural forms with a persuasive (and often manipulative) aim has been widely investigated in the context of discourse studies, especially in media and political discourse (van Dijk, 1991, Fairclough, 1989, 1995; Maitland & Wilson, 1987; Wilson, 1990; Zupnik, 1994; Wodak, 1989, 1997, 2009, pp. 97 ff.; Duszak, 2002; Davies, 2013, and many others). Inclusive *we* is often exploited in political communication to create group cohesion, but the shift from exclusive to inclusive meaning is also a means to obtain adhesion, implicitly extending to the audience values and beliefs initially presented as belonging to an *exclusive* group.

The first-person plural can also be used with speaker-exclusive reference (Santulli, 2020). As the pronoun *we* inherently includes reference to the speaker, this is an interesting case, regularly occurring in certain contexts analysed in research and referred to as condescending-we or nursery-we (De Cock, 2011; Helmbrecht, 2015; Gardelle & Sorlin, 2015). This is when *we* actually means you. Beyond these codified forms, there are other aspects of speaker-exclusive *we* that are particularly relevant in political discourse, which have been indicated as rhetorical-we (Quirk et al., 1985). These forms occur when the enunciator using *we* cannot actually perform the action, and fictively include themselves in a category they actually do not belong to. This generates a conflict between the obvious semantic interpretation and the pragmatic use of the form. An interesting example (quoted in Maitland & Wilson, 1987) is a statement pronounced by Mrs. Thatcher in a 1983 speech: "We shall fight for our freedom in time of peace as fiercely as we have fought in time of war". With this statement, Mrs. Thatcher blurs the boundaries between her (conservative) government and the community at large, including the whole country, and possibly beyond it. The first phrase (*we shall fight*) is clearly a quotation from Churchill's famous wartime speech, but its reference is extremely vague. If we interpret the first-person plural as addressee-exclusive, it refers to the Conservative Government led and represented by Mrs. Thatcher herself. This interpretation, however, needs revision in the light of the interpretation of the *second* form (*we have fought*). Mrs. Thatcher did not actually fight during the war, but she evokes a historical entity of which she wants to be part: Britain as a whole (and even the Allies) are the implicit reference group. This circumstance opens up new perspectives for the interpretation of the first form, and promotes the inclusive reading of its value. Moreover, this inclusive value cannot be limited to the supporters of Mrs.

Thatcher's government. The most obvious solution of the semantic conflict triggered by the speaker-exclusive form is the identification of those who fought (and won) during the war with those who want to fight (and win) now.

This use of speaker-exclusive *we* can be labelled as rhetorical not only for its persuasive (and manipulative) power, but also because it can be interpreted as a grammar metaphor (Santulli, 2020). There is a discrepancy between objective facts and their linguistic representation, through which the enunciator can present themselves as a member of a group they actually cannot belong to. From the pragmatic point of view, forms like this possess a twofold inclusivity: they are metaphorically speaker-inclusive, and they are also addressee-inclusive, i.e. they aim to generate *embrayage* and lead the addressee to identify with the enunciator (or the group they belong to).

As discussed above, the first and the second person belong to the plane of *discours*, while the third person is part of *histoire*, and therefore shifts the attention beyond the enunciative exchange. This has an evaluative effect: the greater the distance from the context of enunciation the lower the involvement and the sense of affiliation. Quite obviously, the third person (singular of plural) identifies the out-group, even the Enemy. *They* are those who do not share *our* traditions and values, i.e. the Other.

The opposition *us-other* plays a fundamental role in the creation of identities. As stated in the Introduction to a volume totally devoted to this topic:

> The pronoun *we* is a prototypical exponent of the speaker-group, as opposed to the distance-establishing *they*. Both *we* and *they* can be skilfully managed in discourse in order to construct, redistribute or change the social values of ingroupness and outgroupness. *We* in particular opens up a number of referential and pragmatic options (esp. the inclusive—exclusive distinction) and enjoys a strong cultural salience across languages and contexts (Duszak, 2002, p. 6).

In the volume edited by Duszak, the use of personal pronouns with this specific aim is investigated in a wide range of languages and cultural contexts, ranging from Soviet Russia (Pyykkö, 2002) to Poland (Skarżyńska, 2002), from the identity of the Hebrews under the Nazi rule (Schmid, 2002) to that of the Argentine Mothers of Plaza de Mayo (Wagner, 2002). Generally speaking, the opposition *we-they* is common practice in political and news discourse, and has frequently been the object of linguistic and discursive analyses (Pennycook, 1994, De Fina, 1995, Postoutenko, 2009, Moberg & Eriksson, 2013, and many others).

From the point of view of agreement, it is important to emphasise that the speaker does not aim to make *them* part of the audience, because it is not possible to find a common ground of agreement, and they are not the target of the persuasive effort. Yet they are crucial, as they *e contrario* reinforce the identity of the in-group. The way they interpret facts and the values they promote are opposite to those belonging to the in-group, and in the political contest, they become an object of criticism and attack.

3.2   Agreement on Facts: Tense

In the New Rhetoric, the objects of agreement pertaining to the realm of the real are
first and foremost *facts*. Yet it has already been observed (Sect. 1.2.3) that, in
discourse, there are no objective facts, but only a linguistic representation of the
outer world conceived by the addresser. In this perspective, facts are actually
narratives, which offer an interpretation of events within the framework of a given
system of values and fundamental beliefs.

The linguistic representation of facts is closely related to the system of transitivity
(Halliday, 1985), in that it concerns *who does what to whom*. The role of *who* and
whom can be performed by pronouns (amply discussed in the previous section),
while *does* brings into the picture predicates, which can be analysed from different
perspectives. Among them, tenses are particularly relevant in this context, since facts
are treated as linguistic objects of the *narrative* type. In Benveniste's theory of
enunciation, the narration of past events is part of the plane of *histoire* (cf. *supra*).
More precisely, events "are characterized as past from the time they have been
recorded and uttered in a historical temporal expression" (Benveniste, 1959/1971:
206). According to the French linguist, the formal markers capable of impressing
temporality (thus enabling the performance of the crucial *historical* function of
language) are two verbal categories, namely tense and person taken together. In
his view, *stricto sensu* historical narration excludes the use of "the formal apparatus
of discourse", primarily the relationship of the persons *I—you*. Moreover, the
historical utterance admits three tenses: the *aorist* (i.e. the simple past), the *imperfect*,
and the *pluperfect* (i.e. the past perfect). For Benveniste *histoire* is expressly a
narrative with no intervention of the speaker including aorist forms:

> As a matter of fact, there is then no longer even a narrator. The events are set forth
> chronologically, as they occurred. No one speaks here; the events seem to narrate them-
> selves. The fundamental tense is the aorist, which is the tense of the event outside the person
> of a narrator (*Ibidem*: 208).

This interpretation of the concept of history excludes autobiographic narratives.
Benveniste investigates the asymmetry in French verb paradigms, showing that
autobiographical narrative is marked by the use of the perfect tense (*J'ai fait*, 'I've
done'), which he calls "the aorist of discourse" (*Ibidem*: 213). The crucial point is
that the aorist "objectifies the event by detaching it from the present", while the
perfect "links the past event with our present" (*Ibidem*).

A wider and more systematic discussion of the use of tenses was proposed by
Weinrich (1964) in an essay fully devoted to this theme and based on the analysis of
a large choice of (literary) texts stemming from different linguistic traditions—
mostly Romance. The book, significantly entitled *Tempus*, has a telling German
subtitle: *besprochene und erzählte Welt* ('the commented and the narrated world'),
which synthetises the contraposition between 'comment' and 'narrative'. It would be
reductive, though, to limit Weinrich's theory to the realm of literature, as despite its
origin, it can be applied to other domains and genres, both oral and written.

In his book, Weinrich observes special patterns of tense distribution in a text or in parts of it. His tense classification is similar to the one produced by Benveniste to distinguish *histoire* from *discourse*. Weinrich admitted he had drawn inspiration from the work of the French linguist, but emphasised that he attributed crucial importance to breaking the link between past and history, which in his opinion do not fully overlap. Weinrich's complete classification assigns simple past (and imperfect), pluperfect and conditional (i.e. future in the past) to narrative; present, perfect and future to comment. Simple past and present represent the "zero grade" in both groups, while pluperfect and perfect mark a *retrospection,* and conditional and future a *prospection.* In other words, they are used to retrieve or anticipate information, respectively. In a text, or in single parts of it, one tense (or a group of tenses) prevails, and switching from one tense or group to another corresponds to a significant change in the structure of the text.

One could be tempted to believe that the strategy governing the use of tenses in texts corresponds to the effort of reproducing a chronological dimension. Yet accurate analyses of tenses show that they are deployed in texts to obtain a given mode of representation, namely narrative or comment, with the intention of stimulating detachment or involvement. The speaker can *narrate* events from a distance, so that they remain detached from both addresser and addressee, or *comment* on them, thus bringing them nearer to the communicative event. While the preterit is the tense of narrative (equivalent to Benveniste's aorist) the perfect is considered inadequate to tell facts "objectively", but is used to present facts from the point of view of a participant or a witness.

This idea of a functional distribution of tenses not related to chronological time was not completely new in the field of literary research. In the French context, Barthes (1953) studied the *passé simple* as the tense typical of narratives of both fictive and historical facts. According to the French philosopher, narratives generate "autarchic universes", with their own space and time constraints, populated by their own objects, people, and myths. No longer functional to expressing time relations, the *passé simple* is the ideal tool for the construction of a universe, for telling myths, cosmogonies, stories and novels. It presupposes the detached construction of a world by a demiurge-like narrator who uses the tense to illustrate and explain their reality. According to Barthes, this tense is typical of *les Belles Lettres*, it is the formal manifestation of a contract between the writer and society as an explicit marker of creation and artistic intention. In other genres, narratives prefer tenses that are nearer to spoken language, with events no longer belonging to Literature nor to History. In this perspective, there is a crucial correspondence between the Novel and History, as they both aim at "alienating" facts, with the *passé simple* enabling a social group to take possession of their past.

The whole theory of tenses has interesting consequences when applied to discourse analysis. In news discourse, for example, the use of narrative tenses in editorials (a genre that does not tell facts but typically comments on facts) is functional to causing a change in the receptive attitude of the reader. This is particularly evident in Romance languages, which make a distinction between preterit and imperfect. The following excerpt from an Italian rightwing newspaper's editorial illustrates the point clearly:

Nell'ottobre scorso, da ogni angolo della penisola *sentimmo* giungere la protesta per una violenza e un tradimento che si *effettuarono* ai danni del corpo elettorale [. . .] Il misfatto *venne compiuto* e un ex comunista *saliva* senza alcuna investitura popolare alla responsabilità di Palazzo Chigi (Santulli, 2001: 76).

(Last October, from every corner of the peninsula, a protest, we heard, against the violence and treason that were carried out at the expense of the electoral body. [. . .] The misdeed was committed, and a former communist ascended, without any popular investment of sorts, to the highest responsibility of Palazzo Chigi [i.e. the seat of the government])

The tone of the excerpt comes through as delusively historical, due to the joint effect of an altogether archaic prose and of tense choices in particular. The use of the preterit forms *sentimmo, effettuarono,* and *venne compiuto* is highly marked in this context, where contemporary Italian would rather have perfect or imperfect tenses. Even more noteworthy is the use of the so-called 'narrative imperfect' (*saliva*), which was once typically employed to describe a punctual action concluded in the past, but seizing it in its most dynamic and worth-telling aspects. At the same time, it signaled a certain detachment from the narrated facts. In this editorial, using simple past in lieu of the perfect and the narrative imperfect contributes to create the impression that the narrated facts belong to history, and are therefore true, objectifying at the same time the values attached to them.

In rhetorical terms, including a (short) *narratio* in the oration has the function of dis-tending the argumentative tension (Santulli, 2001). The status of the facts reported in the narrative is irrelevant: be they 'historical truth' or fictive invention, they are presented in the narrative mode to trigger the desired reaction of the audience.

The adoption of the narrative mode makes it possible to put events into an impersonal dimension, beyond the intervention of the interlocutors who are induced to adopt a detached attitude, which in turn excludes debate. When facts are presented in the 'mythical' perspective of preterit, they become untouchable and incontrovertible, which is tantamount to saying that they are actually *true*. This is how *myths* are generated. A myth is a special form of narrative, which draws authenticity from tradition and is not subject to interpretations; it is truth that can only be observed with detachment, and lies outside the realm of opinions and arguments. Historically, dialectics killed myth, as the two exclude each other and cannot co-exist. You do not discuss myths, you simply contemplate them.

Myths are not limited to the sphere of the sacred, nor do they concern only the great themes of creation and destiny of mankind. In the political domain, myths are narratives of events that have to be made intelligible for an audience. They are considered true, received and transmitted as exemplary history of a group (a nation, a party, etc.). They play a fundamental role in the development of ideologies:

In the modern context, political myth can be defined as an ideologically marked narrative of past, present, or predicted political events. By *ideologically marked*, I mean that the narrative discourse carries the imprint of assumptions, values and goals associated with a specific ideology or identifiable family of ideologies, and that it therefore conveys an explicit or implicit invitation to assent to a particular ideological standpoint (Flood, 1996: 41-42).

The 'narrative' presentation of facts transforms them into a piece of common history, making it possible for the speaker to adopt an 'epic' perspective, and behave as an omniscient narrator, who moves freely from past to future, presenting facts that are often well known to the audience, not judged for their truthfulness, but recognised as common experience and tradition. Quite obviously, mythical narratives lend themselves to be exploited as objects of agreement.

In political discourse, the occurrence of the preterit, the narrative tense *par excellence*, is a clue of myth activation that deserves attention, especially in languages where its use is disappearing from spoken varieties. The cases of French and Italian have already been mentioned above, but the Italian situation is particularly complex, as the *passato remoto* has a diatopic distribution: it is nearly absent in the varieties spoken in the Northern area, but amply used in central and Southern varieties. In grammatical descriptions, it is usually presented as a tense used to refer to facts lying in a 'remote' past, in opposition to the perfect, used for nearer events (see the discussion of the editorial quoted above). This description, however, does not accurately reflect actual use, which is highly influenced not only by the geographical origin of the speaker but also by the 'mode' chosen. A quite remarkable example of narrative mode in conflict with diatopic variety is the use of *passato remoto* in the speeches of Silvio Berlusconi, an Italian politician whose Northern origin was clearly perceivable in his language use, especially in phonetics. Despite this, Berlusconi systematically used the *passato remoto* in his speeches to narrate the story of his own life and of his party, as well as to tell the recent history of the country. In his speeches, the use of the narrative tense corresponded to the adoption of a mythical perspective functional to constructing agreement on 'facts', i.e. events belonging to the past, interpreted and presented from his point of view (Santulli, 2005). Berlusconi's use of *passato remoto* was unusual and marked for two different reasons: it contrasted with the geographical origin of the speaker, and it was frequently used in the first person, which—as stated by Benveniste—usually combines with the perfect (the 'aorist of discourse'). The very use of the past tense combined with the first person confirms its crucial role in the creation of myths and their exploitation for persuasive goals.

Even though we have dealt with person and tenses separately, it is often the combination of the two that has strategic relevance with regard to the construction of agreement. Although Benveniste excluded the possibility of using the tenses of narrative in the first person, autobiographic narrative can occur on the plane of *histoire*, whenever the narrator intends to adopt a detached attitude and present their story (or the story they witnessed) as a *myth*. Actually, in political myth, Flood (1996: 119) singles out three different voices: the extra-diegetic narrator, the intradiegetic narrator, and the narrator who rhetorically identifies with the audience. The extra-diegetic narrator tells facts from the outside and corresponds to the (proto)typical (non)person of a historical narrative. The intradiegetic narrator speaks in the first person as a witness or as an active participant to events that are however presented using the tenses that are typical in the historical mode. Finally, the narrator who rhetorically identifies with the audience uses the inclusive first person plural, encouraging the addressees to adhere to their interpretation of facts, presented as mutually shared. The narrating voice controls the presentation of places, contexts, and people, regulating the access of other figures and other (reported) voices, representing the Other (*they*).

Within the historical mode, the triad *I-we-they* is the enunciative counterpart of the three fundamental political myths singled out by Edelman (1971: 76-80), which will be named here—following Geis (1987)—the Valiant Leader, United-We-Stand, and the Conspiratorial Enemy. The first myth promotes the image of a brave and benevolent Leader, who can protect and save the group in dangerous circumstances; in political speeches, this is the arguer. The second propagates the idea that a group (a nation, a party, etc.) can defeat their enemy with commitment and sacrifice, and thanks to their loyalty and obedience to the leader— in discursive terms, the speaker and the audience. Finally, the third myth identifies a powerful and hostile out-group who conspire against the in-group, i.e. the opposite party, who must be challenged to guarantee peace and prosperity.

3.3   Agreement through Modality

The notion of modality refers to the attenuation or intensification of the speaker's commitment to the propositional content of any given utterance. It can be used with several semantic meanings (jussive, desiderative, intentive, hypothetical, potential, obligative, dubitative, hortatory, exclamative, etc.), all of which in their own respect add a "supplement or overlay of meaning to the most neutral semantic value of the proposition of an utterance" (Bybee & Fleischman, 1995: 2).

In this sub-section, reference will be made to the system of modality developed in Halliday's Functional Grammar, which is the most comprehensive and authoritative theory of language underpinning Discourse Analysis. In the Functional Grammar paradigm, 'modality' refers to the "intermediate degrees, between the positive and negative poles" construing "the region of uncertainty that lies between 'yes' and 'no'". As Halliday and Mathiessen put it,

> In between the certainties of 'it is' and 'it isn't' lie the relative probabilities of 'it must be' (high value modal) 'it will be' (medial value modal), 'it may be' (low value modal). Similarly, in between the definitive 'do!' and 'don't!' lie the discretionary options 'you must do', 'you should do', 'you may do'. (Halliday & Matthiessen, 2004: 144)

This definition (and the attendant examples) reflects the traditional distinction between the two main categories of epistemic and deontic modality (cf. Bybee & Fleischman, 1995). Halliday, though, refers to 'modalization'—modality concerning propositions, where yes-no has the value of asserting or denying, and 'modulation'—modality concerning proposals, where the two poles are "do it / don't do it".

In propositions, between 'it is so', and 'it isn't so' there can be different degrees of probability or different degrees of usuality, both of which can be expressed through a modal verb (or more precisely a "finite modal operator in the verbal group") or by a modal adjunct of probability or usuality (*probably, usually*). Alongside the probability scale, for example, the extent of certainty varies from certain (that must be true), to probable (that will be true), to possible (that may be true), depending on whether the value of the modal used is high or low. It is worth pointing out, though, that however high the value of a modal, its presence will nonetheless mitigate the certainty of the utterance. As Thompson and Hunston affirm, "a proposition without modality is simply one where the inherent option of signalling intermediate degrees of commitment has not been taken up" (2000: 20). This actually corresponds to the highest degree of certainty: *That's certainly John* is less certain than *that's John*, which leads Halliday and Mathiessen to point out that "you only say you are certain when you are not" (Halliday & Matthiessen, 2004: 147).

In a proposal, the intermediate possibilities vary depending on whether the utterance is a command or an offer. In commands there can be different degrees of obligation (*allowed to/supposed to/required to*) while in offers what varies is the degree of inclination (*willing to/anxious to/determined to*). Modulation in proposals can be expressed by finite modal operators (*should, must, ought to*), by passive (impersonal) forms, such as *you're supposed to*, or by an adjective, e.g. *I'm anxious to help them.*

Besides polarity (yes/no), type of modality (modalization vs modulation), and value (high vs low), the system of modality according to the Functional Grammar comprises the dimension of orientation, which refers to whether the source of the conviction is stated explicitly or implicitly and whether it is presented as objective or subjective. Taking the probability scale, examples of implicit and explicit orientation are *it is certain that* vs *I'm certain that*, while objectivity vs subjectivity can be exemplified respectively by *certainly* vs *I'm certain that.*

The four traits of orientation combine to form a matrix of 4 possible combinations, as shown below:

	subjective	objective
implicit	must	certainly
explicit	I'm certain that ...	it is certain that ...

(*Ibidem*: 149)

The most obvious grammatical codification of modality are modal verbs, which can express ability, permission, possibility, willingness, intention, prediction, hypothetical states of affairs, probability, obligation, logical necessity, as well as other minor nuances of such meanings (Quirk et al., 1985: 97–102). However, as shown in the examples above, modality extends well beyond modal verbs, including modal adjectives (*possible, necessary, probable, likely, certain*), modal adverbs (*maybe, necessarily, certainly, probably, likely, perhaps*), projecting clauses like *I think*, or *there is no doubt that* (Halliday & Matthiessen, 2004: 608 ff.), but also nouns (*possibility, necessity*), lexical verbs like *suggest* (Perkins, 1983), and nuances conveyed by the use of aspect with verbs of cognition like *I was thinking* (Stubbs, 1996).

Possibly due to their grammatical codification, modal verbs are of all the modal expressions those that have received greater attention in argumentation theory. They are generally treated as indicators of the extent of commitment to a standpoint, in terms of either certainty or obligation. Epistemic modality—what logicians call doxastic modality—indicates the extent of commitment of the speaker to the "truth or acceptability of the propositional content of his standpoint" (Snoeck Henkemans, 1997: 109), thus performing a metadiscursive function. Other types of modality, like deontic modality, not only express commitment (*must* indicates a stronger commitment than *should*), but are part of the propositional content. According to Rocci, modals can be seen as direct or indirect indicators[4] of specific types of argumentative relations (see Rocci, 2012, 2008a, b for a review of the literature).

3.3.1 Modality in Discourse

From a discursive perspective, modality is often associated with evaluation, as understood by Thompson and Hunston (2000: 5): "Evaluation is the broad cover term for the expression of the speaker or writer's attitude or stance towards a viewpoint on, or feelings about the entities or propositions that he or she is talking about". The speaker's stance towards the propositional content of their message can be expressed bluntly without recourse to modality, or it can be modalized and/or modulated. Evaluation is comprised of two dimensions, along which stance can be expressed in relation to either epistemic or affective values.

From the viewpoint of evaluation, structures that contribute to conveying epistemic or affective stance have been grouped into three areas concerned respectively with comparison, the expression of subjectivity, and the expression of value. Any comparison entails the assessment of something against a comparator or a standard. The value expressed, therefore, is not an absolute one, but is a matter of degree, and as such it shares in the logic of modulation. Comparisons can be realised through comparative adjectives and adverbs (*higher, more quickly, faster, worse*), adverbs of degree (*fairly, very, at all, largely, much, a lot, a good pretty, quite, rather, really, scarcely*), and comparator adverbs (*just, only, at least*). Markers of subjectivity include a very broad array of elements, going from modal verbs and other

---

[4]Houtlosser (2002, 169–170) defines argumentative indicators as words or expressions that "point to speech acts that are instrumental in the various stages of dispute resolution". These are what Rocci refers to as 'direct indicators' (Rocci, 2008b), as is the case for the connective *because*. However, indicators do not necessarily point to a speech act that is instrumental in the dispute resolution, due to the polysemy of language and also to the fact that the indicator may not refer to the argumentative move itself but to some other semantic or pragmatic categories, which can co-occur with that argumentative move. Indicators of this second type are indirect indicators, and account for several items discussed in van Eemeren et al. (2007).

expressions of certainty/uncertainty (*unlikely, probably*) to stance adverbs (*unfortunately, hopefully*) and conjunctions (*although, however*), and marked clause structures, which modulate the allocation of emphasis, deviating from the linear clause structure (clefts and pseudoclefts, extraposition). Thompson and Hunston (2000: 21) also include report and attribution structures, since presenting a proposition as averred or as attributed clearly makes a difference in terms of commitment. However, this specific aspect will be dealt here under the rubric of polyphony (cf. Sect. 3.6). Markers of value, finally, comprise lexical items with a connotation or indications of the existence of goals, but since these are not per se modulated, they will not be dealt with here.

Besides epistemic and affective evaluation, Thompson and Hunston (2000: 24) identify two other parameters of evaluation, i.e. expectedness (*clearly, obviously, surprisingly, interestingly enough*) and importance, or relevance (*even more importantly, significantly*). Whereas epistemic and affective evaluation are mainly 'real-world-oriented', expressing attitude towards some text-external aspects of reality, expectedness and importance are mostly text-oriented, helping the interlocutor to follow the flow of discourse and retrieve internal coherence. This does not mean, though, that their modulating function is simply technical; signalling what comes next as obvious as opposed to unexpected, or on the other hand as more or less significant orients the reception of that content by the audience. Furthermore, with special regard to agreement, signalling something as expected or unexpected presupposes a shared core of expectations between the sender and the receiver, which can be exploited when establishing starting points, and whenever the acceptability of standpoints and premises is posited or negotiated.

3.4 Agreement on Objects and Qualities: Nouns and Adjectives

In the perspective of a linguistic approach to discourse, the choice of words plays a fundamental role. The way of designating people and objects and the way of qualifying them is functional to the representation of the world the arguer intends to promote, which is the general premise to any further argumentative step. In what follows, we focus on the use of nouns as forms of definition and classification of the world and on adjectives (and modifiers in general) as a way of conveying evaluative meaning.

Definition is not a merely linguistic problem, but is intertwined with the concept of categorization, deeply rooted in philosophical and logical concepts. The traditional approach to definition rests on the Aristotelian principle of categorization, which implies the adoption of a model based on the discrete and homogeneous nature of categories. This interpretation of categories has been challenged in modern research, from both the linguistic and cognitive point of view. The implications of these studies lie far beyond the scope of our observations. Yet it is important to emphasise that, whenever the range of application and the boundaries of a category are controversial, assigning a *definiendum* to it has crucial ideological implications. Actually, the importance of classification is not limited to special cases, and never is definition a neutral process. As stated in the NR: "The choice of terms to express the speaker's thought is rarely without significance in the argumentation" (NR: 149). Furthermore:

> In general, an indication of the argumentative intent is given by the use of a term representing a departure from ordinary language. Naturally, selection of the ordinary term may also have argumentative value; on the other hand, one would have to specify when and where use of a particular term can be regarded as ordinary; broadly speaking, a term that passes unnoticed may be considered ordinary. *There is no neutral choice—but there is a choice that appears neutral,* and this can serve as a starting point for the study of modifications for the purpose of argument (*Ibidem*; emphasis added).

The argumentative value of a word can be better perceived through the comparison with other words in the same semantic field, in the context of predominant use in a given situation or domain. In the NR, Perelman and Olbrechts-Tyteca also notice that the analysis of certain variations in expression "can be carried out only in terms of divergence from the expression that goes unnoticed" (NR: 151), which however does not imply that the use of expressions that pass unnoticed is not an argumentative procedure. In other words, assigning to a class and denominating the class are both crucial and unavoidable argumentative steps. Moreover, as they do not usually belong to the explicitly argumentative process, they play a fundamental role in the construction of a shared set of convictions and values to be exploited as objects of agreement. From the rhetorical and discursive viewpoint, Angenot (2014) synthetises: "Raisonner et argumenter, c'est, au plus élémentaire de ses opérations, distinguer, identifier et classer. Tout commence en rhétorique, dans le discours social et dans les idéologies, en donnant des noms aux choses [. . .]."

Anaphoric Encapsulators The importance of classification and denomination is particularly evident when nouns are part of anaphoric processes, syntactically aiming at textual cohesion but discursively useful to promote identification or re-interpretation of classes and concepts. Co-reference or anaphoric encapsulation can be exploited to give alternative denominations of the same object or process that lead to implicit identification, often with an evaluative component. In these cases, it is not uncommon for encapsulators to convey more blunted evaluation than that expressed indirectly or diplomatically in the previous portion of text. The following example is taken from a popularizing article about asthma, which is characterised by sarcasm against science for the many contradictory theories on how to deal with it. The writer tells about how she tried to comply with scientific precepts, while still nourishing doubts as to their efficacy:

> We cleaned the boys' room compulsively and quit using their closets because the asthma books warned that the mere opening and closing of closet doors would stir up pestilential clouds of dust. We *fretted* about whether to open the windows, which would let in fresh air (good) but also pollen (bad). *Should we* use a vacuum cleaner? It would suck up some dust (good), but also blow some around (bad). A humidifier? Moist air soothed the lungs (good), but also helped mold grow (bad).

> We *had no idea* whether any of these fanatical acts ever did a bit of good. Deep down, we wondered whether they were worth the trouble. Our sons still had asthma attacks. But, we thought, maybe they would be even worse if we stopped scrubbing. We were afraid to quit, though eventually we realized that we could make ourselves crazy with this stuff, and we began to run out of steam.
> With all our **bumbling**, though, there was one thing we knew we had done right [....][5]

In the example above, the third paragraph starts with a nominal form (*bumbling*) which encapsulates all the author wrote about their doubts in the two previous paragraphs. While the doubts are first presented as a legitimate reaction of concerned parents, pondering on the pros and cons of each measure they took, referring anaphorically to them as "all our *bumbling*" removes any philosophical dignity to their lack of certainties. Suffice it to consider the example of use for *bumbling* in the Cambridge Online Dictionary: "The players look like bumbling idiots on the field".

The *bumbling* example brings into the picture another important category of discourse analysis, i.e. *loaded words*. They are lexical words with a strong emotional connotation, often used in news discourse to stir a given reaction, most often negative, in the reader.[6] While few words can be considered neutral from the viewpoint of connotation, some are certainly more heavily connoted than others. Referring to some acts as *homicides* or *killing*, for example, evokes per se negative feelings, but if those actions are named *slaughter* or *massacre*, the emotional response they aim to elicit is even more negative (Carter et al. 2008).

The notion of loaded words is partly overlapping with that of dysphemisms and, by extension, of euphemisms, which are intended as pejorative or ameliorative ways of referring to some aspects of reality that are considered taboos in a given culture.

Adjectives Adjectives are *relational concepts* (Prandi, 2004: 123) used for the expression of qualities. The attribution of a quality to a referent can have different implications. Grammars traditionally distinguish between objective and subjective qualifier, the former used for a sort of classification (*She is a blue-eyed girl*, or she belongs to the class of blue-eyed girls), the latter being the expression of a subjective judgement not empirically verifiable (*She is a beautiful girl*). This distinction has been refined by Kerbrat-Orecchioni (1980), who introduces a tripartite classification: affective, axiological and non-axiological. Affective adjectives reflect an emotional state, thus conveying an emotion of the enunciator (*dear, sad, moving*); axiological adjectives are the expression of evaluation in relation to a system of values (*beautiful, important*), while non-axiological adjectives, though implying evaluation, are based on relatively objective criteria, which are generally accepted by the community (*long, hot, heavy*). Despite prototypical examples, the divide between these

---

[5] New York Times, 19 March, 2001 (in Osimo, 2007: 85).

[6] Interestingly enough, this is reminiscent of the notion of *persuasive definition*, "one which gives a new conceptual meaning to a familiar word without substantially changing its emotional meaning" (Stevenson, 1938: 311), to stretch the agreement enjoyed by the original concept to another concept now included in its scope of reference (s. Zarefsky, 2014: 324). In the *bumbling* example, however, the process is reversed, as the speaker maintains the propositional content but connotes it negatively.

categories is not always clear-cut, as an adjective ideally belonging to one class may perform functions typical of another. Non-axiological adjectives are those that most naturally reflect the views and values of a community, but judging something in relation to a norm entails an element of subjectivity (your judgement of how tall a person is depends on the standards in a given context but also on your height), while axiological judgements may reflect cultural or contextual factors (the idea of beauty rests on culturally shared canons: e.g. fat is beautiful or thin is beautiful?).

Collocations and Epithets A special mention deserve collocations and epithets. Collocations are sequences of words that frequently co-occur, thus forming rigid or semi-rigid combinations. Examples of collocations are strings of adjective+noun, verb+noun or adverb+verb. In the first case especially, the existence of a given collocation may reflect aspects of the social context and implicitly convey an evaluation about them. This is the case of the phrase *working mothers*, which has no male counterpart (*working fathers), suggesting that the fact that a mother works is a 'deviation' from a norm. Discursively, this mechanism not only reflects reality, but contributes to maintaining the status quo. In this respect, the movement to cancel sexism in language is an example of how changing language use is considered to be functional to modifying the role of women in society.

In some types of collocations, the adjective does not add much to the semantic value of the noun, and therefore its use is similar to the role of epithets in rhetoric. Epithets describe a property that is presented as inherently pertaining to the noun, as commonly happened in ancient epic poetry (e.g. *rosy-fingered Dawn, swift-footed Achilles*, etc.). The function of adjectives in these contexts may be purely ornamental: they do not add meaning, but simply play a stylistic function (e.g. *Peleiades Achilles*, or 'Achilles son of Peleus'). Yet epithets may have an argumentative value:

> The epithet results from the visible selection of a quality which is emphasized and which is meant to complete our knowledge of the object. This epithet *is used without justification because it is supposed to set forth unquestionable facts;* only the choice of the facts will seem tendentious. It is permissible to call the French Revolution "that bloody revolution," but this is not the only way of qualifying it and other epithets could equally well be chosen. The role of epithets in argumentation is most clearly seen when two symmetrical qualifications with opposite values appear equally possible: by calling Orestes a "mother slayer" or the "avenger of his father," [...] the speaker unmistakably chooses a viewpoint (NR: 126, emphasis added).

In Critical Discourse Analysis, a well-known counterpart to the Orestes' example is the distinction between 'freedom fighter' and 'terrorist' (van Dijk, 1997). Although the latter seems to have eclipsed the former, there was a time in which the two labels were referentially synonyms, which differed solely for the ideological slant in the eyes of a viewer: both referred to non-military forces engaging in some form of asymmetric conflict, but while 'freedom fighter' indicated sympathy with the cause, 'terrorist' conveyed stark condemnation.

In this perspective, epithets can be fallacious, as they can be "a *petitio principii* by the use of a single appellative" (NR: 129). Epithets usually occur in marked position (*the Prince Consort, the Secretary General*), all the more so in languages where the adjective can both precede or follow the noun, In Italian, for example, post-nominal adjectives can attribute intrinsic (and therefore unquestionable) qualities to a referent: *un impero grande* ('a large empire'), for example, denotes the width of an empire, whereas *un grande impero* entails positive evaluation, comparable to that attached to the expression 'a great empire'. The difference was also exploited in an ad, where a painter rode a bicycle burdened with a huge brush and the payoff claimed that to paint a big wall, it does not take a *pennello grande* ('big brush') but a *grande pennello* ('a great brush').

Adjectives as Indicators of Dissociation As mentioned above, adjectives can assign a referent to a class, but when the referent is an uncountable and indivisible notion, they manipulate the notion itself, tearing it apart and thus triggering a form of dissociation. Dissociation is a crucial argumentative technique, which will be discussed in the following Sect. 3.5. Here, it is however worth observing that evaluative adjectives can modify a unitary concept, splitting it into two opposite terms, with contrasting axiological value. This technique can give rise to fossilized phrases or collocates, frequently used in everyday language and common in news discourse, where the adjective does not really add meaning to the noun, but generates implicit assumptions. The use of adjectives like *actual* or *real* is typical of this strategy: *real help* implies that someone may be providing *unreal* help, which obviously wouldn't be help at all. Similarly, in advertising, the payoff of a fragrance by Dior, *féminin absolu*, is extremely suggestive—but, can there actually be a "féminin relatif"?

This technique for positively connoting general values can be interpreted as an attempt to focus on the concept giving it prototypical sharpness (Martin & White, 2005). As a consequence, the existence of the opposite, blurred representation of the same concept is implied: e.g. *real/actual freedom* vs *a sort of/pseudo-freedom*. Different value is obviously attributed to the two versions of the once unitary concept. Modifiers which emphasise the authentic character of a given concept or quality are therefore linked to a form of dissociation (s. *infra*).

A similar strategy is adopted to transform concepts that would be negatively loaded into positive values, or vice versa. The *Holy War* is a consolidated historical concept, but a *humanitarian war* can be coined to justify questionable military intervention. In political discourse, this is common practice. It can even happen that the adjective simply duplicates the meaning of the noun: an interesting example is the Italian phrase *una giustizia giusta* ('a fair justice'), where noun and adjective have the same lexical root. The use of the indefinite article itself implies the existence of *another* justice, thus triggering dissociation of the notion. Furthermore, the adjective, having the same lexical root of the noun, generates an implicit contraposition with 'an unfair justice' (which is obviously an oxymoron). The phrase was actually used by Italian right-wing leader Silvio Berlusconi, who transformed it in one of the pivotal concepts of his policy (Santulli, 2005). The axiological contrast made it possible for the arguer to present himself as the defender of 'fair justice' and attribute the negative and contradictory representation to the adversary. The arguer did not explicitly affirm that the adversary did not pursue justice at all, thus avoiding open attack, but at the same time emphasised the positive values of his party in opposition to the adversary, and implicitly accused the latter of deception.

Semantic Prosody Another phenomenon connected to collocation is semantic prosody, which refers to the connotation that a word may take through frequent association with other words that are positively or negatively connoted. This shows that positive or negative connotations are not necessarily traits internal to a word, but may derive for the "company that words keep" (Firth, 1957). Such an association can be exploited to convey evaluation covertly. For example, the phrasal verb *set in* has a semantic negative connotation, as demonstrated by the expression 'the rot set in'. When it is used with words that are not necessarily negatively connoted, it transfers onto them a negative value, as is the case for the proposition "hot weather set in early that year" (Thompson and Hunston 2000: 38), where the verb conveys negative evaluation of hot weather, which in other contexts may be pleasant indeed. The negative connotation of a word may not lie, then, with the word itself, but may come from its typical collocates. Louw (1993: 172) pointed out that "in many cases semantic prosodies 'hunt in packs' and potentiate and bolster one another". Following Louw, Channel (2000) remarked that words with the same 'polarity' often cluster together forming a mutually supporting web of negative or positive words.

Negative semantic prosody can also concern suffixes or pseudo-suffixes. In the case of *–ism*, its frequent combination with independent morphemes which have always had, or have acquired, a negative connotation (such as *terrorism, fascism, communism, fanaticism*) has led to its negative interpretation in words like *racism, sexism*, etc. Interestingly enough, the negative semantic prosody of this suffix has even brought to the formation of the quite oxymoronic expression *do-goodism*, referred to well-intentioned but naive and often ineffectual (if not counter-productive) attempts of helping others. A negatively-loaded suffix can also be 'created' as morphological re-interpretation of the ending part of a (negative) word: a typical example of this is the pseudo-suffix *–gate*, modeled on *Watergate*, in neologisms like *Sexgate, Irangate*, etc.

3.5 Agreement on Implicit Premises: Presuppositions, Dissociation and Concession

As already discussed in Chap. 1 (cf., in particular, Sect. 1.3) implicitness has a great persuasive potential. The arguer who exploits implicit meaning to lay their premises and obtain agreement can rely on the adhesion of the audience without actually asking for it. What is implicit is more difficult to challenge, as any objection to what is not actually said may jeopardise communication and compromise face (Goffman, 1967). Should the implicit meaning be challenged, arguers can rebut the arguments of interlocutors, refusing the inferences and denying their intention to imply what they are accused of. This process more easily occurs when implicit meaning is conveyed through context-based assumptions, cultural stereotypes or encyclopaedic associations—i.e. when the implicit meaning is not inscribed in the linguistic structure of the message, but comes with the frame that is activated by a given statement. In this respect, the realm of implicitness is huge and extremely vague.

As we have chosen a discursive approach with a linguistic slant, the discussion here will be limited to those forms of implicitness that are linguistically codified, focusing on three main areas: presuppositions, dissociation, and concession.

3.5.1 Linguistic Presupposition

Presuppositions are particularly interesting, as—according to the distinction put forth by Ducrot (1972)—they do not exploit processes of logical inferencing rooted in contextual or encyclopaedic knowledge, but rely on the literal, linguistic meaning of the utterances. The concept of presupposition refers to the fact that a *pre-supposed* meaning is part of the truth conditions of the *posed* meaning. As a consequence, presupposed meaning cannot be cancelled if the posed meaning is negated nor if it is questioned.[7]

From the discursive point of view, this allows the construction of a clearly identifiable context, as the interpretation of the presupposition does not require further knowledge in addition to what is explicitly inscribed in the linguistic structure of the utterance. It is obviously possible to deny also pre-supposed meaning, but this requires an aggressive attitude in interactional terms, as it causes an interruption in the exchange or, in some cases, explicit labelling of the utterance as false (Ducrot, 1972: 106).[8]

It is therefore evident that presuppositions play a crucial role in the presentation of starting points or premises to argumentation proper. If by default presuppositions entail the *a priori* sharing of their content by the interlocutor, in actual communicative interactions this 'maxim' can be flouted. Flouting the maxim produces the most interesting consequences whenever a linguistic trigger conveys as presupposed meaning something that should actually be posed, because there is no guarantee that it is shared *a priori* by the interlocutor. In such a case, the adhesion to the presupposed meaning is surreptitiously induced *a posteriori*. Linguistic triggers play therefore a strategic function, as they present as presuppositions meanings that should actually be posed, thus influencing the perception of the audience and inducing to passive acceptance.

In these cases, the use of presupposition can be fallacious. In particular, in pragma-dialectics it is considered a violation of the starting point rule, according

---

[7] *John's hat is green*: John has a hat (pre-supposed meaning), the hat is green (posed meaning). The pre-supposed meaning is not affected by negation nor by question form (*John's hat is not green, is John's hat green?*).

[8] Considering the example in note 7, it is possible to affirm: "But John has no hat!". This is however an overt challenge to the interlocutor, who is considered to be ill-informed (or, worse, deceptive).

to which the protagonist should not take a proposition as accepted (i.e. as a starting point) if this is not the case (van Eemeren et al., 2002: 128):

> A familiar trick for preventing a proposition from being attacked is to formulate something controversial in such an inconspicuous way that it is not noticed. This can be done by presenting the controversial proposition as a presupposition [...], thus falsely giving the impression that the addition is an established fact (van Eemeren et al., 2002: 129).

In other words, not always is presupposed meaning part of shared knowledge or opinions. Therefore, the arguer actually gives the audience new information, but the implicit presentation, which does not require open discussion, adds the new elements to other, already shared premises. Obviously, this type of informative presuppositions can play an important role in ideology-loaded contexts.

In very general terms, there are numerous convictions about the nature of the world and of society (as to how things are or should be), which are often unconscious or semi-conscious, difficult to prove but not necessarily non-verifiable. If arguers *pose* these convictions, they commit themselves to supporting them with adequate arguments. If, on the other hand, arguers *presuppose* them, they are not explicitly said and do not need argumentation. They appear to be non-rebuttable, and there are important constraints to raising doubts about them. The possibility of transforming implicit presupposed meaning in explicit statements (which can in turn be rebutted) does remain, but this may make the challenger feel uneasy and distressed. Moreover, in the context of monologic speeches, it is excluded out of practical reasons.

Sbisà suggests that presuppositions should be considered "not as shared assumptions, but as assumptions that ought to be shared" (1999: 501). Exploiting linguistic structures that activate presuppositions, the arguer can increase the effectiveness of their premises, which thus escape argumentation and naturally become part of a common ground including speaker and audience.

An exhaustive taxonomy of linguistic forms that can function as presupposition triggers is difficult to sketch. The most common are: nouns or adjectives that trigger existential presuppositions; relative clauses; cleft or semi-cleft sentences; verbs or adverbs indicating change (e.g. *continue, give up, more*); projecting clauses (e.g. *I understand/ know that*) and counter-factual structures (e.g. *They should have/They should have not*) (Levinson, 1983: 181–84).

Presuppositions are frequently used to obtain agreement on values, as they can induce acceptance of principles, beliefs, social norms, ideals. However, they can also offer "perspectives on *facts*" (Sbisà, 1999: 492, emphasis added). The way of telling facts is, as already observed, crucial in the construction of agreement and in the creation of myths. This effect is enhanced by the use of factual presuppositions, triggered by the use of projecting clauses containing a verb of cognition (especially in the first person singular, e.g. *I realized that, I understood that*). This technique reinforces the perception of the narrated facts as unquestionably pre-existing events, whose historical truth is accepted by the audience as an implicit premise. Thus, the arguer can convey their view of the world without entering the space of confrontation and with no argumentative support, so that it cannot be affected by dialectical rebuttal.

3.5.2 Dissociation

The transformation of values into facts through narrative makes them acceptable for the universal audience, as facts in principle go more unchallenged than values, based on the presupposition of their actual existence. Vice versa, values with a universal appeal can be made more specific, transforming them into the banner of a particular audience (e.g. *liberty* vs *liberalism*). The shift is gradual, and arguers can mitigate or emphasise different traits of the potentially universal values they choose to exploit. In this respect, it is worth quoting a passage from the New Rhetoric:

> The actual audience will be able to consider itself all the more close to a universal audience as the particular value seems to fade before the universal value it determines. It is thus by virtue of their being vague that these values appear as universal values and lay claim to a status similar to that of facts. To the extent that they are precisely formulated, they are simply seen to conform to the aspirations of particular groups. Their role is accordingly to justify choices on which there is not unanimous agreement by *inserting these choices in a sort of empty frame with respect to which a wider agreement exists*. Though this agreement is reached over an empty form, it is nonetheless of considerable significance: it is evidence of the fact that one has decided to transcend particular agreements, at least in intention, and that one recognizes the importance attaching to the universal agreement which these values make it possible to achieve (NR: 76, emphasis added).

In political discourse, the shaping of group values starting from general values is a typical expression of the technique described in the NR. General values are presented as a wide and shared background, which is however unspecified and devoid of particular traits (the *empty frame* described in the NR). Though empty, this frame is functional to establishing a contact with a large (and possibly universal) audience. Universal values are then transformed into the values of a particular group not through an explicit argumentative process, but in the preliminary stages of a speech, when agreement is implicitly constructed. The particular-group values are consistent with the ideology and the policy promoted by the arguer and, at the same time, are opposed to the version of the same universal values supported by the adversary. This effect of polarization is effectively obtained with dissociation.

In the NR, argumentative techniques are divided into two broad categories: the association and the dissociation of notions. Perelman and Olbrechts-Tyteca extensively discuss the latter, which is treated as an argumentative technique used to separate elements that are usually assigned to one and the same concept. Dissociation is therefore different from the breaking of a link of association, which consists in the separation of elements that should be kept distinct and are thought to have been improperly associated. Dissociation presupposes the existence of elements *originally* belonging to the same conceptual unit, and designated by the same term. As a consequence, dissociation deeply reshapes the original notions, modifying their conceptual structure (NR: 411–12).

On the basis of the ample discussion included in the NR, dissociation can be considered an argumentative technique able to solve contradictions deriving from a unitary notion, previously designated with a single term, thanks to the possibility of distinguishing different aspects singled out within the notion itself, which are then subsumed under a new common denominator. As the new notion and the old one (deprived of its "dissociated" aspects) are differently evaluated, dissociation can be used for argumentative purposes. It is important to emphasise that dissociation does not entail a mere shift in meaning, nor do the distinctions remain within the domain of one single notion. Dissociated parts are moved outside the notion itself, as there is no equivalence between the different parts and they are attributed different value. A good example is offered by van Rees: "You've got beer and you've got Grolsch" is the payoff of an advertising campaign, in which the promoted product is put outside the category of beers and thus attributed a special value (van Rees, 2005: 55).

Dissociation has been given a prominent role also by scholars working in the area of pragma-dialectics, van Rees in the first place (s., among others, van Rees, 2005, 2009). Dissociation is reflected in linguistic forms that can be considered *indicators* of dissociation. The taxonomy put forth by van Rees (2005) is an interesting tool to identify dissociation in language. Indicators are grouped into three areas: separation, value, and negation.

Separation is mainly obtained through the specification of the meaning of a word thanks to synonyms or modifiers. For example, in 1994 French legislation introduced the concept of "medically assisted procreation", which implied the splitting of the originally unitary notion of procreation into natural vs assisted procreation, and therefore potentially led to different evaluation of the two. To counter that risk, in subsequent legislation the expression has then been replaced with *assistance médicale à la procreation* ('medical assistance to procreation'), thus restoring the unitary nature of procreation, which comprises all forms of reproduction, with no distinction between natural and in-vitro fertilization (cf. Antelmi, 2012).

Dissociation is also produced through the attribution of different values, when one of the two concepts resulting from the split is given prominence or is considered to be *the* authentic representative of the original notion. The pair appearance–reality is analysed as exemplary manifestation of dissociation in the NR. Therefore, in actual language use "any idea can be dissociated by the addition of the adjectives 'apparent' or 'real', or of the adverbs 'apparently' or 'really'" (NR: 436). This corresponds to the opposition *actual* vs *pseudo* (or synonyms), which has already been examined in Sect. 3.4.

Finally, a concept can be dissociated when the arguer considers a statement *true* if one interpretation of the meaning of the word is adopted, and *false* if another interpretation is adopted. This process is frequently marked by the occurrence of the connector *but* combined with a negation. Van Rees (2005: 60) observes that there are two different possibilities. The negation can precede the conjunction, leading to explicit refusal of the one of the two interpretations of the concept, which is replaced with the other (*it is not... but*). On the other hand, the negation can follow the conjunction (*but not*). This is a semi-explicit expression of negation, which makes it possible for the arguer to criticise a statement in one of its interpretations, *but not* in the other. The two structures correspond to two different values of the conjunction: substitutive vs concessive *but*. In political discourse, concessive *but* is particularly effective to emphasise a positive value within a notion that may be too vague and comprehensive. Arguers claim a very general positive notion (e.g. freedom, democracy), which is fundamental, but not sufficiently defined to distinguish their party from the opposition. Through dissociation, they disavow some negative aspects of the notion, which are cast as upheld by the adversary (e.g.: I am a Catholic *but not* a fundamentalist). As explicitly indicated by the denomination, concessive *but* combines dissociation with concession, which is another crucial strategy for the implicit construction of agreement.

3.5.3   Concession

Concession is usually interpreted as a special case of contrast (s., for ex., Rudolph, 1996), expressing the frustration of an expected causal link. The typical concessive utterance can be defined as the relation between a premise p and a consequence $-q$ which frustrates an expected consequence q. Concession is based on an adversative relation opposing two actual facts, which includes two special components: the facts are in temporal succession, and their connection frustrates a causal link; contrast is combined with the implicit frustrated cause (Prandi, 2004: 311–312). The expectation of regularity of a causal link can be falsified under given circumstances, or, in other words, a rule can admit exceptions, and in order to accept exceptions it is not necessary to deny the rule. Thus, the mechanism of concession relies on presupposed and shared expectations, which allow an exception in the case at hand, and can therefore produce interesting pragmatic effects in the argumentative perspective.[9]

As a matter of fact, a concessive construction does not add anything to the propositional content of the two clauses it comprises (p & q), but simply 'illuminates' it in a special fashion. Garzone (2005b), quoting Frege, emphasises that this 'illumination' consists in:

> the signalling of a relation of contrast, conflict or unexpectedness between the two propositions making up the utterance, or, better, in the addition of an implicated proposition presenting one of the two parts of the utterance as divergent from the standard expectation which would normally be elicited by the other (Garzone, 2005b: 133).

As a consequence, concessive constructions are typically used to affirm the validity of two facts that are normally considered to be incompatible or in contrast to each other. What allows the coexistence of two otherwise contradictory statements is the fact that a different weight is attached to them.

From a syntactic point of view, the concessive relation can be conveyed through subordination or coordination. Subordinated clauses are introduced by a concessive

---

[9] Actually, concession is a both rhetoric-argumentative and logic-grammatical concept: researchers sometimes suggest that this is only a fortuitous homonymy, as from the argumentative point of view concession indicates a specific scheme, including temporary approval of a thesis that is then rejected (Stati, 1998, 2002). In the context of argumentation, concession can also be functional to the expression of different voices, polyphonically materialised in discourse (Ducrot, 1984), an aspect which will be discussed in the following Section (Sect. 3.6).

conjunction (*although, even if*), while in coordination two clauses are connected by adverbs (*nevertheless, however, yet*) or by the conjunction *but*. In subordination, the difference between the status of the main and the subordinated clause reflects more clearly that the conceded and the asserted proposition have a different weight (Thompson & Zhou, 2000; Garzone, 2005b), and the distribution of the propositional content between the main and the subordinated clause indicates which of the two is presented as more valid. The subordinated clause contains the conceded proposition, while the main clause will convey the meaning that is asserted. In coordination, it is the order of the two clauses that signals which of the two carries more 'weight', according to the end-weight linguistic principle whereby the content placed in final position receives more prominence. On a similar basis, in an argumentative context, when two statements are juxtaposed, there is an implicit assumption that the second one asserts the speakers' view (Thompson & Zhou, 2000: 126).

From the rhetorical point of view, it is worth noticing that the (frustrated) causal link presupposed in the concession is not necessarily pre-existent, but it can be also conjured up, being actually created the very moment it is frustrated. The effect of the structure is that of *imposing* an implicit relationship between the two statements. In that case, the causal link (which is usually implicitly introduced as a shared, presupposed assumption) is actually part of the convictions of the arguer not necessarily in tune with those of the audience. Consider the following example:

> Although John is an engineer, he loves music.

This statement presupposes that engineers do not (usually) love music, which is far from being a common and widely accepted notion. When used surreptitiously, the real point in resorting to a concession could be the establishment of the presupposed content, rather than asserting the propositional content.

Concessive constructions contain a polyphonic component, as the two propositions that are set in relation actually voice two different points of view, only one of which is actually endorsed by the speaker. The other, which is temporarily accepted, is presented as assumedly upheld by someone else. This polyphonic aspect of concession will be dealt with in the next Section.

3.6 Agreement from Different Voices: Dialogism and Reported Speech

Polyphony and Concession As discussed in the previous Section, the logical (and syntactic) link founding concession can be artfully exploited to convey implicit meaning and construct agreement. Yet *concession* is primarily a move allowing arguers to guide the audience towards what they want them to admit (NR: 159), and can be preliminary to *confutatio*, also in the form of anticipatory refutation (*prolepsis*) (NR: 501). From the pragmatic point of view, utterances including a concession can be analysed as a special form of speech act. According to Leclère (1980), when the addressee declares (only) temporary agreement with the speaker's point of view, a *partial* speech act is performed, which can be transformed into an explicit performative structure (*I concede/ I agree*, etc.). This approach makes it possible to take into consideration the modal elements that may be introduced to reduce vs reinforce the engagement towards the conceded standpoint (*it is true that; although many/some/a few people believe that; I cannot deny that*; etc.).

As mentioned above, concession can be syntactically expressed with different structures, both subordinate and coordinate. In some cases, even mere juxtaposition can be sufficient to convey concession. It is to be noted, however, that a subordinate clause (especially when it precedes the main clause) immediately marks the presence of a concessive structure, thus orienting the receiver towards this interpretation. In other words, while proposing a different point of view and opening a *dialogic* perspective, the arguer at the same time closes it, or at least reduces the impact of what is temporarily conceded. Subordination immediately signals that the arguer is exposing *their own* viewpoint, which they firmly control and adapt into a cohesive syntactic structure, though they modulate their commitment to anticipate and rebut possible objections. In coordination, on the other hand, the lack of an initial concessive marker allows full adhesion to the conceded statement, raising no different expectations in the receiver. The conceded viewpoint can be presented as part of common experience and beliefs, and is temporarily accepted by both arguer and audience. The conceded part can even be introduced with special emphasis (*it is true that/it is certainly the case that*), though this does not actually correspond to genuine commitment by the arguer. As a matter of fact, when a conviction is emphasised, and explicitly considered *true*, this implies a certain degree of uncertainty: "saying explicitly that you believe something to be true admits the possibility of it not being believed true by everyone" (Thompson & Zhou, 2000:130). In coordinated concessive structures, the initial statement is then followed by a 'correction' (*however/ but,* etc.), which actually rebuts what has been affirmed and forces the listener to re-interpret it as a concession (i.e. a merely temporary adhesion), and to re-consider the value of what had been presented as a shared belief.

In the interplay with the audience, arguers can also take distance from what they concede, marking it as an opinion attributed to the audience or to a third party.[10] In doing so, they introduce different voices in the discourse, and concession fully reveals its inherently dialogic nature.

Different Types of Dialogism The notion of dialogism is widely exploited in discourse analysis, and often intertwined with that of polyphony. Yet researchers do not accept a univocal and explicit definition of these two, partially overlapping phenomena, which can be presented from different points of view. Dendale and Coltier (2006) singled out and compared three main approaches: the line of research stemming from Ducrot's polyphonic theory of enunciation, ScaPoLine, and Bres and Nowakowska's prassematics. Despite conceptual and terminological differences, these three branches are to some extent connected and mutually interdependent, as

---

[10] In some languages, this corresponds to a specific modal choice. In Italian, the conditional marks attribution and sometimes reported speech.

they all recognise their common origin from Bakhtin's seminal work. In that perspective, the crucial element is the relation that each utterance establishes with other utterances, a process that is indispensable to generate meaning. This inherent 'dialogicity' is not limited to actual dialogue, but characterises any type of discourse, as any utterance is connected to other utterances, and these dialogic relations pragmatically make up the texture of communication.

Dialogism entails at the same time the enunciator's awareness of their own discourse, of the interlocutor and of the discursive background (i.e. interdiscourse). This threefold metadiscursive competence parallels an interesting classification of different forms of dialogism, distinguishing autodialogism, interlocutive and interdiscursive dialogism (Bres & Nowakowska, 2006: 24). Autodialogism refers to the relation between the enunciator and their own discourse, which is mainly conveyed through modulation of illocutionary forces, limiting the commitment of the enunciator and thus expressing their willingness to negotiate their claims. Both interlocutive and interdiscursive dialogism, on the other hand, entail the involvement of different voices: the co-enunciator (interlocutor) in the former, and, in the latter, other subjects, which may be more or less explicitly and univocally singled out. The different voices can be introduced through various forms of evaluation and implicit meaning, which have been already examined above, as well as through confutation and concession, which (as shown above) is highly codified and widely exploited to this end. Quite obviously and more explicitly, a different voice can also be introduced through reported speech in its different manifestations. In this respect, references and quotes can be functional to an alternative representation of reality, but can also be exploited to reinforce the viewpoint of the arguer, as a form of *argumentum ad verecundiam*.

In the perspective of agreement, autodialogism is a feature of ethos, insofar as it contributes to the representation of the enunciator *in* discourse and of their relationship *with* their own discourse. Interlocutive dialogism, on the other hand, makes it possible to bring forth the stance of the audience as thought construction of the arguer. The possibility of making both similar and, above all, different convictions more explicit is the prerequisite for reinforcement, corrections and even confutations, which can skilfully contribute to the construction of a common ground. Finally, interdiscursive dialogism offers arguers the possibility of sketching the discursive universe of which they intend to be part. Supporting and contrasting voices can be exploited to enhance the image of both arguer and audience, and to strengthen the connection between them that is the most important preliminary step in the process of persuasion.

Rhetorical Questions An expedient to introduce fictive dialogism in a speech is to ask so-called rhetorical questions, which presuppose that the answer is already known to both speaker and addressee. Any question per se materialises the interlocutor in discourse, and when it is not geared to obtain new information it can be functional to other interpersonal aims. It can have a phatic function, reinforcing the relationship between arguer and audience; it can transform argumentation into drama, with important effects on the attention and the involvement of the audience;

having a pre-determined answer, it can be an important source of agreement. As a matter of fact, "research on the use of rhetorical questions [...] has shown that this type of question invites the answer intended by the questioner" (Renkema, 2004: 155). A famous series of rhetorical questions is present in Shakespeare's *Merchant of Venice*, when Shylock intends to prove that Jews are not different from Christians:

> Hath not a Jew eyes? Hath not a Jew hands, organs, dimensions, senses, affections, passions; fed with the same food, hurt with the same weapons, subject to the same diseases, healed by the same means, warmed and cooled by the same winter and summer as a Christian is? If you prick us, do we not bleed? If you tickle us, do we not laugh? If you poison us, do we not die? And if you wrong us, shall we not revenge? (Act III, Scene 1)

The questions asked by Shylock do not allow a negative answer, as they refer to physical, incontrovertible facts. All questions but one. Actually, a positive answer to the last question entails that revenge is a necessary reaction to injustice, which is not a universal assumption. Its acceptability highly depends on cultural factors, which also determine for whom and at which conditions it can be valid. Therefore, even if Shylock's audience were willing to accept the ratio of revenge, say, for a Christian, its extension to a Jew may not have been warranted.

In political discourse, rhetorical questions are often asked, as in the following example taken from Ronald Reagan's Presidential campaign:

> Can anyone look at the record of this Administration and say, "Well done"?
> Can anyone compare the state of our economy when the Carter Administration took office with where we are today and say, "Keep up the good work"?
> Can anyone look at our reduced standing in the world today and say, "Let's have four more years of this"?

The candidate intended to show that the incumbent President (who was his direct adversary in the race) had poorly administered the country. This *fact* is to be taken as a premise to affirm that a change is necessary. Pre-determining the answer to his questions, Reagan constructs a strong agreement with his audience, as they come to share a common view of the US political situation, which leads to a common conclusion: America needs a new President.

Negation A particular case within the frame of polyphony is negation (cf. Ducrot, 1984: 217 ff.) Whenever something is negated, two points of view are co-present in discourse: the negated one and its opposite. In an example quoted by Fairclough (1992: 122), who includes negation in manifest intertextuality,[11] the newspaper headline "I Didn't Murder Squealer!" carries the presupposition that some other text stated that the person quoted here did murder a 'squealer' (police informant). Negative sentences, then, embed other texts only to contradict and refute them (cf. Leech, 1983 for an account of negative sentences). Consequently, they are

---

[11] Manifest intertextuality is an umbrella term for all the cases in which a text overtly draws upon another text, other forms of it being discourse representation, presupposition, metadiscourse and irony (see Fairclough, 1992: 117–23).

frequently used for polemical purposes, but they can also be oriented to the construction of agreement.

From a formal point of view, negation can be expressed grammatically (*not,
hardly*), but also semantically (*lack of, fail*, but also *myth*[12]), morphologically (*un- a-
dis-*), or it can be implicitly conveyed through comparative forms (Thompson &
Hunston, 2000: 21), such as *instead of, rather than*.

From a pragmatic point of view, the sub-maxim of Negative Uninformativeness,
combined with the Maxim of Quantity, has it that a negative statement will be
avoided if a positive one can be used instead. As noted by Jordan (1998), when a
negative statement is used, the speaker must have a good reason for it, which often
comes down to the intention of denying a proposition "which has been put forward
or entertained by someone in the context." (Leech, 1983: 100).

Negation is used, then, when speakers want to deny a presupposition or an
expectation which they assume to be in the mind of the addressee. Such an
assumption can be motivated by something that was stated earlier in the text or on
the ground of some shared cultural or contextual knowledge. The latter is the case
when negation is exploited in advertisements, where constructing an agreement on a
given premise is key to persuading the would-be customer. This is called positive-
assessment negation (*Ibidem*: 717), and it is used to preempt a negative idea that the
addressee might have about the product, which might undermine its value. An
example can be found in the advertisement of a weight-loss product that claimed:

> Only Acu-Stop means No Strenuous Dieting | No Pills | No Nervousness | No Frantic
> Exercises | No Strange Formulas | No Special Food to Buy (*Ibidem:* 717).

That diet, pills, nervousness etc. are undesirable rests on shared evaluation of what is
desirable and what is not, and the writer counts on the fact that the audience will
agree on that assessment.

3.7   Agreement through Patterns of Figuration: Metaphoric Meaning

Figurative language is an important component of the part of rhetoric concerning the
wording—what in classical terms is known as *elocutio* (Latin counterpart of
Gr. *lexis*). Though originally inseparable from the logical structure of a text (Sect.
1.1.1), the aspects of the rhetorical process connected with the actual linguistic
representation have come to be considered as mere stylistic elements imposed on
the argumentative line to obtain various emotional effects (e.g. attract the attention of
the listener; produce wonder, compassion, terror, etc.). This approach has led to the
well-known split between the argumentative (logical) and the oratorical (emotional)

---

[12] As in 'the Soviet threat is a myth', which is tantamount to saying 'the Soviet threat is not a reality'
(Fairclough, 1992: 122)

parts of rhetoric (cf. Reboul, 1994) and, consequently, to a rebirth of the ancient discipline along two different lines of development: argumentation theory on the one hand, poetics on the other (Piazza, 2004). Yet the aim of persuasion was originally pursued through the close intertwining of argumentative and stylistic means, and research has come to recognize the importance of linguistic choices in general, and of figurative language in particular. As a matter of fact, the NR recognized the argumentative role of the latter, and of metaphor in the first place. In this respect, metaphor can be considered the most widely exploited trope.

The problem with metaphor is that it is difficult to define it, and to draw the boundaries of its vast domain. In this respect a useful starting point can be Prandi's *minimal* definition, which "identifies in the first instance the largest common denominator shared by any kind of metaphor", namely the transfer of a concept into an alien domain (Prandi, 2004: 388–389). The general character of this definition makes it possible to include different interpretations of metaphor. Yet, considering only the initial process of transfer that triggers a semantic conflict, it does not give indications concerning the possible reactions to this conflict. To illustrate this point, Prandi draws on a metaphorical definition of a metaphor, dating back to Medieval grammarian Geoffrey de Vinsauf, based on the image of a sheep feeding *in rure alieno* ('in alien field'). When a sheep jumps the fence and starts feeding in a new field, many things, not always predictable, may happen, or—in plain language—if a concept is transferred into an alien domain, different forms of conflict may arise, leading to a wide range of possible solutions. This approach makes it possible to interpret metaphoric meaning along a continuum of possibilities, among which Prandi singles out the distinction between consistent and conflicting meaning. The former occurs when the transferred element adapts to the new domain, suppressing its alien semantic components and thus blocking conflict. The resulting trope can be better described as a lexical catachresis, as the use of a denomination stemming from a different domain does not trigger new interpretations to solve the conflict, but simply entails deprivation of semantic traits incompatible with the new domain: the *wings* of a building do not have feathers nor are they used to fly. On the other hand, when the initially transferred element does not lose its otherness, the struggle for consistency becomes an interesting and creative process. This is when metaphors trigger new interpretations of reality, for example in the case of the 'scientific revolution' used by Kuhn (1962), as it:

> leads one to scan the assumed properties of political revolutions in order to apply the most relevant of them to the history of science. Instead of adapting the concept of revolution to the inherited idea of scientific discovery, the concept of scientific revolution radically challenges the traditional idea that the history of science is a sort of linear progress (*Ibidem*: 392).

Between the two poles of catachresis and creative metaphor lie metaphorical concepts, grounded in conventional but productive schemes of thought, which do not fully integrate the transferred element into the alien domain, but give rise to conventionalized interpretations that become part of our everyday experience: cognitive metaphors, as TIME is SPACE or MONEY is A FLUID ENTITY, are good examples of this. Prandi's interpretation of metaphor emphasizes the scalar dimension of metaphorical meaning, ranging from mere catachresis to ontological conflicts incompatible with consistency. From this point of view, inconsistent, creative metaphors, like "probes launched beyond the borders of consistent thought" (Prandi, 2004: 396), are the most powerful form of semantic transfer, that can induce to reshape our way of interpreting the world.

This approach can be usefully exploited to analyze the evolution of metaphorical meaning, as the adaptation to the alien context can be interpreted as a dynamic process, so that an initially creative metaphor can gradually lose its inconsistency and fossilize into a new lexical denomination. A good example of this type of evolution is offered by a famous metaphor, that of the *iron curtain*, used by Winston Churchill to describe the post-war political situation in Europe: "A shadow has fallen upon the scenes so lately lighted by the Allied victory [. . .]. From Stettin in the Baltic to Trieste in the Adriatic an iron curtain has descended across the Continent".[13] Europe is interpreted as an originally unitary stage (dominated by the Allies), suddenly broken into two separate blocs by an *iron curtain*, which is not functional to avoid the spreading of a fire, but marks an unbridgeable divide, hiding Eastern European countries from Western view. With his words, Churchill actually *creates* a new political order and officially announces the beginning of the Cold War. The reference to an object belonging to theatrical devices, inconsistent with the geo-political domain it is applied to, triggers a subsequent effort to adapt it to the new context, drawing on previous figurative uses (e.g. "the iron curtain of censorship", 1939; the *bamboo curtain*; etc.: cf. OED). The interpretation forwarded by Churchill was rapidly accepted and the metaphor lost its creative power, to become a shared concept, actually a proper name, as revealed by the use of determiner and capital letters: *the Iron Curtain*. This process of erosion of metaphorical meaning seems to lead to a "dead metaphor". Yet, as suggested in the NR, it is more adequate to qualify it as *dormant*, as "this state of inactivity may only be transitory" (NR: 405). Like Sleeping Beauty, dead metaphors can be woken up to life again: for the Iron Curtain, this occurred, for example, in the title (as well as, in multimodal terms, in poster and trailer) of a well-known movie by Hitchcock, *The Torn Curtain*.

Metaphors in Discourse In the light of what we have discussed so far, it is not surprising that, far from being the exclusive province of rhetoric or poetry, metaphors are largely exploited in everyday and specialized discourse alike. In all domains, for classification of metaphorical use special relevance is given to the above mentioned distinction between creative uses of metaphor, in which distant domains are associated in a way which is unexpected, and cognitive metaphors (Lakoff & Johnson, 1980), which contribute to shape our perception of reality and have become common usage in a given language, or even across languages. Cognitive metaphors have accompanied the development of languages and of human beings' ability to categorize and make sense of the world, with the function of

---

[13] Quoted from "The Sinews of Peace", a speech delivered by the former UK Prime Minister in Fulton (Missouri), on March fifth, 1946 (https://winstonchurchill.org/resources/speeches/1946-1 963-elder-statesman/the-sinews-of-peace/)

making new and more complex experience accessible through association with something familiar. Drawing on Raymond W. Gibbs (1994), Carter et al. (2008) pointed out:

> Metaphors in thought [...] and language [...] arise when people struggle to make greater sense of less-well understood aspects of their experience. In Old English poetry, for example, the leader, the ruler and sometimes even God was referred to as the *hlaford* - the bread lord - and the body was the *banhus*, i.e. the bone house (Carter et al., 2008: 68).

In both cases, words and concepts from the everyday life source domain were used to name and thus to bring into the territory of available meanings some constructs which were superordinate, as is the case of body with regard to bones, or related to the social or even religious systems of meanings. Contemporary examples are the book-of-life metaphor for the sequencing of the human genome (Calsamiglia & van Dijk, 2004), or stem cells defined as the 'master cells' of the body, i.e. cells "that can be programmed to become other types of cells", or as the 'mother' of all the other cells (Degano & Sandrelli, 2020)—all cases of a highly complex scientific discovery made easier to grasp for the layman in scientific popularization. All these examples are clearly not argumentative but share an important trait with argumentation: they were used to bring within the area of familiar meanings something which laid outside. Just as these cognitive uses of metaphor started from unproblematic knowledge to update the catalogue of domesticated concepts, arguments rest on accepted premises to extend their acceptability to a standpoint or conclusion.

One main concern of argumentation theory with regard to metaphor is the distinction between metaphors that are argumentatively relevant in a given discussion from those that are not (van Poppel, 2018; Musolff, 2004; Oswald & Rihs, 2014; Perelman & Olbrechts-Tyteca, 1958; Pielenz, 1993; Santibáñez, 2010; Wagemans, 2016; Xu & Wu, 2014). Drawing a divide which parallels that between creative and conventional metaphors, Steen's Deliberate Metaphor Theory (DMT, Steen, 2008, 2011) distinguishes deliberate from non-deliberate metaphors: deliberate metaphors aim to change the interlocutor's perception of the target domain by projecting onto it properties of the source domain, while non-deliberate metaphors do not. Deliberate metaphors are conceived as three-dimensional objects involving a conceptual, a linguistic, and a communicative dimension. Conceptual mappings[14] are activated through the use of words to communicatively exploit the frame associated with the source domain, with a view to, say, clarify complex issues or to persuade.

Van Poppel (2020) addresses the issue of the relevance of metaphors to argumentation drawing on Steen's DMT, pointing out that argumentativeness is not inherent in the word nor in the conceptual dimension, but it is the communicative use made of metaphors that determines whether they are used argumentatively or not. Whether metaphors have an argumentative value can be established relying on

---

[14]"There is a set of systematic correspondences between the source and the target in the sense that constituent conceptual elements of B correspond to constituent elements of A. Technically, these conceptual correspondences are often referred to as mappings" (Kövecses, 2010: 4).

the pragma-dialectical heuristic tools for reconstructing a critical discussion. Deliberate metaphors are often regarded as a form of analogy argumentation (Perelman & Olbrechts-Tyteca, 1958; Garssen & Kienpointner, 2011), but they are not limited to that. Van Poppel lists the functions of metaphors identified in recent studies, which include: material or minor premises (Oswald & Rihs, 2014; Wagemans, 2016), procedural or major premises (Xu & Wu, 2014; Wagemans, 2016), starting points/backing (Pielenz, 1993; Renardel de Lavalette et al., 2019; Santibáñez, 2010; Xu & Wu, 2014).

Metaphors and Evaluative Meaning The potential of metaphors for argumentation lies especially in the evaluative content that is often attached to the source domain chosen. A case in point comes from the use of metaphors in a corpus of newspaper articles about stem cell legislation, where evaluation tended to be positive when referred to the potential of stem cells, and negative when referring to legislation that restricts the use of stem cells for ethical concerns. Generally speaking, positive evaluation is often conveyed by the conventional cognitive metaphor SCIENTIFIC PROGRESS is WALKING FORWARD, as is the case in "Stem cells *open the door* to novel therapies", "Our stem cell lines will be a significant *step forward*". In the corpus, less conventional metaphors presented regenerative medicines as a "game changer", resting on the mappings that scientists are playing a match against diseases, and using stem cells is a winning strategy. On the other hand, the action of restricting research on stem cells was metaphorically associated to illness ("near *paralysis* in the field," "the research has been *handicapped*"), with all the negative implications inherent in such a state. Alternatively, restrictive legislation was likened to a violent act ("increasing regulation is *threatening* the future of pioneering research", "the vote was a *blow* for medical research", "the European Parliament had allowed itself to be *hijacked* by a few zealots opposed to progress") (Degano & Sandrelli, 2020).

The stem cell examples draw attention on the fact that the deliberate vs non-deliberate divide does not perfectly overlap with the creative vs conventional distinction, as also conventional metaphors can be used for persuasion. Even though mapping scientific achievement as progress is quite a worn-out metaphor, it has not lost its evaluative potential. To the contrary: through repetition, the positive connotation has become entrenched and almost indissoluble from the referential content. At the same time, the distinction between creative and non-creative metaphors is at times not so clear-cut. As Kövecses points out, in a work that elaborates on Lakoff and Jonhson's work on cognitive metaphors, the context impacts on the use of metaphors. As an effect of this use in context, even conventional metaphors can be revitalized, drawing attention on the language, which is the opposite of what happens with conventional (or dead) metaphors. For example, it is quite common to cast the enforcement of law as a war on crime, or at least as a fight. In news headlines the police is often reported to *deal a blow* to drug traffickers, on the ground of the cognitive metaphor ADVERSE EVENTS ARE BLOWS, where of course police operations are seen as adverse from the viewpoint of the criminals. Such uses are hardly perceived as creative. However, if the same cognitive metaphor is activated in a headline about doping in boxing, things would change. This is the case of the headline "Double drugs blow" published in *The Sun* (October 6th, 2016) with reference to boxer Tyson Fury failing for the second time drug tests for cocaine, where the context makes it evident that a pun was intended.

In the political domain, the study of metaphors has led to the development of a special form of critical analysis, namely Critical Metaphor Analysis (CMA, Charteris-Black, 2004, 2005, 2013). This approach is founded on the assumption that metaphors can "activate unconscious emotional associations", thus influencing our evaluation of facts and beliefs (Charteris-Black, 2005: 13). In CMA, metaphors connect *ideology*, as "a belief system through which a particular social group creates the meanings that justify its existence to itself" (*Ibidem*: 21), and political *myth*, as "an ideologically marked narrative which purports to give a true account of a set of past, present, or predicted political events and which is accepted as valid in its essentials by a social group" (Flood, 1996: 44). Thus, metaphors function as a bridge between conscious (cognitive, i.e. *logos*) and unconscious (emotional, i.e. *pathos*) means of persuasion, creating a moral perspective on life (i.e. *ethos*). Charteris-Black moves from a definition of metaphor that emphasizes the central role of transfer of meaning and consequent semantic tension, and observes that metaphor, through the association of attributes of the source domain with those of the target domain, causes a conceptual shift with highly persuasive potential. Examples from the discourse of both British and American politicians of the XX century bring forth different patterns of exploitation of metaphorical meaning (Charteris-Black, 2005), which appear relevant also beyond the framework of the specific theoretical approach chosen by the author.

References

Angenot, M. (2014). La rhétorique de la qualification et les controverses d'étiquetage. *Argumentation & Analyse du discours* (13). http://journals.openedition.org/aad/1787. DOI: https://doi.org/10.4000/aad.1787.

Antelmi, D. (2012). *Comunicazione e analisi del discorso*. UTET.

Aristotle, *Ars Rhetorica*, (Rh.). English translation by C.D.C. Reeve (2018). *Rhetoric*. Indianapolis & Cambridge: Hacket Publishing Company.

Barthes, R. (1953). *Le degré zéro de l'écriture*. Seuil.

Benveniste, É. (1946). Structure des relations de personne dans le verb. *Bulletin de la Société de Linguistique* (XLIII/1) [English translation in: Id. (1971). *Problems in General Linguistics* (pp. 195–204). University of Miami Press].

Benveniste, É. (1959). La relation de temps dans le verbe français. *Bulletin de la Société de Linguistique* (LIV/1) [English translation in: Id. (1971). *Problems in General Linguistics* (pp. 205–216). University of Miami Press].

Bres, J., & Nowakowska, A. (2006). Dialogisme: du principe à la matérialité discursive. In L. Perrin (Ed.), *Le sens et le voix. Dialogisme et poliphonie en langue et en discours* (pp. 21–48). Université de Metz.

Brown, R., & Gilman, A. (1960). The pronouns of power and solidarity. In T. A. Sebeok (Ed.), *Style in language* (pp. 253–276). MIT Press.

Bybee, J., & Fleischman, S. (Eds.). (1995). *Modality in grammar and discourse*. John Benjamins.

Calsamiglia, H., & van Dijk, T. A. (2004). Popularization discourse and knowledge about the genome. *Discourse & Society, 15/4*, 369–389.

Carter, R., Goddard, A., & Reah, D. (2008). *Working with texts. A core introduction to language analysis* (2nd ed.). Routledge.

Channel, J. (2000). Corpus-based analysis of evaluative lexis. In S. Hunston & G. Thompson (Eds.), *Evaluation in text. Authorial stance and the construction of discourse* (pp. 38–55). Oxford University Press.

Charteris-Black, J. (2004). *Corpus approaches to critical metaphor analysis*. Palgrave Macmillan.

Charteris-Black, J. (2005). *Politicians and rhetoric. The persuasive power of metaphor*. Palgrave Macmillan.

Charteris-Black, J. (2013). *Analysing political speeches: Rhetoric, discourse, metaphor*. Palgrave Macmillan.

Daniel, M. (2005). Two ways of pronominal number categorization. In M. Haspelmath et al. (Eds.), *World atlas of language structures*. Oxford University Press.

Davies, M. (2013). *Opposition and ideology in news discourse*. Bloomsbury.

De Cock, B. (2011). Why *we* can be *you*: The use of 1st person plural forms with hearer reference in English and Spanish. *Journal of Pragmatics, 43*, 2762–2775.

De Fina, A. (1995). Pronominal choice, identity and solidarity in political discourse. *Text—Interdisciplinary Journal for the Study of Discourse, 15/3*, 379–410.

Degano, C., & Sandrelli, A. (2020). A corpus-based study of ethically sensitive issues in EU directives, national transposition measures and the press. *Lingue e Linguaggi, 34*, 119–136.

Dendale, P., & Coltier, D. (2006). Élements de comparaison de trois théories linguistiques de la polyphonie et du dialogisme. In L. Perrin (Ed.), *Le sens et le voix. Dialogisme et poliphonie en langue et en discours* (pp. 271–295). Université de Metz.

Ducrot, O. (1972). *Dire et ne pas dire*. Hermann.

Ducrot, O. (1984). *Le dire et le dit*. Éditions de Minuit.

Duszak, A. (Ed.) (2002). *Us and others. Social identities across languages, discourses and cultures*. John Benjamins.

Edelman, M. (1971). *Politics as symbolic action*. Academic.

Fairclough, N. (1989). *Language and power*. Longman.

Fairclough, N. (1992). *Discourse and social change*. Longman.

Fairclough, N. (1995). *Media discourse*. Edward Arnold.

Filimova, E. (Ed.). (2005). *Clusivity. Typology and case studies of the inclusive-exclusive distinction*. John Benjamins.

Firth, J. R. (1957/1968). A synopsis of linguistic theory 1930–55. *Studies in linguistic analysis* (special volume of the Philological society). 1–32. Reprinted in F. Palmer (ed.), *Selected Papers of J. R. Firth 1952–59* (pp. 168–205). Longman.

Flood, C. (1996). *Political myth: A theoretical introduction*. Garland.

Gardelle, L., & Sorlin, S. (Eds.). (2015). *The pragmatics of personal pronouns*. John Benjamins.

Garssen, B., & Kienpointner, M. (2011). Figurative analogy in political argumentation. In E. Feteris, B. Garssen, & F. Snoeck Henkemans (Eds.), *Keeping in touch with pragma-dialectics* (pp. 39–58). John Benjamins.

Garzone, G. (2005a). Letters to shareholders and Chairman's statements: Textual variability and generic integrity. In P. Gillaerts & M. Gotti (Eds.), *Genre variation in business letters* (pp. 179–204). Peter Lang.

Garzone, G. (2005b). Pragmatic and discoursal features of annual executive letters: Observations on the rhetorical and evaluative function of concessive constructions. In M. Bondi & N. Maxwell (Eds.), *Cross-cultural encounters: Linguistic perspectives* (pp. 130–143). Officina Edizioni.

Geis, M. L. (1987). *The language of politics*. Springer Verlag.

Gibbs, R. W. (1994). *The poetics of mind*. Cambridge University Press.

Goffman, E. (1967). *Interaction ritual: Essays on face-to-face behavior*. Doubleday.

Goffman, E. (1974). *Frame analysis: An essay on the organization of experience*. Harper & Row.

Goffman, E. (1981). *Forms of talk*. University of Pennsylvania Press.

Halliday, M. A. K. (1985). *An introduction to functional grammar*. Edward Arnold.

Halliday, M. A. K., & Matthiessen, C. M. I. (2004). *An introduction to functional grammar*. Routledge.

Helmbrecht, J. (2015). A typology of non-prototypical uses of personal pronouns: Synchrony and diachrony. *Journal of Pragmatics, 88*, 176–189.

Houtlosser, P. (2002). Indicators of a point of view. In F. van Eemeren (Ed.), *Advances in pragma-dialectics* (pp. 169–184). SicSat/Vale Press.

Jakobs, G. (2003). Reporting annual results. In T. Ensink & C. Sauer (Eds.), *Framing and perspectivising in discourse* (pp. 91–109). John Benjamins.

Jespersen, O. (1924). *The philosophy of grammar*. George Allen & Unvin.

Jordan, M. P. (1998). The power of negation in English: Text, context and relevance. *Journal of Pragmatics, 29*, 705–752.

Kerbrat-Orecchioni, K. (1980). *L'énonciation, de la subjectivité dans le langage*. Armand Colin.

Kövecses, Z. (2010). *Metaphor: A practical introduction*. Oxford University Press.

Kuhn, T. (1962). *The structure of scientific revolutions*. University of Chicago Press.

Lakoff, G., & Johnson, M. (1980). *Metaphors we live by*. University of Chicago Press.

Leclère, P. (1980). La concession: rhétorique et linguistique. *Folia Linguistica, 13*, 63–73.

Leech, G. (1983). *Principles of pragmatics*. Routledge.

Levinson, S. (1983). *Pragmatics*. Cambridge University Press.

Louw, B. (1993). Irony in the text or insincerity in the writer? The diagnostic potential of semantic prosodies. In M. Baker, G. Francis, & E. Tognini-Bognelli (Eds.), *Text and technology. In honour of John Sinclair* (pp. 157–176). John Benjamins.

Maitland, K., & Wilson, J. (1987). Pronominal selection and ideological conflict. *Journal of Pragmatics, 11*(4), 495–512.

Martin, J. R. M., & White, P. R. R. (2005). *The language of evaluation: Appraisal in English*. Pallgrave McMillan.

Moberg, U., & Eriksson, G. (2013). Managing ideological differences in joint political press conferences. A study of the strategic use of the personal pronoun 'we'. *Journal of Language and Politics, 12*(3), 315–334.

Musolff, A. (2004). *Metaphor and political discourse. Analogical reasoning in debates about Europe*. Palgrave Macmillan.

Osimo, B. (2007). *La traduzione saggistica dall'inglese*. Hoepli.

Oswald, S., & Rihs, A. (2014). Metaphor as argument: Rhetorical and epistemic advantages of extended metaphors. *Argumentation, 28/2*, 133–159.

Pennycook, A. (1994). The politics of pronouns. *ELT Journal, 48/2*, 173–178.

Perelman, Ch. & Olbrechts-Tyteca, L. (1958). *Traité de l'argumentation. La nouvelle rhétorique*. Paris: Presses Universitaires de France [English translation by J. Wilkinson & P. Weaver (1969): *The New Rhetoric. A Treatise on Argumentation*. University of Notre Dame Press].

Perkins, M. R. (1983). *Modal expressions in English*. Pinter.

Piazza, F. (2004). *Linguaggio, persuasione e verità. La retorica nel Novecento*. Carocci.

Pielenz, M. (1993). *Argumentation und Metapher*. Gunter Narr Verlag.

Postoutenko, K. (2009). Between 'I' and 'we': Studying the grammar of social identity in Europe (1900–1950). *Journal of Language and Politics, 8/2*, 195–222.

Prandi, M. (2004). *The building blocks of meaning*. John Benjamins.

Prieto, L.J. (1977). Una nota de gramatica : 'Nosotros' plural de 'yo'? In *Estudios ofrecidos a Emilio Alarcos Llorach* (pp. 209–216). Universidad de Oviedo.

Pyykkö, R. (2002). Who is 'us' in Russian political discourse. In A. Duszak (Ed.), *Us and others. Social identities across languages, discourses and cultures* (pp. 233–248). John Benjamins.

Quirk, R., Greenbaum, S., Leech, G., & Svartvik, J. (1985). *A comprehensive grammar of the English language*. Longman.

Reboul, O. (1994). *Introduction à la rhétorique. Théorie et pratique*. Presses Universitaires de France.

Renardel de Lavalette, K. Y., Andone, C., & Steen, G. J. (2019). I did not say that the government should be plundering anybody's savings. Resistance to metaphors expressing starting points in parliamentary debates. *Journal of Language and Politics, 18/5*, 718–738.

Renkema, J. (2004). *Introduction to discourse studies*. John Benjamins.

Rocci, A. (2012). Modality and argumentative discourse relations: A study of the Italian necessity modal *dovere*. *Journal of Pragmatics, 44*, 2129–2149.

Rocci, A. (2008a). Modality and its conversational backgrounds in the reconstruction of argumentation. *Argumentation, 22/2*, 165–189.

Rocci, A. (2008b). Modals as lexical indicators of argumentation. A study of Italian economic-financial news. *L'analisi linguistica e letteraria, XVI*, 577–619.

Rudolph, E. (1996). *Contrast: Adversative and concessive relations and their expression in English, German, Spanish and Portuguese on sentence level and text level*. De Gruyter.

Santibáñez, C. (2010). Metaphors and argumentation: The case of Chilean parliamentarian media participation. *Journal of Pragmatics, 42/4*, 973–989.

Santulli, F. (2001). Narrazione, mito, realtà: scelte temporali e strategie argomentative in alcune forme di linguaggio giornalistico. In C. Bettoni, A. Zampolli, & D. Zorzi (Eds.), *Atti del II Convegno della Associazione Italiana di Linguistica Applicata* (pp. 67–85). Guerra.

Santulli, F. (2005). *Le parole del potere, il potere delle parole. Retorica e discorso politico*. FrancoAngeli.

Santulli, F. (2020). *We shall fight:* Speaker-exclusive *we* as a grammatical metaphor. *International Journal of Linguistics, 12/4*, 43–64.

Sbisà, M. (1999). Ideology and the persuasive use of presupposition. In J. Verschueren (Ed.), *Language and ideology*. Selected papers from the 6th International Pragmatics Conference (pp. 492–509). International Pragmatics Association.

Schmid, M. (2002). Persecution and identity conflicts: The case of German jews. In A. Duszak (Ed.), *Us and others. Social identities across languages, discourses and cultures* (pp. 341–356). John Benjamins.

Siewierska, A. (2004). *Person*. Cambridge University Press.

Silverstein, M. (1976). Shifters, linguistic categories, and cultural description. In K. Basso & H. Selby (Eds.), *Meaning in anthropology* (pp. 11–55). University of New Mexico Press.

Silverstein, M. (2003). Indexical order and the dialectics of sociolinguistic life. *Language & Communication, 23*, 193–229.

Skarżyńska, K. (2002). *We* and *they* in polish political discourse: A psychological approach. In A. Duszak (Ed.), *Us and others. Social identities across languages, discourses and cultures* (pp. 249–264). John Benjamins.

Snoeck Henkemans, A. F. (1997). *Analysing complex argumentation: The reconstruction of multiple and coordinatively compound argumentation in a critical discussion*. Sic Sat.

Stati, S. (1998). La concession: syntaxe, logique et argumentation. *La linguistique*, 119–122.

Stati, S. (2002). *Principi di analisi argomentativa*. Pàtron.

Steen, G. J. (2011). From three dimensions to five steps: The value of deliberate metaphor. *Metaphorik.de, 21*, 83–110.

Steen, G. J. (2008). The paradox of metaphor: Why we need a three-dimensional model of metaphor. *Metaphor Symbol, 23/4*, 213–241.

Stevenson, Ch. (1938). *Persuasive definitions. Mind* (XLVII/ 187). 331–350.

Stubbs, M. (1996). *Text and corpus analysis*. Blackwell.

Thompson, G., & Hunston, S. (2000). Evaluation: An introduction. In I. S. Hunston & G. Thompson (Eds.), *Evaluation in text. Authorial stance and the construction of discourse* (pp. 1–27). Oxford University Press.

Thompson, G., & Zhou, J. (2000). Evaluation and organization in text: The structuring role of evaluative disjuncts. In I. S. Hunston & G. Thompson (Eds.), *Evaluation in text. Authorial Stance and the Construction of Discourse* (pp. 121–141). Oxford University Press.

Urban, G. (1986). Rhetoric of a war chief. *Working Papers and Proceedings of the Centre for Psychosocial Studies, Chicago* (5). 1–27.

van Dijk, T. A. (1991). *Racism in the press: Critical studies in racism and migration*. Routledge.

van Dijk, T. A. (1997). What is political discourse analysis? *Political Linguistics, 11*, 11–52.

van Eemeren, F. H., Houtlosser, P., & Snoeck Henkemans, A. F. (2007). *Argumentative indicators in discourse: A pragma-dialectical study*. Springer.

van Eemeren, F. H., Grootendorst, R., & Snoeck Henkemans, A. F. (2002). *Argumentation: Analysis, evaluation, presentation*. Erlbaum.

van Poppel, L. (2018). Argumentative functions of metaphors: How can metaphors trigger resistance? In S. Oswald & D. Maillat (Eds.), *Argument and inference*. Proceedings of the 2nd European Conference on Argumentation volume II, Fribourg 2017.

van Poppel, L. (2020). The relevance of metaphor in argumentation. Uniting pragma-dialectics and deliberate metaphor theory. *Journal of Pragmatics, 170*, 245–252.

van Rees, A. (2005). Indicators of dissociation. In F. H. van Eemeren & P. Houtlosser (Eds.), *Argumentation in practice* (pp. 53–68). John Benjamins.

van Rees, A. (2009). *Dissociation in argumentative discussions. A pragma-dialectical perspective*. Springer.

Wagemans, J. H. M. (2016). Analyzing metaphor in argumentative discourse. *Rivista Italiana di Filosofia del Linguaggio, 10/2*, 79–94.

Wagner, L. (2002). Strategic alignment in the discourse of La Madres de la plaza de Mayo. In A. Duszak (Ed.), *Us and others. Social identities across languages, discourses and cultures* (pp. 357–374). John Benjamins.

Weinrich, H. (1964). *Tempus. Besprochene und erzählte Welt*. Kohlhammer.

Wilson, J. (1990). *Politically speaking*. Basil Blackwell.

Wodak, R. (1989). *Language, power and ideology: Studies in political discourse*. John Benjamins.

Wodak, R. (1997). Das Ausland and anti-semitic discourse: The discursive construction of the other. In S. H. Higgins (Ed.), *The language and politics of exclusion: Others in discourse* (pp. 65–87). Sage.

Wodak, R. (2009). *The discourse of politics in action. Politics as usual*. Palgrave and McMillan.

Xu, C., & Wu, Y. (2014). Metaphors in the perspective of argumentation. *Journal of Pragmatics, 62*, 68–76.

Zarefsky, D. (2014). *Political argumentation in the United States*. John Benjamins.

Zupnik, Y. J. (1994). A pragmatic analysis of the use of person deixis in political discourse. *Journal of Pragmatics, 21/4*, 339–383.

Chapter 4
The Presidential Announcement: Building Agreement on Disagreement

Abstract The Chapter explores the construction of agreement in a genre of contemporary US politics, the Presidential Announcement (PA), which hinges on the performative act of announcing the decision to run for the Presidency, offering reasons for the choice. For this research, the attention has focused on the seven challenging candidates who managed to win the elections from 1960 to 2010. The diachronic approach, combined with the selection of candidates opposing the incumbent administration, makes it possible to recognize recurring argumentative patterns alongside with elements of variation depending on both contextual facts and personal approach. Challenging candidates single out the need for change and their potential to enact that change as crucial arguments to answer the 'why-me' question. This, in turn, brings forth harsh criticism of the incumbent presidency together with a strong emphasis on personal qualities and values. Widely exploiting the three fundamental political myths, the arguers construct their ethos, transforming the gloomy representation of the present political situation into a shared premise, which then plays a fundamental role in the construction of preliminary agreement. Pronominal choices, presupposition and other forms of implicit meaning, loaded words and metaphors are all functional to both depicting the present problems and prospecting future changes, frequently envisaged as the restoration of a previous Golden Age. Along the timeline, the genre shows a remarkable evolution, mainly linked to the effects of the Watergate scandal, displaying a few similar features across the political divide, as well as interesting common traits shared by individual candidates.

As explained in the Introduction, we have singled out two institutionalized monologic genres in US political discourse to explore how the arguers pursue agreement, with a special attention for the linguistic features most frequently exploited. In this chapter, the focus will be on the Presidential Announcement (PA). This denomination is used to label the formal public launch of a campaign for the Presidency, which has often taken the form of a speech delivered by the candidate. In the course of the XX century, formal campaign announcements have become customary, though they are not the first act in a campaign. Preliminary work by the candidate and their associates "helps to shape the rhetorical situation in which

© The Author(s), under exclusive license to Springer Nature Switzerland AG 2022   89
F. Santulli, C. Degano, *Agreement in Argumentation*, Perspectives in Pragmatics,
Philosophy & Psychology 31, https://doi.org/10.1007/978-3-031-16293-0_4

the announcement address is made" (Trent et al., 2011: 210). In this respect, timing plays a crucial role, also in consideration of financial rules provided by the Federal Elections Commission, which have induced many candidates to delay formal announcements, thus generating ambiguities and consequent criticism.

Although in recent decades many candidates have chosen to reveal their intentions gradually, the announcement speech has not lost its pivotal role in the campaign communication, as it is perceived as a due formal act establishing a special relationship between candidate and voters, often producing considerable press coverage. A distinctive trait of the speech officially starting the campaign is the performative act of *announcing* the intention to run for the Presidency (tossing "the hat in the ring", as stated by Th. Roosevelt in 1912), but there are other significant recurring moves which have become part of the ritual, among them: self-portrait, analysis of selected aspects of the political scenario, indication of objectives. Moreover, challenging candidates usually include criticism of the incumbent presidency. For a candidate, the PA is the first formal appeal to voters, functional to obtaining support and persuading the audience to cast their vote for them. As a genre, it is therefore part of deliberation, from both the Aristotelian and the pragma-dialectical point of view.

The speeches selected for the present analysis, belonging to the post-war period, were all delivered by winning candidates. The qualitative approach has made it necessary to limit the number of selected texts, which include only challenging candidates, both Republican and Democrat. The PA of a president in office is actually a sort of sub-genre, as it is produced in a very special context: almost all US presidents have run for a second term, and therefore their announcement is highly expected and almost due. As the living expression of the incumbent presidency, the candidate-president is in a favourable and at the same time tricky position, as he is naturally held responsible for both positive and negative political decisions. The rhetorical strategy and argumentative line of this type of announcement are therefore less immediately comparable with those adopted by challenging candidates. To emphasise the adversarial approach, candidates belonging to the same party of the incumbent president were also excluded. Therefore, this small corpus comprises the PA delivered by seven candidates who were to become US Presidents: JFK, Nixon, Carter, Reagan, Clinton, GW Bush, and Obama. Limited reference will be made to Trump's Announcement. The speeches span over five crucial decades, which saw profound changes in the US policy and in their image both at home and worldwide. From the Cold War to the War on Terror, this period was marked by a series of momentous events of historical importance: the missile crisis in Cuba, the conquer of the Moon, the Vietnam war, the fall of the Berlin Wall and the collapse of the Soviet Union, the Twin Towers Attack, to name just a few. Other events, though having a more limited impact at a global level, have caused important reactions at home, sometimes dramatically altering traditional feelings and opinions. Among them, the Watergate scandal has certainly marked a discontinuity in the relation between American people and their President, which has left its traces in the evolution of presidential rhetoric.

The historical background is obviously of the utmost importance to understand the intentions of the arguers and their argumentative choices. In particular, the quest for agreement is founded on feelings, values and beliefs that are in their turn the consequence of complex series of intertwined events. Yet the choice to focus on the linguistic tools exploited in discourse will lead us to consider similar phenomena across time and political allegiance, to identify predominant strategies and, at the same time, to investigate if and how the genre has evolved to adapt to the changing needs of both US politics and society at large.

4.1 Kennedy and Nixon: A Statement and a Letter[1]

Chronologically, the first two texts date back to the Sixties, and immediately appear different from the following ones. Though they belong to the PA genre, they are not actual speeches: Kennedy informed of his intention to run for the Presidency in a statement pronounced at a press conference in the Senate Caucus Room,[2] Nixon with a letter addressed to the citizens of New Hampshire. Both texts are short (445 and 407 words, respectively), much shorter than the speeches of the other candidates selected for this analysis. From the point of view of the contents and the organization of the text, they also share a fundamental feature: they do not expose intentions let alone a political programme, but focus only on the importance of the American Presidency and on the conviction of the arguer that he is well-equipped to take this enormous responsibility. Stripped of all disguise, the argumentative line is very simple: the role of the American President is crucial to tackle the difficulties of the moment, I have the qualities required to tackle these difficulties, and *therefore* I can (or *will*) be the next President of the USA.

Given this ethotic approach, one would expect ample details on personal qualities and background, but the information given is actually scanty. Nor does the arguer attempt to establish a strong contact with his audience. While there are several occurrences of the personal pronoun *I*, *you* is almost absent as well as *we* (cf. Sect. 3.1 above). The exploitation of elements of pathos is very limited. A closer look at the two texts will make it clearer how each arguer organizes his speech, and which specific tools he exploits.

The *statement* pronounced by Kennedy, in the framework of a press conference, is actually (and quite obviously) shaped as a press release. A short informative lead, which *in medias res* performs the institutional function (i.e. announcing the

---

[1] Texts are available at https://www.jfklibrary. org/archives/other-resources/john-f-kennedy-speeches/presidential-candidacy-19600102 and at http://www.4president.org/speeches/1968/nixon1968announcement.htm, respectively. They are also included, together with all the other texts analysed for this research, in the Appendix to this volume.

[2] The room, originally intended for party caucuses, has hosted important Senate investigations and is now named after the three brothers Kennedy who served as senators (the Kennedy Caucus Room).

candidacy), is followed by a representation of the challenges of the US presidency and a series of short and clear statements concerning the position of the speaker. The final paragraph, as a sort of boilerplate, gives very neutral information about the personal record of the candidate, but closes with an image of America "as defender of freedom" which re-proposes a crucial word and gives an important clue to understand the whole political programme (cf. Sect. 3.4 above). In this respect, it is interesting to note how Kennedy opens his statement:

> I am announcing today my candidacy for the Presidency of the United States.
>
> The Presidency is the most powerful office in the *Free World*. Through its leadership can come a more vital life for our people. In it are centered the hopes of the globe around us for *freedom* and a more secure life. For it is in the Executive Branch that the most crucial decisions of this century must be made in the next four years--*how* to end or alter the burdensome arms race, where Soviet gains already threaten our very existence--*how* to maintain freedom and order in the newly emerging nations--*how* to rebuild the stature of American science and education--*how* to prevent the collapse of our farm economy and the decay of our cities--*how* to achieve, without further inflation or unemployment, expanded economic growth benefiting all Americans--and *how* to give direction to our traditional moral purpose, awakening every American to the dangers and opportunities that confront us.
>
> *These* are among the *real issues* of 1960. And it is on the basis of these issues that the American people must make their fateful choice for their future. (Kennedy)[3]

The American presidency is seen as the beacon of the Free World, as a crucial instrument in guaranteeing its quintessential quality, which implicitly opposes it to the Communist World: the Cold War is a well-known reality, and is immediately presented as the framework in which the US presidential campaign takes place. Freedom is mentioned several times, and is definitely a value that can be assumed as part of a shared common ground of beliefs and convictions (Perelman & Olbrechts-Tyteca, 1958). The contraposition to the Soviet Union is quite obvious and expected, as is the positive value of freedom. Less expected is the strategy adopted to present the needs of the future. As mentioned above, Kennedy does not present his programme, but gives a list of the actions the new president *must* take. They are introduced with a presupposition, *how to*, so that it is taken for granted that they are necessary (as emphasised also by the choice of the modal *must*) and the propositional content only refers to the means necessary to perform them (cf. Sect. 3.5.1 above). The questions mentioned in the list are then referred to with an anaphora (*these*) and an encapsulator (*real issues*) including an adjective with a potential dissociative value (implying: if someone talks about different issues, those are not *real*, but false) (cf. Sect. 3.5.2 above).

The emphasis on *how* has another semantic implication: it is crucial to choose a president who possesses the right qualities, who is able to perform the required actions. Kennedy proposes himself as the right man, because (after his numerous contacts with other Democrats all over the country) he thinks he can win (after having discussed the *real issues* of the campaign, he states: "My candidacy is

---

[3] In all the quotations from Presidential Announcements, unless differently stated, emphasis is added.

therefore based on the conviction that I can win both the nomination and the election"). The legitimacy does not rely on the qualities of the arguer, but on the implicit judgement of his party-fellows, who are explicitly mentioned. The party faces a historic challenge, Kennedy is only the man who can secure the victory. In Kennedy's announcement, the party of the candidate plays a crucial role, while in the other speeches analysed for this research it is rarely mentioned and never given prominence. Conversely, Kennedy does not refer to the adversary, but the opposite party frequently emerges in other PAs, as the Enemy to combat.

Eight years later, Nixon makes his PA in a letter addressed to the citizens of New Hampshire, the first state to vote in a presidential primary. In the opening lines of the address, the arguer emphasises the voters' responsibility, their spirit of participation and the influential character of their vote. Yet, this is only a preamble, aimed to construct a positive image of the speaker and to obtain the benevolence of the audience (cf. Sect. 1.1.3 above). The crucial appeal to agreement comes in the following paragraph, which is potentially addressed to a much wider audience:

> In 1968, *your* responsibility is greater than ever. The nation is in *grave difficulties*, around the world and here at home. The choices *we* face are larger than any differences among Republicans or among Democrats, larger even than the differences between the parties. They are beyond politics. *Peace* and *freedom* in the world, and *peace* and *progress* here at home, will depend on the decisions of the next President of the United States.
> For these critical years, America needs *new* leadership. (Nixon)

Agreement is founded on facts (vaguely, but evaluatively described as *grave difficulties*) and values (freedom, peace and progress, which are the implicit objectives of the future presidency, and actually depend on its future decisions). The arguer then affirms that America *needs a new leadership*, but does not support his statement with any argument. Yet, this implicitly introduces the idea that the incumbent administration has been unable to cope with the difficulties, and possibly contributed to generate them. This implicit premise is in line with the attitude of a challenging candidate (cf. Sect. 3.5 above). The presentation of the difficulties of the moment is followed by self-presentation:

> During fourteen years in Washington, I learned the awesome nature of the great decisions a President faces. During the past eight years I have had a chance to reflect on the lessons of public office, to measure the nation's tasks and its problems from a fresh perspective. I have sought to apply those lessons to the needs of the present, and to the entire sweep of this final third of the 20th Century.
> And I believe I have found some answers. (Nixon)

Nixon does not talk about his education, nor about his political record: this is not the narrative of facts, rather a sort of *Erziehungsroman*, with the protagonist revealing his thoughts and feelings. This process of initiation is crucial to develop the ability to find the right answers and allows the arguer to justify his decision: "I have decided, *therefore*, to enter the Republican Presidential primary in New Hampshire". The logic conclusion is emphasised by an explicit argumentative connector.

The final part of the Announcement is the expression of the candidate's *will*, referred to the actions he intends to perform during the campaign (*I will*, repeated five times), in relation to the voters (*your comments, your questions,* etc.). He tells something about the recent past (*I have visited New Hampshire*) and about his feelings (*I appreciated, I am grateful*), to emphasise his friendly relationship with his supporters. Yet these feelings are insufficient to ground agreement ("But in asking your support now, I ask it not on the basis of old friendships"), because the stakes go well beyond that: "*We* have entered a *new* era. And I ask *you* to join *me* in helping make this an age of greatness for *our* people and for *our* nation". This final appeal is an attempt to create community with the audience, who are supposed to share the premises (the existence of a new era) to be ready to become part of the project.

As anticipated above, the two Announcements share important features, though Nixon—differently from Kennedy—in the final part of his address shows his willingness to establish a direct contact with his voters, the Republicans involved in primary vote. The choice to communicate his decision in connection to the New Hampshire primary makes it possible for Nixon to focus on a local dimension and create a more direct contact, to extend this special relationship to the American people as a whole (*our nation*). There is however no systematic effort to create a community of (and *with*) supporters. Both candidates stage a story of difficulties and problems for America and the world, where the protagonist is the President, who can tip the scales in favour of accepted positive values. Their argument is simply their conviction that they *will* be elected, and *will* be able to play the role.

4.2   After Watergate: From Carter to Obama

Considering the nature of Kennedy's rhetoric—suffice it to think of his Acceptance Speech, which introduced the concept of the New Frontier—and thinking of other, more recent examples of PA, it is rather surprising that he decided to formulate such a short and essential statement for the formal launch of his presidential campaign. Nor was Nixon's choice more generous. In the Sixties, the PA as a genre of political communication seems to be neglected by the candidates. Things appear to be different in 1976: only 8 years after Nixon's letter, Carter delivered a very long and complex speech, which opens up a new approach to the PA, starting the consolidation of some generic traits as well as showing interest and special care for the very 'ceremony' of announcement. This line of development will reach its climax with Obama's speech, where the structure, the crucial elements, and the wording itself are fully expanded and carefully exploited to create complete agreement and identification with the intended audience.

Between 1968 and 1976, a crucial experience changed the image of the American President and the relationship of American citizens (and voters) with their President: the Watergate scandal. Watergate is a crucial divide, which induces candidates to give renewed importance to their official Announcement, not only in the choice of contents and words, but also in timing and location choices. In this respect, candidates have learnt to disclose their intentions gradually and "the public has come to expect that a serious presidential candidate will likely go through several steps before ultimately delivering an announcement speech" (Trent et al., 2011: 210). They have frequently chosen to deliver their speeches in places that have a special meaning for them and for their audience, to emphasise privileged links without making them exclusive. Clinton, for example, conveniently chose the historic Old State House Museum in Little Rock, Arkansas (his state, where he was Governor), while Obama, following a similar path, made his announcement in Springfield, Illinois, where he worked as a lawyer and a Senator, "in the shadow of the Old State Capitol, where Lincoln once called a house divided to stand together"—as he said in his speech. A very symbolic location for both, and this is not the only element of similarity between their speeches. Reagan, on the other hand, who as an actor had experience of shooting, had his announcement televised in NYC, renouncing an official public event to exploit his special charm in front of the screen.

As for the recurring traits characterizing the announcements we are now considering, they all develop the theme of the *new* (which had already been introduced, though without justification, by Nixon). More precisely, they link the need for the new with criticism of Washington, not simply of the incumbent Presidency (which is obvious for a challenging candidate) but of the Capital as such, as the epitome of (federal) power and source of all evils. There are of course differences among the five candidates, but this aspect is common to all of them, at least to some extent. They also tend to present the new desired course as a *re*newal, which actually consists in re-proposing and re-affirming the values of the past, belonging to a prosperous time, untouched by the evils of the present. Characters from the glorious history of America—from the Founding Fathers to Lincoln and Kennedy—are set on the stage.

In parallel, time is ripe for the personalization of politics. The candidate counts more than the party (Kennedy had a very different approach!) and his image is crucial to obtain approval and, ultimately, to win. As for Carter, we could say that this rule is applied in negative, as he won, according to political analysts, exactly *because* he was fairly unknown to the great public. It has been estimated that before his entering the campaign, only 2% of the Americans knew his name. This circumstance was particularly advantageous when—in the immediate post-Watergate era—it was necessary to have a new face, someone who was not perceived to be compromised with politics and its negative connotations. Though a former Governor of Georgia, Carter was the right man to represent the new, which meant new people for a new approach to political action, first and foremost, to the Presidential Office. The following challengers, on the other hand, laid great emphasis on their own personality and their previous career, on talents and merits. Reagan, the former actor, fully exploited his abilities as a communicator, and so did the others. As a consequence, self-portrait became a pivotal element in the PA, with a combination of facts (performed actions) and values (beliefs and personal qualities), that gradually became the foundation for the very choice to enter the presidential challenge.

These two fundamental aspects combine with sketches of future actions, in the form of a rough programme, mostly centred on a few highly symbolic elements. The analysis of the strategies adopted to present the programme will show important differences among the five considered candidates. Yet each of them plays with the three fundamental political myths (Edelman, 1971): affirming his qualification to become the *Leader*, revealing—with different degrees of explicitness—the faults of the *Enemy*, and trying to aggregate the support and the cooperation with the voters. In this perspective, enunciation choices obviously play a crucial role.

In what follows, the focus will initially be on Jimmy Carter, whose speech has some special traits of 'transition' (Sect. 4.2.1), and then shift onto the two Republican challengers (Sect. 4.2.2) to finish with the two Democrats, who are evidently linked by very strong similarities (Sect. 4.2.3).

4.2.1   Jimmy Carter: The Outsider[4]

The strength of Carter's candidacy lay in his low profile: he was the common man, frank and reliable, not compromised with the intricacies of Washington's politics, an outsider. His PA displays the fundamental features mentioned above: a self-presentation including ample mention of his previous political success; criticism for Washington and politics and therefore the need for a new course, which is actually a historical re-course, a coming back to better times, to the original values that lie at the foundation of America. In his long speech, which curiously does not include the actual performative announcement, he also discusses the crucial problems of the moment, the evils and the steps to be taken in the reorganization of political activities, as well as in various areas of governmental action (energy and environment, welfare and health care, education and agriculture, and obviously international affairs). The presentation is however not linear, structures change, criticism of the past and vision of the future are mingled, and few anaphora help the listener (and even the reader) to recognise the line of thought. Yet there are some linguistic strategies that emphasise the key elements of the speech.

Presupposition (cf. Sect. 3.5.1 above) through iterative verbs (*regain, restore, reaffirm* et sim.) is amply exploited to convey the idea of a Golden Age which must be brought to life again. Presupposition is also introduced with *that*-clauses, also with reference to the interpretation of Watergate ("We have discovered *that* our trust has been betrayed"). Lexical choices (cf. Sect. 3.4 above) condense the ideological point of view of the arguer ("the *shame* of Watergate"), or as anaphoric encapsulators synthesize a detailed description of the present situation ("the *chasm* between people and government").

The most remarkable linguistic trait concerns self-presentation. Though Carter presents himself and his work, there are very few occurrences of the first person pronoun. *I* is often hidden in a plural *we*. The speech opens with "we Americans" (repeated twice), and the speaker emphasises that each person has multiple identities. He presents himself as a farmer, an engineer, a businessman, a planner, a scientist, a governor and a Christian. To have so many different identities is tantamount to

---

[4]Text available at http://www.4president.org/speeches/carter1976announcement.htm

having none and is in tune with the effort of the enunciator to preserve the anonymity that in the contingencies of that election could be a great advantage. He prefers to use the first person plural pronoun, not only with an inclusive value, but also with exclusive implications (cf. Sect. 3.1 above). When he talks about his experience as a Governor and his achievements, he does not emphasise his action and his qualities, but speaks in the plural (*we won, we abolished, we developed* etc.), ideally sharing both merits and responsibilities with his collaborators (and possibly with all the citizens of Georgia). There is one expression, repeated five times, in the first person, but it is a negative statement: "I think not", used as the answer to five different rhetorical questions. The first four rhetorical questions concern desired achievements of the future administration (e.g.: "Is a simplified, fair and compassionate welfare program beyond the capacity of our American government? I think not"). The *subiectio* (or self-answered rhetorical question) induces the listener to agree with the position of the arguer, as the answer is obvious and inevitable. Moreover, acceptance of the fact that it is possible to implement these policies implicitly includes acceptance of the fact that they are desirable, to be pursued in the first place. In the final part of the speech, the fifth occurrence of *I think not,* used as the answer to a series of five different rhetorical questions and in a different context, has a more comprehensive value, which is worth examining in further detail.

The conclusion of the speech is centred on personal memories, which are the vehicle to introduce historical memories. Hints of dialogism (cf. Sect. 3.6 above) and reference to other voices can be found across the speech. For example, the chiasm referring to the lack of confidence in government ("The root of the problem is not so much that our people have lost confidence in government, but that government has demonstrated time and again its lack of confidence in the people") echoes the famous conclusion of Kennedy's Inaugural Address. Furthermore, Carter has again recourse to *subiectio*, posing two crucial questions concerning *policy* and *goals*:

> What is our national policy for the production, acquisition, distribution or consumption of energy in times of shortage or doubtful supply? There is no policy! What are our long-range goals in health care, transportation, land use, economic development, waste disposal or housing? There are no goals! (Carter)

This passage recalls Churchill's famous *Blood, sweat and tears* speech, when the British statesman imagined his audience posing similar questions (*you ask: what is our policy... you ask: what is our goal*), but gave positive and galvanizing answers (*war* and *victory*, respectively). Carter's questions appear as a negative version of that historical appeal, establishing intertextuality but, at the same time, re-proposing his low profile (remember *I think not!*).

The link with history and his positioning in inter-discourse becomes explicit when he tells the audience of his visit to Philadelphia, to celebrate 200 years after the First Continental Congress. Continuity is established between the present leaders who visited Philadelphia and the Founding Fathers ("we heard exactly the same prayer and sat in the same chairs occupied in September 1774 by Samuel Adams, John Jay, John Adams, Patrick Henry, George Washington, and about forty-five other strong and opinionated leaders"). The arguer attributes great values to them, in line with the American tradition. They are a strong common ground for agreement. On that basis, Carter introduces his thoughts:

> I don't know whose chair I occupied, but sitting there *I thought* soberly about their times and ours. Their people were *also* discouraged, disillusioned and confused. But these early leaders acted with purpose and conviction.
>
> I wondered to myself: Were they more competent, more intelligent or better educated than we? Were they more courageous? Did they have more compassion or love for their neighbors? Did they have deeper religious convictions? Were they more concerned about the future of their children than we? *I think not.*
>
> *We are equally capable* of correcting our faults, overcoming difficulties, managing our own affairs and facing the future with justifiable confidence. (Carter)

The opinions about the Founding Fathers (though introduced as Carter's *thoughts*) are part of a definitely shared feeling. Talking about them, Carter uses a presupposition (triggered by *also*) to suggest that present Americans are as "discouraged, disillusioned and confused" as their predecessors. The five rhetorical questions, similar to the other four deployed in the text, entail their obvious answer, which is however proposed as a personal conviction. Indirectly, the qualities required to the next president have been listed, and Carter implicitly claims that he possesses them. He does not say that, but in line with the Aristotelian concept of ethos has tried to *show* these qualities in the course of the speech (cf. Sect. 1.1.3 above).

A positive statement finally recognises the talents of present Americans and raises optimism for the future. Yet the arguer is no longer speaking in the first person, but uses a plural pronoun and shares intentions and merits with his audience (*we are equally capable*). This strategy is in tune with the limited use of the first person singular in the whole speech, but in this context it becomes functional to the construction of a close link between speaker and audience, and hints at the United-we-stand myth (Edelman, 1971; Geis, 1987). At the end of the speech, the Valiant Leader is still in the background; only implicitly does he come to the forefront with the very last question, left unanswered: "For our Nation – for all of us – that question is: 'Why not the best?'". Carter seems to comply with the Maxim of Modesty (Leech, 1983) and leaves it to the interlocutor to identify him as the right man for the necessary renewal. Yet, against all modesty, this man finally is *the best*.

4.2.2 Reagan and G.W. Bush: From the Rosy Scenario to Compassionate Conservatism[5]

Reagan's televised official announcement in 1979 is a long and well-structured speech, which displays a tidy canonical sequence of moves: introduction to present the characters (the self and the adversary), illustration of fundamental points of the

---

[5]Texts available at https://millercenter.org/the-presidency/presidential-speeches/november-13-1 979-announcement-presidential-candidacy and at http://www.4president. org/speeches/2000/georgewbush2000announcement.htm respectively.

political programme, conclusion to create cohesion with supporters. Compared with Carter's speech it is better organized, more direct in the construction of the image of the leader and of the prospects for the future. As Carter, the arguer initially describes himself as possessing different identities, which however correspond to different phases of his life. These identities are consistent with different perspectives on American history, which in turn generate a powerful and optimistic image of a country where "nothing is impossible":

> To me our country is a living, breathing presence, unimpressed by what others say is impossible, proud of its own success, *generous*, yes and naive, sometimes wrong, never mean and always impatient to provide a better life for its people in a framework of a basic *fairness* and *freedom*. (Reagan)

A personal opinion (*to me*) concerning a common entity (*our country*) is founded on values so positive that they are certainly shared, whose co-occurrence is reinforced through alliteration. Their proclamation sheds light on the man who has this high opinion of America, immediately contraposed to "those in our land today who *would have us believe*" that the United States are weak, fearful, and urged by insuperable problems. The problems of the country are presented as a conviction of some "leaders who claim that our problems are too difficult to handle". *They* tell us horrible lies, depict a gloomy scenario, *they* are the Enemy. Agreement is sought on this view, which primarily is a judgement of the incumbent presidency (cf. Sects. 3.1 and 3.2 above).

The contraposition is conveyed with a clear statement: "I don't believe that", a stronger echo to Carter's "I think not", followed by a remarkable specification: "And, I don't believe you do either". The point of view of the arguer coincides with that of his audience. These statements become the very reason for Reagan's choice ("That's *why* I am seeking the presidency"). The present difficulties are not insurmountable, because the present crisis is not the failure of America, it is the failure of present leaders, who therefore need to be replaced. This is the crucial argument to justify change and, in turn, to ask for support. On the other hand, Reagan's refusal to accept the bleak prospects and his faith in the future qualify him as the ideal agent to enact change.

The programme for the future presidency is amply illustrated, including its ideological foundations, presented as obvious and scientific tenets. Suffice it to analyse one example. When talking about the current economic situation—referred to with a loaded encapsulator, *disaster*—Reagan explains why the governmental approach has failed, affirming that "business is not a taxpayer" and "only people pay taxes". His economic doctrine is presented as absolute truth as "it is political *demagoguery* or economic *illiteracy* to try and tell us otherwise". The democratic recipes failed because they are *wrong* and their policies have led to inflation, poverty, and to "*the utter fiasco* we now call the energy crisis" (for the use of evaluative lexicon, cf. Sect. 3.4 above). The programme for the future presidency is direct consequence of these *facts*—actually, a personal conservative reading of contemporary events. A crucial word occurs over and over again: *restore* (cf. Sect. 3.5.1

above). It implies that it is necessary to go back to the pre-Democrat administration, so that problems can be solved and America can be great again.[6]

The long exposition of the program (including a rather detailed discussion of world problems) ends with a coming back to the initial point, to the "leaders in our government who have told us that, we, the people, have lost confidence in ourselves". This ideal short circuit emphasises the importance of false convictions, induced by misleading politicians, a theme which will be exploited also in Obama's announcement. The final part of the speech, similarly to Carter's, plunges into the roots of American history to find the right premises for the construction of a common ground. Tom Paine is Reagan's testimonial, with a quotation form his work: "we have it in our power to begin the world over again" (cf. Sect. 3.6 above).

The ethos of the arguer is grounded in these roots.

> *We--today's living Americans--*have in our lifetime fought harder, paid a higher price for freedom and done more to advance the dignity of man than any people who have ever lived on this Earth. The citizens of this great nation *want* leadership--yes--but *not a "man on a white horse"* demanding obedience to his commands. *They want* someone who believes they can "begin the world over again." A leader who will *unleash* their great strength and remove the roadblocks government has put in their way. *I want* to do that more than anything I've ever wanted. And it's something that I believe with God's help *I can* do. (Reagan)

Tom Paine, speaking from the time "when Washington's men were freezing at Valley Forge", is part of a common heritage and could trigger the metaphoric use of the first person plural (Santulli 2020). Yet, Reagan chooses an inclusive and explicit interpretation of the pronoun *we*, which makes it possible for him to speak in the name of a group, described with hyperbolic qualities, whose wishes he is thus entitled to interpret. The image of the man on a white horse is actually a sort of preterition, because the President the Americans are supposed to want is portrayed in the act of *unleashing* their strength, with a metaphor evoking a context not far from that of a rider. This is the ideal Valiant Leader the Americans want and the arguer *wants* to be. Reagan *can* be the man. Self-confidence contributes crucially to empowerment.

A further testimonial is introduced, with another, longer instance of intertextuality: the Pilgrim John Winthrop, in the act of having "a rendezvous with destiny"[7] and announcing the foundation of "a city upon a hill". Evangelical and historical memories merge to generate mythical prospects for the future:

> A troubled and *afflicted mankind* looks to us, pleading for us to keep our *rendezvous with destiny*; that we will uphold the *principles* of *self-reliance, self-discipline, morality,* and-- above all--*responsible liberty* for every individual that *we will* become that shining city on a hill.
>
>   I believe that *you and I together* can keep this rendezvous with destiny. (Reagan)

---

[6]The campaign payoff actually was: Let's make America great again.

[7]The expression, already used by F. Roosevelt, triggers a double level of dialogism: explicit quotation and interdiscursive allusion (cf. Sect. 3.6 above).

In the final appeal, words are carefully chosen to link present to past, hinting at the evils of the present without mentioning them (*afflicted mankind*), and to enumerate the values that need to be shared. Though presented as self-evident and accepted, these principles are mentioned here for the first time. They belong to the conservative perspective, and even *liberty* (which is typically shared as a value across the political divide) is introduced with a *precization* (*responsible*) (van Rees, 2005), transforming it into a highly connoted banner for the Republicans. Inclusive-we hints at the United-we-stand myth and the closing image explicitly shows arguer and audience, tightly linked (*you and I together*) in the representation of a prosperous future for America.

Two decades later, after 12 years of Republican and eight of Democrat rule, another republican challenged the party of the incumbent President: GW Bush. His announcement, delivered in Iowa, is a well-structured speech, including principles and purposes, with a great emphasis on the construction of the image of the candidate as possessing the right qualities to be the future Leader. There is little room for the construction of a united entity including arguer and audience, and even the representation of the adversary is neglected. *I* is the dominating form, followed by *we*, which is used to refer generically to the Americans (a rather week inclusiveness) or with exclusive reference (s. *supra*, Sect. 3.1). The following example is a recurring scheme: "*We'll* be prosperous if *we* reduce taxes. *I'll* have a plan that reduces marginal rate". The validity of the economic recipe is taken for granted, the focus is on the will of the arguer to be the one who implements it.

The very reason why Bush is running lies in his convictions and his qualities:

> I'm running *because* our country *must be prosperous*. But prosperity *must have* a *purpose*. The purpose of prosperity is to make sure the American dream touches every willing heart. The purpose of prosperity is to leave *no one out*... to leave no one behind. I'm running *because* my party must match a *conservative mind with a compassionate heart*. And I'm running to win. (GW Bush)

The fundamental convictions are not negotiated, they belong to the realm of necessity (s. *supra*, Sect. 3.3). Prosperity is part of that pool of values (or, more precisely, ambitions) that are widely shared. No-one wants to be poor, and it is acceptable to link prosperity (as anything else) to a purpose, which is presented as totally inclusive (*no one out*). These shared notions are transformed into a conservative value and an evangelical principle, the former guiding logical reasoning (*mind*), the latter inspiring noble feelings (*heart*). Bush can (or *must*) run because he strongly believes in this combination, in its *winning* power. An exception among the candidates examined in this section, Bush very marginally exploits the argument of the *new* (very few occurrences of the world are clustered in the final part of the speech and mostly referred to the style of the campaign), nor does he rely much on presuppositions (cf. Sect. 3.5.1 above) triggered by *re-* or *again* (one single, quite significant, exception being "I will *rebuild* military power"). Key in the whole speech is the idea of compassionate conservatism, a label he accepts and is proud of. He implicitly presents himself as the inventor of this combination and wants to be its champion.

From compassionate conservatism stem the goals of his programme: the promotion of responsibility and compassion. The former implies a *moral* approach, a clear-cut distinction between *right* and *wrong,* while the latter is actually not a duty of the government but of "armies of compassion that exist in every community". The tribute to evangelical Christians, who have been indicated as an important component of Bush supporters, is self-evident. To make the concept clearer, the arguer gives examples ("It is conservative to cut taxes. It is compassionate to help people save and give and build"), and presents his experience as a compassionate conservative in Texas. Exclusive-we is used to refer to some important measures adopted in Texas, and paves the way for a self-portrait, which exploits presupposition to induce acceptance of the arguer's viewpoint:

> *I've learned to lead.* I don't run polls to tell me what to think. I make decisions based on a conservative philosophy that is engrained in my heart. Trust local people to make right choices about their schools and cities. *Understand that* private property is the backbone of capitalism. Fight for American interests and American workers in the world. *Know* the importance of family and the need for personal responsibility. These are principles from which I will not vary.
>
> I've learned you *can not lead by dividing people.* This country is hungry for a new style of campaign. *Positive. Hopeful. Inclusive.* A campaign that attracts new faces and new voices. A campaign that unites all Americans toward a better tomorrow. (GW Bush)

He presents his qualities as deriving from experience, and in describing this experience he introduces as pre-suppositions some fundamental tenets of conservatism (private property, capitalism, family and responsibility). He does not want to be divisive, because this is not a good quality for a leader, but he has chosen an approach that can be criticized (as explicitly admitted in the speech itself: "I know this approach has been criticized"). He talks about hope, but he has previously affirmed that "Government can spend money, but it can't put hope in our hearts". His pronominal choices are all but inclusive, yet he uses "inclusive" words, in the final part of the speech, to obtain union and approval. They sound fake. Even his optimism is openly presented as instrumental to consensus:

> I say a better tomorrow *because* I've learned that *people want to follow an optimist.* They don't respond to the message: "Follow me, things are going to get worse." They respond to someone who appeals to our better angels, not our darker impulses. They respond to someone who sees better times – *and I see better times.* (GW Bush)

Optimism for Reagan was a deep conviction, the very reason for his running for President, it came from his heart. For Bush optimism is a tactical decision: he must be optimistic because he wants to be followed (and people follow an optimistic leader). As a Leader he *must be optimistic.* And, as a challenging candidate, he must present this approach as some form of renewal. Here is his conclusion:

> It feels to me like an *old era* of American politics is ending -- like Americans are waiting for *new hopes, new energy, new idealism. We will* prove that someone who is conservative and compassionate can win without sacrificing principle. *We will* show that politics, after a time of tarnished ideals, can be higher and better. *We will* give our country a fresh start after a season of *cynicism.*
>
> *We* have a long way to go, but *we* start today. And *I hope you'll join me.* (GW Bush)

Not differently from optimism, the narrative of the old era contraposed to a new course in politics is introduced at the end of the speech, as a sort of due homage to the arguer's role as a challenging candidate. Also the negative feature of the present season, cynicism, is mentioned here for the first time. Quite remarkably, the verb forms used to sketch the future (*we will*) boost an exclusive interpretation of the first-person plural. The candidate and the circle of his close supporters (not even all the Republicans) are on stage, and the arguer makes a very modest attempt to create a larger group. The very last statement is ambiguous: which reference is to be attributed to *we*? If it included the audience, there would be no need to ask them to join, but if it is (vaguely) exclusive, why should *you* (the audience) join *me* (and not *us*)?

This clumsy effort to aggregate support reveals how far the arguer is from his audience. He is totally unable to evoke the United-we-stand myth, because he has actually chosen to be divisive, to exploit divisive values and to emphasise his personal stand. *I* dominates the scene, sometimes hidden in an exclusive plural: at most, anyone else can merely *join*.

4.2.3   A Red Thread of Empowerment from Clinton to Obama[8]

While the two challenging Republican candidates examined above actually share only limited aspects both in the choice of founding values and in the strategies of self-presentation, a red thread tightly links the two Democrat challengers—Bill Clinton and Barak Obama.

Their speeches show quite remarkable similarities, which will be commented upon without neglecting the analysis of the most significant differences, to shed light on the approach adopted by each candidate and, at the same time, to single out elements of evolution revealing how much Obama owes to his Democrat predecessor.

First of all, the general structure of the text. Both candidates do not open their speech with the performative statement, but their announcement is pronounced after a long introduction, which actually is a process for the construction of their audience and of agreement with them (Perelman & Olbrechts-Tyteca, 1958). Great values, aspects of personal biography and considerations about the present situation are part of this itinerary, which becomes the prerequisite for the announcement itself, the reason that justifies the choice to run. The fundamental aspects of the political programme are illustrated only after the official announcement, followed by a final

---

[8]Texts available at http://www.4president.org/speeches/1992/billclinton1992announcement.htm and at http://www.4president.org/speeches/2008/barackobama2008announcement.htm respectively.

peroratio, which, in line with the tenets of ancient rhetoric, widely exploits ethic and pathetic elements leading to a highly emotional climax.

4.2.3.1   Introduction and Performative Statement

Both arguers start with an informal welcome to anchor their delivery to a shared physical context. Obviously, the address is meant also for a wider audience, which will be reached through media coverage, but the communion with actual people, standing before the speaker, has a strong emotional impact and generates a warm contact that can be easily expanded to include virtual participants. As mentioned above, both speeches have a long introduction, which is however differently organized by the two candidates.

In establishing the contact with the audience, Clinton emphasizes the role played by his interlocutors in determining his choice ("*all of you*, in different ways, have brought me here today"), and immediately gives the gist of his commitment: "Preserving the American *dream*. Restoring the *hopes* of the forgotten middle class. Reclaiming the *future* for our children". He then exploits existential presuppositions triggered by a *that*-structure (cf. Sect. 3.5.1 above) to present his point of view on the present American situation:

> I refuse to be part of a generation *that* celebrates the *death* of Communism abroad with the *loss* of the American Dream at home.
>
> I refuse to be part of a generation *that fails* to compete in the global economy and so condemns hard-working Americans to a life of struggle without reward or security.
>
> That is why I stand here today...because I refuse to stand by and let our children become part of the first generation to do worse than their parents. I don't want my child or your child to be part of a country *that's coming apart* instead of *coming together*. (Clinton)

He then introduces some elements of personal experience and memories, mentioning his role as Governor of Arkansas, meant as an ethotic proof of him being qualified to be a good president. In this respect, he behaves as his predecessors. The political international scenario is dominated by the collapse of the Soviet Union, but this is no guarantee of security, as "we cannot build a safe and secure world unless we can first make America strong at home". The home situation is gloomy, and this is the fault of the incumbent presidency—more precisely, of 12 years of Republican administration. The identification of the Enemy is explicit, and criticism is conveyed by a wide choice of negative linguistic element: open negation (*no vision, no action, no partnership, no leadership*) as well as negatively-loaded words and expressions (*wrong, divide, slipping behind, wash their hands, losing our way*, etc.) (cf. Sect. 3.4 above).

Effectively exploiting anaphoric repetition, the arguer singles out the direct responsibilities of the Republicans in fostering racial conflict, lowering educational standards, denying economic support:

> For 12 years, Republicans have tried to divide us - race against race - so we get mad at each other and not at them. [. . .]

> For 12 years, the Republicans have talked about choice without really believing in it. George Bush says he wants school choice even if it bankrupts the public schools [...]
> For 12 years, the Republicans have been telling us that America's problems aren't their problem. (Clinton)

The harsh judgement of the administration is not supported by arguments, but is part of the accepted premises, that quite obviously lead to the conclusion that things have to change.

Differently from Clinton's, the introduction of Obama's announcement is strongly centred on his biography.[9] While Clinton relies mainly on the construction of the Enemy, Obama focuses on his own image as a Leader whose life is clear evidence of his qualifications and attitudes.

He wants to tell his personal story ("But let me tell you how I came to be here"). In his homodiegetic (and mythical) narrative (cf. Sect. 3.2 above), the arguer tells facts but also shares feelings, and is able to construct a quite effective self-portrait: he is a self-made man, he has moral values and Christian faith, a solid legal background, and large experience of real-life problems. The narrative also includes the first-person plural, when the arguer starts talking about his friends (and other fellow-Democrat senators) to illustrate their achievements (*we were able to reform a death penalty system, we were able to give health insurance*, etc.) and to sketch their ethical qualities:

> I made lasting friendships here, friends that I see here in the audience today. It was here -- It was here where *we* learned to *disagree without being disagreeable*; that it's possible to compromise so long as you know those *principles that can never be compromised*; and that so long as we're willing to *listen to each othe*r, we can *assume the best* in people instead of the worst. (Obama)

The ethical qualities of the arguer are presented as the result of a special process of initiation, shared with long-lasting friends. These are essential elements for the character of a politician; in describing himself and his friends, Obama sketches at the same time the profile of the ideal President. Moreover, his described ethos (*ethos dit*) is turned into *ethos montré* (Maingueneau, 2002), as he shows those very qualities in the act of speaking, above all in the way he represents the adversary. As we have seen, in the initial part of his speech Clinton explicitly mentions the Republicans as agents of evil. Obama, on the other hand, never mentions his adversaries, but introduces the negative attitudes and behaviours indirectly, using passive or impersonal structures (*we have been told...; what's stopped us..., what's filled the void...*). Moreover, he does this mainly after the formal announcement, when he re-examines the history of America. Clearly, he does not want to be *disagreeable*. The Enemy is there, pervasive and dangerous, but it is not a personal, recognisable adversary. It is the dark side of American politics, which has generated "disillusionment and frustration", leaving room for "the cynics, the lobbyist, the special interest".

---

[9]For the analysis of Obama's biography as a rhetorical construction, s. Van Belle (2014).

An anticipation of this presentation of opposing negative forces occurs at the very beginning of the speech, when Obama (before telling his personal story) mentions great values, attributing them to the audience ("You came here because you believe in what this country can be") and opposing them to their negative counterparts implicitly attributed to the other party:

> In the face of *war*, you believe there can be *peace*. In the face of *despair*, you believe there can be *hope*. In the face of a *politics that shut you out*, that's told you to settle, that's *divided* us for too long, you believe that we can be *one* people, reaching for what's possible, building that *more perfect union*. (Obama)

Both Clinton and Obama focus on *hope*, look at the future and care for the next generations. They both pursue *unity*. In particular, Obama links this theme to the founding text of American democracy, claiming the need for *a more perfect union*. Unity in the country mirrors unity of the supporters, and is a way to start constructing the United-we-stand myth.

The official, performative statement comes after the introduction, as a consequence of what has been said in the introduction. Clinton:

> Today, as we stand on the threshold of a *new* era, a *new* millennium, I believe we need a *new* kind of *leadership*, leadership committed to *change*. Leadership *not mired in the politics of the past*, not limited by *old ideologies*...Proven leadership that knows how to *reinvent* government to help solve the real problem of real people.
> *That is why today* I am declaring my candidacy for President of the United States. *Together* I believe *we can* provide leadership that will *restore* the American dream - that will fight for the forgotten middle class - that will provide more opportunity, insist on more responsibility and create a greater sense of community for this great country. (Clinton)

Clinton's decision stems from his criticism of the present government, from his convictions and his commitment for change. The time indication (*today*, repeated twice) links the announcement to the present situation, because it is the present situation that requires this decision. The word *leadership* anticipates the character of the Leader, who however is joined by his supporters in his effort (*together... we can*). They are the *agents* of *change*, though change has a component of re-turning to past, as implied by the presuppositions (*restore, reinvent*) (cf. Sect. 3.5.1 above). As for the Republicans change allegedly means going back to the pre-Democrat era, for Democrat Clinton change is to re-cover values buried by 12 years of Republican administration.

In Obama's speech, the Announcement is the final step of his biography, the first step in a metaphorical *journey* (cf. Sect. 3.7 above) leading to the Presidency:

> It was *here*, in Springfield, where North, South, East, and West come together that I was reminded of the essential *decency* of the American people -- where I came to believe that through this decency, we can build *a more hopeful* America. And that is *why*, in the shadow of the Old State Capitol, where Lincoln once called on a house divided to stand together, where *common hopes and common dreams* still live, *I stand before you* today to *announce my candidacy* for President of the United States of America. (Obama)

The performative utterance is linked to the context of enunciation, both in space (*here*) and time (*today*), and stems from the whole previous story, condensed in a few crucial words: *decency, hopes, dreams*, which are *common*, shared by arguer and audience. This is the reason for Obama's announcement, which is pronounced in the form of a solemn self-appointment, with a historical and interdiscursive link to Lincoln and his House Divided speech.[10]

4.2.3.2   Programmes for Change

The theme of change, which is almost regularly exploited by challenging candidates (and sometimes not only by them), is transformed into the pivotal theme in both Clinton's and Obama's speeches, and, even more interestingly, the enactment of change is not presented as the exclusive job of the future president, but is entrusted also to the responsibility of the audience. The audience possess the right qualities to participate into the project (Obama: "people who love their country *can* change it") and play a crucial role in guaranteeing that change will actually occur. The involvement of the audience, their active participation is a distinguishing trait of both speeches: it emerges in the final part of Clinton's and is transformed into the backbone of Obama's announcement and campaign.

Change is offered as the crucial justification for the candidacy and, as a consequence, for support: the negative forces (more or less explicitly singled out) must be beaten to make change possible. Clinton, with an evident ascending climax: "this election is about change: in our party, in our national leadership, in our country". In this perspective, change is the logical consequence of agreement on facts (the faults of the present and recent past) and on the shared values, which have been betrayed by the adversary administration.

But change is also in opposition to the federal government as such, to "the ways of Washington" (Obama), because "Washington failed us" (Clinton). In this respect, both Democrat candidates echo the criticism expressed by their post-Watergate[11] predecessors, including Republican Reagan. Change is more pervasive than political allegiance. Clinton: "The *change* we must make isn't liberal or conservative. It's both, and it's different. The small towns and main streets of America aren't like *the corridors and backrooms of Washington*". In Obama's view, it is the very essence of America: "The genius of *our Founders* is that they designed a system of *government that can be changed. And we should take heart, because we've changed this country before*". Paradoxically, changing the country is the best way to demonstrate loyalty to the founding tradition of the country itself, and this gives it the strength of an argument from authority (backed by none other than the mythical Founding Fathers).

The material contents of the programme are only the practical and concrete aspect of the founding goal of change. Clinton and Obama share similar objectives:

---

[10]Lincoln is Obama's testimonial, while Clinton mentions Kennedy (explicitly quoting from his famous Inaugural Address), as well as Teddy Roosevelt and Harry Truman, who (differently from the Republicans governing for the previous 12 years) "didn't hesitate to use the bully pulpit of the Presidency" in favour of the weaker.

[11]Obama explicitly mentions Watergate: "I was proud to help lead the fight in Congress that led to the most sweeping ethics reforms since Watergate".

education, health care, social security, the protection of the environment, prosperity are among the primary problems. There are obviously also international issues, more linked to the contingencies of the historical context (the Nineties of post-Cold War as opposed to the post-9.11 period and the Iraq war). Apart from the latter, there are no important differences in the programmes of the two candidates. Yet each of them chooses his own textual strategy to illustrate his intentions and plans.

Clinton wants to *rebuild* America, with a common effort of responsibility, but his use of first-person plural is initially exclusive:

> In a Clinton Administration, we are going to create *opportunity for all. We've got to* grow this economy, not shrink it. *We need to give people* incentives to make long-term investment in America and reward people who produce goods and services, not those who speculate with other people's money. *We've got to invest* more money in emerging technologies to help keep high-paying jobs here at home. *We've got to convert* from a defence to a domestic economy. [...]
>
> In a Clinton Administration, students and parents and teachers will get a real education President. [...] (Clinton)

These actions are typical of the governmental responsibilities of an *Administration*. By repeating "in a Clinton Administration", the arguer illustrates what is going to happen if he becomes president, with each new repetition introducing an argument in support of a pro-Clinton vote, often comparing the envisaged prospects with what has already been done in Arkansas.[12] There is also an inclusion of the audience, but the people are mainly confined to a secondary role: "The government owes our people more opportunity, but *we all* have to make the most of it through responsible citizenship".

On the other hand, Obama presents his programme as a common path, gaining strength from common action and the commitment of all. The progression of the argumentative line is marked by an exhortative form: *let us*. Starting from *let us begin*, the expression is repeated twenty times, marking the crucial steps of this programme for change. Four times the formula is expanded into *let us be the generation that*, emphasising the importance of poverty, health care, energy policies, and national safety, respectively. Echoing Clinton ("I refuse to be part of a generation that"), Obama turns that negative statement into a positive empowerment, so that the most urgent tasks of a new administration become a question of generational change. Parallel to *let us*, another pivotal formula is repeated like a mantra: *we can do that*. The active role of the group leads to success, and here is the core of the campaign, ready to be transformed into the famous payoff: *Yes, we can*. The assertive nature of the statement is emphasised in the payoff (*yes*): structured as an answer, it presupposes that doubts have been raised and then functions as a *confutatio*.

---

[12] There are some digressions: in the excerpt quoted above, for example, Clinton illustrates the different meanings of the expression *opportunity for all,* through the anaphoric repetition of the modal expression *we've got to,* which makes it easier to recognize the argumentative line.

4.2.3.3   Final *Peroratio*

Complying with the canon of ancient rhetoric, Clinton's *peroratio* starts with a short narrative *digressio*. He tells about a visit he and Hillary made to a Los Angeles classroom and compares the worries of contemporary children to the (idyllic) feelings that dominated his own childhood. Things have profoundly, and negatively, changed, and therefore it is time for change, to bring *the American dream* back to life. Sharing responsibility with a whole generation, the arguer finally calls to action:

> That is *our generation's responsibility* - to form a new covenant... more opportunity for all, more responsibility from everyone, and a greater sense of *common* purpose.
>   I believe with all my heart that together, *we can* make this happen. *We can usher in* a new era of progress, prosperity and renewal. *We can – we must*. This is *not just* a campaign for the Presidency – it is a campaign for the *future*, for the forgotten hard-working middle-class families of America who deserve a government that fights for them. A campaign to keep America strong at home and around the world. *Join with us*. *I* ask for *your* prayers, *your* help, *your* hands, and *your* hearts. *Together we can* make America *great again*, and build a *community of hope* that will inspire the world. (Clinton)

The emphasis is on common ideals and purposes, and on the empowerment of a generation who *can*—and *must*—enact change. The Valiant Leader needs the United-we-stand myth. He calls to action in a campaign that is much more than an electoral challenge, which implies that the audience are much more than mere voters. Actually, there is still a shade of ambiguity in the use of the first-person plural. When Clinton says "Join with us", he is addressing the audience who are asked to join an already existing group, giving *us* an exclusive value. Yet in the final appeal, *I* and *you* merge into a *together we*, the inclusive group of supporters and future actors in the process of change. A similar enunciative choice was made also by Reagan, and it is in this perspective that Clinton re-uses Reagan's payoff, which is however transformed from an exhortation (*let's make*) into a bare unquestionable statement, affirming capacity (*we can*) and therefore guaranteeing victory and success.

In Obama's speech the discursive stop that cools down the emotions and prepares *peroratio* takes the form of a *confutatio*. With one of the rare occurrences of the first person singular in the second part of the speech, Obama anticipates objections, attributing them to a vague non-person (*those who*) hidden somewhere between *I* and *we* ("*I* know that there are *those who* don't believe *we* can do all those things"). He recognizes the soundness of these objections and uses a marked form of exclusive first-person plural (*all of us running for President*) to express his personal understanding. There is however a counter-argument against this, namely the fact that the campaign is more than an electoral effort ("this campaign can't only be about *me*. It must be about *us*"). Like Clinton, he emphasises the crucial meaning of the moment, and uses the United-we-stand myth in support of the Valiant Leader. To reach a maximum of unity with his audience, Obama exploits a special discursive move, joining them in an inclusive *we*, and looking at himself from the outside (*he*):

> By ourselves, this change will not happen. Divided, *we* are bound to fail. But the life of a tall, gangly, self-made Springfield lawyer tells us that a different future is possible.
>   *He tells us* that there is *power* in words.

> *He tells us* that there's *power* in conviction. That beneath all the differences of race and region, faith and station, we are *one people*.
>   *He tells us* that there's *power* in *hope*. (Obama)

In this way Obama places himself outside the subjectivity of discourse (Benveniste, 1946, cf. Sect. 3.1), and thus he is able to construct and reinforce his ethical identity of Leader while remaining part of his audience. Anaphora gives further strength to this representation. After this moment of strong unity, the arguer can present himself as a candidate (*I am in this race, I want to win. . .*) separate from the group of supporters, who are in their turn capable of autonomous judgement (*if you will, if you feel, if you sense*). There are however also inclusive forms (*before us, our slumber, our fear, we owe*), engrained in shared feelings and beliefs, which legitimise the arguer to take the role of Leader, in final communion with his audience:

> Then *I am ready* to take up the cause, and march *with you*, and work *with you* – today.
>   *Together we can* finish the work that needs to be done, and *usher in* a new birth of freedom on this Earth. (Obama)

I and *you*, urged by the needs of the present (*today*), become the collective entity (*together we*) enabled to perform a historical task, whose significance expands well beyond American borders. The echo of Clinton's final words is strong, in the choice of pronouns, of values, even of single words (*usher in*).[13] Careful reading of the texts suggests that Obama has learnt Clinton's lesson, chooses to exploit the same fundamental arguments, and manages to develop his discursive line more consistently throughout the speech.

4.3   Final Remarks

To sum up, a line of evolution can be recognized in the Presidential Announcement from the Sixties to the first decade of the XXI century. All challenging candidates construct preliminary agreement with the audience relying on a negative judgement of the incumbent administration, which entails the need for change. And they all present themselves as capable of enacting that change. Yet, before Watergate, Kennedy and Nixon construct their credibility on a line of symptomatic reasoning, emphasising their personal qualities. After Watergate, all challenging candidates widely exploit arguments from alternatives to support the need for change, in combination with the argument from act and person, to support their adequacy to the role. Against this background, each candidate obviously adopts his own approach, and the analysis of individual choices can highlight a thread of interdiscursive connections running across time and political allegiance.

Kennedy and Nixon emphasise the power of the US president and the crucial choices he must make; they feel adequate for the role (because the party recognises

---

[13] This verb actually occurs also in Bush' speech, but not in the final part ("My first goal is to usher in the responsibility era").

this or simply because of personal convictions) and *therefore* they run. After Watergate, more emphasis is laid on current maladministration and on the evils of federal politics. Washington is the epitome of government for its own sake and not for the sake of the people. This concept is differently modulated but it is a constant. The point is to *be able* to change in the face of current government's failures.

Carter runs ultimately *because* he does not believe that *we* are worse than the Founding Fathers. He keeps a low profile, but implicitly suggests that he can be the personification of *the best*. Reagan emphasizes the need for the *new*, as he believes that the incumbent administration is responsible for all evils, first and foremost for constructing non-existing evils, and robbing Americans of their traditional optimism. He runs *because* he still believes that no dream is impossible and with his supporters he can "meet this rendezvous with destiny". Clinton hinges his campaign on change, to oppose the negative actions performed in 12 years of Republican administration. He runs *because* he believes it is possible to *restore* forgotten values, in communion with the whole country. G.W. Bush gives it for granted that compassionate conservatism is the solution to all the problems of America. As the country *must* be prosperous and at the same time compassionate, he runs *because* he is the champion of this ideology, and displays a special manipulative effort to present his divisive values as agents of unification. Finally, Obama recognises the values of the American people, and shares them. He also recognises the presence of negative forces that undermine those values and, at the same time, the power of people to defend them. He runs *because* he knows that change is possible, in a combined effort of the Leader and his supporters.

On the whole, the involvement of the audience tends to become stronger and stronger, the United-We-Stand myth becomes more and more decisive in the quest for support (with GW Bush as an exception). The Valiant Leader is obviously always on stage, though his presence may be mitigated for contingent reasons (Carter), while the Conspiratorial Enemy is constructed with varying degrees of aggressiveness, almost fading away in Obama's speech.

Like a devastating storm, Trump swooped in the presidential contest, defying all the rules developed during the previous decades. Trump's speech will not be the object of a detailed analysis, but a cursory reading of the text is sufficient to perceive the difference. Trump is not far from his predecessors for the big themes he exploits: he *will make America great again*, echoing previous candidates from both parties. He is tough and clear-cut in judging the incumbent President and the Democrat candidate, not differently from Clinton, Reagan, and others. He presents himself as the right man for the presidential office, as any other candidate. Yet his style is totally different, in terms of how the speech is organized, of its wording, its delivery, and— what is more interesting from the viewpoint of agreement—in the foundation of the main ethotic argument.

A crucial difference lies in the image of the future president that emerges (sometimes with brutal explicitness) from his speech, i.e. his self-portrait, which is at the same time the portrait of the ideal president. Trump is, first and foremost, an exceptionally rich man. He is not the representative of a wealthy (upper)middle class, like a farmer, a lawyer or an actor. He is far above the standards. For him, this is a guarantee, because he does not need money, he has no obligations towards donors, lobbyists or special interests. He acknowledges that there are certain "ways" in Washington, that he is part of the system, but his money make him immune from corruption. He talks openly and loosely about these issues, and transforms his huge wealth into the main argument to support his candidacy. The informal presentation includes the dramatization of his negotiation power as a future president, to the point that he reproduces a dialogue between himself and "the head of Ford" concerning the building of a car factory in Mexico, which vividly represents his being beyond corruption and special interests. The well-organized line of argumentation ideally developed along the previous decades is broken. The new course is explicitly declared: people "don't need the rhetoric"; a "cheerleader" instead is Trump's version of the Valiant Leader myth.

It goes without saying that this approach has not survived one single presidential term—so far. Biden's rhetorical choices have been sober and in line with the tradition that had previously dominated presidential campaigns across the political divide. This is however a very recent story, lying outside the time span chosen for the present analysis.

References

Benveniste, É. (1946). Structure des relations de personne dans le verb. Bulletin de la Société de Linguistique (XLIII/1) [English translation in: Id. (1971). *Problems in General Linguistics* (pp. 195–204). Miami: University of Miami Press].

Edelman, M. (1971). *Politics as symbolic action*. Academic.

Geis, M. L. (1987). *The language of politics*. Springer Verlag.

Leech, G. (1983). *Principles of pragmatics*. Longman.

Maingueneau, D. (2002). Problèmes d'ethos. *Pratiques, 113-114*, 55–67.

Perelman, Ch. & Olbrechts-Tyteca, L. (1958). *Traité de l'argumentation. La nouvelle rhétorique*. Paris: Presses Universitaires de France [English translation by J. Wilkinson & P. Weaver (1969): *The New Rhetoric. A Treatise on Argumentation*. Notre Dame (Ind.): University of Notre Dame Press].

Santulli, F. (2020). We shall fight: Speaker-exclusive *we* as a grammatical metaphor. *International Journal of Linguistics, 12/4*, 43–64.

Trent, J., Friedenberg, R., & Denton, R. (2011). *Political campaign communication: Principles and practices*. Rowman & Littlefield.

Van Belle, H. (2014). The bridge. The rhetorical construction of Barak Obama's biography by David Remnik. In H. van Belle et al. (Eds.), *Let's talk politics* (pp. 171–184). John Benjamins.

van Rees, A. (2005). Indicators of dissociation. In F. H. van Eemeren & P. Houtlosser (Eds.), *Argumentation in practice* (pp. 53–68). John Benjamins.

Chapter 5
The Inaugural Address: Fostering Objects of Agreement

Abstract The Inaugural Address is a genre that seeks agreement not expediently, to win the presidential race, but because its very institutional purpose is the 'restoration of ideological normality' after the bitter divisions of the electoral strife. The Chapter provides an analysis of the Inaugural Address divided in two main parts. In the first, the focus is on the cognitive moves of the genre, highlighting recursive structural and ideological elements which are functional to the construction of agreement. In the second part, building on the findings of the first, attention is turned to the eminently argumentative component of the IA. The scope is limited to the Inaugurals of presidents at their first mandate, from Eisenhower to Obama, coming after a predecessor of the opposite party, as these contextual factors are predictive of greater argumentativeness. This notwithstanding, the genre comes through as having a mainly epideictic function, with three out of four main moves bent on fostering the agreement with the audience. For the remaining really argumentative move, a comparison is carried out of how topoi, as intended in the AMT model, are used by the different presidents. The argumentation here is meant to state the main challenge for the years ahead and to present the president's approach as the best suited to the task of facing it. In doing so, the arguer tries to win the audience agreement to the proposed reading of the historical context and of the role of the president in that given contingency.

The Inaugural Address (IA) is the least argumentative of electoral speeches, with the balance definitely hanging on the construction of agreement as opposed to adversariness and confrontation. It comes when the clamour of the electoral campaign fades and the president elect is sworn in, thereby becoming the President, by virtue of the performative value of the oath. The institutional function of the inaugural address has been described as highly symbolic (Hart, 1984; Campbell & Jamieson, 1986; Gronbeck, 1986), aiming in the first place to restore "ideological normality" after the strife of the electoral campaign (WAUDAG, 1990, in Trosborg, 2000, p. 136), but also to invoke the "Plural Presidency". The latter notion is related to the fact that for the first time the president speaks for the institution, and not as an individual, and at the same time he calls the government and single citizens to action (Hart, 1984, p. 58, in Trosborg, 2000, p. 137). The voice of the institution resonates with the words of predecessors, which allows the new president to establish his administration in the tradition of American history. It addresses the audience as a whole, obliterating the partisanship and asperity that had divided voters in the previous months.

A collective identity is sought, as a way to (re)establish a sense of community, and this core element of the Inaugural makes it possible to classify it as a form of epideictic discourse. Nowadays, the notion of epideictic is defined more broadly than in classical rhetoric, where it referred to a specific genre, strictly characterized as a monological speech uttered at ceremonies, praising or attacking someone (Lopez-Pan, 2015). In contemporary views, epideictic speeches are those meant to strengthen the values and the solidarity bonds within a community, which, from this perspective, is defined as "a condition of agreement on certain shared values" (Lopez-Pan, 2015, p. 288). The functions attributed to epideictic argumentation, then, are not deliberative, but cognitive (or heuristic)—geared to the elaboration of opinion and testing them against criticism (Lumer, 1991), so as to reinforce the community's 'state of persuasion' (Micheli, 2012, p. 121). At the same time, it performs an identifying function—through the expression of their opinions the participants "portray themselves" (Doury, 2012, p. 99); and is oriented to the "face-goals" of argumentation, with convergence of opinion generating per se satisfaction (*Ibidem*, p. 110).

This enhanced agreement on values, can then be put to use for future calls to action (Graff & Winn, 2006, p. 51, in Degano 2020), which in the IA translates into harnessing consensus for the new presidency, a sort of open line of credit for the 4 years ahead, with policies and programs only hinted at, as a more thorough discussion would rekindle divisions, which would run counter the very institutional function of the address. It is in this construction of consensus around general objectives that the argumentative potential of the IA lies. Implicitly the speaker asks those who did not vote for him to accept his new institutional role as the President of all Americans, setting aside differences for the sake of a greater good, i.e. the pursuit of a common goal for the nation set by the President in response to the material contingency faced by the nation and the world.

Such an appeal is obviously more tenable on the symbolic plane than on the factual or historical one. It rests on the proposition that there is a collective identity that overrides social differences, holding a common stake that prevails over the interests of particular social groups, who may in fact be antagonistic. The symbolic dimension comes manifestly to the fore through the liturgical aspects of the IA, which mix the political with the religious plane, as shown by the oath taken on the Bible, the final salute "God bless America", but also the biblical references interspersed within the speech – an interdiscursive reference to the puritan origins of the Pilgrim Fathers – and in some cases by the insertion of a prayer opening the address (e.g. Eisenhower: "My friends, before I begin the expression of those thoughts that I deem appropriate to this moment, would you permit me the privilege of uttering a little private prayer of my own. And I ask that you bow your heads. . .").

Directly descending from its institutional function are the moves that characterize the cognitive structure of the genre (Bhatia, 1993), which will be identified and discussed in the first part of this chapter, while the second focuses on prototypical argumentative schemes related to one of such moves in particular.

5.1 Move 1: The Construction of Agreement Through Appeals to Collective Identity and Unity of Purpose

Related to the 'restoration of ideological normality' is a move that we may call 'invoking collective identity and unity of purpose', which emphasizes a collective identity over divisions. It leverages on some well-established objects of agreement, first and foremost the inalienable rights enshrined in the Constitution – freedom, equality and the right to aspire to a better life condition, i.e. the American promise, taking American history as a testimony of those values.

Step 1. Why we are here. Most speeches preliminarily recall the purpose of the Inaugural ceremony, thus linking the speech that is going to follow to the context of situation. This lays the ground for the words of the President to be seen as part of a ritual which takes its meaning from its being repeated and not as a single event. In this sense it is not originality that is valued, but repetition, not differently from what happens in religious rituals. Of course, each IA differs from those of the predecessors in terms of stylistic choices and partly of contents, but it is mostly a variation on the tune. This move aims to establish continuity more than unicity. That is why the context is discursively addressed with explicit deictic references. Eisenhower, after uttering the prayer, comes to what he sees as the urgent matter of their time ("forces of good and evil are massed and armed and opposed as rarely before in history"), linking this historical contingency to the timeless purpose of the Inauguration ceremony:

1. This fact defines the meaning of *this* day. *We are summoned by this honored and historic ceremony*[1] to witness more than the act of one citizen swearing his oath of service, in the presence of God. We are called as a people to give testimony in the sight of the world to our faith that the future shall belong to the free (Eisenhower).

Kennedy incipit reads "We observe today not a victory of a party but a celebration of freedom". Nixon opens his Inaugural saying: "I ask *you* to share with me *today* the Majesty of *this* moment. In the orderly transfer of power we celebrate the unity that keeps us free". Clinton recalls the purpose of the IA by saying *"Today, we* do more than celebrate America; we rededicate ourselves to the very idea of America." GW Bush explicitly mentions the American Promise, and at the same time spells out its content through the values that inspired his vision: *"Today, we* affirm a new commitment to live out our nation's promise through civility, courage, compassion and character" (GW Bush). Obama refers to the institutional purpose of the inaugural address celebrating the spirit of agreement that prevailed at the time of the Founding

---

[1] In all quotations, emphasis is added by the author to highlight relevant discursive features.

Fathers and that still reverberates in the most important ritual of the American Presidency: "On *this* day, *we* gather because we have chosen hope over fear, unity of purpose over conflict and discord". And then, he goes on:

2. The time has come to reaffirm our enduring spirit; to choose our better history; to carry forward that precious gift, that noble idea, passed on from generation to generation: the God-given promise that all are equal, all are free, and all deserve a chance to pursue their full measure of happiness (Obama).

A bit less explicitly, Reagan refers to the context of situation by saying "To a few of *us here today*, this is a solemn and momentous occasion; and yet, in the history of our nation it is a commonplace occurrence," adding to the personal (*us*) and time deictic reference (*today*) also an anchorage to the place (*here*). What is commonplace for the nation is "The orderly transfer of authority as called for in the Constitution" that "routinely takes place as it has for almost two centuries".

At the time of the Founding Fathers the principles so warmly praised by each new president had very concrete counterparts in the groundbreaking political choice of declaring independence, and rejecting monarchy, as well as a social organization that in the rest of the world still had aristocracy placed at the top of the pyramid out of a birth privilege, which would exclude any non-member from achieving an equal status. The success of this 'experiment' is still celebrated in the IA with undiminished wonder as an awesome fact. Reagan states "few of us stop to think how unique we really are. In the eyes of many in the world, this every-4-year ceremony we accept as normal is nothing less than a miracle". GW Bush affirms: "The peaceful transfer of authority is rare in history, yet common in our country"; Obama on a similar tone states "It is because we, all of us, hold to these principles that the political changes accomplished this day do not imply turbulence, upheaval or disorder."

Nowadays, in a changed international context where several countries have since embraced the same constitutive principles, the primacy of such a democratic choice is still invoked as the core of American spirit, which after all is the ground on which American exceptionalism is claimed. Eisenhower, whose presidency was oriented towards internationalism, calls freedom a *faith*, and attributes to it the greatness of the Nation, invoking *the spirit of the free* as a new laical version of religious brotherhood among peoples. Implicitly, the US are thus upgraded to the guardians of such universal value.

3. This *faith* rules our whole way of life. It decrees that we, the people, elect leaders not to rule but to serve. It asserts that we have the right to choice of our own work and to the reward of our own toil. It inspires the initiative that makes our productivity the wonder of the world. And it warns that any man who seeks to deny equality among all his brothers betrays *the spirit of the free* and invites the mockery of the tyrant (Eisenhower).

Step 2. Affirming unity over division. This step contributes to the rhetorical aim of the move by downplaying the risk that actual divides pose for the construction of a collective identity. Two orders of divisions are tackled, economic and ethnic divisions. With regard to the former, work is framed as a social equalizer in an attempt to neutralize class divide. As Romagnuolo (2013) points out, the principles of freedom and equality alone could hardly become forces of inclusion in the pursuit of a common identity in a country where large groups had initially been excluded or marginalized, and immigration from the four corners of the world kept accounting for such a large part in the composition of the social tissue. Freedom and equality, together with individualism, formed the nucleus of Civic Republicanism (Romagnuolo, 2013, p. 120, based on Stucky, 2004, and Beasley, 2004), which was the expression of just a part of the population, i.e. the Anglosaxon settlers, who by the end of the eighteenth century represented 49% of the population, as results from the 1790 census which however did not include the Native Americans (Ricento, 2003, p. 613 in Romagnuolo 2013). They needed to persuade the other half of the population, of different origins, to accept such values as the core of a common national identity, hence the myth of the origins: the values and culture that allowed the settlers to endure and survive, taken together with the success of the American political experiment, were to become the inspiring principles of the nation. Spreading this verb was the task of schools and of the American Presidency, the main organ of US political propaganda (Romagnuolo, 2013, p. 120).

The real social equalizer, though, in Romagnuolo's view, was work, as the only value that could make it possible to overcome the differences and make the American creed become true: whatever the hardships of one's condition, through hard work the promise of a better life could be achieved by anybody. Reference to work as a social equalizer is present in all the Inaugural Addresses analyzed, with slight differences. Eisenhower directly establishes the connection between equality and work clarifying that equality is not to be intended as having equal means (clearly a sensitive issue in the light of the then rampant military and ideological fight against communism) but equal ideals, which are cast as equally cherished by "the most humble and the most exalted":

4. In the light of this equality, we know that the virtues most cherished by free people--love of truth, pride of work, devotion to country--all are treasures equally precious *in the lives of the most humble and of the most exalted*. The men who mine coal and fire furnaces, and balance ledgers, and turn lathes, and pick cotton, and heal the sick and plant corn--all serve as proudly and as profitably for America as the statesmen who draft treaties and the legislators who enact laws (Eisenhower).

The rhetorical expedient of the list is used to stress the idea of unity out of different work and economic conditions, with some work profiles considered more prototypically representative in this respect: the miner, the farmer, the industry worker, clerks, doctors. Interestingly enough from a linguistic point of view, such labels are not used, preferring instead the pattern 'the men who' + predicate (a material verb) describing their job: the men who mine coal, plant corn, fire furnaces, balance ledgers, heal the sick. Each element is linked to the previous one with the conjunction 'and', and not simply through a comma, thus reinforcing the idea of equality through the use of the paratactic conjunction. Reagan (example 5 below) uses the same pattern and names the same staple categories ("men and women who raise our food, man our mines and our factories, heal us when we are sick"), while adding some of his own ("who teach our children, keep our homes, and patrol our streets"), and naming another few using category labels ("professionals, industrialists, shop-keepers, clerks, cabbies, and truckdrivers").

In Reagan's discursive construction, the scope of his Administration's action is announced as coinciding with the interest of workers, whatever the work is. In opposition to politics defending the vested interests of particular social groups, he commits to making the interests of all workers, cutting through social divides:

5. Our concern must be for a special interest group that has been too long neglected. It knows no sectional boundaries or ethnic and racial divisions, and it crosses political party lines. It is made up of *men and women who raise our food, patrol our streets, man our mines and our factories, teach our children, keep our homes, and heal us when we are sick—professionals, industrialists, shopkeepers, clerks, cabbies, and truckdrivers*. They are, in short, "We the people," this breed called Americans (Reagan).

The claim is clearly unrealistic, as politics is notoriously the arena in which conflicting interests are mediated. It can only be made sense of as an appeal to the unifying identity around which most Americans can find an agreement, and in this sense the verbatim quotation from the constitution, "We the people", interdiscursively reinforces the appeal.

At the same time, work was and is still being used as a parameter of exclusion from the in-group. Originally, the target of exclusion were Native Americans – who had to be reclaimed from the "wandering life" (Andrew Jackson, State of the Union Address, 1829), and made "to work like any other man on his own ground" (Theodore Roosevelt, State of the Union Address, 1901), non-hard-working immigrants, the physically unfit, and the 'negroes' (Romagnuolo, 2013). In the more recent examples above, a work divide is implicitly drawn, with an in-group embracing workers, whatever the social prestige of their position, and non-workers implicitly classified as out-group members. Decades later, addressing the audience from the opposite political camp, Obama celebrates Americans' hard-working and enduring spirit as the reason of its greatness:

6. . . .we understand that greatness is never a given. It must be earned. Our journey has never been one of shortcuts or settling for less. It has not been the path for the faint-hearted, for those who prefer leisure over work, or seek only the pleasures of riches and fame. Rather, it has been *the risk-takers, the doers, the makers of things* - some celebrated, but more often men and women obscure in their labor, who have carried us up the long, rugged path towards prosperity and freedom (Obama).

As was the case for Reagan, even for Obama work ethics is what defines American people, proving at once an inclusion and exclusion parameter: while risk-taking and productivity are in-group cherished values, the pursuit of compromise and easy wealth are what define non-members. Work is constructed in association with the frame of sacrifice ("men and women struggled and sacrificed and worked till their hands were raw") as a way to achieve better conditions in one's life and for the posterity ("so that we might live a better life"), and as self-sacrifice for the greater good of the nation ("They saw America as bigger than the sum of our individual ambitions; greater than all the differences of birth or wealth or faction").

As shown by these examples, exclusion strategies are not so marked as they were in the past, and they have partly changed target, but nonetheless mechanisms of in-group vs out-group representations are still exploited.

The enduring and hard-working spirit of the American people are also used argumentatively as warrants of feasibility. Persuading the audience that the action called for is feasible is a typical concern in discourses advocating for a chance of policy (Omar, 2019). In such calls to action, which typically rest on pragmatic arguments (van Eemeren et al., 2002, p. 101), the most stringent critical question is related to the feasibility issue, i.e. whether the advocated measure would actually work. People's willingness to engage in action rests on this prerequisite, as well as on sharing the view that the action advocated would bring desirable results. For American presidents coming after one or two terms of the opposite political color, invoking change is quite natural, and feasibility is often tackled by stating that the American people have the capability of enacting the change of pace that is pushed for. Clinton presented the task of renewing America as *fearsome*, using a loaded word to add momentum, but so, he said, are American strengths ("Though our challenges are *fearsome*, so are our *strengths*"). And this argument is backed by the nation's record, as he says "And Americans have ever been a restless, questing, hopeful people. We must bring to our task today the vision and will of those who came before us". Obama, dealing with the quandary of the subprime financial and economic crisis, quotes American productivity and inventiveness as constant traits of the nation that are a necessary condition for "the work of remaking America":

7. We remain the most prosperous, powerful nation on Earth. Our workers are no less productive than when this crisis began. Our minds are no less inventive, our goods and services no less needed than they were last week or last month or last year. Our capacity remains undiminished (Obama).

On a par with class divide, the heterogeneous origin of the American population could pose a threat to the construction of a common national identity, and warding off the ethnical division has been a long-lasting concern. In the past, efforts were made to preempt the risk that for the newcomers the ties to the culture of origin would be stronger than their sense of belonging to their new homeland. *Hyphen politics* or *hyphenism*, (what today is called *identity politics*) was seen as a grave menace to the US democratic order, with German, Italian, and Irish immigrants accused of refusing to integrate, and Democrats accused of trading on ethnicity to get immigrants' votes. It is in this context that the slogan "America First" was used by three Republican candidates in the 1920s (Warren G. Harding, Calvin Coolidge and Herbert Hoover), becoming a shorthand for anti-hyphenism. A few years earlier, though, it had been used also by Democrat Woodrow Wilson, out of concern that

German-Americans might retain sympathy for Germany in World War I (Churchwell, 2018, p. 85).

The attitude toward US multi-ethnical origin is possibly the greatest element of change in the rhetoric of the IA. The sense of threat that had characterized anti-hyphenism dissolved and made room for praise, so much so that the glorification of differences can now be considered a recurrent step in the cognitive structure of IAs, whereby the democratic coexistence of peoples with different origins is seen as embodying the American creed. Clinton, discussing the 'idea of America', says it is "ennobled by the faith that our nation can summon from its myriad diversity the deepest measure of unity". Obama states: "we know that our patchwork heritage is a strength, not a weakness", and defends this statement adding:

8. We are a nation of Christians and Muslims, Jews and Hindus, and non-believers. We are shaped by every language and culture, drawn from every end of this Earth; and because we have tasted the bitter swill of civil war and segregation, and emerged from that dark chapter stronger and more united, we cannot help but believe that the old hatreds shall someday pass; that the lines of tribe shall soon dissolve; that as the world grows smaller, our common humanity shall reveal itself; and that America must play its role in ushering in a new era of peace (Obama).

With due reformulations, Obama's argument can be reconstructed as follows:

1 Our patchwork heritage is a strength
1.1 Our history taught us that our patchwork heritage is a strength
1.1.1 We emerged from Civil war and segregation stronger and more united
1.1.2 As those division dissolved, current divisions will dissolve 1 day
1.2 We are better equipped (than more homogenous nations) to democratically cope with diversity in a globalized world

Step 3. Unity against an enemy. As earlier stated, the IA is not a speech meant to sow division but to foster unity. A powerful way of fostering unity, though, is through division, not within the intended audience community but pitting it against some common enemy. At times of open conflict with other nations, enemies are easily identified: the Soviet Union for Eisenhower and Kennedy (which they did not name explicitly, though), terrorists for Obama ("We will not apologize for our way of life, nor will we waver in its defense, and for those who seek to advance their aims by inducing terror and slaughtering innocents, we say to you now that our spirit is stronger and cannot be broken; you cannot outlast us, and we will defeat you"). Interestingly enough, Kennedy, at the height of Cold War tensions, and justifying arms race as a way to ward off the risk of an escalation to a full-fledged war, addresses America's enemies with the request that "both sides begin again the quest for peace". He leverages on common spaces of agreement between the two super-powers, reversing in a way the logic of a domestic call to action against an external enemy ("But neither can two great and powerful groups of nations take comfort from our present course--both sides overburdened by the cost of modern weapons, both rightly alarmed by the steady spread of the deadly atom"). Then, a 'call to arms' is made not again a state, but against "the common enemies of men: tyranny, poverty, disease, and war itself" inviting the formation of a "grand and global alliance" to improve life conditions for all mankind.

At times of relative peace, pointing to an enemy outside the national borders would be awkward as the IA reaches well beyond the nation and it does not have to sound like a declaration of war. In these cases, the tones reserved to foreign policy are generally conciliating, reaffirming American partnership with their allies, and reaching out to all peace-loving countries. This said, differences emerge regarding the extent to which each President intends to let the US be involved in foreign policy, the debate between isolationism and interventionism being a long-standing one in American political discourse.

For enemy construction, then, presidents often look at internal enemies, who from within America and from a position of power mine the credibility of the American promise – namely corrupt politicians. They are often referred to metonymically using the name of the capital ("Washington", "the ways of Washington"). The trend started with Woodrow Wilson who redesigned (within the constitutional limits) the power relations between the Congress and the Presidency, in favor of the latter. He leveraged on his lack of a Washington background and used his knowledge of the Constitution and the way the government worked to his advantage.[2] In IAs coming after the Watergate scandal the invective against Washington seems to have become customary, allowing the President to take side with those citizens that are disaffected to politics, while being a politician himself.

5.2   Move 2. Spelling Out What Change Means: Problem Statement and Solution

Logically following from the Renewal of the American promise is another important move in the cognitive structure of the IA, which states what it means, for a given generation, to live up the American promise. As Clinton put this, "Though we march to the music of our time, our mission is timeless. Each generation of Americans must define what it means to be an American". Like in the rest of the speech, the views of the President are constructed as universally acceptable by whoever subscribes to the principles defining the spirit of America. The perception that there is a problem and that tackling it should be the priority of the new administration is presented as shared by the community, and the solution is cast as dictated by the American creed that was recalled and reaffirmed in the previous moves. A direct link is thus established between the values of the past and the actions of the present and the future. As declared by GW Bush "With a simple oath, we affirm old traditions and make new

---

[2] *Woodrow Wilson's long shadow* by Leopold Todd, October 28, 2013 https://edition.cnn.com/2013/10/28/politics/woodrow-wilson-biography-berg/index.html accessed on 8/7/2021.

beginnings." Past and present are set in relation, presenting American history as a coherent effort of living up the American promise:

9. American story. A story of flawed and fallible people, united across the generations by grand and enduring ideals. The grandest of these ideals is an unfolding American promise that everyone belongs, that everyone deserves a chance, that no insignificant person was ever born. Americans are called upon to enact this promise in our lives and in our laws (GW Bush).

In some cases the problem-solution structure is presented in terms of a much needed change, whose ratio is traced back to a view of American history as a journey towards progress (Clinton calls it America's *heroic journey*), where progress inherently contains the idea of change. In Clinton's first Inaugural the idea of change is the central theme, which pivots around the extended metaphor of spring as a moment of renewal. A spring that has not came as a result of the perpetual alternation of seasons, but as an effect of vote, ("you [...] have forced the spring").

10. When our founders boldly declared America's independence to the world and our purposes to the Almighty, they knew that America, to endure, would have to change. Not change for change's sake, but change to preserve America's ideals; life, liberty, the pursuit of happiness... Thomas Jefferson believed that to preserve the very foundations of our nation, we would need dramatic change from time to time (Clinton).

At the same time, change is presented, quite paradoxically, as renewal, which presupposes going back to an unspecified previous era, a sort of Golden Age where the current predicament did not affect American society. Stripped of this aura of universal consensus, however, this move is the most markedly argumentative in the Inaugural, as at heart it consists in a problem statement, which indicates the presidency's priority in relation to the contingent situation, and the proposal of a solution. Generally, if the problem is likely to be perceived as such by the audience at large, the solutions are clearly a matter of political choice, hence more prone to controversy. The problems can be formulated as such more or less explicitly. Reagan, for example, explicitly identified the problem ("an economic affliction of great proportions") of the United States at the time of his first mandate in the inflation and the taxes:

11. These United States are confronted with an *economic affliction of great proportions*. We suffer from the longest and one of the worst sustained *inflations* in our national history. It distorts our economic decisions, penalizes thrift, and crushes the struggling young and the fixed- income elderly alike. It threatens to shatter the lives of millions of our people (Reagan).

At traits he mixes a description of the effects of the crisis ("the worst sustained inflations in our national history", "Idle industries have cast workers into unemployment, causing human misery and personal indignity") with explanations of the causes, which necessarily entails a given reading of reality, without marking the difference between the two ("Those who do work are denied a fair return for their labor by a tax system which penalizes successful achievement and keeps us from maintaining full productivity. But great as our tax burden is, it has not kept pace with public spending"). Nixon labels the problems as such, calling them "troubles" and "crisis" through a reversed analogy with Roosevelt's predicaments:

12. Standing in this same place a third of a century ago, Franklin Delano Roosevelt addressed a Nation ravaged by depression and gripped in fear. He could say in surveying the Nation's *troubles*: "They concern, thank God, only material things." Our *crisis* today is the reverse (Nixon).

He then uses a chiastic pattern to contrapose the status quo (qualified through its wants) and the unfulfilled needs of America:

13. We have found ourselves rich in goods, but ragged in spirit; reaching with magnificent precision for the moon, but falling into raucous discord on earth. We are caught in war, wanting peace. We are torn by division, wanting unity. We see around us empty lives, wanting fulfillment. We see tasks that need doing, waiting for hands to do them (Nixon).

Obama takes on, among other things, sterile political and ideological divisions, by saying "we come to proclaim an end to the petty grievances and false promises, the recriminations and worn-out dogmas, that for far too long have strangled our politics", implying that what is to be terminated is a problem. Clinton uses an anaphora (repetition of 'when' in clause-initial position, associated to a concessive structure signaled by 'but'), to introduce the problems he intends to tackle during his presidency:

14. This new world has already enriched the lives of millions of Americans who are able to compete and win in it. *But when* most people are working harder for less; *when* others cannot work at all; *when* the cost of health care devastates families and threatens to bankrupt many of our enterprises, great and small; *when* fear of crime robs law-abiding citizens of their freedom; and *when* millions of poor children cannot even imagine the lives we are calling them to lead, we have not made change our friend (Clinton).

The solutions as well can be explicitly formulated ("It is time to check and reverse the growth of government which shows signs of having grown beyond the consent of the governed", Reagan) or implied by the negative description of the status quo, together with vague statements about the course of action that needs to be taken ("We must act today in order to preserve tomorrow" and "the solutions we seek must be equitable", Reagan; "Today we pledge an end to an era of deadlock and drift", Clinton). Nixon explicitly introduces his solution as "an answer to the crisis", but then, again the solution is very vaguely worded, and certainly does not qualify as a political solution.

By virtue of its more intrinsically argumentative nature, this move will be given attention in the second part of this chapter, where prototypical argumentative schemes for the inaugural are discussed.

5.3 Move 3. Invoking the Plural Presidency as a Call to Action

As already said, the plural presidency refers both to the president using for the first time an institutional voice, and to a call to the citizens to take an active part in the renewal of America. Differences here can be pinned down simply to the choices made in terms of role representation. The unmarked form of pronominal reference for a collective endeavor involving both the speaker and the addressees would be the inclusive first-person plural (*we/us*), which is actually used by some presidents. Reagan appeals to common responsibility saying, "All of us together, in and out of government, must bear the burden". Interestingly enough, this appeal in inserted in an argument, which touches a typical topos (in the sense of common place) of populist discourse (Degano/Sicurella 2019), rejecting the government of the elite, and challenging at the same time the role of experts, and expertise, on the ground that 'the people' has within itself all it takes to govern the nation. His argument goes as follows:

15. From time to time, we have been tempted to believe that society has become too complex to be managed by self-rule, that government by an elite group is superior to *government for, by, and of the people. But if no one among us is capable of governing himself, then who among us has the capacity to govern someone else? All of us together, in and out of government, must bear the burden*. The solutions we seek must be equitable, with no one group singled out to pay a higher price (Reagan).

Also Clinton and Obama use an inclusive first-person plural, without Reagan' populist drive. Clinton uses the exhortative form ("*Let us all take more responsibility*, not only for ourselves and our families but for our communities and our country") jointly with the obligational modal *must* ("To renew America, *we must* revitalize our democracy"). Obama uses an impersonal passive referred to an inclusive *us* ("What is required of us now is a new era of responsibility") inserted in a cleft structure, which presupposes that the people is required to do something. Two other presuppositions are triggered by nominalized forms of verbs of cognition—what Levinson calls *factive verbs* (Levinson, 1983, p. 181)—i.e. recognition and knowledge, in the two appositional constructs "a *recognition* on the part of every American, that *we* have duties to ourselves, *our* nation, and the world" and "duties that *we* do not grudgingly accept but rather seize gladly, firm in the *knowledge* that there is nothing so satisfying to the spirit, so defining of our character, than giving *our* all to a difficult task". Nixon has recourse to a first-person plural pronoun subtly, and sometimes ambiguously, mixing audience-inclusive and exclusive uses:

16. But *we* are approaching the limits of what government alone can do.
    Our greatest need now is to reach beyond government, and to enlist the legions of the concerned and the committed.

>   What has to be done, has to be done by *government and people together* or it will not be done at all. The lesson of past agony is that *without the people we can do nothing*; *with the people we can do everything*.
>
>   To match the magnitude of *our* tasks, *we* need the energies of *our people*—enlisted not only in grand enterprises, but more importantly in those small, splendid efforts that make headlines in the neighborhood newspaper instead of the national journal.
>
>   With these, we can build a great cathedral of the spirit—*each of us raising* it one stone at a time, as he reaches out to his neighbor, helping, caring, doing.
>
>   I do not offer a life of uninspiring ease. I do not call for a life of grim sacrifice. *I ask you to join* in a high adventure—one as rich as humanity itself, and as exciting as the times *we* live in (Nixon).

The needs can be assumed to be collective ("we are approaching the limits of what government alone can do, our greatest need now is…"), but the one who can felicitously reach out beyond government is only the president, thus suggesting an audience-exclusive use of *we*. Pronominal reference is clearly audience-exclusive in the statement "without the people we can do nothing", as the third-person reference of 'the people' logically excludes them from the subject *we*. In the next few lines the use of pronouns constructs an institutional role for Nixon as president, referred to with the first person singular pronoun ("I do not offer, I ask you"), and a role for Nixon as a citizen who on a par with other men ("each of us") is called to build "a cathedral of the spirit" to answer the call of the time *we live in*.

As shown by Nixon's example, the range of personal reference is not limited to the first person plural, but includes impersonal codification through third-person personal reference, with the government on the one hand and the people on the other, as well as first-person singular plus second person address (*you*). In the following examples from GW Bush the move is realized through impersonal forms, where a concession acknowledges the responsibilities of the government, as if to preempt criticism, but *yet* frustrates the ensuing inference that this should free citizen from personal engagement. The deontic appeal to the citizens comes as an indirect speech act, since an instruction (be compassionate) is presented as a statement, ("compassion is the work of a nation, not just a government"):

17. Government has great responsibilities for public safety and public health, for civil rights and common schools. *Yet compassion is the work of a nation, not just a government* (GW Bush).

Later on the same strategy is used with third-person reference to the "government" (in the premodified string "government program"):

18. Americans are generous and strong and decent, *not because* we believe in ourselves, *but because* we hold beliefs beyond ourselves. When this spirit of *citizenship* is missing, no *government program* can replace it. When this spirit is present, no wrong can stand against it (GW Bush).

Once more, negation is used to emphasize the endorsement of one view and the rejection of its contrary (*not because. . . ., but because. . .*). Third person reference is used also by Obama, with regard to the responsibility of government in the utterance "For *as much as government can* do and must do, it is ultimately the faith and determination of *the American people* upon which this nation relies". The second person form of address (*you*) occurs both in Clinton and Obama's Inaugurals. Clinton uses "you my fellow Americans" constructing the whole American people as his addressee, even if actually the action associated to *you* was not accomplished by all the Americans, but just by those who voted for him (*"you, my fellow Americans have forced the spring"*). This ambiguity allows him to address his call to action to all Americans, as shown by the second part of that statement, where he has recourse to *we* ("Now, *we must do the work* the season demands"). Later on in the speech, the counterpart to *you* is *I/me*, referred to the president, and then, interestingly, third-person reference is used for the Congress:

19. To that work *I* now turn, with all the authority of *my* office. *I* ask the Congress to join with *me*. But no president, no Congress, no government, can undertake this mission alone. *My fellow Americans, you, too, must play your part in our renewal.* I challenge a new generation of young Americans to a season of service; to act on *your* idealism by helping troubled children, keeping company with those in need, reconnecting our torn communities (Clinton).

In this way Clinton implies that each party, in its own role, should work to make the renewal of America possible. At the same time, though, as an effect of the reference choices, the presidents' role of leadership and authority is emphasized, the *people* is constructed as the president's privileged interlocutor (*you*) and the Congress is set apart from the communion between himself and the people (technically, *we* is the sum of *I* and *you*). The Congress is thus subtly excluded them from the ratified participants proper, in line with the diffidence towards the 'ways of Washington' mentioned earlier.

5.4   Move 4. Final Exhortation and Historic Quotation

The final slot in any textual unit – be it a sentence, a paragraph or a whole speech – is per se a privileged position, as coming last confers prominence to its content. This is all the more so in speeches with a strong persuasive component, and it is not a coincidence that towards the end of the speech the president's tone goes back to the solemnity of the opening lines with its appeal to the founding values, in a sort of circular structure. In several cases, solemnity is achieved quoting the words of some source of authority, like the Founding Fathers or the Bible. In this way, the gist of the president's speech is conveyed in a nutshell, while bestowing on it the authoritativeness of an entity whose status is beyond political divisions and beyond discussion. At the same time, it allows the president to construct his ethos in the light of that of the predecessor he quotes, further contributing to the construction of the plural presidency, as far as the use of an institutional voice is concerned. The selection of the authoritative person to quote from, however, leaves room to each new president to characterize his profile and his presidency, also in opposition to his predecessor, while remaining within the boundaries of tradition and of the genre.

Kennedy and Clinton quote from the Bible, both verbatim ("rejoicing in hope, patient in tribulation" – Romans 12:12, Kennedy; *The scripture say,* Clinton) and drawing tropes from it, namely the mountain top, and the valley; the trumpets calling to service, the vigilant guard:

20. Now *the trumpet summons us* again—not as a call to bear arms, though arms we need—not as a call to battle, though embattled we are—but a call to bear the burden of a long twilight struggle, year in and year out, *"rejoicing in hope, patient in tribulation"*—a struggle against the common enemies of man: tyranny, poverty, disease and war itself (Kennedy).

21. And so, my fellow Americans, at the edge of the twenty-first century, let us begin with energy and hope, with faith and discipline, and let us work until our work is done. *The scripture says,* "And let us not be weary in well-doing, for *in due season,* we shall reap, if we faint not" (Clinton).

From this joyful *mountaintop* of celebration, we hear *a call to service in the valley.* We have heard the *trumpets.* We have *changed the guard.* And now, each in our way, and with God's help, we must *answer the call* (Clinton).

The latter quotations are meant to give force to Clinton's call to action, while providing a hook to the extended metaphor of seasons ("in due season we shall reap") that pervades his Inaugural.

GW Bush quotes a message sent to Jefferson, mentioning also the Declaration of Independence, as the ultimate source of authority, and thus closing with a recall of the very purpose of the Inauguration, i.e. the renewal of the American promise contained in the Declaration:

22. After the Declaration of Independence was signed, Virginia statesman John Page wrote to Thomas Jefferson, "We know the race is not to the swift nor the battle to the strong. Do you not think an angel rides in the whirlwind and directs this storm?" Much time has passed since Jefferson arrived for his inauguration. The years and changes accumulate, but the themes of this day he would know, "our nation's grand story of courage and its simple dream of dignity" (GW Bush).

Through this quotation, Bush contributes to an anti-heroic representation of America's force, which lies in idealism, and not in perfection ("flawed and fallible people, united across the generations by grand and enduring ideals").

Obama quotes the words of "the father of our nation" without naming him, and so implying that the common background between him and his audience will allow the receiver to decode the message correctly, thus emphasizing a solidarity bond with the audience.

23. So let us mark this day with remembrance, of who we are and how far we have traveled. In the year of America's birth, in the coldest of months, a small band of patriots huddled by dying campfires on the shores of an icy river. The capital was abandoned. The enemy was advancing. The snow was stained with blood. At a moment when the outcome of our revolution was most in doubt, *the father of our nation* ordered these words be read to the people:

> Let it be told to the future world that in the depth of winter, when nothing but hope and virtue could survive that the city and the country, alarmed at one common danger, came forth to meet it.

> America. In the face of our common dangers, in this winter of our hardship, let us remember these timeless words... (Obama).

The words Obama quotes were written by the pamphleteer Thomas Paine in the first one of a series of essays known as *The Crisis*, which started to appear at the end of 1776, to exhort the revolutionary troops commanded by George Washington, the father of the nation, not to give up, at a time when the chances of defeating the British Army, and actually of survival, had become minimal. Such a closing amplifies the anchorage to the constitutive principle of America advocated throughout his speech. The threat to the very existence of the US project contained in Obama's final quotation can be read as a reference to the threat posed by the attack to the Twin Towers, but also to a greater risk coming from within. Such risk comes from a perception insinuating in the American spirit after 2001 that the values of the United States (i.e. freedom, the rights of men, the rule of law) are what makes the country vulnerable to the attacks of those who defy the way of life inspired by those very values.

Occasionally the president decides not to borrow words from the Founding Fathers, but for some other source of authority. Nixon, for example closed his IA with a quote from a poet celebrating the landing of the man on the Moon.

24. As the Apollo astronauts flew over the moon's gray surface on Christmas Eve, they spoke to us of the beauty of earth--and in that voice so clear across the lunar distance, we heard them invoke God's blessing on its goodness.

    In that moment, their view from the moon moved poet Archibald MacLeish to write:

> To see the earth as it truly is, small and blue and beautiful in that eternal silence where it floats, is to see ourselves as riders on the earth together, brothers on that bright loveliness in the eternal cold--brothers who know now they are truly brothers (Nixon)-

Reagan quotes an unknown soldier from WW1, buried in the Arlington Cemetery:

25. Under one such marker lies a *young man*--Martin Treptow--who left his job in a small town barber shop in 1917 to go to France with the famed Rainbow Division. There, on the western front, he was killed trying to carry a message between battalions under heavy artillery fire.

    We are told that on his body was found a diary. On the flyleaf under the heading, "My Pledge," he had written these words: "America must win this war. Therefore, I will work, I will save, I will sacrifice, I will endure, I will fight cheerfully and do my utmost, as if the issue of the whole struggle depended on me alone" (Reagan).

The spirit of sacrifice of that soldier is used by Reagan as an exemplum for contemporary Americans, who are called to solve, with Gods help (invoking God' help being another fixed step at the end of the Inaugurals) the problems that America faced at the time. The choice of quoting this *young man* is consistent with the motif of the layman hero that Reagan celebrated earlier in his speech, and that ties up with the populist challenge of the elite and experts discussed above:

26. We have every right to dream heroic dreams. Those who say that we are in a time when there are no heroes just don't know where to look. You can see heroes every day going in and out of factory gates. Others, a handful in number, produce enough food to feed all of us and then the world beyond. You meet heroes across a counter--and they are on both sides of that counter. There are entrepreneurs with faith in themselves and faith in an idea who create new jobs, new wealth and opportunity. . .(Reagan).

Interestingly enough, Reagan makes a meta-linguistic remark on his verbal construction of the hero, stating: "I have used the words 'they' and 'their' in speaking of these heroes. I could say 'you' and 'your' because I am addressing the heroes of whom I speak--you, the citizens of this blessed land".

Finally, Eisenhower does not end the speech with a quotation, but nonetheless the tone becomes highly poetical in the closing lines, thus underlining the solemnity of the passage.

27. For this truth must be clear before us: whatever America hopes to bring to pass in the world must first come to pass in the heart of America.

    The peace we seek, then, is nothing less than the practice and fulfillment of our whole faith among ourselves and in our dealings with others. This signifies more than the stilling of guns, casing the sorrow of war. More than escape from death, it is a way of life. More than a haven for the weary, it is a hope for the brave (Eisenhower).

The four moves discussed so-far are common to all the speeches analyzed, deriving directly from the institutional function of the IA of restoring ideological unity after the strife of the electoral campaign, while at the same time announcing the priorities of the new Administration and calling others to action. It is therefore reasonable to expect that beyond differences in content and style they feature common patterns of argumentation, which will be the topic of the next section.

5.5   Argumentative Schemes in the IA: Value-Based Reasoning and Endoxa

As stated in Chap. 2, the potential for agreement construction lies mostly in establishing starting points that are then exploited argumentatively. The selection of starting points is therefore crucial to win the receiver's acceptance of a standpoint, and quite obviously the most effective starting points are those that are shared a-priori by the speaker and the audience. They include values and beliefs but also factual knowledge of the world (material starting points), as well as recurrent patterns of reasoning that are commonly used in a given field of human activity (procedural starting points), thus becoming crystallized into schemes or topoi, which are used mostly unawarely by the members of a community. It is within schemes that material starting points, whether preliminary established or not, are put to use, thus trying to capitalize on the agreement they enjoy, to elicit the transfer of acceptability from the premises to the conclusion. Since real-life argumentation is often enthymematic, starting points are not necessarily mentioned explicitly, but may be simply entailed, which makes it easier for a speaker to present them as tacitly agreed, even if this is not the case (van Eemeren et al. 2007, cf. § 2.2).

Attention is now turned to the use of argumentative schemes in the IA, reconstructing them according to the Argumentum Model of Topoi (Rigotti & Greco Morasso, 2010), which places special emphasis on the implicit premises of argumentation. Prior to that a reconstruction is made of the argumentation that prototypically underlies the Inaugural Address as a genre, following the pragma-dialectical conventions, which differently from the AMT model allows for a general view of the argumentation (cf. Degano, 2021 for a comparison of the two models). The archetypical reasoning underlying the argumentation in the Inaugural Address can be reconstructed as follows:

1 Let's set aside divisions
1.1a We have a common goal *and*
1.1b Only working together can we achieve this goal
1.1a.1 our goal is based on our common values
1.1a.1' (our common values are more important than our divisions)

Put more discursively, the orator asks the people to be accepted as the new president of all Americans placing commonalities before differences (standpoint). The defense of such standpoint has a coordinative structure. The first argument defending the exhortation to set divisions apart is that now there is a goal to achieve (the goal varies depending on the historical and political contingency), which can be accepted as a common goal by all citizens, whatever their vote was (1.1a). The other argument that jointly with the former defends the standpoint is that only if everybody contributes to it, can the goal be achieved (1.1b). The claim that the goal ahead is common to all (1.1a) is in turn defended on the ground that it derives from the founding values of the United States (1.1a.1), which are implicitly taken as an undiscussed object of agreement. The inference that justifies the passage from the common values claim to the common goal claim, and eventually the acceptance of the standpoint, is that the founding values of America, which are cast as common to all citizens, are more important than differences (1.1a.1′).

This argumentation seems to find a formal counterpart in the argument from value-based practical reasoning, which, following Walton et al.'s compendium of schemes (Walton et al., 2008, p. 324), is as follows:

Premise 1: I have a goal G
Premise 2: G is supported by set of values V
Premise 3: Bringing about A is necessary (or sufficient) for me to bring about G
Conclusion: Therefore, I should (practically ought to) bring about A

The AMT representation of the scheme that underlies the argumentation in Inaugural Addresses can then be represented as follows.

As discussed with reference to the moves, the problem that must be tackled changes from one president to another, mostly as a result of the historical context, and of the president's political allegiance.

For Eisenhower the problem is the risk coming from the Soviet Union and the Cold War. In this sense his speech sounds like a call to war, a war which was not, as yet, a waged war, but a prospective one. The excerpt below contains the explicitation of the problem:

28. This fact defines the meaning of this day... We are called as a people to give testimony in the sight of the world to our faith that the future shall belong to the free.

    The enemies of this faith know no god but force, no devotion but its use. They tutor men in treason. They feed upon the hunger of others. Whatever defies them, they torture, especially the truth.

    Here, then, is joined no argument between slightly differing philosophies. This conflict strikes directly at the faith of our fathers and the lives of our sons. No principle or treasure that we hold, from the spiritual knowledge of our free schools and churches to the creative magic of free labor and capital, nothing lies safely beyond the reach of this struggle.

    Freedom is pitted against slavery; lightness against the dark.

    [...]

    We must be ready to dare all for our country... We must be willing, individually and as a Nation, to accept whatever sacrifices may be required of us. A people that values its privileges above its principles soon loses both (Eisenhower).

Stripping it of its discursive form, the reasoning rests on the value-based practical reasoning outlined in Fig. 5.1. Filling in the relevant content in the AMT slots for the material premises and the conclusion deriving from them, the scheme can be reconstructed as follows (Fig. 5.2):

Here, the action called for in the maxim (A) translates into urging American people to be ready to sacrifice their privilege (the comfortable way of life warranted by freedom and peace), should the fight against communism require that. The material premises supporting this request are that freedom is at risk because of

Material starting point   Procedural starting point

ENDOXON   LOCUS:
The American principles entail...   Value-based practical reasoning

DATUM   MAXIM
Problem X is contrary to   If bringing about A (tackling
/threatens/ betrays the   PROBLEM) is necessary for me
American promise   to bring about goal G [and G is
                                                   supported by founding
                                                   principle], then I should bring
                                                   about A

         FIRST CONCLUSION   MINOR PREMISE

              tackling PROBLEMS is necessary
              for us to live out American principles

                        CONCLUSION

                      We must tackle
                      PROBLEMS

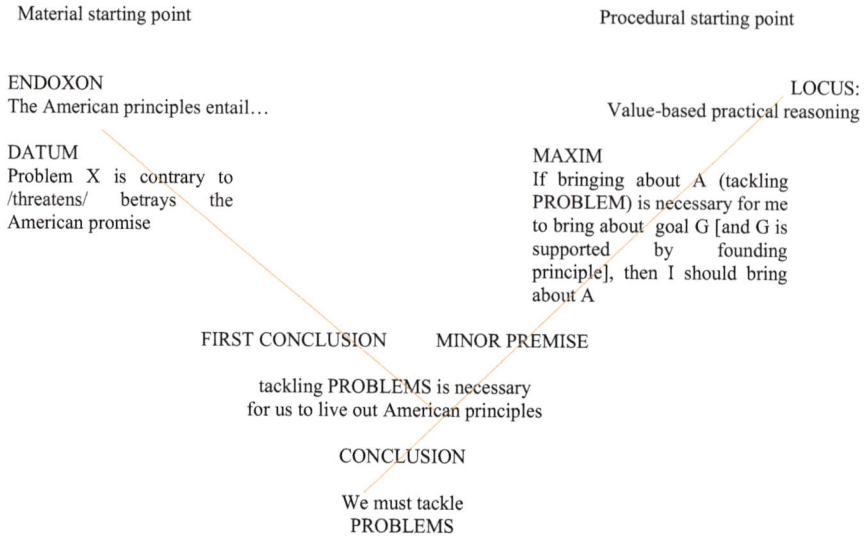

Fig. 5.1 Prototypical scheme underlying the IA

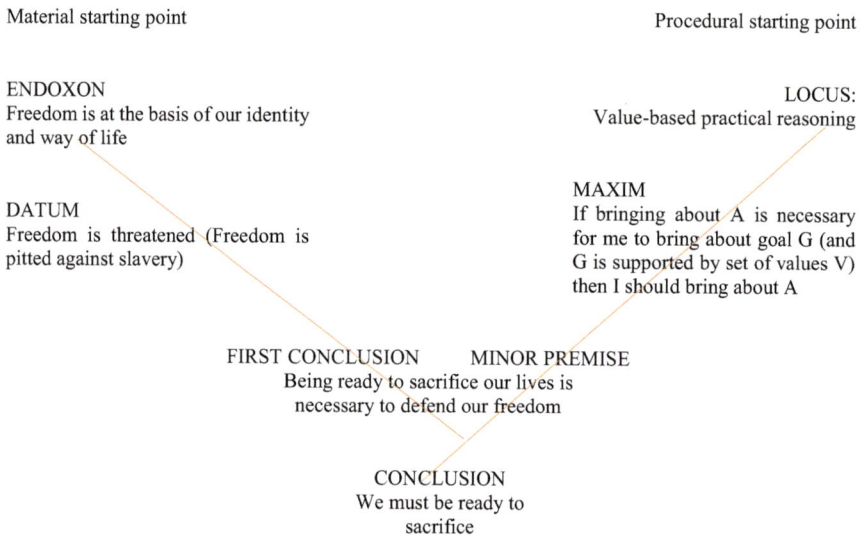

Material starting point   Procedural starting point

ENDOXON   LOCUS:
Freedom is at the basis of our identity   Value-based practical reasoning
and way of life

                                                   MAXIM
DATUM   If bringing about A is necessary
Freedom is threatened (Freedom is   for me to bring about goal G (and
pitted against slavery)   G is supported by set of values V)
                                                   then I should bring about A

         FIRST CONCLUSION   MINOR PREMISE
              Being ready to sacrifice our lives is
              necessary to defend our freedom

                        CONCLUSION
                      We must be ready to
                      sacrifice

Fig. 5.2 Eisenhower

communism and the Cold War (datum) and that the whole American way of living, highly valued by all citizens, depends on freedom. Interestingly enough, Eisenhower's call to arms enacts a partial reframing of the struggle against communism as a fight for freedom against slavery, leveraging on the emotionally loaded connotation of the concept of slavery in general, and all the more so in American history. Slavery therefore is used as a catalyst of agreement, which would resonate powerfully with all the people who abhor slavery, without need of precisely mapping out the analogies between the two constructs.

Kennedy.

Having established the preliminary starting point that neither group of nations can in the long run benefit from the shaky and fearful balance achieved through arms race, Kennedy exhorts his counterpart (the Soviet Union) to take together with the US a number of actions, all meant to a de-escalation:

> 29. So let us begin anew--remembering on both sides that civility is not a sign of weakness, and sincerity is always subject to proof. Let us never negotiate out of fear. But let us never fear to negotiate.
>
> [...]
>
> *Let both sides, for the first time, formulate serious and precise proposals for the inspection and control of arms--and bring the absolute power to destroy other nations under the absolute control of all nations.*
>
> Let both sides seek to invoke the wonders of science instead of its terrors. Together let us explore the stars, conquer the deserts, eradicate disease, tap the ocean depths and encourage the arts and commerce.
>
> Let both sides unite to heed in all corners of the earth the command of Isaiah--to "undo the heavy burdens . . . (and) let the oppressed go free."
>
> And if a beachhead of cooperation may push back the jungle of suspicion, let both sides join in creating a new endeavor, not a new balance of power, but a new world of law, where the strong are just and the weak secure and the peace preserved.

The main practical action invited by Kennedy is bringing arms race under control, so that the worst scenario of mankind's self-destruction, be it planned or accidental, can be warded off. A reconstruction of this argument is given below (Fig. 5.3):

Per se, this form of practical reasoning is not particularly value-based, except of course for the moral imperative of preserving mankind from destruction. However, in the list of actions introduced by the exhortative "let us", there are actions that are more specifically value-based: the progress of science and knowledge, the eradication of diseases, freeing the oppressed. More generally, then, the call for both parties to begin 'a new quest for peace', which deescalates the risk of total destruction posed by the arms race, is seen as a prerequisite to achieve the goal of fighting the plagues that still afflict mankind across national borders, i.e. "the common enemies of man", mentioned above (Sect. 5.4),

Nixon's first Inaugural Address opens on a lighter note, with a celebration of the time in which it takes place as a "moment of beginning, in which courses are set that shape decades or centuries." Even though both the Cold War and the Vietnam War were still going on, Nixon sees peace as within reach ("For the first time, because the people of the world want peace, and the leaders of the world are afraid of war, the times are on the side of peace"). Material problems do not seem to afflict America, or at least technological breakthroughs promise solutions to them ("Forces now are converging that make possible, for the first time, the hope that many of man's deepest aspirations can at last be realized. The spiraling pace of change allows us to contemplate, within our own lifetime, advances that once would have taken

LOCUS:
Practical reasoning

ENDOXON
The absolute power to destroy other
nations can only be restrained by
absolute control of all nations

MAXIM
If bringing about A is necessary
for me to bring about goal G, then
I should bring about A

DATUM
Arms race as is, i.e. without control,
can bring mankind to destruction

FIRST CONCLUSION   MINOR PREMISE

Formulating serious proposals for the control and inspection of arms is necessary to preempt the risk of
total destruction

CONCLUSION
We must formulate
serious proposals for the
control and inspection of
arms

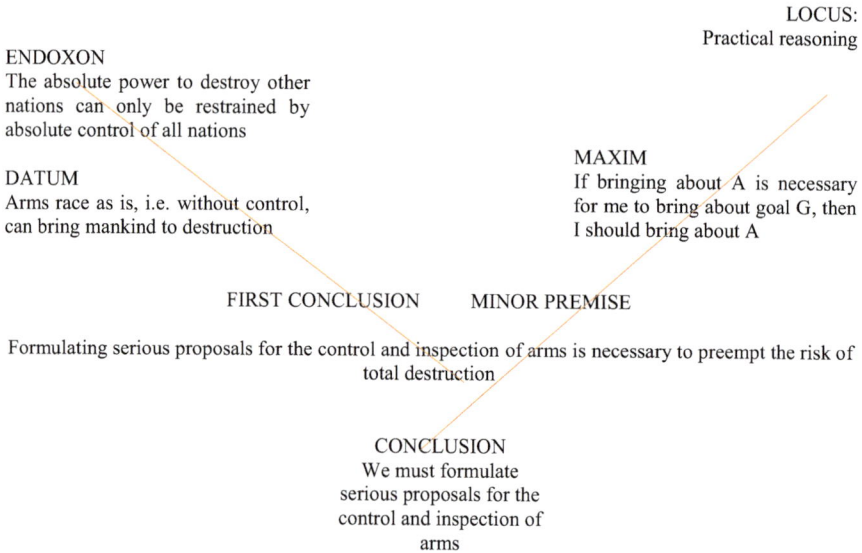

Fig. 5.3 Kennedy

centuries"). The problem, in his view, lies outside material things, as it affects the
spirit, and is embodied in war (per se quite a material thing!), division, futility of life,
and lack of action:

30. We have found ourselves rich in goods, but ragged in spirit; reaching with
    magnificent precision for the moon, but falling into raucous discord on earth.
       We are caught in war, wanting peace. We are torn by division, wanting
    unity. We see around us empty lives, wanting fulfillment. We see tasks that
    need doing, waiting for hands to do them.
       To a crisis of the spirit, we need an answer of the spirit.
       To find that answer, we need only look within ourselves.
       When we listen to "the better angels of our nature," we find that they
    celebrate the simple things, the basic things--such as goodness, decency,
    love, kindness (Nixon).

The 'action' advocated for is listening to "the better angels of our nature", as a
solution to the current crisis of the spirit. In spite of the immateriality of the action
called for, the value-based practical scheme still applies, as shown below (Fig. 5.4):

The quotation "the better angels of our nature" is taken from Lincoln's Inaugural
Address, where the metaphor referred to the praiseworthy qualities in human
temperament. In Lincoln's words, uttered on the eve of the Civil War, those qualities
were meant as an antidote to the bitter division between North and South. They were
themselves a quotation, plausibly from Shakespeare's Othello, where they refer to
the effect that the death of Desdemona by Othello's hand might have had on her
father, had he been still alive. The news might have led him to "curse his better angel
from his side, And fall to reprobation" (Othello V, ii, 206.). The lack of attribution of

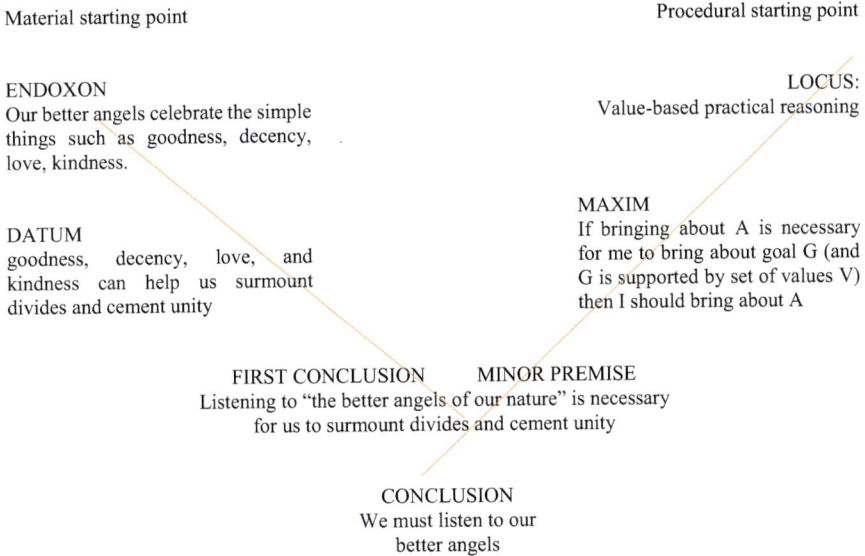

Material starting point   Procedural starting point

ENDOXON   LOCUS:
Our better angels celebrate the simple   Value-based practical reasoning
things such as goodness, decency,
love, kindness.

                                                                   MAXIM
DATUM   If bringing about A is necessary
goodness,   decency,   love,   and   for me to bring about goal G (and
kindness can help us surmount   G is supported by set of values V)
divides and cement unity   then I should bring about A

              FIRST CONCLUSION   MINOR PREMISE
              Listening to "the better angels of our nature" is necessary
              for us to surmount divides and cement unity

                            CONCLUSION
                          We must listen to our
                            better angels

Fig. 5.4 Nixon

the quote testifies to its being common ground to the orator and the audience, which justifies the use of the set of values it refers to (goodness, decency, love and kindness) as an endoxon. The fact that the quotation is common ground and that the values it refers to are positively connoted invites a perception of Nixon's point as the natural consequence of shared premises. The receiver would have a hard time in trying to deny that goodness, decency, kindness, and love are an antidote to division, but might still challenge the choice of such intimate qualities (as opposed to more socially-oriented values) as the foundation of a political vision. Of course one can always challenge a starting point that is entailed as endoxical, but disentangling from it would require an extent of critical testing by the receiver, who is otherwise 'co-opted' to accept the speaker's entailments.

For Reagan, the problem was inflation and a stagnant economy, which in his plans for the new Administration could only be revitalized by cutting taxes and reducing the power of the Federal Government, so as to unleash private initiative. The scheme below only concerns the first part of Reagan's reasoning, i.e. the identification of inflation as the problem, which entails that its end is desirable. How to obtain that result is another argument, which will not be considered here.

31. Well, this administration's objective will be a healthy, vigorous, growing *economy that* provides *equal opportunity* for all Americans, with no barriers born of bigotry or discrimination. … Ending inflation *means* freeing all Americans from the terror of runaway living costs. All *must* share in the productive work of this "new beginning" and all *must* share in the bounty of a revived economy (Reagan).

Translating this argument in AMT terms, the reasoning goes as follows (Fig. 5.5):

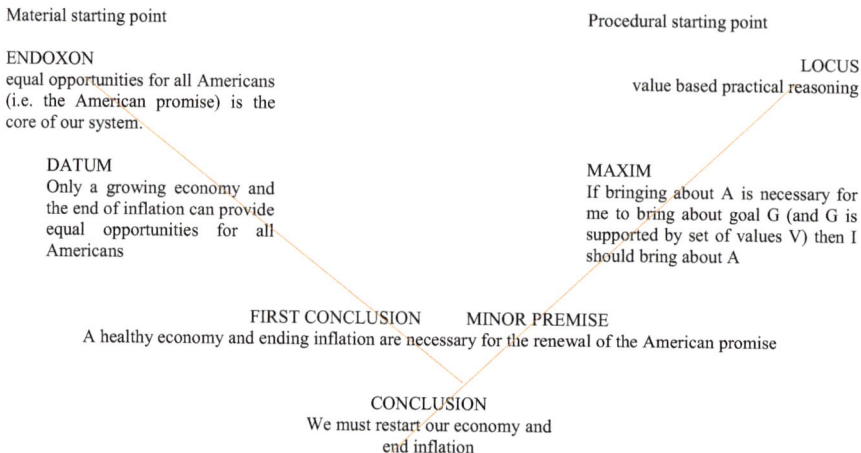

Material starting point   Procedural starting point

ENDOXON   LOCUS
equal opportunities for all Americans   value based practical reasoning
(i.e. the American promise) is the
core of our system.

    DATUM   MAXIM
    Only a growing economy and   If bringing about A is necessary for
    the end of inflation can provide   me to bring about goal G (and G is
    equal opportunities for all   supported by set of values V) then I
    Americans   should bring about A

              FIRST CONCLUSION   MINOR PREMISE
    A healthy economy and ending inflation are necessary for the renewal of the American promise

                        CONCLUSION
                  We must restart our economy and
                        end inflation

Fig. 5.5   Reagan

The necessity of restarting economy is here defended establishing a direct cause-effect relation between economic growth and the possibility of realizing the American promise. This nexus is presented as self-evident, and as such highly acceptable to the audience, even though it is far from factual, as a growing economy does not per se warrant an equitable redistribution of the wealth that would come from such a "new beginning". However the level of certainty attributed to the causal relation is very high, as a resultant of different discursive choices related to the area of modality: first and foremost the defining relative clause that post-modifies *economy* ("a growing economy *that* provides equal opportunity for all Americans"), jointly with the absence of modalization, which, expresses the highest commitment (see §3.3 above). The verb *means* (still without modalization) links the cause (*a growing economy*) and the effect ("freeing all Americans from the terror of runaway living costs"), and the high-value modal of obligation *must* is repeated in the pattern *all must share* ("All must share in the productive work of this "new beginning" and all must share in the bounty of a revived economy"). The epistemic certainty attached to the procedural reasoning is coupled with an extent of semantic indefiniteness on the plane of the material premises, as the concept of *equal opportunities* used as endoxon is per se quite ambiguous. As Zarefsky points out, the notion has gone through a process of semantic change, started in the late 1960s, from the initial meaning of the absence of barriers to social mobility imposed on the individual at birth (cf. slavery) to a new meaning which entails an active role of the government to be attained (Zarefsky, 2014, p. 323). Using the expression as endoxon, Reagan can cast it as having just one referential meaning which is immediately understood by the receiver, thus exploiting its inherent ambiguity to try and establish it as an object of agreement both for liberalist-oriented receivers, who object to state intervention in society and the economy, and for more progressive-minded audiences, who believe in the role of state to reduce socio-economic disparity imposed at birth.

Clinton's first Inaugural Address pivoted around the contraposition of old and new, which is rendered mostly through the metaphor of winter and spring discussed above, but also by the repetition or the prefix *re-* (e.g. *reborn*), of the modal *will* and of the adjective *new*. His Inaugural was uttered at the time of epochal changes, first and foremost the end of the Cold War (it is the first Inaugural Address after the fall of the Berlin Wall), but also the beginning of globalization, and great technological advances. Clinton celebrates such change, but at the same time warns his "fellow citizens" that resisting change or failing to keep pace with it would have serious consequences. Hence the need to make "change our friend, not our enemy". In particular, Clinton's worries concern the economy and its fallout on the life of American workers, and consequently on social cohesion, but also medical care – a Democratic flagship – and security, as expressed in the following lines:

32. Raised in unrivaled prosperity, we inherit an economy that is still the world's strongest, but is weakened by business failures, stagnant wages, increasing inequality, and deep divisions among our people.

    [...] when most people are working harder for less; when others cannot work at all; when the cost of health care devastates families and threatens to bankrupt many of our enterprises, great and small; when fear of crime robs law-abiding citizens of their freedom; and when millions of poor children cannot even imagine the lives we are calling them to lead, we have not made change our friend (Clinton).

The argument can be reconstructed according to the AMT conventions as follows (Fig. 5.6):

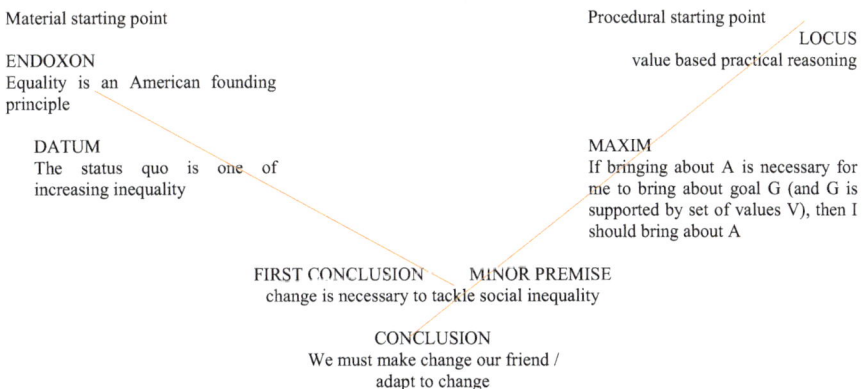

Material starting point		Procedural starting point
		LOCUS
ENDOXON		value based practical reasoning
Equality is an American founding principle		
DATUM		MAXIM
The status quo is one of increasing inequality		If bringing about A is necessary for me to bring about goal G (and G is supported by set of values V), then I should bring about A
	FIRST CONCLUSION MINOR PREMISE	
	change is necessary to tackle social inequality	
	CONCLUSION	
	We must make change our friend / adapt to change	

Fig. 5.6 Clinton

In line with the spirit of the Inaugural as a genre, the proposition that inequality is increasing is treated as self-evident (the datum), either because it was actually under everybody's eyes, or because its acceptability had already been prepared during the campaign. Differently from Reagan's case, where the datum expresses a general rule (the fulfilment of the American promise depends on a strong economy), here the datum describes a state of things (growing inequality) as factual. The use of figurative language in the expression "make change our friend" is at a time evocative and vague enough to allow Clinton to exploit the positive connotation of the word *friend* without feeding any political content into this statement, thus maximizing its potential appeal to establish agreement with the audience.

With G.W. Bush the variation on the tune is minimal. In touch with the doctrine of compassionate conservatism, he places emphasis on the fallibility of the American people, whose greatness lies in the ideals that lead them through history, but when it comes to problem spotting and the attendant proposal of solution, the reasoning is not so different from Clinton's:

33. We have a place, all of us, in a long story. . . . It is the American story. A story of flawed and fallible people, united across the generations by grand and enduring ideals. The grandest of these ideals is an unfolding American promise that everyone belongs, that everyone deserves a chance, that no insignificant person was ever born. Americans are called upon to enact this promise in our lives and in our laws.

    While many of our citizens prosper, others doubt the promise, even the justice, of our own country. The ambitions of some Americans are limited by failing schools and hidden prejudice and the circumstances of their birth; and sometimes our differences run so deep, it seems we share a continent, but not a country. We do not accept this, and we will not allow it. Our unity, our union, is the serious work of leaders and citizens in every generation; and this is my solemn pledge, "I will work to build a single nation of justice and opportunity" (GW Bush).

Where Clinton selected equality as a founding principle, GW Bush mentions the American promise as the founding value on which the practical reasoning rests. Obstacles to meeting the promise are inequalities ("sometimes our differences run so deep, it seems we share a continent but not a country"; "While many of our citizens prosper, others doubt the promise, even the justice, of our own country"), especially in terms of opportunity. The education system and latent prejudice are blamed as a limiting factor for self-realization, which – as was the case for Reagan – is seen as the means to reach prosperity. Plotting this reasoning in the AMT matrix, the argument unfolds as illustrated in Fig. 5.7.

So far, the analysis of the most argumentative part of the Inaugural Addresses has shown a considerable consistency among presidents in procedural terms, as shown by the recourse to the same argument scheme, and some variation in the selection of material component. The founding value which lends force and authority to the acceptability claim is mostly chosen among the American principles enshrined in the

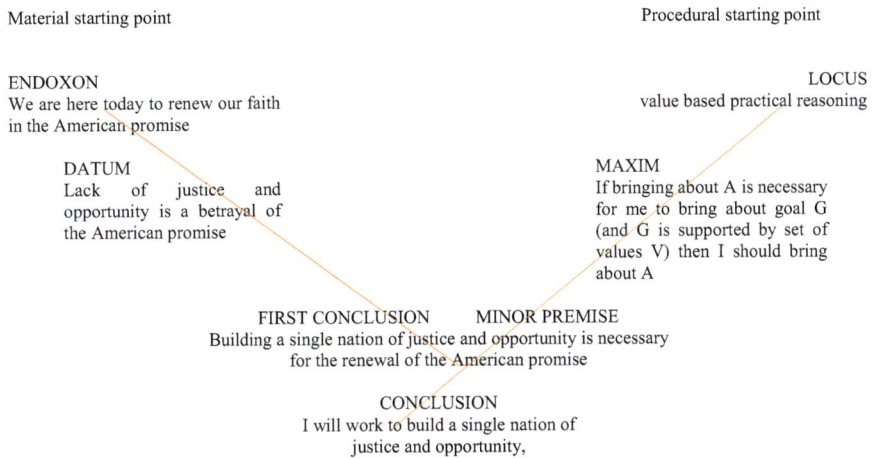

Material starting point   Procedural starting point

ENDOXON   LOCUS
We are here today to renew our faith   value based practical reasoning
in the American promise

            DATUM   MAXIM
            Lack   of   justice   and   If bringing about A is necessary
            opportunity is a betrayal of   for me to bring about goal G
            the American promise   (and G is supported by set of
                                                    values V) then I should bring
                                                    about A

                FIRST CONCLUSION   MINOR PREMISE
              Building a single nation of justice and opportunity is necessary
                        for the renewal of the American promise

                            CONCLUSION
                    I will work to build a single nation of
                         justice and opportunity,

Fig. 5.7 G.W. Bush

Constitution, the choice fell on freedom for Eisenhower, on equality for Reagan and Clinton, and on the more broadly scoped American promise for Bush.

Obama's Inaugural address is equally imbued with American principles, but the scheme used to defend his advocated course of action is the practical argument based on analogy (Walton et al., 2008, p. 316), which goes as follows:

Base premise: The right thing to do in S_1 was to carry out action x
Similarity premise: S_2 is similar to S_1
Conclusion: Therefore, the right thing to do in S_2 is to carry out action x.

While all the presidents discussed so far take for granted that the American core values and ideals are objects of agreement, Obama argues for the necessity of remaining faithful to their ideals. Faithfulness to the ideals in not used as an endoxon, i.e. an unchallenged common starting point, but is made per se the object of argumentation, calling for a respect of those ideals as a way to get out of the crisis that America was undergoing at the time, as a long wave of the 2001 terrorist attacks:

34. At these moments, America has carried on not simply because of the skill or vision of those in high office, but because We the People have remained faithful to the ideals of our forbearers, and true to our founding documents. *So it has been. So it must be with this generation of Americans* (Obama).

Referring to previous crises in American history, Obama affirms that they were overcome precisely because his predecessors chose to abide by their founding principles, and did not think that they were not suitable for times of crises. The argument goes as follows (Fig. 5.8):

The analogy with history and with the forebears can be seen as a variation on the tune of the value-based pragmatic arguments, where the authority of the mythical figures of the Founding Fathers added force to the authority normally given by the

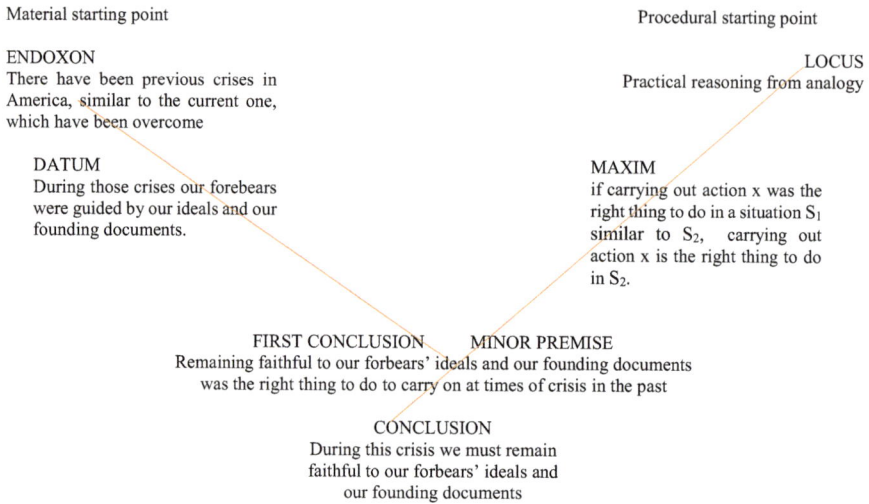

Material starting point   Procedural starting point

ENDOXON   LOCUS
There have been previous crises in   Practical reasoning from analogy
America, similar to the current one,
which have been overcome

    DATUM   MAXIM
    During those crises our forebears   if carrying out action x was the
    were guided by our ideals and our   right thing to do in a situation S_1
    founding documents.   similar to S_2,   carrying out
                                                        action x is the right thing to do
                                                        in S_2.

            FIRST CONCLUSION   MINOR PREMISE
        Remaining faithful to our forbears' ideals and our founding documents
            was the right thing to do to carry on at times of crisis in the past

                    CONCLUSION
                During this crisis we must remain
                faithful to our forbears' ideals and
                    our founding documents

Fig. 5.8 Obama

founding values. Particularly significant is the repetition of the same scheme later on
in the Address, in the part dealing with defense, which is the most directly connected
with the theme of the deviation from the founding values, especially as far as the
violation of human rights in Guantanamo was concerned:

35. As for our common defense, we reject as false the choice between our safety
    and our ideals. Our Founding Fathers faced with perils we can scarcely
    imagine, drafted a charter to assure the rule of law and the rights of man, a
    charter expanded by the blood of generations. Those ideals still light the world,
    and we will not give them up for expedience's sake (Obama).

The fact that Obama defended the need to stick to American founding ideals
suggests counter-factuality, i.e. that the previous administration failed to uphold
them. Focusing on established rules (what it should be) as opposed to what has not
been allows Obama to avoid a fiercely adversarial style, in line with his commitment
to "disagree without being disagreeable" (see Sect. 4.2.3.1).

Only Kennedy's speech, among the ones analyzed here, appealed to a value cast
as universal, i.e. the moral imperative of assuring a "more fruitful life to all
mankind", in touch with his request to the nations "who would make themselves"
the enemies of America to join in a "new quest for peace, before the dark powers of
destruction unleashed by science engulf all humanity in planned or accidental self-
destruction".

5.5.1 Signaling Agreement in the Schemes

As shown above, the founding values are the main source of agreement in the Inaugurals, and as such they are generally taken for granted. In most cases they are just mentioned presupposing their existence and general acceptance. In some cases, though, they are spelt out beforehand, making them explicit starting points, so as to be able to rely on them argumentatively immediately afterwards or later on in the speech. Sometimes the status of starting point is marked by the use of verbs of cognition in a projecting clause, which is followed by a formulation of the principle, as is the case in this example taken from an IA that actually falls outside the time range of this analysis, but is particularly eloquent in this respect: "*Remember, remember* always, *that* all of us, and you and I especially, are descended from immigrants and revolutionists" (Truman 1 march 1947). Obama stated: "In reaffirming the greatness of our nation we *understand that* greatness is never a given. It must be earned". Reagan, explicitly recalled the founding values and principles on which his decisions as president descend, by saying:

36. So, as we begin, let us take inventory. We are a nation that has a government--not the other way around. And this makes us special among the nations of the Earth. Our Government has no power except that granted it by the people. It is time to check and reverse the growth of government which shows signs of having grown beyond the consent of the governed (Reagan).

The choice of presenting political choices as directly descending from the values that inspire them reached a peak in Eisenhower's speech. Faced with the possibility of a devastating war against the Soviet Union, his presentational choices suggest his intention to justify war within the ethical limits of American ideals. He thus spelt out seven 'rules of conduct' concerning war and other aspects of foreign policy:

37. In pleading our just cause before the bar of history and in pressing our labor for world peace, we shall be guided by certain fixed principles. These principles are:

    (a) *Abhorring* war as a chosen way to balk the purposes of those who threaten us, *we hold* it to be the first task of statesmanship to develop the strength that will deter the forces of aggression and promote the conditions of peace.
        . . .
    (b) *Realizing* that common sense and common decency alike dictate the futility of appeasement, *we shall* never try to placate an aggressor by the false and wicked bargain of trading honor for security. . .
    (c) *Knowing* that only a United States that is strong and immensely productive can help defend freedom in our world, *we view* our Nation's strength and security as a trust upon which rests the hope of free men everywhere. . .
    (d) *Honoring* the identity and the special heritage of each nation in the world, *we shall* never use our strength to try to impress upon another people our own cherished political and economic institutions.

(e) *Assessing* realistically the needs and capacities of proven friends of free-dom, *we shall* strive to help them to achieve their own security and well-being. . . .

(f) *Recognizing* economic health as an indispensable basis of military strength and the free world's peace, *we shall* strive to foster everywhere, and to practice ourselves, policies that encourage productivity and profitable trade. ...

(g) *Appreciating* that economic need, military security and political wisdom combine to suggest regional groupings of free peoples, *we hope*, within the framework of the United Nations, to help strengthen such special bonds the world over. . .

By these rules of conduct, we hope to be known to all peoples.

By their observance, an earth of peace may become not a vision but a fact.

This hope--this supreme aspiration--*must rule* the way we live.

We must be ready to dare all for our country. . . .

We must be willing, individually and as a Nation, to accept whatever sacrifices may be required of us. A people that values its privileges above its principles soon loses both.

The pattern repeated throughout this 'code of conduct' is present participle [secondary clause] + *we shall* + material verb / we + verb of cognition (*hold, hope*). The present participle in the secondary clause, preceding the main clause, discursively constructs the propositional content as a timeless truth, shared by the audience, from which facts, be they material or cognitive processes, are derived. Agreement on the rules is thus constructed as acceptable to the audience, and on this ground the final set of deontic standpoints ("This hope must rule the way we live. We must be ready to dare all for our country. . . .We must be willing. . .") is legitimated.

5.6   Conclusion

The chapter has focused on the Inaugural Address from the dual perspective of linguistic-based Genre Analysis and of argumentation schemes. The first part ana-lyzed the main moves and steps forming the backbone of the IA cognitive structure, thus identifying its institutional preconditions and purpose, as called for by the pragma-dialectical approach to the study of argumentation in context. Four main moves have emerged, three of which are directly related to purposes of the IA already indicated in the literature (healing the divisions of the electoral strife and invoking the plural presidency). These are mostly geared to constructing or reinforcing agreement with the audience, so as to reframe the previous candidate of one political party as the president of all Americans. The remaining move (Move 2) is more properly argumentative, as it spells out *the* problem that the

Administration sets to tackle and outlines a solution, or at least some guiding principle that will inspire it.

The regularities observed in the first part of the analysis have prepared the ground for the identification of a prototypical pattern of reasoning (van Eemeren, 2018, p. 150) that brings together the moves oriented to fostering objects of agreement with the argumentative move proper, setting in relation past and present, the goal of the new Administration and the founding values, the new president and his predecessors. Such a prototypical pattern has a formal counterpart in the value-based practical reasoning scheme, which underpins most of the speeches analyzed (Eisenhower, Nixon, Reagan, Bush, and Clinton). Obama has recourse to a slightly different scheme: practical reasoning based on analogy, but with the same effect of setting generally accepted founding values at the center of the stage. Kennedy, on the other hand, has no explicit recourse to the constitutive values of the United States as premises giving justificatory force to the core argument of his speech (i.e. the necessity of de-escalation to preserve humanity from destruction). He appeals to values that are akin to those enshrined in the American constitution, but formulating them in a way that is less immediately recognizable as culturally connotated, so as to pose them as a common starting point to both parties in the Cold War.

The AMT model, with its attention for material starting points, has made it possible to pinpoint the value(s) that each president selects as a material starting point, most of which come from the constitutive values of the United States, that are *the* final repository of agreement for this genre, testifying to its highly liturgical, epideictic function.

References

Beasley, V. B. (2004). *You, the People: American National Identity in Presidential Rhetoric*. Texas A&M University Press.

Bhatia, V. K. (1993). *Analysing Genre: Language Use in Professional Settings*. Longman.

Campbell, K. K., & Jamieson, K. H. (1986). Inaugurating the Presidency. In H. W. Simons & A. A. Agazarian (Eds.), *Form, Genre, and the Study of Political Discourse* (pp. 203–225). University of South Carolina Press.

Degano, C. (2021). Argumentative Topoi Seen from a Discourse Analytic Perspective. *Lingue Linguaggi, 42*, 51–75.

Doury, M. (2012). Preaching to the Converted. Why Argue When Everyone Agrees? *Argumentation, 26*, 99–114.

Graff, R., & Winn, W. (2006). Presencing 'communion' in Chaïm Perelman's new rhetoric. *Philosophy & Rhetoric, 39/1*, 45–71.

Gronbeck, B. E. (1986). Ronald Reagan's Enactment of the Presidency in Inaugural Address. In H. W. Simons & A. A. Agazarian (Eds.), *Form, Genre, and the Study of Political Discourse* (pp. 226–245). University of South Carolina Press.

Hart, R. P. (1984). *Verbal Style and the Presidency*. Academic.

Levinson, S. C. (1983). *Pragmatics*. Cambridge University Press.

Lopez-Pan, F. (2015). The Newspaper as an Epideictic Meeting Point. On the Epidictic Nature of the Newspaper Argumentation. *Argumentation, 29*, 285–303.

Lumer, C. (1991). Structure and Function of Argumentations. An Epistemological Approach to Determining Criteria for the Validity and Adequacy of Argumentations. In F. H. van Eemeren et al. (Eds.), *Proceedings of the Second International Conference on Argumentation* (pp. 98–107). Sicsat.

Micheli, R. (2012). Arguing without trying to persuade? Elements for a Non-Persuasive definition of argumentation. *Argumentation, 26*, 115–126.

Omar, A. A. (2019). *Strategic Maneuvering for Political Change. A Pragma-Dialectical Analysis of Egyptian Anti-Regime Columns*. John Benjamins.

Ricento, T. (2003). The Discursive Construction of Americanism. *Discourse and Society, 14/5*, 611–637.

Rigotti, E., & Greco Morasso, S. (2010). Comparing the Argumentum Model of Topics to other Contemporary Approaches to Argument Schemes: The Procedural and Material Components. *Argumentation, 24*, 489–512.

Romagnuolo, A. (2013). L'America nella retorica presidenziale: identità (con)divise, perdute e ritrovate. *Fictions, 12*, 119–128.

Churchwell, S. (2018). *Behold, America: A History of America First and the American Dream*. Bloomsbury Publishing.

Stuckey, M. (2004). *Defining Americans. The Presidency and the National Identity*. University Press of Kansas.

Trosborg, A. (2000). The inaugural address. In A. Trosborg (Ed.), *Analysing Professional Genres* (pp. 121–144). John Benjamins.

van Eemeren, F. H. (2018). *Argumentation Theory: A Pragma-Dialectical Perspective*. Springer.

van Eemeren, F. H., Grootendorst, R., & Snoeck Henkemans, F. (2002). *Argumentation: Analysis, Evaluation, Presentation*. Erlbaum.

van Eemeren, F. H., Houtlosser, P., & Snoeck Henkemans, A. F. (2007). *Argumentative indicators in discourse: A pragma-dialectical study*. Springer.

Walton, D., Reed, C., & Macagno, F. (2008). *Argumentation schemes*. Cambridge University Press.

WAUDAG. (1990). The rhetorical construction of a President. *Discourse & Society, 1/2*, 189–200.

Zarefsky, D. (2014). *Political Argumentation in the United States*. Jonh Benjamins.

Chapter 6
A Presidential Debate: Exploiting Agreement in an Adversarial Context

Abstract In this Chapter, the first presidential debate in the history of US elections, opposing Kennedy as challenging candidate to Nixon as incumbent Vice-President, is analyzed. Argument reconstruction is combined with a discourse perspective, against the backdrop of both contextual factors and generic traits. The main argumentative schemes exploited by the candidates are singled out, namely arguments from: alternatives, value-based practical reasoning, interaction of act and person, and group-member relation. Special emphasis is placed on the choice of premises and their rebuttal by the adversary. Two different strategies seem to characterize the discourse of either candidate. Nixon seeks agreement with as broad an audience as possible on the *needs*, often acknowledging a unity of judgment with his competitor, while emphasising differences from the adversary on the *means* that must be used to address them. Kennedy, on his part, stresses differences between the parties that he and Nixon represent. In the rhetorical perspective, the advantage Kennedy obtained from this debate may stem not only from his look or from his ability to play with the medium, but crucially also from his capacity of constructing the right audience. He showed a big view, appealed to widely shared values, well aware of speaking to people not familiar with the technicalities of politics or the economy– the large prime time TV audience. Conversely, Nixon lost not only for his inadequate approach to TV broadcasting, for his being underweight and pale, nor for his perspiration. Actually, he did not consider the nature of his potential audience, speaking to a small fraction of that big viewership, who were able to understand and to follow him in his punctual rebuttal of his adversary's convictions.

In the previous Chapters, we have explored the quest for agreement in two institutionalised genres of political communication in the US context. Both the Presidential Announcement and the Inaugural Address are crucial steps along the road to the White House, marking the official launch of the campaign and the formal beginning of the presidential office, respectively. As genres, they both include recurring features in their general structure, in the choice of most frequently exploited themes and linguistic devices, which often occur across the political divide. In the chronological dimension, they have proved to be subject to evolution, though preserving a few distinguishing traits.

In the US electoral and institutional system, launching the campaign and taking office are two acts that include a linguistic performance, whose ceremonial component imposes unwritten norms and—though obviously leaving room for personal interpretation—limits the scope for argumentative moves. Belonging to deliberation, the Announcement does include argumentation proper, which however often boils down to giving an *ethotic* reason for claiming support. The Inaugural, on the other hand, is inherently epideictic as it draws on common ground values and history to recast the newly elected President in his institutional role.

For this last Chapter, we have chosen to focus on a genre that, emphasising the adversarial component, is more likely to offer instances of actual argumentative effort, possibly also with reference to politically divisive specific issues: the Presidential Debate. The genuinely dialogical nature of debates makes them a more complex object of analysis than a speech, as chains of arguments here form through interaction, and reconstructing them requires looking at the sequence in which they occur. This would be hardly compatible with the approach taken in the previous chapters, where moves were compared across speeches, privileging the identification of patterns over in-depth analysis of single excerpts. Therefore, having decided to single out just one debate for analysis, we chose the one that marked a milestone for the genre, i.e. the first televised presidential debate in a US presidential campaign, which in 1960 opposed Richard Nixon, as the incumbent Vice-President, to John Fitzgerald Kennedy, the challenging Democrat nominee.

6.1 US Presidential Debates: Context and Genre

In the last few decades, TV debates between the nominated candidates have gradually become customary in the presidential campaign. They are usually scheduled in the last part of the campaign, devoted to different topical issues (typically: home affairs, international affairs, etc.) and governed by rules agreed between the candidates. Format, sponsorship and broadcasting rules have changed, but debates have come to be considered a crucial means to reach mainly undecided voters to the point that they can tip the scales in favour of the candidate who manages to 'win' them. Actually, winning a debate is a matter of audience perception, as measured through opinion polls, and of pundits awarding the contest to one of the contenders.

The first televised debate ever, dating back to the Nixon-Kennedy campaign in 1960, is thought to have played a crucial role in giving the final victory to the challenging candidate. For this reason, in the following elections candidates were reluctant to accept this challenge and it was not until 16 years later that President Ford and his Democrat challenger Jimmy Carter accepted to be engaged in three face-to-face debates. Also in that case, debates (and particularly the second, which was devoted to foreign policy) are believed to have produced dramatic effects, crucially contributing to Carter's very close election. Since 1976, each presidential election has featured a series of debates, sometimes also confronting the candidates for vice-president. In 1987, a Commission on Presidential Debates was established, an independent organization which sponsors and produces the general election presidential debates, carrying out research on this theme.[1] The Commission has made all efforts to guarantee voters the opportunity to watch debates between leading candidates, recommending the two major parties to cooperate in order to avoid the candidates declining to debate. Thus, the direct face-to-face confrontation between the candidates has become a permanent—and fundamental—part of the electoral process.

US presidential debates have been studied form different points of view, in the realm of both social and political studies. As a genre of political communication, they have attracted the attention of discourse analysts, who have explored how they manage to influence the campaign, promising "insight into what the candidates are like" (Myers, 2008, p. 121). They have been considered a hybrid genre, combining aspects of political interviews with traits typical of speeches (Halmari, 2008). In Myers' view (Myers, 2008, p. 140), they are situated on a continuum between speeches and interviews, where the former display more oratorical features while the latter adopt a typically conversational style. Actually, as noted by Boyd (2013) in his introduction to the analysis of the Obama-McCain final 2008 debate, the pre-determined format of presidential debates makes them different from more spontaneous exchanges between adversaries. The context, the structure and, above all, the aim influence the adversarial structure of the exchange, as the two participants, though forming a speaker/addressee relationship, are primarily interested in the reactions of the audience.

Beside the two candidates, participants (cf. Goffman, 1967) to a debate are the moderator (and possibly a panel of journalists asking questions), and a complex structure of audiences: a physically present primary audience, a larger secondary audience watching the broadcast, and a tertiary audience watching the debate in a later transmission. Therefore, in rhetorical terms the audience extends far beyond the TV studio where a debate takes place, reaching out to a large viewership and a much larger number of people (world-wide) who will watch the highlights or read summaries and quotations in all types of media. In this context, the aim of the candidates to construct and maintain their public self-image is crucial, and, in pragmatic terms, face work plays a fundamental role. So does alignment with the audience, especially as far as judgements about problems to be tackled are concerned. The questions asked to the candidates generally point out an unsatisfactory status quo, which the candidate is called to comment on, providing a solution to it. For incumbent candidates, this can reveal tricky, as simply answering the question would presuppose acceptance of the judgement that the status quo is unsatisfactory, which in turn entails an acceptance of responsibility for such state of things. On the other hand, denying the problem to avoid the blame would create a misalignment with the portion of the audience who perceive that there is a problem, thus failing to establish a fundamental object of agreement (Degano, 2016).

---

[1] The Commission's website (https://www.debates.org/) is a useful and reliable source for information about the debates. Texts and videos are available at: https://www.debates.org/debate-history/.

In debates, communication takes place in the context of a medium which broadcasts images as well as voices—and images may be even more important than words. The exploitation of body language, mimics, gesture together with paralinguistic elements (e.g. tone of voice, speech rate, etc.) can make a difference, producing a more convincing message. The analysis of these semiotic aspects of debates lies, however, outside the scope of this research, which will exclusively focus on transcribed texts.

6.1.1 Nixon Vs Kennedy: The First Challenge

The first televised debate in the history of the US presidency (and, actually, of the world) was broadcast on September 26th, 1960. It took place in Chicago at the studios of CBS's WBBM-TV. It was moderated by Howard Smith, of CBS News, and included a panel of four journalists. The format, agreed by the two candidates, included 8 mins opening statements by each of them, 2′30″ answers to the questions, optional rebuttal and 3′20″ closing statements each. It was expected that Nixon would profit from his better knowledge of foreign policy issues and his experience with radio debates. Yet he was unfamiliar with the new medium and initially underestimated its peculiarities: he did not pay adequate attention to his appearance and clothing, refused makeup, and behaved as if he were talking in a radio debate. Kennedy, on the contrary, carefully considered all visual aspects, had his brother Bob make an inspection of the studios to evaluate light effects and appeared in full control of the potential of the new medium. It has been argued that a drop of sweat appearing on Nixon's chin during the first debate played a decisive role in tipping the balance in favour of his adversary. Actually, in the following three debates the Vice-President was better equipped for a televised confrontation, but the viewership numbers of these were much lower than the first's, which with 66.4 million viewers is considered one of the most watched broadcasts in the history of US television.

As already mentioned above, the non-verbal aspects will not be examined here, but the analysis will exclusively take into consideration the texts.

In the next paragraphs we will first look for recurrent argument schemes, thus identifying procedural and material premises, for which an audience agreement is presupposed or sought. A fine-grained discursive analysis is carried out of the opening statements and the final appeals delving on candidates' self-presentation strategies, and their interrelation with the identified argumentative schemes. In this frame, emphasis is also placed on the fundamental issue of leadership, examining the presentation choices made by each candidate for ethos-centered argument schemes. The integration of the argumentative and the discursive perspectives is meant to highlight how agreement is strategically pursued (van Eemeren & Houtlosser, 2002, 2006; van Eemeren, 2010), with a focus on the choice of premises and their challenge by the adversary.

6.2 Reconstruction of Argumentative Patterns

From the viewpoint of genre analysis, the institutional aim of the debate is to emphasise differences entering in the merits of programs, so as to give voters a chance to make a vote decision. Agreement, then, cannot be sought having the universal audience (i.e. all Americans) in mind, as discussing policies immediately creates the conditions for division. The programmes for the years ahead descend from ideologies and their discussion necessarily sets up interdiscursive relations with the backdrop of beliefs that characterise a party's identity and vision, thus automatically selecting a part of the audience as the intended addressee and excluding another.

The debate is organized into opening statements by either candidate, sets of questions and answers (questions are asked by the journalists addressing one candidate at a time, the answers are followed by the comment of the other contender), and the final summation. Broadly speaking, within this structure three functions are performed, according to the Functional Theory of political campaigns: praising own party, attacking the other party, and defending from attacks (Benoit, 2003, 2007). At a closer look, several finer-grained moves and steps can be identified. *Praising* mainly pertains to the moves oriented to presenting the candidate and the program as preferable. Thus, it can concern (a) the candidate themselves, (b) the party, or (c) the policies. Taken together, these moves are meant to defend the view that one candidate is preferable to the other, which is a matter of ethos construction (cf. 1.1.3 above). *Attacks*, as well, can target the opponent on a personal ground, the programs, or the party. *Defences* can come as a rejection *tout court* of the claim made by the other party (be it candidate or journalist), or as a partial rejection, where distinctions or a reframing are actuated. In all this, the pursuit of agreement with the intended audience is the driving force, within constraints imposed by the candidate status as a challenger or incumbent.

Within praises, the ethos of the candidate as a person capable of running the country is primarily constructed through the identification of a problem and the proposal of solutions to tackle it. The schemes associated to this pattern fall in the realm of practical reasoning.

6.2.1 Challenger's Prototypical Reasoning: Agreement on the Poor Performance of the Incumbent Government

In the specific debate at issue, Kennedy's priority is fighting Communism (cf. Chaps. 4 and 5), at home and abroad. His point, as a challenger, is that the current Administration has not done enough to create the growth that is a precondition to win the race against the Soviet Union, and therefore a change of pace is needed. This is a realization of the argumentation prototypically enacted by the challenger in the presidential race (cf. Chap. 4), where the standpoint *vote for me* is

1. Vote for me

1.1a We need change

1.1b I am the one who
can bring about change

Fig. 6.1 Prototypical reasoning for challenging candidates

defended on the ground of coordinative argumentation (van Eemeren et al., 2002, p. 63 ff). One argument is that change is needed (causal argumentation of the pragmatic subtype), the other is that the speaker is the one who is best suited to make change happen (symptomatic argument) (Fig. 6.1).

Following the AMT, the scheme used to justify the transition from argument 1.1a to the standpoint (1.) is based on the locus from alternatives, which at the same time implies the need to terminate the current government experience and to give trust to the opposition party:

Premise 1: either X or Y can be required.
Premise 2: X is not required.
Conclusion: Y is required (Walton et al., 2008, p. 318).

Plotted in the AMT Y-shaped scheme, it can be reconstructed as follows:

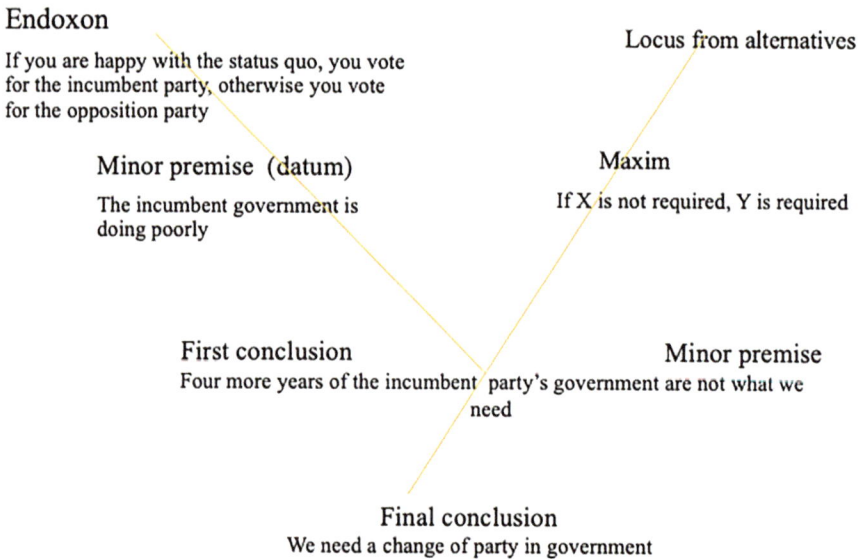

Endoxon

Locus from alternatives

If you are happy with the status quo, you vote
for the incumbent party, otherwise you vote
for the opposition party

Minor premise (datum)

Maxim

The incumbent government is
doing poorly

If X is not required, Y is required

First conclusion

Minor premise

Four more years of the incumbent party's government are not what we
need

Final conclusion
We need a change of party in government

This is a sort of implicit argument inherent in the debate situation, as well as in other genres of the electoral campaign, as shown in Chap. 4 with regard to the Announcement. Then each challenging candidate needs to make the case for the proposition that the incumbent government is doing poorly, pointing out major problems with the current Administration. The datum in the scheme above, then, becomes the standpoint of further discussion, where new schemes are employed, as we will discuss in the next sections.

6.2.2   Agreement on the Datum: The Growth Issue

Kennedy's attack to Nixon. For the first debate, it had been agreed that the subject matter be restricted to "internal or domestic American matters", as stated by the moderator in his opening remarks. Yet Kennedy, who was given the floor first, managed to shift the attention onto the international scenario, opening up a much wider perspective. Drawing inspiration from Lincoln, Kennedy compares the question posed in 1860—"whether this nation could exist half-slave or half-free"—to the question he considers crucial in 1960: "whether *the world* will exist half-slave or half-free, whether it will *move in the direction* of *freedom*, in the direction of the *road* that we are taking, or whether it will move in the direction of *slavery*".[2]

With this opening, the arguer manages to introduce his leitmotiv and keyword: *freedom* as opposed to slavery, exploiting at the same time the metaphor of the journey (a trope frequently occurring in political discourse and in particular in electoral speeches). Freedom and the journey are the backbone of Kennedy's opening: the former is the banner of the US in opposition to Communism,[3] a crucial value and the very essence of any reasonable policy; the latter activates the idea of a movement, in space and time, marking both the progression of historical events and the expansion of political ideals. The exploitation of the then dominant international issue is evidently functional to obtaining agreement. The debate is meant to revolve around domestic issues, but Kennedy preliminarily makes it clear that it is impossible to separate home policies from international affairs, because the Cold War must be waged—and can be won—at home. "If we fail, freedom fails" is a short and clear assertion, emphasised through alliteration and repetition, which attributes world-level responsibility to all Americans in the contemporary world scenario.

In the confrontation with the Soviet Union, home policies are crucial, insofar as the US productive power should not lag behind that of the USSR and of the other Communist countries. Therefore, Kennedy in his opening statement attacks Nixon on the growth issue, spelling out the problem in the following terms:

1. The kind of country we have here, the kind of society we have, the kind of strength we build in the United States will be *the defense of freedom*. If we do well here, if we meet our obligations, if we're *moving ahead*, then I think freedom will be secure around the world. *If we fail, then freedom fails*. Therefore, I think the question before the American people is: Are we doing as *much* as *we can do*? Are we as *strong* as *we should be*? Are we as strong as *we must be* if we're going to maintain our independence, and if we're going to maintain and hold out the hand of friendship to those who look to us for assistance, to those who look to us for survival? (Kennedy)

---

[2]Unless differently stated, emphasis in quotations is added by the Authors.

[3]Impossible to forget the opposition between the *free world* and the *Communist world* Kennedy would represent 3 years later, in his famous *Ich bin ein Berliner* speech.

His argumentation can be reconstructed as having a complex structure, where the standpoint is defended by the two coordinated arguments: 1.1a We need more growth, and 1.1b Of the two candidates I am the one who can bring more growth. Each of them is in turn defended by further supporting arguments (subordinative argumentation), as summed up below:

1 Vote for me
1.1a We need more growth
1.1a.1a We are not as strong as we should be
1.1a.1b Being strong is the only way to warrant our freedom
1.1b I am the candidate who can bring about more growth
1.1b.1a Nixon is part of the current government
1.1b.1b The current government has not produced as much growth as we need

Two argument schemes can be identified here (see also Chap. 5): Value-based practical reasoning underpins argument 1.1a, and Argumentation from interaction of act and person (Walton et al., 2008, p. 321) underpins 1.1b. The value-based practical reasoning scheme is as follows:

Premise 1: I have a goal G.
Premise 2: G is supported by set of values V.
Premise 3: Bringing about A is necessary (or sufficient) for me to bring about G.

Conclusion: Therefore, I should (practically ought to) bring about A (Walton et al., 2008, p. 324).

According to the AMT conventions, Kennedy's first line of defense (1.1a) can be reconstructed as follows:

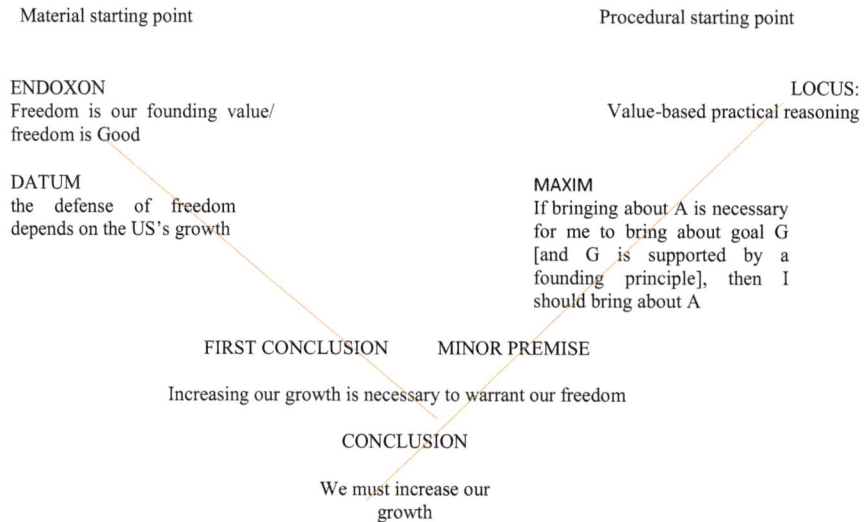

Material starting point   Procedural starting point

ENDOXON   LOCUS:
Freedom is our founding value/   Value-based practical reasoning
freedom is Good

DATUM   MAXIM
the defense of freedom   If bringing about A is necessary
depends on the US's growth   for me to bring about goal G
                                                   [and G is supported by a
                                                   founding principle], then I
                                                   should bring about A

          FIRST CONCLUSION   MINOR PREMISE

       Increasing our growth is necessary to warrant our freedom

                        CONCLUSION

                     We must increase our
                           growth

This conclusion sets growth as a benchmark against which Nixon's adequacy for the role should be judged. The part of the scheme that receives greater emphasis in Kennedy's speech is the datum, which does not express a fact, but a causal relation among facts ("The kind of country we have here, the kind of society we have, the kind of strength we build in the United States will be the defence of freedom"). Once the interdependency is established between US success and the success of the freedom-based model they champion, an inverted parallelism is used ("If we do well here [...] freedom will be secure around the world. If we fail, then freedom fails") to heighten the urgency of the choice.

Building on the sense of urgency thus created, Kennedy moves on to establishing himself as the only credible candidate who can secure the necessary growth (argument 1.1b), not by praising his qualities (he lacks a record in this sense), but discrediting his opponents' capacity to do so, through the use of the act and person scheme:

Premise 1: person P has done acts A.
Premise 2: to acts A is attributed the value V.
Conclusion: person P is V (Walton et al., 2008, p. 321).

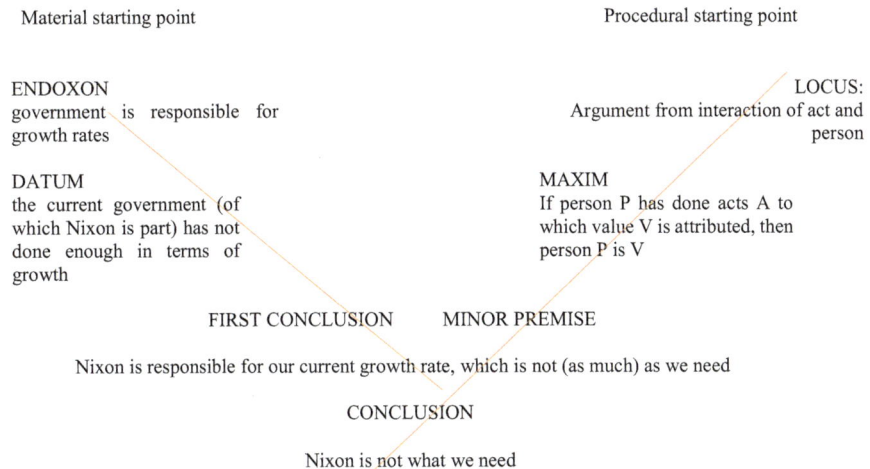

Material starting point   Procedural starting point

ENDOXON   LOCUS:
government is responsible for   Argument from interaction of act and
growth rates   person

DATUM   MAXIM
the current government (of   If person P has done acts A to
which Nixon is part) has not   which value V is attributed, then
done enough in terms of   person P is V
growth

            FIRST CONCLUSION   MINOR PREMISE

        Nixon is responsible for our current growth rate, which is not (as much) as we need

                          CONCLUSION

                    Nixon is not what we need

From a discursive point of view, the use of three rhetorical questions in a row in excerpt (1) is meant to establish agreement on the premise that the status quo is not satisfactory. This agreement is then exploited as a datum, the material minor premise that jointly with the common wisdom of how democracy should work (*endoxon*) leads to the first, preliminary, conclusion, that another term of the same Administration is not what the US need. Modality is a useful means to modulate the concept in a careful crescendo: "Therefore, I think the question before the American people is: Are we doing as much as we *can* do? Are we as strong as we *should* be? Are we as strong as we *must* be if we're going to maintain our independence? [. . .]".

These questions imply an involvement of the audience through the use of the first-person plural, which is only a short preamble to the expression of personal convictions, introduced with a formula repeated many times: "I am not satisfied (when/until)". The answer invited through the three rhetorical questions is thus given as Kennedy's personal position, which, in terms of presentation choices, marks his distance from the adversary very sharply: "I should make it very clear that I do not think we're doing enough, that I am not satisfied as an American with the progress that we're making". Each anaphoric repetition of "I'm not satisfied when. . ." introduces a problem for which the current administration has failed to find an adequate solution:

2. *I'm not satisfied* to have 50% of our steel-mill capacity unused. *I'm not satisfied* when the United States had last year the lowest rate of economic growth of any major industrialized society in the world. [. . .] *I'm not satisfied* when the Soviet Union is turning out twice as many scientists and engineers as we are. *I'm not satisfied* when many of our teachers are inadequately paid, or when our children go to school part-time shifts. (Kennedy)

This structure conveys (*poses*) a judgement, and at the same time *presupposes* the propositional content of the following clause. It is chosen to illustrate all the faults of the incumbent Presidency, which are therefore taken for granted, and not offered for debate.

Kennedy thus exploits Nixon's continuity argument (cf. journalist's preamble to a question "Mr. Vice President, your campaign stresses the value of your eight-year experience"), turning it against him: Such growth rate, Kennedy's reasoning goes, is what Nixon's party could do, which is not enough. If electors agree that more growth is needed, they can only vote for the other candidate. From the viewpoint of argumentation quality, a change of government does not per se warrant that the new Administration will do better than the previous one, nor Kennedy quantifies the amount of growth that his government would pursue to stay ahead of the Soviet Union. He uses expressions like "Are we doing *as much as* we *can* do? Are we *as strong as* we *should* be?" where the comparison is between the status quo and an unspecified ideal (*we can do, we should be*), the desirability of which people can adhere to, without raising issues of feasibility. However, the vagueness in Kennedy's attack is not pointed out by his adversary, who limits to a defense of the incumbent Administration against the accusation of scarce growth, as discussed below.

Nixon's refutation. Nixon's opening statement is actually a refutation of the arguments Kennedy brought against him, where there is a tension between the necessity of rejecting accusations of a lack of growth during the incumbent Republican Administration and the necessity of saving agreement with the audience on the irrefutable premise that America needs more growth. Ancient theories of refutation envisaged three ways of attacking (and refuting) an argument, challenging respectively the premise, the conclusion or the connection between the premise and the conclusion (Walton et al., 2008, p. 222). Among contemporary approaches, the New

Rhetoric (Perelman & Olbrechts-Tyteca, 1958) sees refutation as connected with techniques based on the dissociation of elements that were associated in the argument that is being challenged (e.g. in the case of an argument from example a counterexample can be brought, or in an argument from rule, an exception may be claimed).

In his response Nixon cannot deny the need for growth, as it would cast him as a defender of the status quo—hardly a winning position at elections –, but at the same time he cannot show agreement with the representation depicted by Kennedy. He thus accepts his challenger's point of view on the key role played by the US internationally. Nixon "subscribe[s] completely" to the spirit of Kennedy's words, and admits that "the United States should move ahead". Kennedy, after all, has shifted the discussion onto a very high and general level, where it is difficult to disagree, reason why Nixon is obliged to find differences and emphasize them. "Where do we disagree?"—he asks. To answer this crucial question, he must challenge the presupposed meanings of Kennedy's statements. He explicitly says that: "I think we disagree on the *implication* of his remarks tonight and on the statements that he has made on many occasions during his campaign to the effect that the United States has been standing still". And he embarks on a consistent confutation of the data given by the adversary. He talks about the GNP, electric power, schools, highways. He compares the achievements of Eisenhower's administration to Truman's. He asks precise questions and gives answers based on a large number of figures. The key question is: "Is the United States standing still?" The answer is *no*, because, looking at "the record", figures show that "this is not standing still". Nixon does not directly rebut Kennedy's standpoint; he defies its premises.

3. When we compare the growth in this Administration with that of the previous Administration that then there was a total growth of 11% over 7 years [sic!]; in this Administration there has been a total growth of 19% over 7 years. That shows that there's been *more growth in this Administration than in its predecessor*. But let's not put it there; let's put it in terms of the average family. What has happened to you? We find that your wages have gone up five times as much in the Eisenhower Administration as they did in the Truman Administration. What about the prices you pay? We find that the prices you pay went up five times as much in the Truman Administration as they did in the Eisenhower Administration. What's the net result of this? This means that the average family income went up 15% in the Eisenhower years as against 2% in the Truman years. Now, *this is not standing still*. (Nixon)

Mere disagreement on figures is however not enough to mark the difference between the views of the two candidates. To distinguish his programme from that of the challenger, Nixon introduces the opposition between *goals* and *means*. Kennedy has sketched noble aims nurtured with universal values, which are difficult to replace. Nixon shares the aims and confines disagreement to the means, namely actual policies.

Shifting the attention onto the means makes it possible for Nixon to emphasise that his feelings are not different from those of the challenger, and that they both are sincere in their motives. After implicitly accusing Kennedy of lying, Nixon restores the face of his adversary, recognising the authenticity of his feelings. The real topic of the debate will be *how* the goals set by both candidates can be reached.

Another example of a dissociative technique can be seen below, where Nixon uses it to reject just part of Kennedy's argument:

4. We heard tonight, for example, the statement made that our growth in national product last year was the lowest of any industrial nation in the world. Now last year, of course, was 1958. That happened to be a recession year. *But* when we look at the growth of G.N.P. this year, a year of recovery, we find that it's six and nine-tenths per cent and one of the highest in the world today. (Nixon)

Here the national product, treated as a unitary whole in Kennedy's datum, is divided into two different notions: the Gross National Product of 1958 (a recession year) and the GNP of 1959, a recovery year, and the most salient, as the Administration's record must be considered in its entirety. And whereas Kennedy's claims are accepted with regard to GNP in 1958, they are rejected for 1959.

6.2.3 The Incumbent's Viewpoint: Party Stereotypes as Starting Points in Group-Member Argumentation

In his opening statements Nixon attacks his adversary challenging the idea of Kennedy as an innovator, which in a way reveals great concern for the fact that Kennedy was perceived as 'the new':

5. [...] when we look at the various programs that he offers, *they do not seem to be new*. They seem to be simply *retreads* of the programs of the Truman Administration which preceded it. [...] *I will concede* that in all the areas to which I have referred Senator Kennedy would have the federal government spend more than I would have it spend. (Nixon)

His argumentation can be reconstructed as follows:

1. Vote for me

   1.1 Kennedy's programs are not that new
   1.2 His programs would reach the same goal as ours but with greater expenditure

We will just focus on the second line of defence (1.2), in which the scheme of the Interaction of group and its members is used, in its variant 2 (Walton et al., 2008, p. 322):

Premise 1: Group G has quality Q.
Premise 2: M is a member (idea, habit, custom, product, method) of G.

Premise 3: if G has Q, its member M (ideas, habits, customs, products, methods) is Q.
Conclusion: M is Q.

Indirectly attributed to Kennedy, on the ground of group-member association, is the misconception that the goodness of a program lies in its cost: the more costly the better.

6. Now, when *we* look at these programs, *might I suggest* that in evaluating them we often have a *tendency* to say that the test of a program is how much you're spending. I will *concede* that in all the areas to which I have referred Senator Kennedy would have the federal government spend more than I would have it spend. (Nixon)

Nixon concedes that Kennedy as president would spend more than he would. But the amount of federal spending is not a correct measure of success, as the question is "which government does the most". Kennedy's *means* are considered dangerous because they would "stifle creative energies", leading to "the stagnation of the motive power that we need in this country to get progress".

Incidentally, this is a variation on the tune of another leitmotiv of Republican attacks to the Democrats, i.e. the Big Government argument—the bigger and the more controlling of citizens' life, the better for the Democrats, but Big Government stifles citizens' initiative (cf., for example, Reagan's Inaugural Address, Chap. 5).

Reconstructed following AMT conventions, the argument looks like this:

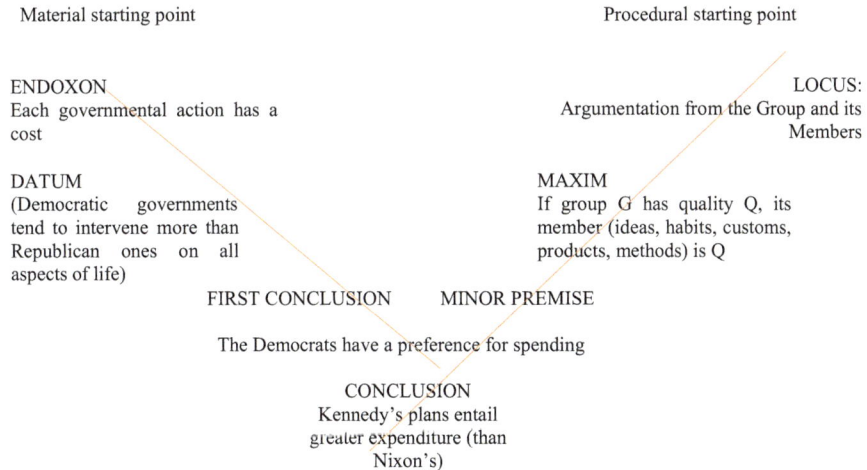

Material starting point	Procedural starting point
ENDOXON Each governmental action has a cost	LOCUS: Argumentation from the Group and its Members
DATUM (Democratic governments tend to intervene more than Republican ones on all aspects of life)	MAXIM If group G has quality Q, its member (ideas, habits, customs, products, methods) is Q

FIRST CONCLUSION   MINOR PREMISE

The Democrats have a preference for spending

CONCLUSION
Kennedy's plans entail
greater expenditure (than
Nixon's)

Interestingly enough, the datum is left unexpressed in Nixon's argument, and can be reconstructed only inferentially on the ground of one of the Republicans staple arguments against the Democrats. As for the expressed part of the scheme, the view attributed to Kennedy (i.e. the more costly the better) was never professed by him during the debate, nor plausibly on other occasions during the campaign, but his membership to the Democratic Party makes the allegation of higher expenditure credible against the backdrop of interdiscursive remarks attached to the Party. As far as presentation devices are concerned, the vagueness used in the attribution of the view that "the test of a program is how much you spend" makes it less likely to be met with a disavowing remark (e.g. I've never said that). The view (ex. 6 above) is generally attributed to an inclusive *we*, and a series of linguistic hedges contribute to reducing its epistemic force: the modal *might* associated to the low-modality verb *suggest* (cf. Sect. 3.3), and the nominalized form *tendency* (cf. Sect. 3.4) together reduce chances of disproof. Furthermore, the projecting clause "I will concede that" introduces an element of purported dialogism with an ironical function—you normally concede something that you are unwilling to admit, which is definitely not the case for Nixon, who intendedly accuses his adversary of high-spending policies. At the same time, the act of conceding generates the implicature that someone uttered that view, and in the context of the presidential race the invited meaning is that Kennedy uttered it, as concessions are made to adversaries. These strategies qualify Nixon's attack as a rebuttal of a view fallaciously attributed to his opponent, which is a violation of the Unexpressed Premise Rule (van Eemeren, 2018, p. 635). The Rule is violated when an antagonist produces a reconstruction of a protagonist's unexpressed premise "that goes beyond the pragmatic optimum to which the protagonist may be supposed to be committed when pragmatic factors like the context and the available background information are duly taken into account" (*Ibidem*). All in all, these linguistic choices, together with other aspects which will be examined in the following section, suggest Nixon's preference for an indirect style of communication, which was possibly not so fine-tuned for a televised event.

6.2.4   *The* **Leadership** *Issue: Agreement on the Leader's Experience*

Attacks to Kennedy and the related defense. If the two candidates have similar objectives but imagine different means to reach them, the ability of the leader to pursue and enact adequate policies is crucial. Kennedy in his Announcement founded his very decision to run on his (and his party's) conviction that he was the right man for the delicate job of a president (s. Sect. 4.1). On the other hand, Nixon's electoral brochure had the telling opening statement "We need a President who knows the job", and recognized Nixon as the best-equipped candidate as "only Richard Nixon already has the knowledge required, based on eight years of direct experience". Nixon capitalized on his role as Vice-President, Kennedy on the consensus of the Democrats.

Against this background, questions concerning the leadership were expected, and were actually asked. Bob Fleming, of ABC News, raised the issue in his first question for Kennedy:

7. Senator, the Vice President in his campaign has said that you were *naive* and at times *immature*. He has raised the question of leadership. On this issue, *why* do you think people should vote for you rather than the Vice President? (Fleming)

The question is introduced with an expression of interdiscursivity: the panellist reports Nixon's opinion, and uses two adjectives, *naïve* and *immature*, which are not a compliment—to say the least. The question proper is focused on the *reason* why Kennedy should be preferred to the (implicitly) more experienced adversary. In the case of Kennedy, the difference of opinion started by the journalist's question concerns whether he is fit for the position he is racing for, against allegation of naivety and at times immaturity.

In his answer, Kennedy exploits this implicitness to compare his personal record to the Vice-President's:

8. Well, the Vice President and I came to the Congress *together* in 1946; we *both* served in the Labor Committee. I've been there now for *14 years, the same period of time* that he has, so that our experience in government is *comparable*. (Kennedy)

Different linguistic elements (*together, both, the same*) emphasise that the two candidates have a lot in common. Numbers tell that their experience is *comparable*. This is the first line of defence used by Kennedy, which is complemented with another argument based on the party record, in a complex structure that can be reconstructed as follows:

1 Kennedy is a fit leader
1.1a Kennedy's experience in politics is as long as Nixon's
1.1b Nobody would question Nixon's experience
1.2a Kennedy comes from the Democratic Party
1.2b the Democratic Party has a record (i.e. is more experienced) for social policies

The standpoint is defended by two pairs of coordinative arguments forming multiple lines of defence: (1.1a) taken together with the implicit argument (1.1b), and (1.2a) jointly with (1.2b). Agreement-wise, the first line of defence rests on the starting point that Nixon is, instead, mature and experienced, as these were the qualities leveraged on by Nixon himself throughout the campaign. The duration of Kennedy's experience (14 years, as many as Nixon's) is used as a supporting argument, in a scheme from analogy, which, following the pragma-dialectical conventions[4] (van Eemeren et al., 2002, p. 99) can be paraphrased as follows:

---

[4]Insofar as an argument rests on one of the three main schemes of pragma-dialectics, this three-level representation is enough, as it is possible to plot all the elements of the argument (standpoint, premise and inferential reasoning connecting them). When an argument does not correspond to one of the three main schemes, but to a subtype of them, the AMT model (cf. Chap. 2) allows an easier identification of the locus from existing repertoires of schemes, which in turn makes it possible to derive a maxim that suits the discursive context to which the scheme is applied.

Kennedy is an experienced leader,
Because Nixon is an experienced leader.
And Kennedy's experience in politics is as long as Nixon's.[5]

This is, however, only the first part of the answer, after which Kennedy continues as follows:

9. Secondly, I think the question is what are the programs that we advocate, what is *the party record* that we lead? I come out of the Democratic Party, which in this century has produced Woodrow Wilson and Franklin Roosevelt and Harry Truman, and which supported and sustained these programs which I've discussed tonight. Mr. Nixon comes out of the Republican Party. He was nominated by it. And it is a fact that through most of these last 25 years the Republican leadership has opposed federal aid for education, medical care for the aged, development of the Tennessee Valley, development of our natural resources. I think Mr. Nixon is an effective leader of his party. I hope he would grant me the same. The question before us is: *which point of view and which party* do we want to lead the United States? (Kennedy)

Kennedy arbitrarily reformulates the question, in order to have the opportunity of saying what he wants and foster a more favourable picture of himself as a president, which by the way is actually a fallacious behaviour, in the form of *ignoratio elenchi.* Having focused on the party he represents and leads, Kennedy can find authoritative predecessors—Wilson, Roosevelt, Truman—who supported programmes similar to the one he now proposes. Nixon, on the contrary, cannot rely on a positive record welfare-wise, as his party has constantly opposed the reforms he now advocates. Kennedy's line of reasoning is quite explicit: the Democrats have a positive record on Welfare (unlike the Republicans); I "come out of the Democratic Party" (while Nixon "is an effective leader of his party"); therefore, who wants the reforms should vote Kennedy. The starting point it rests on, i.e. that the Democratic Party is the champion of social/progressive policies, is entailed in the reasoning but is not made explicitly. By the way, this entailment is actually justified against common knowledge of US parties' positioning along the political divide, so the move cannot be considered manipulative, in that what is presented as a starting point can be considered such. However, the entailment that the Democratic Party is the champion of social/progressive policies would hold the same even if it weren't justified against common knowledge. This shows how implicitness can induce the acceptance of controversial starting points by an unsavvy audience.

The starting point of the party record is used argumentatively, based on a subtype of symptomatic reasoning, namely the group and its member scheme, which we have

---

[5]In fact, this formulation is a reader friendly version of the actual pragma-dialectical formalized scheme based on analogy, which would go as follows:
  Y (being an experienced leader) is true of X (Kennedy)
  Because Y (being an experienced leader) is true of Z (Nixon)
  And X (Kennedy) and Z (Nixon) are comparable.

already analyzed above. In this case, however, party allegiance is claimed by the candidate and not turned against him. Despite his right of rebuttal, Nixon does not immediately comment on Kennedy's answer, though this shift from personal qualities to party policies turns out to be an advantage for Kennedy.

Attacks to Nixon and the related defence. The issue of political experience and leadership is raised also in other questions, with more attention to the specific quality of political experience. The following question is addressed to Nixon by Stuart Novins of CBS:

> 10. Mr. Vice President, your campaign stresses the value of your 8 year *experience*, and the question arises as to whether that experience was as an *observer* or as a *participant* or as an *initiator* of policy-making. Would you tell us please specifically what major proposals you have made in the last 8 years that have been adopted by the Administration? (Novins)

The panellist asks for detailed information concerning Nixon's job as a Vice-President, to prove whether he is actually qualified for political action. The answer is very vague. Nixon mentions his foreign trips, and recommendations he made when coming back, concerning specific policies. He also mentions the Committee on Price Stability and Economic Growth he chairs, which has made recommendations successively adopted by the Administration. Nixon dialogically reports Kennedy's negative opinion concerning that commission, but rebuts it.

After Nixon's answer, Kennedy does not renounce his right to reply, but he uses his time to go back to Nixon's introductory statement, and comment on the comparison between Truman's and Eisenhower's Administrations. Again, *ignoratio elenchi*.

A further question is centred on "the question of executive leadership", asked this time to Nixon by Sander Vancour, NBC News. It is a rather long question, which aims to explore the reliability of Republican slogans emphasising the role of experience and implying that Nixon had "more governmental executive decision-making experience" than his opponent. The panellist questions the Republican claims, using a short, anecdotal narrative:

> 11. Now, in his news conference on August 24th, President Eisenhower was asked to give one example of a major idea of yours that he adopted. His reply was, and I'm quoting; "If you give me a week I might think of one. I don't remember." Now that was a month ago, sir, and the President hasn't brought it up since, and I'm wondering, sir, if you can clarify *which version is correct* - the one put out by Republican campaign leaders or the one put out by President Eisenhower? (Vancour)

The protagonist of the episode is President Eisenhower, and this gives the reported words a special weight. The prestige of the source is a strong element implicitly in favour of the second alternative indicated in the question proper. It is thus suggested that the narrative aims to discredit the actual experience of the Vice-President, who, according to the model put forth by Novins in the previous question, seems to have never been an *initiator* (nor, possibly, a *participant*) of policy-making.

Nixon's answer is complex and well-organised. First of all, he classifies the President's words as "a facetious remark", thus depriving them of their authority. In doing so, he includes an incidental comment ("if you know the President, that was probably a facetious remark"), which suggests that the panellist actually does not know the President (while Nixon does), or—which is even worse—is trying to manipulate his intentions. Beyond this, Nixon expands on this episode and gives a concise and clear lesson on both constitutional rules and institutional etiquette. It is the President who takes the decisions, the President "has always maintained and *very properly*" that he can get advice from different individuals or bodies and is not obliged to reveal them. Nixon is blunt: "I do not say that I have made the decision. And I would say *no President should ever allow* anybody else to make the major decisions". In other words, it is the question that is ill-conceived, because it offers an improper interpretation of a joke, and because it implicitly admits (and positively evaluates) constitutionally improper behaviour. In that perspective, the facetious answer of the President is justified by the fact that also the *other* question (the one posed to Eisenhower in the narrated episode) is wrong.

Finally, Nixon refers back to Kennedy's viewpoint (cf. above), conceding the data (they both entered the Congress in the same year), but confuting the conclusion that they have the same experience, because Kennedy has been "in the legislative branch", he in the executive. The concept of political experience is thus split into two different notions: legislative vs executive record, and only the latter is attributed value as crucial background for a would-be President. Through this dissociation Nixon manages to focus the attention of the voters on his *executive* experience. In his final discursive move Nixon emphasises the role of the audience ("both he [Kennedy] and I are going to abide by whatever the people decide") aiming at obtaining their benevolence. At the same time, in representing both candidates as respectful and faithful to institutional principles, Nixon politely defends his adversary's positive face, which in turn makes him appear as a gentleman, with a deep sense of fair play.

Argumentatively, the difference between legislative and executive experience can have a role in the decision of voters, if they accept the implicit premise that a President needs *specific* experience. On the basis of this assumption, they can conclude in favour of the Vice-President. Kennedy's comment on Nixon's answer hinges on the rebuttal of this premise. The ability to implement the goals is different from mere experience, because "there's no certain *road* to the presidency". The metaphor of the journey re-activates the idea of movement and evolution, as if the life of a would-be President were a sort of *Bildungsroman*. In this process, results may come unexpected and experience, after all, is not predictive of the success of a candidate as a president. This proposition is defended bringing forth the example of Lincoln, who had hardly any administrative experience when he was elected president, and is still acclaimed as one of the greatest presidents. This further remark can be inserted in the argumentation structure examined above (Sect. 6.2.3) as an alternative line of defence (1.3), should argument 1.1.a be defeated. Possibly this view is also closer to Kennedy's real conviction, but using it as a first counterargument in reply to the journalist's challenge might have created a misalignment with the audience expectation that a candidate must have experience, an object of agreement which is realistically part of the pragmatic commitments (see Sect. 2.1) related to the presidential race.

6.3   Closing Statements: A Final Bid to Establish Agreement on the Status Quo

According to the rules governing the debate, each candidate had $3'20''$ for summation, functioning as a final *peroratio*. Reading the TV debate in the light of the analytic stages of the critical discussion model, the closing statements are as far as the genre can go in terms of reaching a conclusion.

Nixon uses most of his time to come back to some of the points he has already made in the introductory remarks and while answering some questions. First of all, he wants to discuss "where we *really do* stand" in comparison with the Soviet Union. As anticipated by the emphasis (conveyed with both an adverb and a morphological means), he maintains that Kennedy's interpretation is not acceptable. The Senator looks at percentages, while he considers absolute figures and thus confutes Kennedy's premises once again. He recognises shared goals, but emphasises different means, and suggests that the Democratic proposals will not be effective to guarantee growth. In that respect, he focuses on specific issues and, once more, on the question of government spending, which to him does not spell success. Namely, Truman's spending policies led to inflation and consequent difficulties for the people "who could least afford it". Which leads to the conclusion: "I stand for programs that will mean growth and progress. But it is also essential that he [the President] not allow a dollar spent that could be better spent by the people themselves".

Kennedy, on the other hand, starts his final statement with data, contrasting Nixon on his own ground. He accepts the numbers but reads them in a long-term perspective. He also apparently accepts Nixon's claim that "the means are at question", and hinges his final appeal to voters on the effectiveness of the means adopted by the incumbent Presidency:

12. *If you feel* that everything that is being done now is *satisfactory*, that the relative power and prestige and strength of the United States is *increasing* in relation to that of the Communists; that we've *gaining* more security, that we are *achieving* everything as a nation that we should achieve, that we are achieving a *better life* for our citizens and *greater strength*, *then I agree. I think you should vote for Mr. Nixon.* (Kennedy)

Kennedy is (ironically) exploiting the Locus from termination, namely the Maxim that, if something is of value, it must not be interrupted (s. Sect. 2.3.1), inviting the audience to assess the *status quo* which he ostensibly presents from the point of view of the incumbent administration. Once that interpretation is accepted, the present policies are to be considered valuable, and *therefore* they must not be interrupted. This means that voters have to choose Nixon.

This scenario is however rejected, and to it Kennedy opposes his interpretation:

13. *But if you feel* that we have to move again in the 60s, that the function of the president is to set before the people the unfinished business of our society as *Franklin Roosevelt* did in the 30s, the agenda for our people—what we must do as a society to meet our needs in this country and protect our security and help *the cause of freedom* [sic!]. (Kennedy)

He does not fully develop the reasoning. It is enough to present a different viewpoint, which does not simply confute the previous, but also widens to include reference to a prestigious testimonial (Roosevelt) and considers US problems in the framework of the international context where freedom is the key issue. Thus, Kennedy manages to go back to his initial words, putting freedom at the centre and opening up a glorious historical perspective:

14. As I said at the beginning, the question before us all, that faces all Republicans and all Democrats, is: can freedom *in the next generation* conquer, or are the Communists going to be successful? That's the great issue. And if we meet our responsibilities I think freedom will conquer. If we fail, if we fail to move ahead, if we fail to develop sufficient military and economic and social strength here in this country, then I think that uh - the *tide could begin to run against us*. And I don't want historians, 10 years from now, to say, these were the years when *the tide ran out* for the United States. I want them to say these were the years when *the tide came in*; these were the years when the United States *started to move again*. (Kennedy)

He looks at present events from the point of view of future observers, and is so able to offer two possible alternatives, epitomised in the image of the tide, which could run out or come in for the United States. The metaphor activates the idea of cyclical movement, but also the opposition between low and high moments in the history of a country. If this has to be a *high* moment, the United Stated must "move *again*". The presupposition re-affirms Kennedy's interpretation of the current situation as characterized by a lack of movement/growth. The final appeal actually concerns the goals and not the mere means:

15. That's the question before the American people, and only you can decide what you want, *what you want this country to be*, what you want *to do with the future*. I think *we're* ready to move. And it is to that great task, if *we're* successful, that *we will address ourselves*. (Kennedy)

Kennedy's very last words include interesting first-person plural forms: the audience is entitled to decide, then if the Democrats win (if *we* are successful), they will work to implement the chosen course. The plural forms are exclusive of the audience. Yet the pathos conveyed by the closing images (movement, a great task, success) enhances the inclusive interpretation of pronominal reference, paving the way for the involvement of all citizens in the process, and thus anticipating the all too famous reversal of the dominant perspective Kennedy will call for in his Inaugural Address "and so, my fellow Americans: ask not what your country can do for you--ask what you can do for your country".

6.4   Conclusion

The passages of the debate we have commented give quite a clear image of the approach chosen by each candidate. Kennedy is able to shift the focus on the themes he prefers, preliminary establishing agreement on the 'fact' that domestic affairs cannot be severed from the international context. He looks beyond the US borders, and analyzes domestic issues for their worldwide significance. He repeatedly uses presupposition to offer a gloomy view of the present American situation. He has a key word: freedom. All domestic policies have crucial consequences for the world, and therefore for the future of freedom in the world. Nixon relies on data, reporting and commenting on them to challenge the premises of the adversary; he is rigorous, institutionally correct, able to unveil manipulative questioning, and generous with his adversary. Yet he does not have the big picture. His analyses are difficult to follow for the viewers who do not have enough knowledge of the issues.

The scheme analysis suggests that the dominant pattern of reasoning for the challenger rests on the argument from alternatives (or its germane scheme based on the Locus from Termination), associated with value-based pragmatic reasoning (which is actually used also by Nixon). Other schemes, used by both the contenders, are the argument from interaction of act and person, and the group-member scheme.

For what concerns the argument from alternatives, the need of change is justified on the ground that the current government's performance is not satisfactory. This proposition is the datum in the AMT reconstruction that we proposed of the prototypical challenger's reasoning, which in turn is backed by mentioning problems that allegedly have not been properly tackled by the current Administration. Kennedy does so arguing in broad strokes, with an international drive, occasionally interspersing the big picture with data (e.g. industry working to its half-capacity). In his strategy, this is associated with vagueness, which is exploited acting as a facilitator of agreement. Suffices it to mention the growth issue, where Kennedy does not state the amount of growth that is needed to win the battle against communism, which would at the same time set a benchmark for measuring his future government's performance.

In the frame of the battle for survival between freedom and slavery, his adversary's reliance on exact data of domestic growth is presented as petty and unsuitable to the stake. Nixon defends the government performance challenging the premises. He cannot say that further growth is not desirable, but refuses to subscribe to the view that there has been no growth, and does so attacking the selection of data made by his adversary, and proposing instead a different selection of data which assumedly allows a more correct reading and interpretation of the status quo.

As for the scheme based on the interaction of act and person, the material premise on which audience agreement is assumed is that government requires experience. On this ground, Kennedy is depicted as immature, compared to his older and definitely experienced adversary, and therefore unfit for the role of president. Kennedy refutes the premise that he is less experienced than Nixon, arguing that they have as many years of experience in Congress, to which Nixon replies raising the stake. Through a dissociation, he claims that what is required is not generic Congress experience, but experience in the executive. In turn, the journalists' question to Nixon in this respect concerns his actual experience as a decision maker, thus challenging the premise that having experience as a vice-president warrants that he is suitable for the role, and implying an even higher stake: what counts is having made important decisions, adopted by the president. Nixon defeats this argument, attacking the question (constitutionally, it is just for the president to make decisions). At this point, Kennedy goes a step further, denying altogether the premise that he has so far apparently accepted: experience is not needed, after all, as Lincoln's case demonstrates.

Finally, reasoning based on the group-member relation is used by Nixon to attack Kennedy based on the presumably higher costs of his program, absent any actual record of the challenger's performance as an administrator. However, it is also exploited in praises by Kennedy, to establish the credibility of his reform program against the Democratic record as the champion of welfare-oriented policies.

In all cases, Kennedy's tone is grand, framing the US presidential election in the momentous battle for the survival of the United States and the free world. At the same time, he is vague and does not require an understanding of the details. He manages to exploit the agreement constructed by his adversary on some key premises, in the course of the campaign or of the debate, but bending it to his own purposes: Nixon is experienced—and so is Kennedy; Nixon has created a certain rate of growth—that is as far as he can go, which is not *enough* to win the race against the Soviet Union. Nixon's argumentation is more punctual, he shows partial agreement with his adversary, rejecting the *means* but not the *goals*; he uses dissociation to defend himself from attacks, showing recognition for his adversary and at times saving his face. Nonetheless, he does not come out the 'winner' of the debate.

Though Kennedy's advantage was mainly attributed to his ability to play with the new medium, his victory has an authentically rhetoric component, namely his ability to create and exploit agreement with the TV audience actually watching the debate. His big view, his careful exploitation of both exemplary events of the past and appealing prospects for the future are able to attract the average prime-time viewer, happy enough with vague promises rather than interested in the technical evaluation of sheer facts and numbers.

References

Benoit, W. L. (2003). Presidential campaign discourse as a causal factor in election outcome. *Western Journal of Communication, 67*, 97–112.

Benoit, W. L. (2007). *Communication in political campaigns*. Peter Lang.

Boyd, M. (2013). Reframing the American Dream. Conceptual metaphor and personal pronouns in the 2008 US presidential debates. In P. Cap & U. Okulska (Eds.), *Analyzing genres in political communication* (pp. 297–319). John Benjamins.

Degano, C. (2016). Corpus linguistics and argumentation: Retrieving argumentative patterns in UK prime ministerial debates. *Journal of Argumentation in Context, 5/2*, 114–138.

Goffman, E. (1967). *Interaction ritual*. Doubleday.

Halmari, H. (2008). On the language of the Clinton-Dole presidential campaign debates: General tendencies and successful strategies. *Journal of Language and Politics, 7/2*, 247–270.

Myers, G. (2008). Analysing interaction in broadcast debates. In R. Wodak & M. Krzyżanokski (Eds.), *Qualitative discourse analysis in the social sciences* (pp. 121–144). Palgrave Macmillan.

Perelman, Ch. & Olbrechts-Tyteca, L. (1958). *Traité de l'argumentation. La nouvelle rhétorique*. Paris: Presses Universitaires de France [English translation by J. Wilkinson & P. Weaver (1969). *The New Rhetoric. A Treatise on Argumentation*. University of Notre Dame Press].

van Eemeren, F. H. (2010). *Strategic Manoeuvring in argumentative discourse: Extending the pragma-dialectical theory of argumentation*. John Benjamins.

van Eemeren, F. H. (2018). *Argumentation theory: A pragma-dialectical perspective*. Springer.

van Eemeren, F. H., & Houtlosser, P. (2002). Strategic maneuvering in argumentative discourse: Maintaining a delicate balance. In F. H. van Eemeren & P. Houtlosser (Eds.), *Dialectic and rhetoric. The warp and woof of argumentation analysis* (pp. 131–159). Kluwer Academic.

van Eemeren, F. H., & Houtlosser, P. (2006). Strategic maneuvering: A synthetic recapitulation. *Argumentation, 20*, 381–392.

van Eemeren, F. H., Grootendorst, R., & Snoeck Henkemans, F. (2002). *Argumentation: Analysis, evaluation, presentation*. Lawrence Erlbaum.

Walton, D., Reed, C., & Macagno, F. (2008). *Argumentation Schemes*. Cambridge University Press.

Chapter 7
Conclusion

Abstract The chapter draws some conclusions from the analysis of agreement in US electoral discourse carried out in the book, explored along the twofold argumentative and rhetorical dimensions, the latter with a focus on the construction of the speaker's credibility (ethos). The analysis concerns three genres marking respectively the beginning of the race (the Announcement Speech), the core (the televised debate) and the end (the Inaugural Address), resting on a composite theoretical framework that brings together linguistics (with regard to personal reference, verb tense, modality, presuppositions, concessive constructions, dissociations, and figurative language), with views on agreement from classical Aristotelian rhetoric, the New Rhetoric, the pragma-dialectical approach to argumentation and the Argumentum Model of Topics.

The analysis led to identify variation in the construction of agreement within and across genres as a function of each genre's institutional aim and more generally of their situational context, namely intended audience, monologic or dialogic mode and channel. In the Announcement a change occurred diachronically, with the Watergate Scandal as a watershed in the way ethos construction and alignment with the audience are pursued, with growing importance given to enemy construction. In the Inaugural Address, where genre integrity prevails over political partisanship, agreement is sought on the ground of founding national values, which are taken as common starting points on the ground of which the main political vision of each new president for the term ahead should be accepted. In the debate, where the adversary is physically present and the large prime time TV audience often lacks political expertise, the choice of premises shows a focus on the needs of as broad an audience as possible. A unity of judgment with the competitor can be shown, while emphasising differences from the adversary on the merits of how problems should be solved. At the same time the quick dialogic exchange allows for an appropriation of the adversary's arguments only to turn them against their originator.

Methodologically, the analytic categories of argumentation theory favour the observation of patterns and regularities while the integration of the linguistic components allows for the identification of fine-grained variation, all with a view to setting in relation the forms of discourse and the conditions set by extra-textual factors.

F. Santulli, C. Degano, *Agreement in Argumentation*, Perspectives in Pragmatics, Philosophy & Psychology 31, https://doi.org/10.1007/978-3-031-16293-0_7

In this volume, the discussion of agreement as a notion relies on the conviction that it can be explored along two different dimensions, one more eminently argumentative, oriented to the transfer of acceptability from the premises to the conclusion, the other more interpersonal, related to the credibility of the speaker (i.e. ethos). The latter is a prerequisite to the former, but is not chronologically precedent: credibility is created as the discourse unfolds and therein lies, in the first place, the persuasive force of discourse. If the audience does not deem the speaker credible, every effort of persuasion would be vain.

The two dimensions of agreement were investigated starting from their historical evolution. The first chapter dwelled on the construction of the speaker's ethos, setting the Aristotelian notion in relation to the contemporary pragmatic concepts of face and politeness.

In the Aristotelian view, ethos actually is the most important means of proof, and the persuasive strength of the speaker directly connects to three fundamental characters (i.e. wisdom, virtue and goodwill). These qualities need to be displayed from the very beginning of a speech, thus creating the conditions for the three prerequisites of agreement (referred to in the *Rhetoric* as audience's attention, goodwill and ease of learning). The discourse analytical approach, on the other hand, has emphasized that ethos is always constructed for an audience, and this produces an effect of mirroring between arguer and addressees, making it a crucial component both in the production and in the reception of discourse.

The chapter also tackled agreement on facts and values from the perspective of the New Rhetoric, where the selection of objects of agreement (grouped into the two categories of facts and values) is functional to the very process of audience construction. The pivotal role of the audience in NR emphasizes that agreement is obtained between the arguer (*I*) and the addressees (*you*), thus confirming the contribution of ethos in the interpersonal dimension of agreement. From the enunciative viewpoint, a maximum of concordance is obtained when I and You collide into an inclusive we, a collective entity made up of individuals displaying similar characters and sharing similar convictions, which can be exploited as a safe foothold to develop argumentation proper. Quite evidently, both ethos and agreement become more and more important as discourse shifts from the solid ground of demonstrative reasoning into the realm of disputation.

The second chapter pondered on the notion of agreement in the pragma-dialectical approach to argumentation, focusing on starting points (facts and values on which an agreement exists or is assumed between the parties), and topoi as formalized patterns for the transfer of agreement from the premises to the conclusion. Particular emphasis was placed on the implicitness of starting points, a fact of language at large that responds to the principle of economy in communication. On this ground, whenever premises are inferable from the context or from encyclopedic or previous knowledge, they are left implicit, as is the case with the enthymeme (Sect. 1.3.2), taking for granted that the other party will be able to inferentially retrieve them. This is also the mechanism that accounts for the often-implicit realization of the opening stage in actual discourse counterparts of the critical discussion model. Since starting points are shared premises used argumentatively, establishing them explicitly beforehand and then using them as supporting arguments in the argumentation stage would create a redundancy. However, the implicitness of premises can also be used manipulatively, generating the false impression that whatever is not brought up for discussion has actually been agreed beforehand or is not disputable. This is the case of unexpressed premises that are actually disputable for the other party, and therefore fail to qualify as starting points, but are taken as such, leaving them out of the spotlight. In some other cases, however, explicitly seeking agreement on one starting point beforehand can actually hide attempts of surreptitiously distracting the other party from another more controversial premise, which is left implicit, but is used argumentatively as a starting point. Reconstructing the structure of argumentation through formalized models permits a critical scrutiny, which at the same time makes the unexpressed parts explicit. In particular, the chapter argued that in the broader frame of pragma-dialectics the AMT model can prove a useful bridge between discourse analysis and argumentation theory, facilitating the comparison of real uses of arguments with formalized lists of topoi/schemes derived from the rhetorical tradition.

Since rhetoric is by definition persuasion through discourse (*dia tou logou*) there is a fundamental linguistic component in it. Chapter 3 presents a selection of linguistic devices that are more frequently put to use for the discursive construction of agreement.

Given the pragmatic nature of persuasive discourse, personal reference plays a fundamental role, as it is functional to the linguistic representation of the participants in the communicative event (strictly speaking, I and You as deictic pronouns). Moreover, other entities can be represented through the third person or through definite descriptions. In political discourse, in particular, the third person is often attributed to a party cast as the enemy. Each form of reference in its own respect contributes to the creation of agreement either impinging on solidarity within in-group members or on the exclusion of the out-group. Beyond identities, agreement concerns facts, whose representation revolves around the transitivity system. Central to the transitivity system is the verb and the related system of tenses. The past tense in particular can be exploited for the creation of agreement through narratives, where subjective representations of events can acquire the status of facts. This mechanism underlies the creation of (political) Myths.

Facts are inherently considered to be true. However, in discourse different extents of factuality can be conferred through epistemic modality, just as different degrees of commitment can be expressed through deontic modality. Both dimensions of modality favor the acceptability of contested propositions, making it possible to invite partial acceptance of a given view. At the same time, the possibility of obtaining acceptance relies on the choice of words referring to objects and attributing qualities. In this respect, definition and denomination are powerful persuasive instruments as are adjectives, in particular when they have an axiological value. Choices at the level of the noun phrase are relevant in terms of frame activation, eliciting agreement not only on the semantic content but also on the wealth of implicit connections associated to them.

Frames are just one of the mechanisms through which implicit meaning can be conjured up, other widely exploited devices being presupposition and concession. Through presupposition, the arguer invites the acceptance of the posed propositional content of an utterance, while also entailing the acceptance of some implicit meaning on which the truth value of the former depends. Concession on its part relies by definition on an implicit frustrated cause, i.e. it entails the acceptance of a judgement concerning what is considered the normal relation between two co-occurring facts. Furthermore, implicit value judgements can be conveyed through dissociation, or the splitting of a unitary notion into parts that are attributed different value. This technique is frequently exploited in political discourse, to distinguish one's own position from that of the adversary when the adherence to universally accepted values is at stake, or to solve a contradiction deriving from the interpretation of such general values. All linguistic devices impinging on implicitness have the advantage of blurring the borders of the objects of agreement, thus increasing their chances of being accepted. Just as communication is possible not *in spite of* vagueness but *because of* vagueness, the exploitation of implicit meanings is not per se a deviation from an ideal norm of communication, but is what makes communication possible. Yet the use of implicit can be bent to manipulative ends, when contested meanings are conveyed implicitly to enhance chances that they escape critical scrutiny. Both concession and dissociation entail a certain degree of polyphony, a feature of discourse which is prototypically associated with explicit dialogic devices such as quotation, but is often realized more covertly, e.g. through rhetorical questions, negation and irony. The point of dialogism with regard to agreement is that it allows a fictive dialogue where opposite positions are engaged, preempting potential criticism or defeating anticipated objections, and thus favoring the acceptance of the arguer's premises and their validity in the defense of a standpoint.

Tangential to the devices discussed so far, figurative language—metaphors in the first place—concurs to the pursuit of agreement through its capacity of evoking alternative frames that are deemed more effective for the construction of a common ground between the arguer and the audience.

In the second part of the book, the composite methodological frame delineated above was applied to a selection of texts belonging to three genres of US political communication. From a methodological point of view, the sample selection was underpinned by the conviction that genre characterization emerges more clearly through the comparison with other genres, and at the same time, within each genre, a diachronic perspective makes it possible to identify both recurring elements and variation. Furthermore, looking at a series of events belonging to the same genre, as opposed to a single specimen, wards off the risk that discourse analysis may simply come down to an isolated comment of the latest headline-hitting speech, without advancing the understanding of that specific activity type and its interaction with the historical context.

The first two application chapters dovetail, each of them being prevalently informed by one of the theoretical perspectives outlined in the first chapters. Chapter 4, on Announcements, mainly rests on ethos and audience construction, while Chapter 5 foregrounds the moves typical of the Inaugural Address as a genre, setting them in relation to the attendant argument schemes. Chapter 6, finally, combines the two perspectives, applying them to the close reading of just one textual instance, i.e. the first, iconic, televised presidential debate in the history of US politics, between J.F. Kennedy and Richard Nixon.

In reason of the different prevailing perspectives, Chaps. 4 and 5 follow a different organization of the analysis, which in turn bears an influence on the type of results obtained. On the one hand, the prevalently chronological order of the Announcement chapter allows the emergence of diachronic variation, with a focus on rhetorical preferences. On the other hand, Chap. 5 is driven by the search for communal traits across the Inaugural Addresses, leading to the identification of constitutive moves and the related schemes, which provide insight into the deep textual structure and the structure of the arguments. In both approaches, constant attention is given to the linguistic presentation devices, continually moving between the macro-textual level of the moves and the micro-level of their linguistic realization.

The choice of the respective approaches to the analysis is further justified based on historical considerations influencing the characterization of the two genres. The inaugural is an older, more consolidated and institutionally conventionalized genre, as testified not only by its interdiscursivity with previous inaugurals, but also by the frozenness of the context in which it takes place, both time- and place-wise. The address, which is today delivered from the West front of the Capitol on the 20th of January, follows the oath that officially swears in the new president, adding to its character of utmost solemnity. The ceremonial value attached to the repetition characterizing the genre makes it reasonable to look for regularities across single instances of the speech.

The announcement, instead, lacking the ceremonial fixity imposed on inaugurals, allows greater freedom to the single candidates, both in terms of physical context and medium. A wide range of different possibilities were actually exploited: Nixon's Announcement was a letter to the electors of Pennsylvania; Kennedy made his announcement during a press conference in the Senate's Caucus Room; Regan had his televised official announcement broadcast by NYC. In the last few decades, however, most candidates have opted for a speech, often delivering it in a symbolic location. Thus the context, freely chosen by the candidate, acquires a rhetorical value. The choice for establishing a physical relationship with the attending audience, who is actually before the candidate, allows a special representation of the relation between arguer and audience. The warmth created through physical proximity is then projected onto a broader audience through media coverage. This opportunity, however, was not exploited by Reagan, whose TV broadcast made it possible for him to capitalize on his experience as an actor (giving him an advantage in exploiting the affordance of the means) and on the familiarity people had with seeing him enter their homes through the screen.

The different contextual variables, combining with the adoption of a usually marked personal style, underpin the decision of looking for elements of variation, with a special focus on the diachronic dimension.

Chapter 4 focused on agreement in ethos construction and alignment with the audience, analyzing the Presidential Announcements by seven challenging candidates who managed to win the election. The analysis revealed an evolution over time, with the Watergate scandal as a watershed. In the two Announcements before it, the candidate's credibility as a prospective president was constructed on the basis of symptomatic reasoning, asserting that such a crucial position on the domestic and international scene requires a fit candidate, and the candidate has the needed qualities. After the Watergate, a crisis ensued in the relation between the people and politicians, and the loss of trust seems to have determined a change in the discursive construction of the people-president relation. Challenging candidates have placed more emphasis on decrying the 'Ways of Washington' and calling for change, from the very beginning of their campaign, kicked off by the Announcement. From the viewpoint of argumentation, this translates in a preference for arguments from alternatives, to defend the need-of-change standpoint, complemented with the argument from act and person, to persuade voters of the candidate adequacy for the position. Interestingly enough, the call for change was sometimes constructed as a restoration of a previous 'state of grace'.

Parallel to the change in the candidate's ethos construction, greater importance started too be given to the construction of the Enemy, on the one hand, and to the creation of communion with the audience, on the other, in a metaphorical replication of the call to arms frame (Clinton and Obama).

Chapter 5 produced an analysis of the cognitive structure of the Inaugural Adress, characterizing it as the least confrontational and argumentative activity type of electoral discourse, performing mostly an epideictic function. Four main moves were identified, three of which aimed at constructing or reinforcing agreement with the audience on the founding values of the United States, to fulfil the institutional aim of reframing the winner as the President of all Americans. To this end past and present are constantly set in relation, through references to history and by means of interdiscursive allusions echoing both previous presidents and the Bible. Just one of the moves qualified as properly argumentative, consisting in the enunciation of the main challenges the new Presidency will have to tackle and of the approach needed to find a solution. The scheme used to realize the move's rhetorical purpose is typically value-based practical reasoning, retrieved in five of the seven speeches. In the remaining Address, the practical reasoning was based on analogy, but nonetheless it performed the same function of justifying current judgements on the ground of the founding values relied on as starting points also in the other speeches. Within these institutionalized constraints, variation exists regarding the choice of specific values used as material starting points, and their wording. The results of the analysis also suggest that when new presidents are sworn in, the saliency of their inaugural address can only be appreciated if read against the backdrop of its interdiscursive relations with the genre and with specific instances of it by predecessors.

Chapter 6 focused on a genre emphasizing the adversarial approach, namely the Presidential Debate. The first presidential debate in the history of US elections, opposing Kennedy as challenging candidate to Nixon as incumbent Vice-President, was analyzed from both the argumentative and the discursive perspectives. On the plain of argumentation, four main patterns of reasoning were identified resting on: the argument from alternatives, value-based pragmatic reasoning, the argument from interaction of act and person and the argument from group-member relation. They were analyzed in their both material and procedural components, with special attention for the choice of premises and their rebuttal by the adversary.

The analysis reveals that each candidate relies on a different strategy, which partly depends on their different status. Kennedy as a challenger attacks the incumbent Administration for an unsatisfactory status quo. Nixon seeks agreement with as broad an audience as possible on the desirability of further improving the status quo, often acknowledging a unity of judgment with his competitor, while emphasising differences from the adversary on how to achieve this goal. At the same time, he embarks on a punctual defense of the government. Both candidates stress differences between the parties they represent, Nixon to attack Kennedy, Kennedy to construct his ethos in the line of the Democratic tradition. Moreover, Kennedy seems to consistently appropriate Nixon's arguments, only to turn them against him. Nixon emphasises his experience; Kennedy counters that he has as many years of experience. Nixon demonstrates that there has been growth during his term as a Vice-President, provided certain parameters are taken into consideration; Kennedy retorts that the growth rate achieved is not enough. Kennedy does not deny Nixon's claim that there has been growth, but uses the data brought by Nixon himself to make the point that Nixon would not be able to do better than that as a president. The vagueness of the formulation (Kennedy stays away of figures in that respect) possibly contributes to gaining him acritical acceptance of the argument by the audience.

In the rhetorical perspective, the advantage Kennedy obtained from this debate may stem not only from his look or from his ability to play with the medium. Kennedy had the big view, talked about the world, the future, evoked well-known historical events. He was speaking to people who were not familiar with the technicalities of politics, the large prime time TV audience. Nixon lost not only for his inadequate approach to TV broadcasting, for his being underweight and pale, nor for his perspiration. Actually, he lost because he did not consider the nature of his potential audience. He spoke to a small fraction of that big viewership, to those who were able to understand and to follow him in his punctual rebuttal of his adversary's convictions.

In other words, the results of the first televised Presidential Debate anticipate a feature that has characterized them until today: they are not meant to convince those who are interested in politics and already have their own political opinions. They address, first and foremost, the people who are usually far from political issues, who often do not even cast their vote. These people watch debates because a Presidential Debate is a popular event with wide media coverage. These people get lost amid too much data, want to be guided through a text and rarely recognise manipulative language: anaphora, metaphor, presupposition, and pathos are among the most effective arguer's strengths, the silver bullet that can knock down the adversary.

Drawing the threads together, the construction of agreement has been shown to play a crucial role in the three genres analyzed, each with its own specificities.

Differences can be pinned down to the function of each speech within the constellation of electoral campaign discourse and, of course, to the mode.

The two genres belonging to the race proper, i.e. the Announcement and the debate, differ clearly for one being monologic, and the other dialogic. In the monologic genre of the Announcement, agreement is sought on a broad basis of positive and negative values, seeking as full an adherence as possible with the intended audience. Agreement is created also at the expense of the adversary, but the enemy construction is purely discursive—the adversary not being physically there and hence not being able to counteract. The other candidates' voice is brought into the picture through polyphony, either referring to previous statements by the adversary or by ascribing him to a group, and attaching to the person propositions that are part of the group's ideological repertoire. The debate, instead, imposes the contenders to take issue with the propositions put forth by the adversary, which may steer the discussion onto uncomfortable ground. Candidates seem to prototypically cope with this predicament by taking the adversary's premises, and qualifying them by making distinctions, using dissociations and concessions. Also modality is exploited to this end, allowing a candidate to grade his commitment to a given proposition, and thus making it possible to seek or show partial acceptance or rejection of it. As a result of these discursive strategies, agreement comes through the debate as a matter of relative preferability, as opposed to an absolute ideal. Even polyphony plays a role in the debates, allowing the candidates to address statements made by their adversary on a different occasion, rather than those made during the debate. They can thus choose to engage those parts of the adversary's discourse that are more functional to their own purposes.

At the same time, the Announcement Speech and the Debate differ from the Inaugural Address, in the first place for the audience they imply. The Inaugural Address does not seek the particular audience of potential electors, but a potentially universal audience, intended as all reasonable Americans. As a result, agreement in the Inaugural is sought around a broadly sketched goal, which is cast as directly informed by one or more founding principles of the United States. This contributes to the highly conventional tone of the Inaugural Address, which requires each new specimen of it to be read against the backdrop of previous instances of the genre.

Methodologically, our study of agreement leverages on the reconstruction of argumentation coupled with the analysis of the forms of discourse, benefiting from such an integrated approach. The analytic categories of argumentation theory facilitate the task of pinpointing patterns and regularities that would risk escaping the net of purely linguistics-informed models. The argumentative component of the analytic frame adopted in this book favours the integration of the macro- and micro-levels of discourse, setting in relation the forms of discourse and the conditions set by extra-textual factors into recognizable patterns. Detecting patterns is per se crucial to any discourse-oriented qualitative study of argumentation, but is also a preliminary step for quantitative analysis of argumentative discourse, as it may lead to identifying indicators of argumentation. Sharpening the tools for a quantitative turn is a challenge for future research, in which the analytic frame set out here is further integrated with Corpus Linguistics and Text Mining.

Appendix A: Presidential Announcements

John F. Kennedy

US Senate Caucus Room, Washington, D.C.

January 02, 1960

I am announcing today my candidacy for the Presidency of the United States.

The Presidency is the most powerful office in the Free World. Through its leadership can come a more vital life for our people. In it are centered the hopes of the globe around us for freedom and a more secure life. For it is in the Executive Branch that the most crucial decisions of this century must be made in the next 4 years–how to end or alter the burdensome arms race, where Soviet gains already threaten our very existence–how to maintain freedom and order in the newly emerging nations–how to rebuild the stature of American science and education–how to prevent the collapse of our farm economy and the decay of our cities–how to achieve, without further inflation or unemployment, expanded economic growth benefiting all Americans–and how to give direction to our traditional moral purpose, awakening every American to the dangers and opportunities that confront us.

These are among the real issues of 1960. And it is on the basis of these issues that the American people must make their fateful choice for their future.

In the past 40 months, I have toured every state in the Union and I have talked to Democrats in all walks of life. My candidacy is therefore based on the conviction that I can win both the nomination and the election.

I believe that any Democratic aspirant to this important nomination should be willing to submit to the voters his views, record and competence in a series of primary contests. I am therefore now announcing my intention of filing in the New Hampshire primary and I shall announce my plans with respect to the other primaries as their filing dates approach.

F. Santulli, C. Degano, *Agreement in Argumentation*, Perspectives in Pragmatics, Philosophy & Psychology 31, https://doi.org/10.1007/978-3-031-16293-0

I believe that the Democratic Party has a historic function to perform in the winning of the 1960 election, comparable to its role in 1932. I intend to do my utmost to see that that victory is won.

For 18 years, I have been in the service of the United States, first as a naval officer in the Pacific during World War II and for the past 14 years as a member of the Congress. In the last 20 years, I have traveled in nearly every continent and country—from Leningrad to Saigon, from Bucharest to Lima. From all of this, I have developed an image of America as fulfilling a noble and historic role as the defender of freedom in a time of maximum peril—and of the American people as confident, courageous and persevering.

It is with this image that I begin this campaign.

https://www.jfklibrary.org/archives/other-resources/john-f-kennedy-speeches/presidential-candidacy-19600102

Richard Nixon

January 31, 1968

To the Citizens of New Hampshire:

I hardly need to remind you of the importance of the New Hampshire Presidential primary—both to the candidates and to the country. This importance stems from more than the fact of its being first. It stems also from the spirit in which New Hampshire's voters approach the election, keenly aware of their special responsibility, of the broad influence of their votes.

In 1968, your responsibility is greater than ever. The nation is in grave difficulties, around the world and here at home. The choices we face are larger than any differences among Republicans or among Democrats, larger even than the differences between the parties. They are beyond politics. Peace and freedom in the world, and peace and progress here at home, will depend on the decisions of the next President of the United States.

For these critical years, America needs new leadership.

During 14 years in Washington, I learned the awesome nature of the great decisions a President faces. During the past 8 years I have had a chance to reflect on the lessons of public office, to measure the nation's tasks and its problems from a fresh perspective. I have sought to apply those lessons to the needs of the present, and to the entire sweep of this final third of the twentieth Century.

And I believe I have found some answers.

I have decided, therefore, to enter the Republican Presidential primary in New Hampshire.

I will try to meet as many of you as I can—Republicans, Democrats and Independents, those who will vote in March and those who will vote in November. I will invite your comments. I will answer your questions. I will discuss with you my own vision of America's future, and I will ask for yours.

I have visited New Hampshire often—as a candidate, as a public official, and as a private citizen. I appreciate the many courtesies you have paid me. I am deeply grateful for your support in past elections. But in asking your support now, I ask it not on the basis of old friendships. We have entered a new age.

And I ask you to join me in helping make this an age of greatness for our people and for our nation.

Sincerely,

Richard Nixon

http://www.4president.org/speeches/1968/nixon1968announcement.htm

Jimmy Carter

Address to the National Press Club

December 12, 1974

We Americans are a great and diverse people. We take full advantage of our right to develop wide-ranging interests and responsibilities. For instance, I am a farmer, an engineer, a businessman, a planner, a scientist, a governor and a Christian. Each of you is an individual and different from all the others.

Yet we Americans have shared one thing in common: a belief in the greatness of our Country.

We have dared to dream great dreams for our Nation. We have taken quite literally the promises of decency, equality, and freedom—of an honest and responsible government.

What has now become of these great dreams? That all Americans stand equal before the law? That we enjoy a right to pursue health, happiness and prosperity in privacy and safety? That government be controlled by its citizens and not the other way around? That this Country set a standard within the community of nations of courage, compassion, integrity, and dedication to basic human rights and freedoms?

Our commitment to these dreams has been sapped by debilitating compromise, acceptance of mediocrity, subservience to special interests, and an absence of executive vision and direction.

Having worked during the last 20 years in local, state and national affairs, I have learned a great deal about our people.

I tell you that their great dreams still live within the collective heart of this Nation.

Recently we have discovered that our trust has been betrayed. The veils of secrecy have seemed to thicken around Washington. The purposes and goals of our country are uncertain and sometimes even suspect.

Our people are understandably concerned about this lack of competence and integrity. The root of the problem is not so much that our people have lost confidence in government, but that government has demonstrated time and again its lack of confidence in the people.

Our political leaders have simply underestimated the innate quality of our people.

With the shame of Watergate still with us and our 200th birthday just ahead, it is time for us to reaffirm and to strengthen our ethical and spiritual and political beliefs.

There must be no lowering of these standards, no acceptance of mediocrity in any aspect of our private or public lives.

In Our homes or at worship we are ever reminded of what we ought to do and what we ought to be. Our government can and must represent the best and the highest ideals of those of us who voluntarily submit to its authority.

Politicians who seek to further their political careers through appeals to our doubts, fears and prejudices will be exposed and rejected.

For too long political leaders have been isolated from the people. They have made decisions from an ivory tower. Few have ever seen personally the direct impact of government programs involving welfare, prisons, mental institutions, unemployment, school busing or public housing. Our people feel that hey have little access to the core of government and little influence with elected officials.

Now it is time for this chasm between people and government to be bridged, and for American citizens to join in shaping our Nation's future.

Now is the time for new leadership and new ideas to make a reality of these dreams, still held by our people.

To begin with, the confidence of people in our own government must be restored. But too many officials do not deserve that confidence.

There is a simple and effective way for public officials to regain public trust - be trustworthy!

But there are also specific steps that must be taken.

We need an all-inclusive sunshine law in Washington so that special interests will not retain their exclusive access behind closed doors. Except in a few rare cases, there is no reason for secret meetings of regulatory agencies, other executive departments or congressional committees. Such meetings must be opened to the public, all votes recorded, and complete news media coverage authorized and encouraged.

Absolutely no gifts of value should ever again be permitted to a public official.

Complete revelation of all business and financial involvements of major officials should be required, and none should be continued which constitute a possible conflict with the public interest.

Regulatory agencies must not be managed by representatives of the industry being regulated, and no personnel transfers between agency and the industry should be made within a period of four full years.

Public financing of campaigns should be extended to members of Congress.

The activities of lobbyists must be more thoroughly revealed and controlled.

Minimum secrecy within government should be matched with maximum personal privacy for private citizens.

All federal judges, diplomats and other major officials should be selected on a strict basis of merit.

For many years in the State Department we have chosen from among almost 16,000 applicants about 110 of our Nation's finest young leaders to represent us in the international world. But we top this off with the disgraceful and counterproductive policy of appointing unqualified persons to major diplomatic posts as political payoffs. This must be stopped immediately.

Every effort should be extended to encourage full participation by our people in their own governments' processes, including universal voter registration for elections.

We must insure better public understanding of executive policy, and better exchange of ideas between Congress and the White House. To do this, Cabinet members representing the President should meet in scheduled public interrogation sessions with the full bodies of Congress.

All our citizens must know that they will be treated fairly.

To quote from my own inauguration speech of 4 years ago: "The time for racial discrimination is over. Our people have already made this major and difficult decision, but we cannot underestimate the challenge of hundreds of minor decisions yet to be made. No poor, rural, weak or black person should ever have to bear the additional burden of being deprived of the opportunity of an education, a job or simple justice."

We must meet this firm national commitment without equivocation or timidity in every aspect of private and public life.

As important as honesty and openness are -they are not enough. There must also be substance and logical direction in government.

The mechanism of our government should be understandable, efficient and economical...and it can be.

We must give top priority to a drastic and thorough revision of the federal bureaucracy, to its budgeting system and to the procedures for analyzing the effectiveness of its many varied services. Tight businesslike management and planning techniques must be instituted and maintained, utilizing the full authority and personal involvement of the President himself.

This is no job for the fainthearted. It will be met with violent opposition from those who now enjoy a special privilege, those who prefer to work in the dark, or those whose private fiefdoms are threatened.

In Georgia we met that opposition head on -and we won! We abolished 278 of our 300 agencies. We evolved clearly defined goals and policies in every part of government. We developed and implemented a remarkably effective system of zero base budgeting. We instituted tough performance auditing to insure proper conduct and efficient delivery of services.

Steps like these can insure a full return on our hard-earned tax dollars. These procedures are working in state capitols around the Nation and in our succcssful businesses, both large and small. They can and they will work in Washington.

Our Nation now has no understandable national purpose, no clearly defined goals, and no organizational mechanism to develop or achieve such purposes or goals. We move from one crisis to the next as if they were fads, even though the previous one hasn't been solved.

The Bible says: "If the trumpet give an uncertain sound, who shall prepare himself to the battle." As a planner and a businessman, and a chief executive, I know from experience that uncertainty is also a devastating affliction in private life and in government. Coordination of different programs is impossible. There is no clear vision of what is to be accomplished, everyone struggles for temporary advantage, and there is no way to monitor how effectively services are delivered.

What is our national policy for the production, acquisition, distribution or consumption of energy in times of shortage or doubtful supply? There is no policy! What are our long-range goals in health care, transportation, land use, economic development, waste disposal or housing? There are no goals!

The tremendous resources of our people and of our chosen leaders can be harnessed to devise effective, understandable and practical goals and policies in every realm of public life.

A government that is honest and competent, with clear purpose and strong leadership can work with the American people to meet the challenges of the present and the future.

We can then face together the tough long-range solutions to our economic woes. Our people are ready to make personal sacrifices when clear national economic policies are devised and understood.

We are grossly wasting our energy resources and other precious raw materials as though their supply was infinite. We must even face the prospect of changing our basic ways of living. This change will either be made on our own initiative in a planned and rational way, or forced on us with chaos and suffering by the inexorable laws of nature.

Energy imports and consumption must be reduced, free competition enhanced by rigid enforcement of antitrust laws, and general monetary growth restrained. Pinpointed federal programs can ease the more acute pains of recession, such as now exist in the construction industry. We should consider extension of unemployment compensation, the stimulation of investments, public subsidizing of employment, and surtaxes on excess profits.

We are still floundering and equivocating about protection of our environment. Neither designers of automobiles, mayors of cities, power companies, farmers, nor those of us who simply have to breathe the air, love beauty, and would like to fish or swim in pure water have the slightest idea in God's world what is coming out of Washington next! What does come next must be a firm commitment to pure air, clean water and unspoiled land.

Almost 20 years after its conception we have not finished the basic interstate highway system. To many lobbyists who haunt the capitol buildings of the Nation, ground transportation still means only more highways and more automobiles—the bigger, the better. We must have a national commitment to transportation capabilities which will encourage the most efficient movement of American people and cargo.

Gross tax inequities are being perpetuated. The most surely taxed income is that which is derived from the sweat of manual labor. Carefully contrived loopholes let the total tax burden shift more and more toward the average wage earner. The largest corporations pay the lowest tax rates and some with very high profits pay no tax at all.

When a business executive can charge off a $50 luncheon on a tax return and a truck driver cannot deduct his $1.50 sandwich - when oil companies pay less than 5% on their earnings while employees of the company pay at least three times this rate - when many pay no taxes on incomes of more than $100,000 - then we need basic tax reform!

Every American has a right to expect that laws will be administered in an evenhanded manner, but it seems that something is wrong even with our system of justice. Defendants who are repeatedly out on bail commit more crimes. Aggravating trial delays and endless litigation are common.

Citizens without influence often bear the brunt of prosecution while violators of antitrust laws and other white collar criminals are ignored and go unpunished.

Following recent presidential elections, our U.S. Attorney General has replaced the Postmaster General as the chief political appointee; and we have recently witnessed the prostitution of this most important law enforcement office. Special prosecutors had to be appointed simply to insure enforcement of the law! The Attorney General should be removed from politics.

The vast bureaucracy of government often fails to deliver needed social services to our people. High ideals and good intentions are not matched with rational, businesslike administration. The predictable result is frustration and discouragement among dedicated employees, recipients of services, and the American taxpayers.

There are about 25 million Americans who are classified as poor, two-thirds of whom happen to be white and half of whom receive welfare benefits. At least 10% of these are able to work. A massive bureaucracy of two million employees at all levels of government is attempting to administer more than 100 different programs of bewildering complexity. Case workers shuffle papers in a morass of red tape. Often it is financially profitable not to work and even to have a family disrupted by forcing the father to leave home. Some combined welfare payments exceed the average working family's income, while other needy families have difficulty obtaining a bare subsistence.

The word "welfare" no longer signifies how much we care, but often arouses feelings of contempt and even hatred.

Is a simplified, fair and compassionate welfare program beyond the capacity of our American government? I think not.

The quality of health care in this Nation depends largely on economic status. It is often unavailable or costs too much. There is little commonality of effort between private and public health agencies or between physicians and other trained medical personnel. I expect the next Congress to pass a national health insurance law. But present government interest seems to be in merely shifting the costs of existing services to the federal taxpayer or to the employers. There is little interest in preventing the cripplers and killers of our people and providing improved health care for those who still need it most.

Is a practical and comprehensive national health program beyond the capacity of our American government? I think not.

Federal education laws must be simplified to substitute education for paper-shuffling grantsmanship. Local systems need federal funds to supplement their programs for students where wealth and tax base are inadequate.

Is a comprehensive education program beyond the capacity of the American people? I think not.

As a farmer, I have been appalled at the maladministration of our Nation's agricultural economy. We have seen the elimination of our valuable food reserves, which has contributed to wild fluctuations in commodity prices and wiped out dependable trade and export capabilities. Grain speculators and monopolistic processors have profited, while farmers are going bankrupt trying to produce food that consumers are going broke trying to buy.

I know this Nation can develop an agricultural policy which will insure a fair profit to our farmers and a fair price to consumers.

It is obvious that domestic and foreign affairs are directly interrelated. A necessary base for effective implementation of any foreign policy is to get our domestic house in order.

Coordination of effort among the leaders of our Nation should be established so that our farm production, industrial development, foreign trade, defense, energy and diplomatic policies are mutually supportive and not in conflict.

The time for American intervention in all the problems of the world is over. But we cannot retreat into isolationism. Ties of friendship and cooperation with our friends and neighbors must be strengthened. Our common interests must be understood and pursued. The integrity of Israel must be preserved. Highly personalized and narrowly focused diplomatic efforts, although sometimes successful, should be balanced with a more wide-ranging implementation of foreign policy by competent foreign service officers.

Our Nation's security is obviously of paramount importance, and everything must be done to insure adequate military preparedness. But there is no reason why our national defense establishment cannot also be efficient.

Waste and inefficiency are both costly to taxpayers and a danger to our own national existence. Strict management and budgetary control over the Pentagon should reduce the ratio of officers to men and of support forces to combat troops. I see no reason why the Chief of Naval Operations needs more Navy captains on his staff than we have serving on ships!

Misdirected efforts such as the construction of unnecessary pork-barrel projects by the Corps of Engineers must be terminated.

The biggest waste and danger of all is the unnecessary proliferation of atomic weapons throughout the world. Our ultimate goal should be the elimination of nuclear weapon capability among all nations. In the meantime, simple, careful and fim1 proposals to implement this mutual arms reduction should be pursued as a prime national purpose in all our negotiations with nuclear powers -present or potential.

Is the achievement of these and other goals beyond the capacity of our American government? I think not.

Our people are hungry for integrity and competence in government. In this confused and fast-changing, technological world we still have within us the capability for national greatness.

About 3 months ago I met with the governors of the other 12 original states in Philadelphia. Exactly 200 years after the convening of the First Continental Congress we walked down the same streets, then turned left and entered a small building named Carpenter's Hall. There we heard exactly the same prayer and sat in the same chairs occupied in September of 1774 by Samuel Adams, John Jay, John Adams, Patrick Henry, George Washington, and about 45 other strong and opinionated leaders.

They held widely divergent views and they debated for weeks. They and others who joined them for the Second Continental Congress avoided the production of timid compromise resolutions. They were somehow inspired, and they reached for greatness. Their written premises formed the basis on which our Nation was begun.

I don't know whose chair I occupied, but sitting there I thought soberly about their times and ours. Their people were also discouraged, disillusioned and confused. But these early leaders acted with purpose and conviction.

I wondered to myself: Were they more competent, more intelligent or better educated than we? Were they more courageous? Did they have more compassion or love for their neighbors? Did they have deeper religious convictions? Were they more concerned about the future of their children than we? I think not.

We are equally capable of correcting our faults, overcoming difficulties, managing our own affairs and facing the future with justifiable confidence.

I am convinced that among us 200 million Americans there is a willingness - even eagerness - to restore in our Country what has been lost - if we have understandable purposes and goals and a modicum of bold and inspired leadership.

Our government can express the highest common ideals of human .beings—*if* we demand of it standards of excellence.

It is now time to stop and to ask ourselves the question which my last commanding officer, Admiral Hyman Rickover, asked me and every other young naval officer who serves or has served in an atomic submarine.

For our Nation—for all of us—that question is: "Why not the best?"
http://www.4president.org/speeches/carter1976announcement.htm

Ronald Reagan

New York Hilton, New York, NY
    November 13, 1979
    Good evening. I am here tonight to announce my intention to seek the Republican nomination for President of the United States.
    I'm sure that each of us has seen our country from a number of viewpoints depending on where we've lived and what we've done. For me it has been as a boy growing up in several small towns in Illinois. As a young man in Iowa trying to get a

start in the years of the Great Depression and later in California for most of my adult life.

I've seen America from the stadium press box as a sportscaster, as an actor, officer of my labor union, soldier, officeholder and as both a Democrat and Republican. I've lived in America where those who often had too little to eat outnumbered those who had enough. There have been four wars in my lifetime and I've seen our country face financial ruin in the Depression. I have also seen the great strength of this nation as it pulled itself up from that ruin to become the dominant force in the world.

To me our country is a living, breathing presence, unimpressed by what others say is impossible, proud of its own success, generous, yes and naive, sometimes wrong, never mean and always impatient to provide a better life for its people in a framework of a basic fairness and freedom.

Someone once said that the difference between an American and any other kind of person is that an American lives in anticipation of the future because he knows it will be a great place. Other people fear the future as just a repetition of past failures. There's a lot of truth in that. If there is one thing we are sure of it is that history need not be relived; that nothing is impossible, and that man is capable of improving his circumstances beyond what we are told is fact.

There are those in our land today, however, who would have us believe that the United States, like other great civilizations of the past, has reached the zenith of its power; that we are weak and fearful, reduced to bickering with each other and no longer possessed of the will to cope with our problems.

Much of this talk has come from leaders who claim that our problems are too difficult to handle. We are supposed to meekly accept their failures as the most which humanly can be done. They tell us we must learn to live with less, and teach our children that their lives will be less full and prosperous than ours have been; that the America of the coming years will be a place where–because of our past excesses–it will be impossible to dream and make those dreams come true.

I don't believe that. And, I don't believe you do either. That is why I am seeking the presidency. I cannot and will not stand by and see this great country destroy itself. Our leaders attempt to blame their failures on circumstances beyond their control, on false estimates by unknown, unidentifiable experts who rewrite modern history in an attempt to convince us our high standard of living, the result of thrift and hard work, is somehow selfish extravagance which we must renounce as we join in sharing scarcity. I don't agree that our nation must resign itself to inevitable decline, yielding its proud position to other hands. I am totally unwilling to see this country fail in its obligation to itself and to the other free peoples of the world.

The crisis we face is not the result of any failure of the American spirit; it is failure of our leaders to establish rational goals and give our people something to order their lives by. If I am elected, I shall regard my election as proof that the people of the United States have decided to set a new agenda and have recognized that the human spirit thrives best when goals are set and progress can be measured in their achievement.

During the next year I shall discuss in detail a wide variety of problems which a new administration must address. Tonight I shall mention only a few.

No problem that we face today can compare with the need to restore the health of the American economy and the strength of the American dollar. Double-digit inflation has robbed you and your family of the ability to plan. It has destroyed the confidence to buy and it threatens the very structure of family life itself as more and more wives are forced to work in order to help meet the ever-increasing cost of living. At the same time, the lack of real growth in the economy has introduced the justifiable fear in the minds of working men and women who are already overextended that soon there will be fewer jobs and no money to pay for even the necessities of life. And tragically as the cost of living keeps going up, the standard of living which has been our great pride keeps going down.

The people have not created this disaster in our economy; the federal government has. It has overspent, overestimated, and over-regulated. It has failed to deliver services within the revenues it should be allowed to raise from taxes. In the 34 years since the end of World War II, it has spent $448 billion more than it has collected in taxes–$448 billion of printing-press money, which has made every dollar you earn worth less and less. At the same time, the federal government has cynically told us that high taxes on business will in some way "solve" the problem and allow the average taxpayer to pay less. Well, business is not a taxpayer; it is a tax collector. Business has to pass its tax burden on to the customer as part of the cost of doing business. You and I pay taxes imposed on business every time we go to the store. Only people pay taxes and it is political demagoguery or economic illiteracy to try and tell us otherwise.

The key to restoring the health of the economy lies in cutting taxes. At the same time, we need to get the waste out of federal spending. This does not mean sacrificing essential services, nor do we need to destroy the system of benefits which flow to the poor, elderly, the sick and the handicapped. We have long since committed ourselves, as a people, to help those among us who cannot take care of themselves. But the federal government has proven to be the costliest and most inefficient provider of such help we could possibly have.

We must put an end to the arrogance of a federal establishment which accepts no blame for our condition, cannot be relied upon to give us a fair estimate of our situation and utterly refuses to live within its means. I will not accept the supposed "wisdom" which has it that the federal bureaucracy has become so powerful that it can no longer be changed or controlled by any administration. As President I would use every power at my command to make the federal establishment respond to the will and the collective wishes of the people.

We must force the entire federal bureaucracy to live in the real world of reduced spending, streamlined function and accountability to the people it serves. We must review the function of the federal government to determine which of those are the proper province of levels of government closer to the people.

The tenth article of the Bill of Rights is explicit in pointing out that the federal government should do only those things specifically called for in the Constitution. All others shall remain with the states or the people. We haven't been observing that tenth article of late. The federal government has taken on functions it was never intended to perform and which it does not perform well. There should be a planned, orderly transfer of such functions to states and communities and a transfer with them of the sources of taxation to pay for them.

The savings in administrative overhead would be considerable and certainly there would be increased efficiency and less bureaucracy.

By reducing federal tax rates where they discourage individual initiative–especially personal income tax rates–we can restore incentives, invite greater economic growth and at the same time help give us better government instead of bigger government. Proposals such as the Kemp-Roth bill would bring about this kind of realistic reductions in tax rates.

In short, a punitive tax system must be replaced by one that restores incentive for the worker and for industry; a system that rewards initiative and effort and encourages thrift.

All these things are possible; none of them will be easy. But the choice is clear. We can go on letting the country slip over the brink to financial ruin with the disaster that it means for the individual or we can find the will to work together to restore confidence in ourselves and to regain the confidence of the world. I have lived through one Depression. I carry with me the memory of a Christmas Eve when my brother and I and our parents exchanged our modest gifts–there was no lighted tree as there has been on Christmases past. I remember watching my father open what he thought was a greeting from his employer. We all watched and yes, we were hoping it was a bonus check. It was notice that he no longer had a job. And in those days the government ran the radio announcements telling workers not to leave home looking for jobs–there were no jobs. I'll carry with me always the memory of my father sitting there holding that envelope, unable to look at us. I cannot and will not stand by while inflation and joblessness destroy the dignity of our people.

Another serious problem which must be discussed tonight is our energy situation. Our country was built on cheap energy. Today, energy is not cheap and we face the prospect that some forms of energy may soon not be available at all.

Last summer you probably spent hours sitting in gasoline lines. This winter, some will be without heat and everyone will be paying much more simply to keep home and family warm. If you ever had any doubt of the government's inability to provide for the needs of the people, just look at the utter fiasco we now call "the energy crisis." Not one straight answer nor any realistic hope of relief has come from the present administration in almost 3 years of federal treatment of the problem. As gas lines grew, the administration again panicked and now has proposed to put the country on a wartime footing; but for this "war" there is no victory in sight. And, as always, when the federal bureaucracy fails, all it can suggest is more of the same. This time it's another bureau to untangle the mess by the ones we already have.

But, this just won't work. Solving the energy crisis will not be easy, but it can be done. First we must decide that "less" is not enough. Next, we must remove government obstacles to energy production. And, we must make use of those technological advantages we still possess.

It is no program simply to say "use less energy." Of course waste must be eliminated and efficiently promoted, but for the government simply to tell people to conserve is not an energy policy. At best it means we will run out of energy a little more slowly. But a day will come when the lights will dim and the wheels of industry will turn more slowly and finally stop. As President I will not endorse any course which has this as its principal objective.

We need more energy and that means diversifying our sources of supply away from the OPEC countries. Yes, it means more efficient automobiles. But it also means more exploration and development of oil and natural gas here in our own country. The only way to free ourselves from the monopoly pricing power of OPEC is to be less dependent on outside sources of fuel.

The answer, obvious to anyone except those in the administration it seems, is more domestic production of oil and gas. We must also have wider use of nuclear power within strict safety rules, of course. There must be more spending by the energy industries on research and development of substitutes for fossil fuels.

In years to come solar energy may provide much of the answer but for the next two or three decades we must do such things as master the chemistry of coal. Putting the market system to work for these objectives is an essential first step for their achievement. Additional multi-billion-dollar federal bureaus and programs are not the answer.

In recent weeks there has been much talk about "excess" oil company profits. I don't believe we've been given all the information we need to make a judgment about this. We should have that information. Government exists to protect us from each other. It is not government's function to allocate fuel or impose unnecessary restrictions on the marketplace. It is government's function to determine whether we are being unfairly exploited and if so to take immediate and appropriate action. As President I would do exactly that.

On the foreign front, the decade of the 1980s will place severe pressures upon the United States and its allies. We can expect to be tested in ways calculated to try our patience, to confound our resolve and to erode our belief in ourselves. During a time when the Soviet Union may enjoy nuclear superiority over this country, we must never waiver in our commitment to our allies nor accept any negotiation which is not clearly in the national interest. We must judge carefully. Though we should leave no initiative untried in our pursuit of peace, we must be clear voiced in our resolve to resist any unpeaceful act wherever it may occur. Negotiation with the Soviet Union must never become appeasement.

For the most of the last 40 years, we have been preoccupied with the global struggle–the competition–with the Soviet Union and with our responsibilities to our allies. But too often in recent times we have just drifted along with events, responding as if we thought of ourselves as a nation in decline. To our allies we seem to appear to be a nation unable to make decisions in its own interests, let alone in the common interest. Since the Second World War we have spent large amounts of money and much of our time protecting and defending freedom all over the world. We must continue this, for if we do not accept the responsibilities of leadership, who will? And if no one will, how will we survive?

The 1970s have taught us the foolhardiness of not having a long-range diplomatic strategy of our own. The world has become a place where, in order to survive, our country needs more than just allies–it needs real friends. Yet, in recent times we often seem not to have recognized who our friends are. This must change. It is now time to take stock of our own house and to resupply its strength.

Part of that process involves taking stock of our relationship with Puerto Rico. I favor statehood for Puerto Rico and if the people of Puerto Rico vote for statehood in their coming referendum I would, as President, initiate the enabling legislation to make this a reality.

We live on a continent whose three countries possess the assets to make it the strongest, most prosperous and self-sufficient area on Earth. Within the borders of this North American continent are the food, resources, technology and undeveloped territory which, properly managed, could dramatically improve the quality of life of all its inhabitants.

It is no accident that this unmatched potential for progress and prosperity exists in three countries with such long-standing heritages of free government. A developing closeness among Canada, Mexico and the United States–a North American accord– would permit achievement of that potential in each country beyond that which I believe any of them–strong as they are–could accomplish in the absence of such cooperation. In fact, the key to our own future security may lie in both Mexico and Canada becoming much stronger countries than they are today.

No one can say at this point precisely what form future cooperation among our three countries will take. But if I am elected President, I would be willing to invite each of our neighbors to send a special representative to our government to sit in on high level planning sessions with us, as partners, mutually concerned about the future of our continent. First, I would immediately seek the views and ideas of Canadian and Mexican leaders on this issue, and work tirelessly with them to develop closer ties among our peoples. It is time we stopped thinking of our nearest neighbors as foreigners.

By developing methods of working closely together, we will lay the foundations for future cooperation on a broader and more significant scale. We will put to rest any doubts of those cynical enough to believe that the United States would seek to dominate any relationship among our three countries, or foolish enough to think that the governments and peoples of Canada and Mexico would ever permit such domination to occur. I for one, am confident that we can show the world by example that the nations of North America are ready, within the context of an unswerving commitment to freedom, to see new forms of accommodation to meet a changing world. A developing closeness between the United States, Canada and Mexico would serve notice on friends and foe alike that we were prepared for a long haul, looking outward again and confident of our future; that together we are going to create jobs, to generate new fortunes of wealth for many and provide a legacy for the children of each of our countries. Two hundred years ago, we taught the world that a new form of government, created out of the genius of man to cope with his circumstances, could succeed in bringing a measure of quality to human life previously thought impossible.

Now let us work toward the goal of using the assets of this continent, its resources, technology, and foodstuffs in the most efficient ways possible for the common good of all its people. It may take the next 100 years but we can dare to dream that at some future date a map of the world might show the North American continent as one in which the people's commerce of its three strong countries flow more freely across their present borders than they do today.

In recent months leaders in our government have told us that, we, the people, have lost confidence in ourselves; that we must regain our spirit and our will to achieve our national goals. Well, it is true there is a lack of confidence, an unease with things the way they are. But the confidence we have lost is confidence in our government's policies. Our unease can almost be called bewilderment at how our defense strength has deteriorated. The great productivity of our industry is now surpassed by virtually all the major nations who compete with us for world markets. And, our currency is no longer the stable measure of value it once was.

But there remains the greatness of our people, our capacity for dreaming up fantastic deeds and bringing them off to the surprise of an unbelieving world. When Washington's men were freezing at Valley Forge, Tom Paine told his fellow Americans: "We have it in our power to begin the world over again," we still have that power.

We–today's living Americans–have in our lifetime fought harder, paid a higher price for freedom and done more to advance the dignity of man than any people who have ever lived on this Earth. The citizens of this great nation want leadership–yes– but not a "man on a white horse" demanding obedience to his commands. They want someone who believes they can "begin the world over again." A leader who will unleash their great strength and remove the roadblocks government has put in their way. I want to do that more than anything I've ever wanted. And it's something that I believe with God's help I can do.

I believe this nation hungers for a spiritual revival; hungers to once again see honor placed above political expediency; to see government once again the protector of our liberties, not the distributor of gifts and privilege. Government should uphold and not undermine those institutions which are custodians of the very values upon which civilization is founded–religion, education and, above all, family. Government cannot be clergyman, teacher and patriot. It is our servant, beholden to us.

We who are privileged to be Americans have had a rendezvous with destiny since the moment in 1630 when John Winthrop, standing on the deck of the tiny Arbella off the coast of Massachusetts, told the little band of Pilgrims, "We shall be a city upon a hill. The eyes of all people are upon us so that if we shall deal falsely with our God in this work we have undertaken and so cause Him to withdraw His present help from us, we shall be made a story and a byword throughout the world."

A troubled and afflicted mankind looks to us, pleading for us to keep our rendezvous with destiny; that we will uphold the principles of self-reliance, self-discipline, morality, and–above all–responsible liberty for every individual that we will become that shining city on a hill.

I believe that you and I together can keep this rendezvous with destiny.

Thank you and good night.

Bill Clinton

Old State House, Little Rock, Arkansas.

October 3, 1991.

Thank you all for being here today, for your friendship and support, for giving me the opportunity to serve as your Governor for 11 years, for filling my life full of blessings beyond anything I ever deserved.

I want to thank especially Hillary and Chelsea for taking this big step in our life's journey together. Hillary, for being my wife, my friend, and my partner in our efforts to build a better future for the children and families of Arkansas and America. Chelsea, in ways she is only now coming to understand, has been our constant joy and reminder of what our public efforts are really all about: a better life for all who will work for it, a better future for the next generation.

All of you, in different ways, have brought me here today, to step beyond a life and a job I love, to make a commitment to a larger cause: Preserving the American Dream ... Restoring the hopes of the forgotten middle class... Reclaiming the future for our children.

I refuse to be part of a generation that celebrates the death of Communism abroad with the loss of the American Dream at home.

I refuse to be part of a generation that fails to compete in the global economy and so condemns hard-working Americans to a life of struggle without reward or security.

That is why I stand here today...because I refuse to stand by and let our children become part of the first generation to do worse than their parents. I don't want my child or your child to be part of a country that's coming apart instead of coming together.

Over 25 years ago, I had a professor at Georgetown who taught me that America was the greatest country in history because our people believed in and acted on two simple ideas: first, that the future can be better than the present; and second, that each of us has a personal, moral responsibility to make it so.

That fundamental truth has guided my public career, and brings me here today. It is what we've devoted ourselves to here in Arkansas. I'm proud of what we've done here in Arkansas together. Proud of the work we've done to become a laboratory of democracy and innovation. And proud that we've done it without giving up the things we cherish and honor most about our way of life. Solid, middle-class values of work, Will, family, individual responsibility, and community.

As I've traveled across our state, I've found that everything we believe in, everything we've fought for, is threatened by an administration that refuses to take care of our own, has turned its back on the middle class, and is afraid to change while the world is changing.

The historic events In the Soviet Union in recent months teach us an important lesson: National security begins at home. For the Soviet Empire never lost to us on the field of battle. Their system rotted from the inside out, from economic, political and spiritual failure.

To be sure, the collapse of communism requires a new national security policy. I applaud the President's recent initiative in reducing nuclear weapons. It is an important beginning. But make no mistake - the end of the Cold War is not the end of threats to America. The world is still a dangerous and uncertain place. The first and most solemn obligation of the president is to keep America strong and safe from foreign dangers, and promote democracy around the world.

But we cannot build a safe and secure world unless we can first make America strong at home. It is our ability to take care of our own at home that gives us the strength to stand up for what we believe around the world.

As governor for 11 years, working to preserve and create jobs in a global economy, I know our competition for the future is Germany and the rest of Europe, Japan and the rest of Asia. And I know that we are losing America's leadership in the world because we're losing the American dream right here at home.

Middle class people are spending more hours on the job, spending less time with their children, bringing home a smaller paycheck to pay more for health care and housing and education. Our streets are meaner, our families are broken, our health care is the costliest in the world and we get less for it.

The country is headed in the wrong direction fast, slipping behind, losing our way...and all we have out of Washington is status quo paralysis. No vision, no action. Just neglect, selfishness, and division.

For 12 years, Republicans have tried to divide us—race against race—so we get mad at each other and not at them. They want us to look at each other across a racial divide so we don't turn and look to the White House and ask, why are all of our incomes going down, why are all of us losing jobs? Why are we losing our future?

Where I come from we know about race-baiting. They've used it to divide us for years. I know this tactic well and I'm not going to let them get away with it.

For 12 years, the Republicans have talked about choice without really believing in it. George Bush says he wants school choice even if it bankrupts the public schools, and yet he's more than willing to make it a crime for the women of America to exercise their individual right to choose.

For 12 years, the Republicans have been telling us chat America's problems aren't their problem. They washed their hands of responsibility for the economy and education and health care and social policy and turned it over to 50 states and a 1000 points of light. Well, here in Arkansas we've done our best to create jobs and educate our people. And each of us has tried to be one of those 1000 points of light But I can tell you, where there is no national vision, no national partnership, no national leadership, a 1000 points of light leaves a lot of darkness.

We must provide the answers...the solutions. And we will. We're going to turn this country around and get it moving again, and we're going to fight for the hard-working middle-class families of America for a change.

Make no mistake—this election is about change: in our party, in our national leadership, and in our country.

And we're not going to get positive change just by Bush-bashing. We have to do a better job of the old-fashioned work of confronting the real problems of real people and pointing the way to a better future. That is our challenge in 1992.

Today, as we stand on the threshold of a new era, a new millennium, I believe we need a new kind of leadership, leadership committed to change. Leadership not mired in the politics of the past, not limited by old ideologies...Proven leadership that knows how to reinvent government to help solve the real problem of real people.

That is why today I am declaring my candidacy for President of the United States. Together I believe we can provide leadership that will restore the American dream - that will fight for the forgotten middle class - that will provide more opportunity, Insist on more responsibility and create a greater sense of community for this great country.

The change we must make isn't liberal or conservative. It's both, and it's different. The small towns and main streets of America aren't like the corridors and backrooms of Washington. People out here don't care about the idle rhetoric of "left" and "right" and "liberal" and "conservative" and all the other words that have made our politics a substitute for action. These families are crying out desperately for someone who believes the promise of America is to help them with their struggle to get ahead, to offer them a green light instead of a pink slip.

This must be a campaign of ideas, not slogans. We don't need another President who doesn't know what he wants to do for America. I'm going to tell you in plain language what I intend to do as President. How we can meet the challenges we face—that's the test for all the Democratic candidates in this campaign. Americans know what we're against Let's show them what we're for.

We need a new covenant to rebuild America. It's just common sense. Government's responsibility is to create more opportunity. The people's responsibility is to make the most of it.

In a Clinton Administration, we are going to create opportunity for all. We've got to grow this economy, not shrink it. We need to give people Incentives to make long-term investment in America and reward people who produce goods and services, not those who speculate with other people's money. We've got to invest more money in emerging technologies to help keep high-paying jobs here at home. We've got to convert from a defense to a domestic economy.

We've got to expand world trade, tear down barriers, but demand fair trade policies if we're going to provide good jobs for our people. The American people don't want to run from the world. We must meet the competition and win.

0pportunity for all means world-class skills and world-class education. We need more than photo ops and empty rhetoric - we need standards and accountability and excellence in education. On this issue, I'm proud to say that Arkansas has led the way.

In a Clinton Administration, students and parents and teachers will get a *real* education President.

Opportunity for all means pre-school for every child who needs it, and an apprenticeship program for kids who don't want to go to college but do want good jobs. It means teaching everybody with a job to read, and passing a domestic GI Bill that would give every young American the chance to borrow the money necessary to go to college and ask them to pay it back either as a small percentage of their income over time, or through national service as teachers or policemen or nurses or child care workers.

In. a Clinton Administration, everyone will be able to get a college loan as long as they're willing to give something back to their country In return.

Opportunity for all means reforming the health care system to control costs, improve quality, expand preventive and long-term care, maintain consumer choice, and cover everybody. And we don't have to bankrupt the taxpayers to do it. We do have to take on the big insurance companies and health care bureaucracies and get some real cost control into the system. I pledge to the American people that in the first year of a Clinton Administration, we will present a plan to Congress and the American people to provide affordable, quality health care for all Americans.

Opportunity for all means making our cities and our streets safe from crime and drugs. Across America, citizens are banding together to take their streets and neighborhoods back. In a Clinton Administration, we'll be on their side with new initiatives like community policing, drug treatment for those who need it, and boot camps for first-time offenders.

Opportunity for all means making taxes fair. I'm not out to soak the rich. I wouldn't mind being rich. But I do believe the rich should pay their fair share. For 12 years, the Republicans have raised taxes on the middle class. It's time to give the middle class tax relief.

Finally, opportunity for all means we must protect our environment and develop an energy policy that relies more on conservation and clean natural gas so all our children will inherit a world that is cleaner, safer, and more beautiful.

But hear me now. I honestly believe that if we try to do these things, we will still not solve the problems of today or move into the next century with confidence unless we do what President Kennedy did and ask every American citizen to assume personal responsibility for the future of our country.

The government owes our people more opportunity, but we all have to make the most of it through responsible citizenship.

We should insist that people move off welfare rolls and onto work rolls. We should give people on welfare the skills they need to succeed, but we should demand that everybody who can work and become a productive member of society.

We should insist on the toughest possible child support enforcement. Governments don't raise children, parents do. And when they don't, their children pay forever and so do we.

And we have got to say, as we've tried to do in Arkansas, that students have a responsibility to stay in school. If you drop out for no good reason, you should lose your driver's license. But its important to remember that the most irresponsible people of all in the 1980s were those at the top...not those who were doing worse, not the hard-working middle class, but those who sold out our savings and loans with bad deals and spent billions on wasteful takeovers and mergers - money that could have been spent to create better products and new jobs.

Do you know that in the 1980s, while middle-class income went down, charitable giving by working people went up? And while rich peoples incomes went up, charitable giving by the wealthy went down. Why? Because our leaders had an ethic of get it while you can and to heck with everybody else.

How can you ask people who work or who are poor to behave responsibly, when they know that the heads of our biggest companies raised their own pay in the last decade by four times the percentage their workers' pay went up? Three times as much as their profits went up. When they ran their companies into the ground and their employees were on the street, what did they do? They bailed out with golden parachutes to a cushy life. That's just wrong.

Teddy Roosevelt and Harry Truman and John Kennedy didn't hesitate to use the bully pulpit of the Presidency. They changed America by standing up for what's right. When Salomon Brothers abused the Treasury markets, the President was silent. When the.

rip-off artists looted our S&L's the President Was Silent. In a Clinton Administration, when people sell their companies and their workers and their country down the river, they'll get called on the carpet. We're going to insist that they invest In this country and create jobs for our people.

In the 1980s, Washington failed us too. We spent more money on the present and the past and less on the future. We spent $500 billion to recycle assets in the S&L mess, but we couldn't afford $5 billion for unemployed workers or to give every kid in this country the chance to be in Head Start. We can do better than that, and we will.

A Clinton Administration won't spend our money on programs that don't solve problems and a government that doesn't work. I want to reinvent government to make it more efficient and more effective. I want to give citizens more choices in the services they get, and empower them to make those choices. That's what we've tried to do in Arkansas. We've balanced the budget every year and improved services. We've treated taxpayers like our customers and our bosses, because they are.

I want the American people to know that a Clinton Administration will defend our national interests abroad, put their values into our social policy at home, and spend their tax money with discipline. Well put government back on the side of the hard-working middle-class families of America who think most of the help goes to those at the top of the ladder, some goes to the bottom, and no one speaks for them.

But we need more than new laws, new promises, or new program. We need a new spirit of community, a sense that we are all in this together. If we have no sense of community the American dream will continue to wither. Our destiny is bound up with the destiny of every other American. Were all in this together, and we will rise or fail together.

A few years ago, Hillary and I visited a classroom in Los Angeles, in an area plagued by drugs and gangs. We talked to a dozen sixth graders, whose number one concern was being shot going to and from school. Their second worry was turning

12 or 13 and being forced to join a gang or be beaten. And finally, they were worried about their own parents' drug abuse.

Newly half a century ago, I was born not far from here in Hope, Arkansas. My mother had been widowed 3 months before I was born. I was raised for 4 years by my grandparents, while she went back to nursing school. They didn't have much money. I spent a lot of time with my great-grandparents. By any standard, they were poor. But we didn't blame other people. We took responsibility for ourselves and for each other because we knew we could do better. I was raised to believe In the American dream, in family values, in individual responsibility, and in the obligation of government to help people who were doing the best they could.

Its a long way in America from that loving family which is embodied today in a picture on my wall in the Governor's office of me at the age of six holding my great-grandfather's hand to an America where children on the streets of our cities don't know who their grandparents are and have to worry about their own parents' drug abuse.

I tell you, by making common cause with those children, we give new life to the American dream. And that is our generation's responsibility—to form a new covenant... more opportunity for all, more responsibility from everyone, and a greater sense of common purpose.

I believe with all my heart that together, we can make this happen. We can usher in a new era of progress, prosperity and renewal. We can—we must. This is not just a campaign for the Presidency—it is a campaign for the future, for the forgotten hard-working middle class families of America who deserve a government that fights for them. A campaign to keep America strong at home and around the world. Join with us. I ask for your prayers, your help, your hands, and your hearts. Together we can make America great again, and build a community of hope that will inspire the world.

http://www.4president.org/speeches/1992/billclinton1992announcement.htm

George W. Bush

Cedar Rapids, Iowa
June 12, 1999
What a pleasure it is to visit with you, to shake your hands. Laura and I are so grateful for your welcome, your enthusiasm, your confidence.

There will come a time for formal speeches and ten point plans. But I know the question on your mind: Why are you thinking about running for president? So I'll tell you what's on my heart.

I'll have a formal announcement sometime in the Fall. I have come here today to tell you this: I am running for President of the United States. There's no turning back, and I intend to be the next President of the United States.

I'm running because our country must be prosperous. But prosperity must have a purpose. The purpose of prosperity is to make sure the American dream touches every willing heart. The purpose of prosperity is to leave no one out... to leave no one behind. I'm running because my party must match a conservative mind with a compassionate heart. And I'm running to win.

Prosperity is not a given. Some in this administration think they invented it. But they did not invent prosperity, any more than they invented the Internet. Governments don't create wealth. Wealth is created by Americans—by creativity and enterprise and risk-taking. But government can create an environment where businesses and entrepreneurs and families can dream and flourish.

We'll be prosperous if we reduce taxes. I'll have a plan that reduces marginal rates to create jobs, but a plan that also helps struggling families on the outskirts of poverty. I believe that after we meet priorities, all that remains must be passed back to Americans, so it will not be spent by Washington.

We'll be prosperous if we reduce the regulations that strangle enterprise. And I will do what I did in Texas: fight for meaningful, real tort reform.

We'll be prosperous if we embrace free trade. I'll work to end tariffs and break down barriers everywhere, entirely, so the whole world trades in freedom. The fearful build walls. The confident demolish them. I am confident in American workers and farmers and producers. And I am confident that America's best is the best in the world.

We must be prosperous to keep our commitments to the health and security and dignity of the elderly. And we should trust Americans by giving them the option of investing part of their Social Security contributions in private accounts.

And we must be prosperous to keep the peace. This is still a world of terror and missiles and madmen. And we are challenged by aging weapons and failing intelligence.

I will rebuild our military power – because a dangerous world still requires a sharpened sword.

I will move quickly to defend our people and our allies against missiles and blackmail.

And I will have a foreign policy with a touch of iron – driven by American values and American interests.

America must seize this moment. America must lead. Because America's greatest export to the world is, and always will be, freedom.

America will be prosperous and strong if we do the right things. But prosperity alone is simple materialism. Prosperity must have a greater purpose. The success of America has never been proven by cities of gold, but by citizens of character. Men and women who work hard, dream big, love their family, serve their neighbor. Values that turn a piece of earth into a neighborhood, a community, a chosen nation.

That dream is so vivid – but still many are saying: The dream is not for me. Kids who turn schoolyards into battlefields. Children who corrupt their wills and souls with drugs, who limit their ambitions by having children themselves. Failed schools are creating two societies: one that reads and one that can't; one that dreams and one that doesn't.

These are burdens on the conscience of a successful nation. The next president must close this gap of hope. It is the great challenge to America's good heart.

I want to be a president who sets a tone, a direction, an agenda. I will be an activist president, who sets goals worthy of a great nation. I won't use my office as a mirror to reflect public opinion. And I'll be guided by conservative principles. Government should do a few things, and do them well. Government should not try to be all things to all people.

My first goal is to usher in the responsibility era. An era that stands in stark contrast to the last few decades, when the culture has clearly said: If it feels good, do it. If you've got a problem, blame someone else. Each of us must understand we are responsible for the choices we make in life. We're responsible for the children we bring into the world. We're responsible to love our neighbor as we want to be loved ourselves.

And we must pass this message to our children—teach them there are right choices in life and wrong choices in life. Drugs will destroy you. Alcohol will ruin your life. And having a child out of wedlock is a sure fire way to fall behind. We'll love the babies. But the message must be clear: It is not the definition of a man to father a child out of wedlock and say, "They're not my problem, they're yours."

Some people think it's inappropriate to draw a moral line. Not me. For our children to have the lives we want for them, they must learn to say yes to responsibility, yes to family, yes to honesty and work. I have seen our culture change once in my lifetime, so I know it can change again.

What can be done? Government can help. We can write laws to give schools and principals more authority to discipline children and protect the peace of classrooms. We must encourage states to reform their juvenile justice laws. We must say to our children, "We love you, but discipline and love go hand in hand, and there will be bad consequences for bad behavior."

But changing our culture requires more than laws. Cultures change one heart, one soul, one conscience at a time. Government can spend money, but it can't put hope in our hearts or a sense of purpose in our lives. This is done by churches and synagogues and mosques and charities that warm the cold of life. A quiet river of goodness and kindness that cuts through stone.

So my second goal—one of the biggest jobs for the next president—is to rally these armies of compassion that exist in every community. To nurture. To mentor. To comfort. To perform their commonplace miracles of renewal.

As president, I will lift the regulations that hamper them. I will involve them in after-school programs, maternity group homes, drug treatment, prison ministries. I will lay out specific incentives to encourage an outpouring of giving in America. Supporting these men and women—the soldiers in the army of compassion—is the next, bold step of welfare reform. Because changing hearts will change our entire society.

And my third goal. We should make a solemn commitment in this country: That every child will be educated. That no child will be left behind.

I believe in the power of high standards and high hopes. I have seen what works in my state. Raise the bar of expectations. Measure progress. Insist on results. Blow the whistle on failure. Don't give up on anyone.

As president, I will give more flexibility and authority to states—but encourage local folks to measure results for every child. I will praise success – but shine a spotlight of shame on failure. If schools fail, we must be bold enough to challenge the status quo. And I am going to change Head Start—to teach our youngest children phonics so they can read, and the basics, so they can add.

Everyone must have a first rate education, because there are no second rate children, no second rate dreams.

You've heard me talk about compassionate conservatism. These goals are what I mean.

It is conservative to cut taxes. It is compassionate to help people save and give and build.

It is conservative to reform welfare by insisting on work. It is compassionate to take the side of charities and churches that confront the suffering which remains.

It is conservative to confront illegitimacy. It is compassionate to offer practical help to women and children in crisis.

It is conservative to insist on education standards, basics and local control. It is compassionate to make sure that not one single child gets left behind.

I know this approach has been criticized. But why? Is compassion beneath us? Is mercy below us? Should our party be led by someone who boasts of a hard heart? I know Republicans—across the country—are generous of heart. I am confident the American people view compassion as a noble calling. The calling of a nation where the strong are just and the weak are valued.

I am proud to be a compassionate conservative. I welcome the label. And on this ground I'll take my stand.

It is the ground I've stood as governor of Texas, a job I really love. I know it isn't the same as being president. But if Texas were a country, it would be the 11th largest economy in the world. And I've had some successes. We passed the two biggest tax cuts in Texas history. We reformed our welfare and tort laws. We improved test scores for all the children in our schools, especially African-American and Hispanic kids.

I've learned to lead. I don't run polls to tell me what to think. I make decisions based on a conservative philosophy that is engrained in my heart. Trust local people to make right choices about their schools and cities. Understand that private property is the backbone of capitalism. Fight for American interests and American workers in the world. Know the importance of family and the need for personal responsibility. These are principles from which I will not vary.

I've learned you cannot lead by dividing people. This country is hungry for a new style of campaign. Positive. Hopeful. Inclusive. A campaign that attracts new faces and new voices. A campaign that unites all Americans toward a better tomorrow.

I say a better tomorrow because I've learned that people want to follow an optimist. They don't respond to the message: "Follow me, things are going to get worse." They respond to someone who appeals to our better angels, not our darker impulses. They respond to someone who sees better times—and I see better times.

I want you to imagine a campaign that carries this message. We will defend the American dream with sound economic policies and tax cuts. But we will also tell every American, "The dream is for you." Tell forgotten children in failed schools, "The dream is for you." Tell families, from the barrios of LA to the Rio Grande Valley: "El sueno americano es para ti." Tell men and women in our decaying cities, "The dream is for you." Tell confused young people, starved of ideals, "The dream is for you." This is the kind of campaign we must run.

For my part, I'm running, and I'm running hard. I know that this race will be competitive. I know the other candidates are good and talented people. And I know I'm late. But now that the Texas legislative session is over, I'm taking my front porch campaign to every front porch in this state. I will tell people exactly what I told you here today. Face to face. Eye to eye. And I cannot wait.

It feels to me like an old era of American politics is ending—like Americans are waiting for new hopes, new energy, new idealism. We will prove that someone who is conservative and compassionate can win without sacrificing principle. We will show that politics, after a time of tarnished ideals, can be higher and better. We will give our country a fresh start after a season of cynicism.

We have a long way to go, but we start today. And I hope you'll join me.

Thank you.

http://www.4president.org/speeches/2000/georgewbush2000announcement.htm

Barack Obama

Springfield, Illinois

10 February 2007

Hello Springfield! ...Look at all of you. Look at all of you. Goodness. Thank you so much. Thank you so much. Giving all praise and honor to God for bringing us here today. Thank you so much. I am—I am so grateful to see all of you. You guys are still cheering back there? [to audience on left.]

Let me—Let me begin by saying thanks to all you who've traveled, from far and wide, to brave the cold today. I know it's a little chilly—but I'm fired up.

You know, we all made this journey for a reason. It's humbling to see a crowd like this, but in my heart I know you didn't just come here for me. You...came here because you believe in what this country can be. In the face of war, you believe there can be peace. In the face of despair, you believe there can be hope. In the face of a politics that shut you out, that's told you to settle, that's divided us for too long, you believe that we can be one people, reaching for what's possible, building that more perfect union.

That's the journey we're on today. But let me tell you how I came to be here. As most of you know, I'm not a native of this great state. I—I moved to Illinois over two decades ago. I was a young man then, just a year out of college. I knew no one in Chicago when I arrived, was without money or family connections. But a group of churches had offered me a job as a community organizer for the grand sum of 13,000 dollars a year. And I accepted the job, sight unseen, motivated then by a single, simple, powerful idea: that I might play a small part in building a better America.

My work took me to some of Chicago's poorest neighborhoods. I joined with pastors and lay-people to deal with communities that had been ravaged by plant closings. I saw that the problems people faced weren't simply local in nature, that the decisions to close a steel mill was made by distant executives, that the lack of textbooks and computers in a school could be traced to skewed priorities of politicians a thousand miles away, and that when a child turns to violence—I came to realize that—there's a hole in that boy's heart that no government alone can fill.

It was in these neighborhoods that I received the best education that I ever had, and where I learned the meaning of my Christian faith.

After 3 years of this work, I went to law school, because I wanted to understand how the law should work for those in need. I became a civil rights lawyer, and taught constitutional law, and after a time, I came to understand that our cherished rights of liberty and equality depend on the active participation of an awakened electorate. It was with these ideas in mind that I arrived in this capital city as a state Senator.

It—It was here, in Springfield, where I saw all that is America converge—farmers and teachers, businessmen and laborers, all of them with a story to tell, all of them seeking a seat at the table, all of them clamoring to be heard. I made lasting friendships here, friends that I see here in the audience today. It was here—It was here where we learned to disagree without being disagreeable; that it's possible to compromise so long as you know those principles that can never be compromised; and that so long as we're willing to listen to each other, we can assume the best in people instead of the worst.

That's why we were able to reform a death penalty system that was broken; that's why we were able to give health insurance to children in need; that's why we made the tax system right here in Springfield more fair and just for working families; and that's why we passed ethics reform that the cynics said could never, ever be passed.

It was here, in Springfield, where North, South, East, and West come together that I was reminded of the essential decency of the American people—where I came to believe that through this decency, we can build a more hopeful America. And that is why, in the shadow of the Old State Capitol, where Lincoln once called on a house divided to stand together, where common hopes and common dreams still live, I stand before you today to announce my candidacy for President of the United States of America.

Now—Now, listen, I—I...—thank you, thank you, thank you, thank you. [to audience chanting "Obama"].

Look, I—I...recognize that there is a certain presumptuousness in this, a certain audacity, to this announcement. I know that I haven't spent a lot of time learning the ways of Washington. But I've been there long enough to know that the ways of Washington must change.

The genius of our Founders is that they designed a system of government that can be changed. And we should take heart, because we've changed this country before. In the face of tyranny, a band of patriots brought an empire to its knees. In the face of secession, we unified a nation and set the captives free. In the face of Depression, we put people back to work and lifted millions out of poverty. We welcomed immigrants to our shores. We opened railroads to the west. We landed a man on the moon. And we heard a King's call to let "justice roll down like waters, and righteousness like a mighty stream."

We've done this before: Each and every time, a new generation has risen up and done what's needed to be done. Today we are called once more, and it is time for our generation to answer that call. For that is our unyielding faith—that in—in the face of impossible odds, people who love their country can change it.

That's what Abraham Lincoln understood. He had his doubts. He had his defeats. He had his skeptics. He had his setbacks. But through his will and his words, he moved a nation and helped free a people. It's because of the millions who rallied to his cause that we're no longer divided, North and South, slave and free. It's because men and women of every race, from every walk of life, continued to march for freedom long after Lincoln was laid to rest, that today we have the chance to face the challenges of this millennium together, as one people—as Americans.

All of us know what those challenges are today: a war with no end, a dependence on oil that threatens our future, schools where too many children aren't learning, and families struggling paycheck to paycheck despite working as hard as they can. We know the challenges. We've heard them. We've talked about them for years.

What's stopped us from meeting these challenges is not the absence of sound policies and sensible plans. What's stopped us is the failure of leadership, the smallness—the smallness of our politics—the ease with which we're distracted by the petty and trivial, our chronic avoidance of tough decisions, our preference for scoring cheap political points instead of rolling up our sleeves and building a working consensus to tackle the big problems of America.

For the past six years we've been told that our mounting debts don't matter. We've been told that the anxiety Americans feel about rising health care costs and stagnant wages are an illusion. We've been told that climate change is a hoax. We've been told that tough talk and an ill-conceived war can replace diplomacy, and strategy, and foresight. And when all else fails, when Katrina happens, or the death toll in Iraq mounts, we've been told that our crises are somebody else's fault. We're distracted from our real failures, and told to blame the other Party, or gay people, or immigrants.

And as people have looked away in disillusionment and frustration, we know what's filled the void: the cynics, the lobbyists, the special interests—who've turned our government into a game only they can afford to play. They write the checks and you get stuck with the bill. They get the access while you get to write a letter. They think they own this government, but we're here today to take it back. The time for that kind of politics is over. It is through. It's time to turn the page—right here and right now.

Now look—

[Audience chants "Obama...Obama...Obama"].

Okay. Alright. Thank you. Thank you. Thank you.

Look, look, we have made some progress already. I was proud to help lead the fight in Congress that led to the most sweeping ethics reforms since Watergate. But Washington has a long way to go, and it won't be easy. That's why we'll have to set priorities. We'll have to make hard choices. And although government will play a crucial role in bringing about the changes that we need, more money and programs alone will not get us to where we need to go. Each of us, in our own lives, will have to accept responsibility—for instilling an ethic of achievement in our children, for adapting to a more competitive economy, for strengthening our communities, and sharing some measure of sacrifice.

So let us begin. Let us begin this hard work together. Let us transform this nation. Let us be the generation that reshapes our economy to compete in the digital age. Let's set high standards for our schools and give them the resources they need to succeed. Let's recruit a new army of teachers, and give them better pay and more support in exchange for more accountability. Let's make college more affordable, and let's invest in scientific research, and let's lay down broadband lines through the heart of inner cities and rural towns all across America. We can do that.

And as our economy changes, let's be the generation that ensures our nation's workers are sharing in our prosperity. Let's protect the hard-earned benefits their companies have promised. Let's make it possible for hardworking Americans to save for retirement. Let's allow our unions and their organizers to lift up this country's middle-class again. We can do that.

Let's be the generation that ends poverty in America. Every single person willing to work should be able to get job training that leads to a job, and earn a living wage that can pay the bills, and afford child care so their kids can have a safe place to go when they work. We can do this.

And let's be the generation that finally, after all these years, tackles our health care crisis. We can control costs by focusing on prevention, by providing better treatment to the chronically ill, and using technology to cut the bureaucracy. Let's be the generation that says right here, right now: We will have universal health care in America by the end of the next President's first term. We can do that.

Let's be the generation that finally frees America from the tyranny of oil. We can harness homegrown, alternative fuels like ethanol and spur the production of more fuel-efficient cars. We can set up a system for capping greenhouse gases. We can turn this crisis of global warming into a moment of opportunity for innovation, and job creation, and an incentive for businesses that will serve as a model for the world. Let's be the generation that makes future generations proud of what we did here.

Most of all, let's be the generation that never forgets what happened on that September day and confront the terrorists with everything we've got. Politics doesn't have to divide us on this anymore; we can work together to keep our country safe. I've worked with the Republican Senator Dick Lugar to pass a law that will secure and destroy some of the world's deadliest weapons. We can work together to track down terrorists with a stronger military. We can tighten the net around their finances. We can improve our intelligence capabilities and finally get homeland security right. But let's also understand that ultimate victory against our enemies will only come by rebuilding our alliances and exporting those ideals that bring hope and opportunity to millions of people around the globe.

We can do those things.

But all of this cannot come to pass until we bring an end to this war in Iraq. Most of you know—Most of you know that I opposed this war from the start. I thought it was a tragic mistake. Today we grieve for the families who have lost loved ones, the hearts that have been broken, and the young lives that could have been. America, it is time to start bringing our troops home. It's time—It's time to admit that no amount of American lives can resolve the political disagreement that lies at the heart of someone else's civil war. That's why I have a plan that will bring our combat troops home by March of 2008. Let the Iraqis know—Letting the Iraqis know that we will not be there forever is our last, best hope to pressure the Sunni and Shia to come to the table and find peace.

And there's one other thing that it's not too late to get right about this war, and that is the homecoming of the men and women, our veterans, who have sacrificed the most. Let us honor their courage by providing the care they need and rebuilding the military they love. Let us be the generation that begins that work.

I know there are those who don't believe we can do all these things. I understand the skepticism. After all, every four years, candidates from both Parties make similar promises, and I expect this year will be no different. All of us running for President will travel around the country offering ten-point plans and making grand speeches; all of us will trumpet those qualities we believe make us uniquely qualified to lead this country. But too many times, after the election is over, and the confetti is swept away, all those promises fade from memory, and the lobbyists and special interests move in, and people turn away, disappointed as before, left to struggle on their own.

That's why this campaign can't only be about me. It must be about us. It must be about what we can do together. This campaign must be the occasion, the vehicle, of your hopes, and your dreams. It will take your time, your energy, and your advice to push us forward when we're doing right, and let us know when we're not. This campaign has to be about reclaiming the meaning of citizenship, restoring our sense of common purpose, and realizing that few obstacles can withstand the power of millions of voices calling for change.

By ourselves, this change will not happen. Divided, we are bound to fail. But the life of a tall, gangly, self-made Springfield lawyer tells us that a different future is possible.

He tells us that there is power in words.

He tells us that there's power in conviction.

That beneath all the differences of race and region, faith and station, we are one people.

He tells us that there's power in hope.

As Lincoln organized the forces arrayed against slavery, he was heard to say this: "Of strange, discordant, and even hostile elements, we gathered from the four winds, and formed and fought to battle through."[1]

That is our purpose here today. That is why I am in this race—not just to hold an office, but to gather with you to transform a nation. I want—I want to win that next battle—for justice and opportunity. I want to win that next battle—for better schools, and better jobs, and better health care for all. I want us to take up the unfinished business of perfecting our union, and building a better America.

And if you will join with me in this improbable quest, if you feel destiny calling, and see as I see, the future of endless possibility stretching out before us; if you sense, as I sense, that the time is now to shake off our slumber, and slough off our fears, and make good on the debt we owe past and future generations, then I am ready to take up the cause, and march with you, and work with you—today.

Together we can finish the work that needs to be done, and usher in a new birth of freedom on this Earth.

Thank you very much everybody—let's get to work! I love you. Thank you.

http://www.4president.org/speeches/2008/barackobama2008announcement.htm

Appendix B: Inaugural Addresses

All texts are available on the website of the American Presidency Project (UC Santa Barbara):

https://www.presidency.ucsb.edu/

Dwight D. Eisenhower

January 20, 1953.

My friends, before I begin the expression of those thoughts that I deem appropriate to this moment, would you permit me the privilege of uttering a little private prayer of my own. And I ask that you bow your heads:

Almighty God, as we stand here at this moment my future associates in the Executive branch of Government join me in beseeching that Thou will make full and complete our dedication to the service of the people in this throng, and their fellow citizens everywhere.

Give us, we pray, the power to discern clearly right from wrong, and allow all our words and actions to be governed thereby, and by the laws of this land. Especially we pray that our concern shall be for all the people regardless of station, race or calling.

May cooperation be permitted and be the mutual aim of those who, under the concepts of our Constitution, hold to differing political faiths; so that all may work for the good of our beloved country and Thy glory. Amen.

My fellow citizens:

The world and we have passed the midway point of a century of continuing challenge. We sense with all our faculties that forces of good and evil are massed and armed and opposed as rarely before in history.

This fact defines the meaning of this day. We are summoned by this honored and historic ceremony to witness more than the act of one citizen swearing his oath of

F. Santulli, C. Degano, *Agreement in Argumentation*, Perspectives in Pragmatics, Philosophy & Psychology 31, https://doi.org/10.1007/978-3-031-16293-0

service, in the presence of God. We are called as a people to give testimony in the sight of the world to our faith that the future shall belong to the free.

Since this century's beginning, a time of tempest has seemed to come upon the continents of the earth. Masses of Asia have awakened to strike off shackles of the past. Great nations of Europe have fought their bloodiest wars. Thrones have toppled and their vast empires have disappeared. New nations have been born.

For our own country, it has been a time of recurring trial. We have grown in power and in responsibility. We have passed through the anxieties of depression and of war to a summit unmatched in man's history. Seeking to secure peace in the world, we have had to fight through the forests of the Argonne to the shores of Iwo Jima, and to the cold mountains of Korea.

In the swift rush of great events, we find ourselves groping to know the full sense and meaning of these times in which we live. In our quest of understanding, we beseech God's guidance. We summon all our knowledge of the past and we scan all signs of the future. We bring all our wit and all our will to meet the question:

How far have we come in man's long pilgrimage from darkness toward the light? Are we nearing the light—a day of freedom and of peace for all mankind? Or are the shadows of another night closing in upon us?

Great as are the preoccupations absorbing us at home, concerned as we are with matters that deeply affect our livelihood today and our vision of the future, each of these domestic problems is dwarfed by, and often even created by, this question that involves all humankind.

This trial comes at a moment when man's power to achieve good or to inflict evil surpasses the brightest hopes and the sharpest fears of all ages. We can turn rivers in their courses, level mountains to the plains. Oceans and land and sky are avenues for our colossal commerce. Disease diminishes and life lengthens.

Yet the promise of this life is imperiled by the very genius that has made it possible. Nations amass wealth. Labor sweats to create—and turns out devices to level not only mountains but also cities. Science seems ready to confer upon us, as its final gift, the power to erase human life from this planet.

At such a time in history, we who are free must proclaim anew our faith. This faith is the abiding creed of our fathers. It is our faith in the deathless dignity of man, governed by eternal moral and natural laws.

This faith defines our full view of life. It establishes, beyond debate, those gifts of the Creator that are man's inalienable rights, and that make all men equal in His sight.

In the light of this equality, we know that the virtues most cherished by free people—love of truth, pride of work, devotion to country—all are treasures equally precious in the lives of the most humble and of the most exalted. The men who mine coal and fire furnaces, and balance ledgers, and turn lathes, and pick cotton, and heal the sick and plant corn—all serve as proudly and as profitably for America as the statesmen who draft treaties and the legislators who enact laws.

This faith rules our whole way of life. It decrees that we, the people, elect leaders not to rule but to serve. It asserts that we have the right to choice of our own work and to the reward of our own toil. It inspires the initiative that makes our productivity the wonder of the world. And it warns that any man who seeks to deny equality among all his brothers betrays the spirit of the free and invites the mockery of the tyrant.

It is because we, all of us, hold to these principles that the political changes accomplished this day do not imply turbulence, upheaval or disorder. Rather this change expresses a purpose of strengthening our dedication and devotion to the precepts of our founding documents, a conscious renewal of faith in our country and in the watchfulness of a Divine Providence.

The enemies of this faith know no god but force, no devotion but its use. They tutor men in treason. They feed upon the hunger of others. Whatever defies them, they torture, especially the truth.

Here, then, is joined no argument between slightly differing philosophies. This conflict strikes directly at the faith of our fathers and the lives of our sons. No principle or treasure that we hold, from the spiritual knowledge of our free schools and churches to the creative magic of free labor and capital, nothing lies safely beyond the reach of this struggle.

Freedom is pitted against slavery; lightness against the dark

The faith we hold belongs not to us alone but to the free of all the world. This common bond binds the grower of rice in Burma and the planter of wheat in Iowa, the shepherd in southern Italy and the mountaineer in the Andes. It confers a common dignity upon the French soldier who dies in Indo-China, the British soldier killed in Malaya, the American life given in Korea.

We know, beyond this, that we are linked to all free peoples not merely by a noble idea but by a simple need. No free people can for long cling to any privilege or enjoy any safety in economic solitude. For all our own material might, even we need markets in the world for the surpluses of our farms and our factories. Equally, we need for these same farms and factories vital materials and products of distant lands. This basic law of interdependence, so manifest in the commerce of peace, applies with thousand-fold intensity in the event of war.

So we are persuaded by necessity and by belief that the strength of all free peoples lies in unity; their danger, in discord.

To produce this unity, to meet the challenge of our time, destiny has laid upon our country the responsibility of the free world's leadership.

So it is proper that we assure our friends once again that, in the discharge of this responsibility, we Americans know and we observe the difference between world leadership and imperialism; between firmness and truculence; between a thoughtfully calculated goal and spasmodic reaction to the stimulus of emergencies.

We wish our friends the world over to know this above all: we face the threat—not with dread and confusion—but with confidence and conviction.

We feel this moral strength because we know that we are not helpless prisoners of history. We are free men. We shall remain free, never to be proven guilty of the one capital offense against freedom, a lack of stanch faith.

In pleading our just cause before the bar of history and in pressing our labor for world peace, we shall be guided by certain fixed principles. These principles are:

1. Abhorring war as a chosen way to balk the purposes of those who threaten us, we hold it to be the first task of statesmanship to develop the strength that will deter the forces of aggression and promote the conditions of peace. For, as it must be the supreme purpose of all free men, so it must be the dedication of their leaders, to save humanity from preying upon itself.

In the light of this principle, we stand ready to engage with any and all others in joint effort to remove the causes of mutual fear and distrust among nations, so as to make possible drastic reduction of armaments. The sole requisites for undertaking such effort are that—in their purpose—they be aimed logically and honestly toward secure peace for all; and that—in their result—they provide methods by which every participating nation will prove good faith in carrying out its pledge.

2. Realizing that common sense and common decency alike dictate the futility of appeasement, we shall never try to placate an aggressor by the false and wicked bargain of trading honor for security. Americans, indeed, all free men, remember that in the final choice a soldier's pack is not so heavy a burden as a prisoner's chains.

3. Knowing that only a United States that is strong and immensely productive can help defend freedom in our world, we view our Nation's strength and security as a trust upon which rests the hope of free men everywhere. It is the firm duty of each of our free citizens and of every free citizen everywhere to place the cause of his country before the comfort, the convenience of himself.

4. Honoring the identity and the special heritage of each nation in the world, we shall never use our strength to try to impress upon another people our own cherished political and economic institutions.

5. Assessing realistically the needs and capacities of proven friends of freedom, we shall strive to help them to achieve their own security and well-being. Likewise, we shall count upon them to assume, within the limits of their resources, their full and just burdens in the common defense of freedom.

6. Recognizing economic health as an indispensable basis of military strength and the free world's peace, we shall strive to foster everywhere, and to practice ourselves, policies that encourage productivity and profitable trade. For the impoverishment of any single people in the world means danger to the well-being of all other peoples.

7. Appreciating that economic need, military security and political wisdom combine to suggest regional groupings of free peoples, we hope, within the framework of the United Nations, to help strengthen such special bonds the world over. The nature of these ties must vary with the different problems of different areas.

In the Western Hemisphere, we enthusiastically join with all our neighbors in the work of perfecting a community of fraternal trust and common purpose.

In Europe, we ask that enlightened and inspired leaders of the Western nations strive with renewed vigor to make the unity of their peoples a reality. Only as free

Europe unitedly marshals its strength can it effectively safeguard, even with our help, its spiritual and cultural heritage.

8. Conceiving the defense of freedom, like freedom itself, to be one and indivisible, we hold all continents and peoples in equal regard and honor. We reject any insinuation that one race or another, one people or another, is in any sense inferior or expendable.
9. Respecting the United Nations as the living sign of all people's hope for peace, we shall strive to make it not merely an eloquent symbol but an effective force. And in our quest for an honorable peace, we shall neither compromise, nor tire, nor ever cease.

By these rules of conduct, we hope to be known to all peoples.

By their observance, an earth of peace may become not a vision but a fact.

This hope—this supreme aspiration—must rule the way we live.

We must be ready to dare all for our country. For history does not long entrust the care of freedom to the weak or the timid. We must acquire proficiency in defense and display stamina in purpose.

We must be willing, individually and as a Nation, to accept whatever sacrifices may be required of us. A people that values its privileges above its principles soon loses both.

These basic precepts are not lofty abstractions, far removed from matters of daily living. They are laws of spiritual strength that generate and define our material strength. Patriotism means equipped forces and a prepared citizenry. Moral stamina means more energy and more productivity, on the farm and in the factory. Love of liberty means the guarding of every resource that makes freedom possible—from the sanctity of our families and the wealth of our soil to the genius of our scientists.

And so each citizen plays an indispensable role. The productivity of our heads, our hands and our hearts is the source of all the strength we can command, for both the enrichment of our lives and the winning of the peace.

No person, no home, no community can be beyond the reach of this call. We are summoned to act in wisdom and in conscience, to work with industry, to teach with persuasion, to preach with conviction, to weigh our every deed with care and with compassion. For this truth must be clear before us: whatever America hopes to bring to pass in the world must first come to pass in the heart of America.

The peace we seek, then, is nothing less than the practice and fulfillment of our whole faith among ourselves and in our dealings with others. This signifies more than the stilling of guns, casing the sorrow of war. More than escape from death, it is a way of life. More than a haven for the weary, it is a hope for the brave. This is the hope that beckons us onward in this century of trial. This is the work that awaits us all, to be done with bravery, with charity, and with prayer to Almighty God.

My citizens—I thank you.

John F. Kennedy

January 20, 1961.

Vice President Johnson, Mr. Speaker, Mr. Chief Justice, President Eisenhower, Vice president Nixon, President Truman, Reverend Clergy, fellow citizens:

We observe today not a victory of party but a celebration of freedom–symbolizing an end as well as a beginning–signifying renewal as well as change. For I have sworn before you and Almighty God the same solemn oath our forebears prescribed nearly a century and three quarters ago.

The world is very different now. For man holds in his mortal hands the power to abolish all forms of human poverty and all forms of human life. And yet the same revolutionary beliefs for which our forebears fought are still at issue around the globe–the belief that the rights of man come not from the generosity of the state but from the hand of God.

We dare not forget today that we are the heirs of that first revolution. Let the word go forth from this time and place, to friend and foe alike, that the torch has been passed to a new generation of Americans–born in this century, tempered by war, disciplined by a hard and bitter peace, proud of our ancient heritage–and unwilling to witness or permit the slow undoing of those human rights to which this nation has always been committed, and to which we are committed today at home and around the world.

Let every nation know, whether it wishes us well or ill, that we shall pay any price, bear any burden, meet any hardship, support any friend, oppose any foe to assure the survival and the success of liberty.

This much we pledge–and more.

To those old allies whose cultural and spiritual origins we share, we pledge the loyalty of faithful friends. United, there is little we cannot do in a host of cooperative ventures. Divided, there is little we can do–for we dare not meet a powerful challenge at odds and split asunder.

To those new states whom we welcome to the ranks of the free, we pledge our word that one form of colonial control shall not have passed away merely to be replaced by a far more iron tyranny. We shall not always expect to find them supporting our view. But we shall always hope to find them strongly supporting their own freedom-and to remember that, in the past, those who foolishly sought power by riding the back of the tiger ended up inside.

To those peoples in the huts and villages of half the globe struggling to break the bonds of mass misery, we pledge our best efforts to help them help themselves, for whatever period is required–not because the communists may be doing it, not because we seek their votes, but because it is right. If a free society cannot help the many who are poor, it cannot save the few who are rich.

To our sister republics south of our border, we offer a special pledge–to convert our good words into good deeds–in a new alliance for progress–to assist free men and free governments in casting off the chains of poverty. But this peaceful revolution of hope cannot become the prey of hostile powers. Let all our neighbors know that we shall join with them to oppose aggression or subversion anywhere in the Americas. And let every other power know that this Hemisphere intends to remain the master of its own house.

To that world assembly of sovereign states, the United Nations, our last best hope in an age where the instruments of war have far outpaced the instruments of peace, we renew our pledge of support–to prevent it from becoming merely a forum for invective–to strengthen its shield of the new and the weak–and to enlarge the area in which its writ may run.

Finally, to those nations who would make themselves our adversary, we offer not a pledge but a request: that both sides begin anew the quest for peace, before the dark powers of destruction unleashed by science engulf all humanity in planned or accidental self-destruction.

We dare not tempt them with weakness. For only when our arms are sufficient beyond doubt can we be certain beyond doubt that they will never be employed.

But neither can two great and powerful groups of nations take comfort from our present course–both sides overburdened by the cost of modern weapons, both rightly alarmed by the steady spread of the deadly atom, yet both racing to alter that uncertain balance of terror that stays the hand of mankind's final war.

So let us begin anew–remembering on both sides that civility is not a sign of weakness, and sincerity is always subject to proof. Let us never negotiate out of fear. But let us never fear to negotiate.

Let both sides explore what problems unite us instead of belaboring those problems which divide us.

Let both sides, for the first time, formulate serious and precise proposals for the inspection and control of arms–and bring the absolute power to destroy other nations under the absolute control of all nations.

Let both sides seek to invoke the wonders of science instead of its terrors. Together let us explore the stars, conquer the deserts, eradicate disease, tap the ocean depths and encourage the arts and commerce.

Let both sides unite to heed in all corners of the earth the command of Isaiah–to "undo the heavy burdens . . . (and) let the oppressed go free."

And if a beach-head of cooperation may push back the jungle of suspicion, let both sides join in creating a new endeavor, not a new balance of power, but a new world of law, where the strong are just and the weak secure and the peace preserved.

All this will not be finished in the first 100 days. Nor will it be finished in the first 1000 days, nor in the life of this Administration, nor even perhaps in our lifetime on this planet. But let us begin.

In your hands, my fellow citizens, more than mine, will rest the final success or failure of our course. Since this country was founded, each generation of Americans has been summoned to give testimony to its national loyalty. The graves of young Americans who answered the call to service surround the globe.

Now the trumpet summons us again-not as a call to bear arms, though arms we need-not as a call to battle, though embattled we are-but a call to bear the burden of a long twilight struggle, year in and year out, "rejoicing in hope, patient in tribulation"–a struggle against the common enemies of man: tyranny, poverty, disease and war itself.

Can we forge against these enemies a grand and global alliance, North and South, East and West, that can assure a more fruitful life for all mankind? Will you join in that historic effort?

In the long history of the world, only a few generations have been granted the role of defending freedom in its hour of maximum danger. I do not shrink from this responsibility–I welcome it. I do not believe that any of us would exchange places with any other people or any other generation. The energy, the faith, the devotion which we bring to this endeavor will light our country and all who serve it–and the glow from that fire can truly light the world.

And so, my fellow Americans: ask not what your country can do for you–ask what you can do for your country.

My fellow citizens of the world: ask not what America will do for you, but what together we can do for the freedom of man.

Finally, whether you are citizens of America or citizens of the world, ask of us here the same high standards of strength and sacrifice which we ask of you. With a good conscience our only sure reward, with history the final judge of our deeds, let us go forth to lead the land we love, asking His blessing and His help, but knowing that here on earth God's work must truly be our own.

Richard Nixon

January 20, 1969

Senator Dirksen, Mr. Chief Justice, Mr. Vice president, President Johnson, Vice president Humphrey, my fellow Americans-and my fellow citizens of the world community:

I ask you to share with me today the majesty of this moment. In the orderly transfer of power, we celebrate the unity that keeps us free.

Each moment in history is a fleeting time, precious and unique. But some stand out as moments of beginning, in which courses are set that shape decades or centuries.

This can be such a moment.

Forces now are converging that make possible, for the first time, the hope that many of man's deepest aspirations can at last be realized. The spiraling pace of change allows us to contemplate, within our own lifetime, advances that once would have taken centuries.

In throwing wide the horizons of space, we have discovered new horizons on earth.

For the first time, because the people of the world want peace, and the leaders of the world are afraid of war, the times are on the side of peace.

Eight years from now America will celebrate its 200th anniversary as a nation. Within the lifetime of most people now living, mankind will celebrate that great new year which comes only once in a 1000 years–the beginning of the third millennium.

What kind of a nation we will be, what kind of a world we will live in, whether we shape the future in the image of our hopes, is ours to determine by our actions and our choices.

The greatest honor history can bestow is the title of peacemaker. This honor now beckons America–the chance to help lead the world at last out of the valley of turmoil and onto that high ground of peace that man has dreamed of since the dawn of civilization.

If we succeed, generations to come will say of us now living that we mastered our moment, that we helped make the world safe for mankind.

This is our summons to greatness.

I believe the American people are ready to answer this call.

The second third of this century has been a time of proud achievement. We have made enormous strides in science and industry and agriculture. We have shared our wealth more broadly than ever. We have learned at last to manage a modern economy to assure its continued growth.

We have given freedom new reach. We have begun to make its promise real for black as well as for white.

We see the hope of tomorrow in the youth of today. I know America's youth. I believe in them. We can be proud that they are better educated, more committed, more passionately driven by conscience than any generation in our history.

No people has ever been so close to the achievement of a just and abundant society, or so possessed of the will to achieve it. And because our strengths are so great, we can afford to appraise our weaknesses with candor and to approach them with hope.

Standing in this same place a third of a century ago, Franklin Delano Roosevelt addressed a nation ravaged by depression and gripped in fear. He could say in surveying the Nation's troubles: "They concern, thank God, only material things." Our crisis today is in reverse.

We find ourselves rich in goods, but ragged in spirit; reaching with magnificent precision for the moon, but failing into raucous discord on earth.

We are caught in war, wanting peace. We are torn by division, wanting unity. We see around us empty lives, wanting fulfillment. We see tasks that need doing, waiting for hands to do them.

To a crisis of the spirit, we need an answer of the spirit.

And to find that answer, we need only look within ourselves.

When we listen to "the better angels of our nature," we find that they celebrate the simple things, the basic things–such as goodness, decency, love, kindness.

Greatness comes in simple trappings. The simple things are the ones most needed today if we are to surmount what divides us, and cement what unites us.

To lower our voices would be a simple thing.

In these difficult years, America has suffered from a fever of words; from inflated rhetoric that promises more than it can deliver; from angry rhetoric that fans discontents into hatreds; from bombastic rhetoric that postures instead of persuading.

We cannot learn from one another until we stop shouting at one another—until we speak quietly enough so that our words can be heard as well as our voices.

For its part, government will listen. We will strive to listen in new ways—to the voices of quiet anguish, the voices that speak without words, the voices of the heart—to the injured voices, the anxious voices, the voices that have despaired of being heard.

Those who have been left out, we will try to bring in.

Those left behind, we will help to catch up.

For all of our people, we will set as our goal the decent order that makes progress possible and our lives secure.

As we reach toward our hopes, our task is to build on what has gone before—not turning away from the old, but turning toward the new.

In this past third of a century, government has passed more laws, spent more money, initiated more programs than in all our previous history.

In pursuing our goals of full employment, better housing, excellence in education; in rebuilding our cities and improving our rural areas; in protecting our environment and enhancing the quality of life—in all these and more, we will and must press urgently forward.

We shall plan now for the day when our wealth can be transferred from the destruction of war abroad to the urgent needs of our people at home.

The American dream does not come to those who fall asleep.

But we are approaching the limits of what government alone can do.

Our greatest need now is to reach beyond government, to enlist the legions of the concerned and the committed.

What has to be done, has to be done by government and people together or it will not be done at all. The lesson of past agony is that without the people we can do nothing—with the people we can do everything.

To match the magnitude of our tasks, we need the energies of our people—enlisted not only in grand enterprises, but more importantly in those small, splendid efforts that make headlines in the neighborhood newspaper instead of the national journal.

With these, we can build a great cathedral of the spirit—each of us raising it one stone at a time, as he reaches out to his neighbor, helping, caring, doing.

I do not offer a life of uninspiring ease. I do not call for a life of grim sacrifice. I ask you to join in a high adventure—one as rich as humanity itself, and exciting as the times we live in.

The essence of freedom is that each of us shares in the shaping of his own destiny.

Until he has been part of a cause larger than himself, no man is truly whole.

The way to fulfillment is in the use of our talents. We achieve nobility in the spirit that inspires that use.

As we measure what can be done, we shall promise only what we know we can produce; but as we chart our goals, we shall be lifted by our dreams.

No man can be fully free while his neighbor is not. To go forward at all is to go forward together.

This means black and white together, as one nation, not two. The laws have caught up with our conscience. What remains is to give life to what is in the law: to insure at last that as all are born equal in dignity before God, all are born equal in dignity before man.

As we learn to go forward together at home, let us also seek to go forward together with all mankind.

Let us take as our goal: Where peace is unknown, make it welcome; where Peace is fragile, make it strong; where peace is temporary, make it permanent.

After a period of confrontation, we are entering an era of negotiation.

Let all nations know that during this administration our lines of communication will be open.

We seek an open world–open to ideas, open to the exchange of goods and people–a world in which no people, great or small, will live in angry isolation.

We cannot expect to make everyone our friend, but we can try to make no one our enemy.

Those who would be our adversaries, we invite to a peaceful competition–not in conquering territory or extending dominion, but in enriching the life of man.

As we explore the reaches of space, let us go to the new worlds together–not as new worlds to be conquered, but as a new adventure to be shared.

With those who are willing to join, let us cooperate to reduce the burden of arms, to strengthen the structure of peace, to lift up the poor and the hungry.

But to all those who would be tempted by weakness, let us leave no doubt that we will be as strong as we need to be for as long as we need to be.

Over the past 20 years, since I first came to this Capital as a freshman Congressman, I have visited most of the nations of the world. I have come to know the leaders of the world and the great forces, the hatreds, the fears that divide the world.

I know that peace does not come through wishing for it–that there is no substitute for days and even years of patient and prolonged diplomacy.

I also know the people of the world.

I have seen the hunger of a homeless child, the pain of a man wounded in battle, the grief of a mother who has lost her son. I know these have no ideology, no race.

I know America. I know the heart of America is good.

I speak from my own heart, and the heart of my country, the deep concern we have for those who suffer and those who sorrow.

I have taken an oath today in the presence of God and my countrymen to uphold and defend the Constitution of the United States. To that oath I now add this sacred commitment: I shall consecrate my Office, my energies, and all the wisdom I can summon to the cause of peace among nations.

Let this message be heard by strong and weak alike:

The peace we seek–the peace we seek to win–is not victory over any other people, but the peace that comes "with healing in its wings"; with compassion for those who have suffered; with understanding for those who have opposed us; with the opportunity for all the peoples of this earth to choose their own destiny.

Only a few short weeks ago we shared the glory of man's first sight of the world as God sees it, as a single sphere reflecting light in the darkness.

As the Apollo astronauts flew over the moon's gray surface on Christmas Eve, they spoke to us of the beauty of earth-and in that voice so clear across the lunar distance, we heard them invoke God's blessing on its goodness.

In that moment, their view from the moon moved poet Archibald MacLeish to write: "To see the earth as it truly is, small and blue and beautiful in that eternal silence where it floats, is to see ourselves as riders on the earth together, brothers on that bright loveliness in the eternal cold–brothers who know now they are truly brothers."

In that moment of surpassing technological triumph, men turned their thoughts toward home and humanity-seeing in that far perspective that man's destiny on earth is not divisible; telling us that however far we reach into the cosmos, our destiny lies not in the stars but on earth itself, in our own hands, in our own hearts.

We have endured a long night of the American spirit. But as our eyes catch the dimness of the first rays of dawn, let us not curse the remaining dark. Let us gather the light.

Our destiny offers not the cup of despair, but the chalice of opportunity. So let us seize it not in fear, but in gladness-and "riders on the earth together," let us go forward, firm in our faith, steadfast in our purpose, cautious of the dangers, but sustained by our confidence in the will of God and the promise of man.

Ronald Reagan

January 20, 1981

Senator Hatfield, Mr. Chief Justice, Mr. President, Vice President Bush, Vice President Mondale, Senator Baker, Speaker O'Neill, Reverend Moomaw, and my fellow citizens:

To a few of us here today this is a solemn and most momentous occasion, and yet in the history of our nation it is a commonplace occurrence. The orderly transfer of authority as called for in the Constitution routinely takes place, as it has for almost two centuries, and few of us stop to think how unique we really are. In the eyes of many in the world, this every 4-year ceremony we accept as normal is nothing less than a miracle.

Mr. President, I want our fellow citizens to know how much you did to carry on this tradition. By your gracious cooperation in the transition process, you have shown a watching world that we are a united people pledged to maintaining a political system which guarantees individual liberty to a greater degree than any other, and I thank you and your people for all your help in maintaining the continuity which is the bulwark of our Republic.

The business of our nation goes forward. These United States are confronted with an economic affliction of great proportions. We suffer from the longest and one of the worst sustained inflations in our national history. It distorts our economic decisions, penalizes thrift, and crushes the struggling young and the fixed-income elderly alike. It threatens to shatter the lives of millions of our people.

Idle industries have cast workers into unemployment, human misery, and personal indignity. Those who do work are denied a fair return for their labor by a tax system which penalizes successful achievement and keeps us from maintaining full productivity.

But great as our tax burden is, it has not kept pace with public spending. For decades we have piled deficit upon deficit, mortgaging our future and our children's future for the temporary convenience of the present. To continue this long trend is to guarantee tremendous social, cultural, political, and economic upheavals.

You and I, as individuals, can, by borrowing, live beyond our means, but for only a limited period of time. Why, then, should we think that collectively, as a nation, we're not bound by that same limitation? We must act today in order to preserve tomorrow. And let there be no misunderstanding: We are going to begin to act, beginning today.

The economic ills we suffer have come upon us over several decades. They will not go away in days, weeks, or months, but they will go away. They will go away because we as Americans have the capacity now, as we've had in the past, to do whatever needs to be done to preserve this last and greatest bastion of freedom.

In this present crisis, government is not the solution to our problem; government is the problem. From time to time we've been tempted to believe that society has become too complex to be managed by self-rule, that government by an elite group is superior to government for, by, and of the people. Well, if no one among us is capable of governing himself, then who among us has the capacity to govern someone else? All of us together, in and out of government, must bear the burden. The solutions we seek must be equitable, with no one group singled out to pay a higher price.

We hear much of special interest groups. Well, our concern must be for a special interest group that has been too long neglected. It knows no sectional boundaries or ethnic and racial divisions, and it crosses political party lines. It is made up of men and women who raise our food, patrol our streets, man our mines and factories, teach our children, keep our homes, and heal us when we're sick—professionals, industrialists, shopkeepers, clerks, cabbies, and truck drivers. They are, in short, "We the people," this breed called Americans.

Well, this administration's objective will be a healthy, vigorous, growing economy that provides equal opportunities for all Americans, with no barriers born of bigotry or discrimination. Putting America back to work means putting all Americans back to work. Ending inflation means freeing all Americans from the terror of runaway living costs. All must share in the productive work of this "new beginning," and all must share in the bounty of a revived economy. With the idealism and fair play which are the core of our system and our strength, we can have a strong and prosperous America, at peace with itself and the world.

So, as we begin, let us take inventory. We are a nation that has a government—not the other way around. And this makes us special among the nations of the Earth. Our government has no power except that granted it by the people. It is time to check and reverse the growth of government, which shows signs of having grown beyond the consent of the governed.

It is my intention to curb the size and influence of the Federal establishment and to demand recognition of the distinction between the powers granted to the Federal Government and those reserved to the States or to the people. All of us need to be reminded that the Federal Government did not create the States; the States created the Federal Government.

Now, so there will be no misunderstanding, it's not my intention to do away with government. It is rather to make it work–work with us, not over us; to stand by our side, not ride on our back. Government can and must provide opportunity, not smother it; foster productivity, not stifle it.

If we look to the answer as to why for so many years we achieved so much, prospered as no other people on Earth, it was because here in this land we unleashed the energy and individual genius of man to a greater extent than has ever been done before. Freedom and the dignity of the individual have been more available and assured here than in any other place on Earth. The price for this freedom at times has been high, but we have never been unwilling to pay that price.

It is no coincidence that our present troubles parallel and are proportionate to the intervention and intrusion in our lives that result from unnecessary and excessive growth of government. It is time for us to realize that we're too great a nation to limit ourselves to small dreams. We're not, as some would have us believe, doomed to an inevitable decline. I do not believe in a fate that will fall on us no matter what we do. I do believe in a fate that will fall on us if we do nothing. So, with all the creative energy at our command, let us begin an era of national renewal. Let us renew our determination, our courage, and our strength. And let us renew our faith and our hope.

We have every right to dream heroic dreams. Those who say that we're in a time when there are not heroes, they just don't know where to look. You can see heroes every day going in and out of factory gates. Others, a handful in number, produce enough food to feed all of us and then the world beyond. You meet heroes across a counter, and they're on both sides of that counter. There are entrepreneurs with faith in themselves and faith in an idea who create new jobs, new wealth and opportunity. They're individuals and families whose taxes support the government and whose voluntary gifts support church, charity, culture, art, and education. Their patriotism is quiet, but deep. Their values sustain our national life.

Now, I have used the words "they" and "their" in speaking of these heroes. I could say "you" and "your," because I'm addressing the heroes of whom I speak— you, the citizens of this blessed land. Your dreams, your hopes, your goals are going to be the dreams, the hopes, and the goals of this administration, so help me God.

We shall reflect the compassion that is so much a part of your makeup. How can we love our country and not love our countrymen; and loving them, reach out a hand when they fall, heal them when they're sick, and provide opportunity to make them self-sufficient so they will be equal in fact and not just in theory?

Can we solve the problems confronting us? Well, the answer is an unequivocal and emphatic "yes." To paraphrase Winston Churchill, I did not take the oath I've just taken with the intention of presiding over the dissolution of the world's strongest economy.

In the days ahead I will propose removing the roadblocks that have slowed our economy and reduced productivity. Steps will be taken aimed at restoring the balance between the various levels of government. Progress may be slow, measured in inches and feet, not miles, but we will progress. It is time to reawaken this industrial giant, to get government back within its means, and to lighten our punitive tax burden. And these will be our first priorities, and on these principles there will be no compromise.

On the eve of our struggle for independence a man who might have been one of the greatest among the Founding Fathers, Dr. Joseph Warren, president of the Massachusetts Congress, said to his fellow Americans, "Our country is in danger, but not to be despaired of — On you depend the fortunes of America. You are to decide the important questions upon which rests the happiness and the liberty of millions yet unborn. Act worthy of yourselves."

Well, I believe we, the Americans of today, are ready to act worthy of ourselves, ready to do what must be done to ensure happiness and liberty for ourselves, our children, and our children's children. And as we renew ourselves here in our own land, we will be seen as having greater strength throughout the world. We will again be the exemplar of freedom and a beacon of hope for those who do not now have freedom.

To those neighbors and allies who share our freedom, we will strengthen our historic ties and assure them of our support and firm commitment. We will match loyalty with loyalty. We will strive for mutually beneficial relations. We will not use our friendship to impose on their sovereignty, for our own sovereignty is not for sale.

As for the enemies of freedom, those who are potential adversaries, they will be reminded that peace is the highest aspiration of the American people. We will negotiate for it, sacrifice for it; we will not surrender for it, now or ever.

Our forbearance should never be misunderstood. Our reluctance for conflict should not be misjudged as a failure of will. When action is required to preserve our national security, we will act. We will maintain sufficient strength to prevail if need be, knowing that if we do so we have the best chance of never having to use that strength.

Above all, we must realize that no arsenal or no weapon in the arsenals of the world is so formidable as the will and moral courage of free men and women. It is a weapon our adversaries in today's world do not have. It is a weapon that we as Americans do have. Let that be understood by those who practice terrorism and prey upon their neighbors.

I'm told that tens of thousands of prayer meetings are being held on this day, and for that I'm deeply grateful. We are a nation under God, and I believe God intended for us to be free. It would be fitting and good, I think, if on each Inaugural Day in future years it should be declared a day of prayer.

This is the first time in our history that this ceremony has been held, as you've been told, on this West Front of the Capitol. Standing here, one faces a magnificent vista, opening up on this city's special beauty and history. At the end of this open mall are those shrines to the giants on whose shoulders we stand.

Directly in front of me, the monument to a monumental man, George Washington, father of our country. A man of humility who came to greatness reluctantly. He led America out of revolutionary victory into infant nationhood. Off to one side, the stately memorial to Thomas Jefferson. The Declaration of Independence flames with his eloquence. And then, beyond the Reflecting Pool, the dignified columns of the Lincoln Memorial. Whoever would understand in his heart the meaning of America will find it in the life of Abraham Lincoln.

Beyond those monuments to heroism is the Potomac River, and on the far shore the sloping hills of Arlington National Cemetery, with its row upon row of simple white markers bearing crosses or Stars of David. They add up to only a tiny fraction of the price that has been paid for our freedom.

Each one of those markers is a monument to the kind of hero I spoke of earlier. Their lives ended in places called Belleau Wood, The Argonne, Omaha Beach, Salerno, and halfway around the world on Guadalcanal, Tarawa, Pork Chop Hill, the Chosin Reservoir, and in a hundred rice paddies and jungles of a place called Vietnam.

Under one such marker lies a young man, Martin Treptow, who left his job in a small town barbershop in 1917 to go to France with the famed Rainbow Division. There, on the western front, he was killed trying to carry a message between battalions under heavy artillery fire.

We're told that on his body was found a diary. On the flyleaf under the heading, "My Pledge," he had written these words: "America must win this war. Therefore I will work, I will save, I will sacrifice, I will endure, I will fight cheerfully and do my utmost, as if the issue of the whole struggle depended on me alone."

The crisis we are facing today does not require of us the kind of sacrifice that Martin Treptow and so many thousands of others were called upon to make. It does require, however, our best effort and our willingness to believe in ourselves and to believe in our capacity to perform great deeds, to believe that together with God's help we can and will resolve the problems which now confront us.

And after all, why shouldn't we believe that? We are Americans.

God bless you, and thank you.

Bill Clinton

January 20, 1993

My fellow citizens, today we celebrate the mystery of American renewal. This ceremony is held in the depth of winter, but by the words we speak and the faces we show the world, we force the spring, a spring reborn in the world's oldest democracy that brings forth the vision and courage to reinvent America. When our Founders boldly declared America's independence to the world and our purposes to the Almighty, they knew that America, to endure, would have to change; not change for change's sake but change to preserve America's ideals: life, liberty, the pursuit of happiness. Though we marched to the music of our time, our mission is timeless. Each generation of Americans must define what it means to be an American.

On behalf of our Nation, I salute my predecessor, President Bush, for his half-century of service to America. And I thank the millions of men and women whose steadfastness and sacrifice triumphed over depression, fascism, and communism.

Today, a generation raised in the shadows of the cold war assumes new responsibilities in a world warmed by the sunshine of freedom but threatened still by ancient hatreds and new plagues. Raised in unrivaled prosperity, we inherit an economy that is still the world's strongest but is weakened by business failures, stagnant wages, increasing inequality, and deep divisions among our own people.

When George Washington first took the oath I have just sworn to uphold, news traveled slowly across the land by horseback and across the ocean by boat. Now, the sights and sounds of this ceremony are broadcast instantaneously to billions around the world. Communications and commerce are global. Investment is mobile. Technology is almost magical. And ambition for a better life is now universal.

We earn our livelihood in America today in peaceful competition with people all across the Earth. Profound and powerful forces are shaking and remaking our world. And the urgent question of our time is whether we can make change our friend and not our enemy. This new world has already enriched the lives of millions of Americans who are able to compete and win in it. But when most people are working harder for less; when others cannot work at all; when the cost of health care devastates families and threatens to bankrupt our enterprises, great and small; when the fear of crime robs law-abiding citizens of their freedom; and when millions of poor children cannot even imagine the lives we are calling them to lead, we have not made change our friend.

We know we have to face hard truths and take strong steps, but we have not done so; instead, we have drifted. And that drifting has eroded our resources, fractured our economy, and shaken our confidence. Though our challenges are fearsome, so are our strengths. Americans have ever been a restless, questing, hopeful people. And we must bring to our task today the vision and will of those who came before us. From our Revolution to the Civil War, to the Great Depression, to the civil rights movement, our people have always mustered the determination to construct from these crises the pillars of our history. Thomas Jefferson believed that to preserve the very foundations of our Nation, we would need dramatic change from time to time. Well, my fellow Americans, this is our time. Let us embrace it.

Our democracy must be not only the envy of the world but the engine of our own renewal. There is nothing wrong with America that cannot be cured by what is right with America. And so today we pledge an end to the era of deadlock and drift, and a new season of American renewal has begun.

To renew America, we must be bold. We must do what no generation has had to do before. We must invest more in our own people, in their jobs, and in their future, and at the same time cut our massive debt. And we must do so in a world in which we must compete for every opportunity. It will not be easy. It will require sacrifice, but it can be done and done fairly, not choosing sacrifice for its own sake but for our own sake. We must provide for our Nation the way a family provides for its children.

Our Founders saw themselves in the light of posterity. We can do no less. Anyone who has ever watched a child's eyes wander into sleep knows what posterity is. Posterity is the world to come: the world for whom we hold our ideals, from whom we have borrowed our planet, and to whom we bear sacred responsibility. We must do what America does best: offer more opportunity to all and demand more responsibility from all. It is time to break the bad habit of expecting something for nothing from our Government or from each other. Let us all take more responsibility not only for ourselves and our families but for our communities and our country.

To renew America, we must revitalize our democracy. This beautiful Capital, like every capital since the dawn of civilization, is often a place of intrigue and calculation. Powerful people maneuver for position and worry endlessly about who is in and who is out, who is up and who is down, forgetting those people whose toil and sweat sends us here and pays our way. Americans deserve better. And in this city today there are people who want to do better. And so I say to all of you here: Let us resolve to reform our politics so that power and privilege no longer shout down the voice of the people. Let us put aside personal advantage so that we can feel the pain and see the promise of America. Let us resolve to make our Government a place for what Franklin Roosevelt called bold, persistent experimentation, a Government for our tomorrows, not our yesterdays. Let us give this Capital back to the people to whom it belongs.

To renew America, we must meet challenges abroad as well as at home. There is no longer a clear division between what is foreign and what is domestic. The world economy, the world environment, the world AIDS crisis, the world arms race: they affect us all. Today, as an older order passes, the new world is more free but less stable. Communism's collapse has called forth old animosities and new dangers. Clearly, America must continue to lead the world we did so much to make.

While America rebuilds at home, we will not shrink from the challenges nor fail to seize the opportunities of this new world. Together with our friends and allies, we will work to shape change, lest it engulf us. When our vital interests are challenged or the will and conscience of the international community is defied, we will act, with peaceful diplomacy whenever possible, with force when necessary. The brave Americans serving our Nation today in the Persian Gulf, in Somalia, and wherever else they stand are testament to our resolve. But our greatest strength is the power of our ideas, which are still new in many lands. Across the world we see them embraced, and we rejoice. Our hopes, our hearts, our hands are with those on every continent who are building democracy and freedom. Their cause is America's cause.

The American people have summoned the change we celebrate today. You have raised your voices in an unmistakable chorus. You have cast your votes in historic numbers. And you have changed the face of Congress, the Presidency, and the political process itself. Yes, you, my fellow Americans, have forced the spring. Now we must do the work the season demands. To that work I now turn with all the authority of my office. I ask the Congress to join with me. But no President, no Congress, no Government can undertake this mission alone.

My fellow Americans, you, too, must play your part in our renewal. I challenge a new generation of young Americans to a season of service: to act on your idealism by helping troubled children, keeping company with those in need, reconnecting our torn communities. There is so much to be done; enough, indeed, for millions of others who are still young in spirit to give of themselves in service, too. In serving, we recognize a simple but powerful truth: We need each other, and we must care for one another.

Today we do more than celebrate America. We rededicate ourselves to the very idea of America, an idea born in revolution and renewed through two centuries of challenge; an idea tempered by the knowledge that, but for fate, we, the fortunate, and the unfortunate might have been each other; an idea ennobled by the faith that our Nation can summon from its myriad diversity the deepest measure of unity; an idea infused with the conviction that America's long, heroic journey must go forever upward.

And so, my fellow Americans, as we stand at the edge of the twenty-first century, let us begin anew with energy and hope, with faith and discipline. And let us work until our work is done. The Scripture says, "And let us not be weary in well doing: for in due season we shall reap, if we faint not." From this joyful mountaintop of celebration we hear a call to service in the valley. We have heard the trumpets. We have changed the guard. And now, each in our own way and with God's help, we must answer the call.

Thank you, and God bless you all.

George W. Bush

January 20, 2001

Thank you, all. Chief Justice Rehnquist, President Carter, President Bush, President Clinton, distinguished guests, and my fellow citizens. The peaceful transfer of authority is rare in history, yet common in our country. With a simple oath, we affirm old traditions and make new beginnings.

As I begin, I thank President Clinton for his service to our Nation, and I thank Vice President Gore for a contest conducted with spirit and ended with grace.

I am honored and humbled to stand here where so many of America's leaders have come before me, and so many will follow. We have a place, all of us, in a long story, a story we continue but whose end we will not see. It is a story of a new world that became a friend and liberator of the old, the story of a slaveholding society that became a servant of freedom, the story of a power that went into the world to protect but not possess, to defend but not to conquer.

It is the American story, a story of flawed and fallible people united across the generations by grand and enduring ideals. The grandest of these ideals is an unfolding American promise that everyone belongs, that everyone deserves a chance, that no insignificant person was ever born.

Americans are called to enact this promise in our lives and in our laws. And though our Nation has sometimes halted and sometimes delayed, we must follow no other course.

Through much of the last century, America's faith in freedom and democracy was a rock in a raging sea. Now it is a seed upon the wind, taking root in many nations. Our democratic faith is more than the creed of our country. It is the inborn hope of our humanity, an ideal we carry but do not own, a trust we bear and pass along. Even after nearly 225 years, we have a long way yet to travel.

While many of our citizens prosper, others doubt the promise, even the justice of our own country. The ambitions of some Americans are limited by failing schools and hidden prejudice and the circumstances of their birth. And sometimes our differences run so deep, it seems we share a continent but not a country. We do not accept this, and we will not allow it.

Our unity, our Union, is a serious work of leaders and citizens and every generation. And this is my solemn pledge: I will work to build a single nation of justice and opportunity. I know this is in our reach because we are guided by a power larger than ourselves, who creates us equal, in His image, and we are confident in principles that unite and lead us onward.

America has never been united by blood or birth or soil. We are bound by ideals that move us beyond our backgrounds, lift us above our interests, and teach us what it means to be citizens. Every child must be taught these principles. Every citizen must uphold them. And every immigrant, by embracing these ideals, makes our country more, not less, American.

Today we affirm a new commitment to live out our Nation's promise through civility, courage, compassion, and character. America at its best matches a commitment to principle with a concern for civility. A civil society demands from each of us good will and respect, fair dealing and forgiveness.

Some seem to believe that our politics can afford to be petty because in a time of peace the stakes of our debates appear small. But the stakes for America are never small. If our country does not lead the cause of freedom, it will not be led. If we do not turn the hearts of children toward knowledge and character, we will lose their gifts and undermine their idealism. If we permit our economy to drift and decline, the vulnerable will suffer most.

We must live up to the calling we share. Civility is not a tactic or a sentiment; it is the determined choice of trust over cynicism, of community over chaos. And this commitment, if we keep it, is a way to shared accomplishment.

America at its best is also courageous. Our national courage has been clear in times of depression and war, when defeating common dangers defined our common good. Now we must choose if the example of our fathers and mothers will inspire us or condemn us. We must show courage in a time of blessing by confronting problems instead of passing them on to future generations.

Together we will reclaim America's schools before ignorance and apathy claim more young lives. We will reform Social Security and Medicare, sparing our children from struggles we have the power to prevent. And we will reduce taxes to recover the momentum of our economy and reward the effort and enterprise of working Americans.

We will build our defenses beyond challenge, lest weakness invite challenge. We will confront weapons of mass destruction, so that a new century is spared new horrors. The enemies of liberty and our country should make no mistake: America remains engaged in the world, by history and by choice, shaping a balance of power that favors freedom.

We will defend our allies and our interests. We will show purpose without arrogance. We will meet aggression and bad faith with resolve and strength. And to all nations, we will speak for the values that gave our Nation birth.

America at its best is compassionate. In the quiet of American conscience, we know that deep, persistent poverty is unworthy of our Nation's promise. And whatever our views of its cause, we can agree that children at risk are not at fault.

Abandonment and abuse are not acts of God; they are failures of love. And the proliferation of prisons, however necessary, is no substitute for hope and order in our souls. Where there is suffering, there is duty. Americans in need are not strangers; they are citizens—not problems but priorities. And all of us are diminished when any are hopeless.

Government has great responsibilities for public safety and public health, for civil rights and common schools. Yet, compassion is the work of a nation, not just a government. And some needs and hurts are so deep they will only respond to a mentor's touch or a pastor's prayer. Church and charity, synagogue and mosque lend our communities their humanity, and they will have an honored place in our plans and in our laws.

Many in our country do not know the pain of poverty. But we can listen to those who do. And I can pledge our Nation to a goal: When we see that wounded traveler on the road to Jericho, we will not pass to the other side.

America at its best is a place where personal responsibility is valued and expected. Encouraging responsibility is not a search for scapegoats; it is a call to conscience. And though it requires sacrifice, it brings a deeper fulfillment. We find the fullness of life not only in options but in commitments. And we find that children and community are the commitments that set us free.

Our public interest depends on private character, on civic duty and family bonds and basic fairness, on uncounted, unhonored acts of decency, which give direction to our freedom.

Sometimes in life we're called to do great things. But as a saint of our times has said, "Every day we are called to do small things with great love." The most important tasks of a democracy are done by everyone.

I will live and lead by these principles: to advance my convictions with civility, to serve the public interest with courage, to speak for greater justice and compassion, to call for responsibility and try to live it, as well. In all these ways, I will bring the values of our history to the care of our times.

What you do is as important as anything Government does. I ask you to seek a common good beyond your comfort, to defend needed reforms against easy attacks, to serve your Nation, beginning with your neighbor. I ask you to be citizens: Citizens, not spectators; citizens, not subjects; responsible citizens building communities of service and a nation of character.

Americans are generous and strong and decent, not because we believe in ourselves but because we hold beliefs beyond ourselves. When this spirit of citizenship is missing, no Government program can replace it. When this spirit is present, no wrong can stand against it.

After the Declaration of Independence was signed, Virginia statesman John Page wrote to Thomas Jefferson, "We know the race is not to the swift, nor the battle to the strong. Do you not think an angel rides in the whirlwind and directs this storm?"

Much time has passed since Jefferson arrived for his inauguration. The years and changes accumulate, but the themes of this day, he would know: our Nation's grand story of courage and its simple dream of dignity.

We are not this story's author, who fills time and eternity with his purpose. Yet, his purpose is achieved in our duty. And our duty is fulfilled in service to one another. Never tiring, never yielding, never finishing, we renew that purpose today, to make our country more just and generous, to affirm the dignity of our lives and every life. This work continues, the story goes on, and an angel still rides in the whirlwind and directs this storm.

God bless you all, and God bless America.

Barack Obama

January 20, 2009

My fellow citizens, I stand here today humbled by the task before us, grateful for the trust you have bestowed, mindful of the sacrifices borne by our ancestors. I thank President Bush for his service to our Nation, as well as the generosity and cooperation he has shown throughout this transition.

Forty-four Americans have now taken the Presidential oath. The words have been spoken during rising tides of prosperity and the still waters of peace. Yet every so often, the oath is taken amidst gathering clouds and raging storms. At these moments, America has carried on not simply because of the skill or vision of those in high office, but because we the people have remained faithful to the ideals of our forebears and true to our founding documents.

So it has been; so it must be with this generation of Americans.

That we are in the midst of crisis is now well understood. Our Nation is at war against a far-reaching network of violence and hatred. Our economy is badly weakened, a consequence of greed and irresponsibility on the part of some, but also our collective failure to make hard choices and prepare the Nation for a new age. Homes have been lost, jobs shed, businesses shuttered. Our health care is too costly. Our schools fail too many. And each day brings further evidence that the ways we use energy strengthen our adversaries and threaten our planet.

These are the indicators of crisis, subject to data and statistics. Less measurable but no less profound is a sapping of confidence across our land, a nagging fear that America's decline is inevitable, that the next generation must lower its sights. Today I say to you that the challenges we face are real. They are serious, and they are many. They will not be met easily or in a short span of time. But know this, America: They will be met.

On this day, we gather because we have chosen hope over fear, unity of purpose over conflict and discord. On this day, we come to proclaim an end to the petty grievances and false promises, the recriminations and worn-out dogmas that for far too long have strangled our politics.

We remain a young nation, but in the words of Scripture, the time has come to set aside childish things. The time has come to reaffirm our enduring spirit, to choose our better history, to carry forward that precious gift, that noble idea passed on from generation to generation: the God-given promise that all are equal, all are free, and all deserve a chance to pursue their full measure of happiness.

In reaffirming the greatness of our Nation, we understand that greatness is never a given. It must be earned. Our journey has never been one of shortcuts or settling for less. It has not been the path for the fainthearted, for those who prefer leisure over work or seek only the pleasures of riches and fame. Rather, it has been the risk-takers, the doers, the makers of things—some celebrated, but more often men and women obscure in their labor—who have carried us up the long, rugged path toward prosperity and freedom.

For us, they packed up their few worldly possessions and traveled across oceans in search of a new life. For us, they toiled in sweatshops and settled the West, endured the lash of the whip, and plowed the hard Earth. For us, they fought and died in places like Concord and Gettysburg, Normandy and Khe Sanh.

Time and again, these men and women struggled and sacrificed and worked 'til their hands were raw so that we might live a better life. They saw America as bigger than the sum of our individual ambitions, greater than all the differences of birth or wealth or faction.

This is the journey we continue today. We remain the most prosperous, powerful nation on Earth. Our workers are no less productive than when this crisis began. Our minds are no less inventive. Our goods and services no less needed than they were last week or last month or last year. Our capacity remains undiminished. But our time of standing pat, of protecting narrow interests and putting off unpleasant decisions, that time has surely passed. Starting today, we must pick ourselves up, dust ourselves off, and begin again the work of remaking America.

For everywhere we look, there is work to be done. The state of the economy calls for action, bold and swift, and we will act not only to create new jobs but to lay a new foundation for growth. We will build the roads and bridges, the electric grids and digital lines that feed our commerce and bind us together. We will restore science to its rightful place and wield technology's wonders to raise health care's quality and lower its cost. We will harness the sun and the winds and the soil to fuel our cars and run our factories. And we will transform our schools and colleges and universities to meet the demands of a new age. All this we can do. All this we will do.

Now, there are some who question the scale of our ambitions, who suggest that our system cannot tolerate too many big plans. Their memories are short, for they have forgotten what this country has already done, what free men and women can achieve when imagination is joined to common purpose and necessity to courage.

What the cynics fail to understand is that the ground has shifted beneath them, that the stale political arguments that have consumed us for so long no longer apply. The question we ask today is not whether our Government is too big or too small, but whether it works; whether it helps families find jobs at a decent wage, care they can afford, a retirement that is dignified. Where the answer is yes, we intend to move forward. Where the answer is no, programs will end. And those of us who manage the public's dollars will be held to account to spend wisely, reform bad habits, and do our business in the light of day, because only then can we restore the vital trust between a people and their government.

Nor is the question before us whether the market is a force for good or ill. Its power to generate wealth and expand freedom is unmatched. But this crisis has reminded us that without a watchful eye, the market can spin out of control. The Nation cannot prosper long when it favors only the prosperous. The success of our economy has always depended not just on the size of our gross domestic product, but on the reach of our prosperity, on our ability to extend opportunity to every willing heart, not out of charity, but because it is the surest route to our common good.

As for our common defense, we reject as false the choice between our safety and our ideals. Our Founding Fathers, faced with perils that we can scarcely imagine, drafted a charter to assure the rule of law and the rights of man, a charter expanded by the blood of generations. Those ideals still light the world, and we will not give them up for expedience's sake. And so to all the other peoples and governments who are watching today, from the grandest capitals to the small village where my father was born, know that America is a friend of each nation and every man, woman, and child who seeks a future of peace and dignity, and we are ready to lead once more.

Recall that earlier generations faced down fascism and communism not just with missiles and tanks but with sturdy alliances and enduring convictions. They understood that our power alone cannot protect us, nor does it entitle us to do as we please. Instead, they knew that our power grows through its prudent use. Our security emanates from the justness of our cause, the force of our example, the tempering qualities of humility and restraint.

We are the keepers of this legacy. Guided by these principles once more, we can meet those new threats that demand even greater effort, even greater cooperation and understanding between nations. We will begin to responsibly leave Iraq to its people and forge a hard-earned peace in Afghanistan. With old friends and former foes, we will work tirelessly to lessen the nuclear threat and roll back the specter of a warming planet. We will not apologize for our way of life, nor will we waver in its defense. And for those who seek to advance their aims by inducing terror and slaughtering innocents, we say to you now that our spirit is stronger and cannot be broken. You cannot outlast us, and we will defeat you.

For we know that our patchwork heritage is a strength, not a weakness. We are a nation of Christians and Muslims, Jews and Hindus and nonbelievers. We are shaped by every language and culture, drawn from every end of this Earth. And because we have tasted the bitter swill of civil war and segregation and emerged from that dark chapter stronger and more united, we cannot help but believe that the old hatreds shall someday pass, that the lines of tribe shall soon dissolve; that as the world grows smaller, our common humanity shall reveal itself, and that America must play its role in ushering in a new era of peace.

To the Muslim world, we seek a new way forward based on mutual interest and mutual respect. To those leaders around the globe who seek to sow conflict or blame their society's ills on the West, know that your people will judge you on what you can build, not what you destroy. To those who cling to power through corruption and deceit and the silencing of dissent, know that you are on the wrong side of history, but that we will extend a hand if you are willing to unclench your fist.

To the people of poor nations, we pledge to work alongside you to make your farms flourish and let clean waters flow, to nourish starved bodies and feed hungry minds. And to those nations like ours that enjoy relative plenty, we say we can no longer afford indifference to suffering outside our borders, nor can we consume the world's resources without regard to effect, for the world has changed, and we must change with it.

As we consider the road that unfolds before us, we remember with humble gratitude those brave Americans who, at this very hour, patrol far-off deserts and distant mountains. They have something to tell us today, just as the fallen heroes who lie in Arlington whisper through the ages. We honor them not only because they are guardians of our liberty, but because they embody the spirit of service, a willingness to find meaning in something greater than themselves. And yet at this moment, a moment that will define a generation, it is precisely this spirit that must inhabit us all.

For as much as Government can do and must do, it is ultimately the faith and determination of the American people upon which this Nation relies. It is the kindness to take in a stranger when the levees break, the selflessness of workers who would rather cut their hours than see a friend lose their job, which sees us through our darkest hours. It is the firefighter's courage to storm a stairway filled with smoke, but also a parent's willingness to nurture a child, that finally decides our fate.

Our challenges may be new. The instruments with which we meet them may be new. But those values upon which our success depends–honesty and hard work, courage and fair play, tolerance and curiosity, loyalty and patriotism–these things are old. These things are true. They have been the quiet force of progress throughout our history. What is demanded then is a return to these truths. What is required of us now is a new era of responsibility, a recognition on the part of every American that we have duties to ourselves, our Nation, and the world. Duties that we do not grudgingly accept but, rather, seize gladly, firm in the knowledge that there is nothing so satisfying to the spirit, so defining of our character, than giving our all to a difficult task.

This is the price and the promise of citizenship. This is the source of our confidence, the knowledge that God calls on us to shape an uncertain destiny. This is the meaning of our liberty and our creed; why men and women and children of every race and every faith can join in celebration across this magnificent Mall, and why a man whose father less than 60 years ago might not have been served at a local restaurant can now stand before you to take a most sacred oath.

So let us mark this day with remembrance of who we are and how far we have traveled. In the year of America's birth, in the coldest of months, a small band of patriots huddled by dying campfires on the shores of an icy river. The Capital was abandoned. The enemy was advancing. The snow was stained with blood. At a moment when the outcome of our Revolution was most in doubt, the Father of our Nation ordered these words be read to the people:

"Let it be told to the future world . . . that in the depth of winter, when nothing but hope and virtue could survive…that the city and the country, alarmed at one common danger, came forth to meet [it]."

America, in the face of our common dangers, in this winter of our hardship, let us remember these timeless words. With hope and virtue, let us brave once more the icy currents and endure what storms may come. Let it be said by our children's children that when we were tested, we refused to let this journey end; that we did not turn back, nor did we falter. And with eyes fixed on the horizon and God's grace upon us, we carried forth that great gift of freedom and delivered it safely to future generations.

Thank you. God bless you, and God bless the United States of America.